ABRIELE
ÜNTER

SCHAFT

EINE KÜNSTLERIN

PAULA BECKER-MODERSOHN
BRIEFE UND TAGEBUCHBLÄTTER

1919
VERLAG VON FRANZ LEUWER
IN BREMEN

GALERIE NEUE KUNST FIDES
LEITUNG RUDOLF PROBST

VERTRETUNG
VON
JUSSUF ABBO
POL CASSEL
OTTO DIX
FEININGER
JAWLENSKY
KANDINSKY
PAUL KLEE
E. L. KIRCHNER
W. KRIEGEL
FRANZ MARC
EWALD MATARÉ
EMIL NOLDE

JUNI / JULI 1929 NOCH BESONDERS AUSGESTELLT
PAULA BECKER-MODERSOHN
GEMÄLDE UND HANDZEICHNUNGEN

DRESDEN-A. / STRUVESTRASSE 6

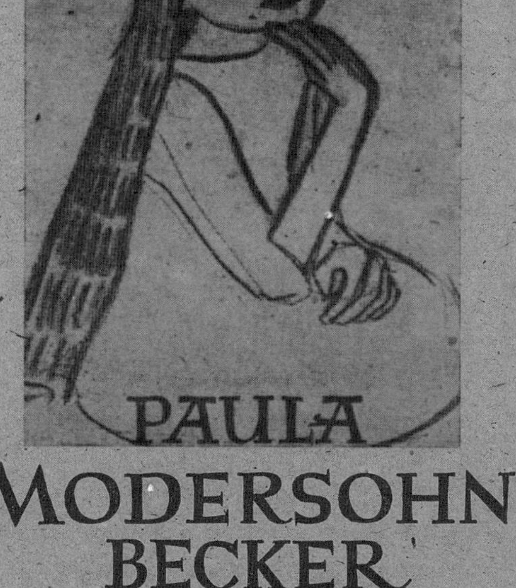

PAULA
MODERSOHN
BECKER

KUNSTHALLE BREMEN · MAI-JUNI 1947

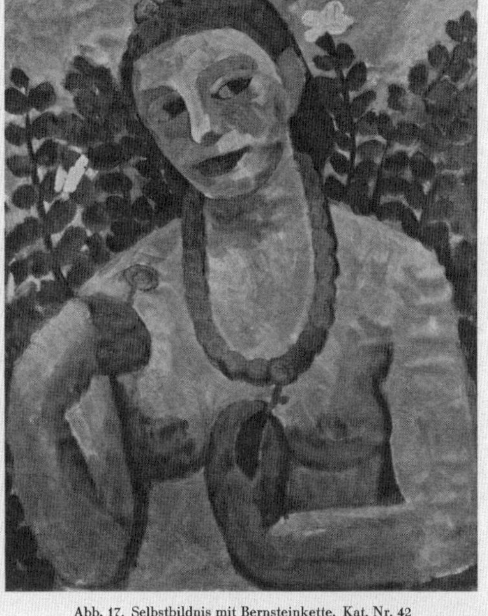

Abb. 17. Selbstbildnis mit Bernsteinkette. Kat. Nr. 42

DIE
PAULA BECKER-MODERSOHN-
SAMMLUNG DES LUDWIG ROSELIUS
IN DER BÖTTCHERSTRASSE
IN BREMEN

HE
WALT

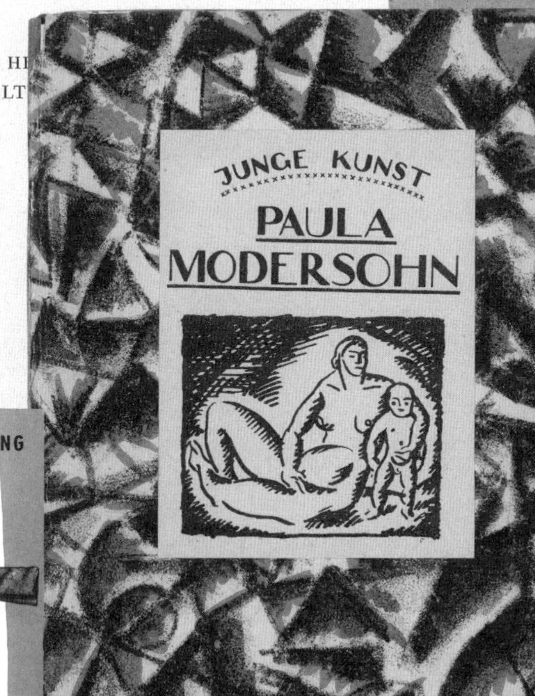

JUNGE KUNST
PAULA
MODERSOHN

ERSTE
AUSSTELLUNG

JAMES ENSOR
PAULA
MODERSOHN=BECKER
ALT=TIBETANISCHES
KUNSTGEWERBE

OKTOBER
1920

PAULA MODERSOHN-BECKER GEDÄCHTNISAUSSTELLUNG

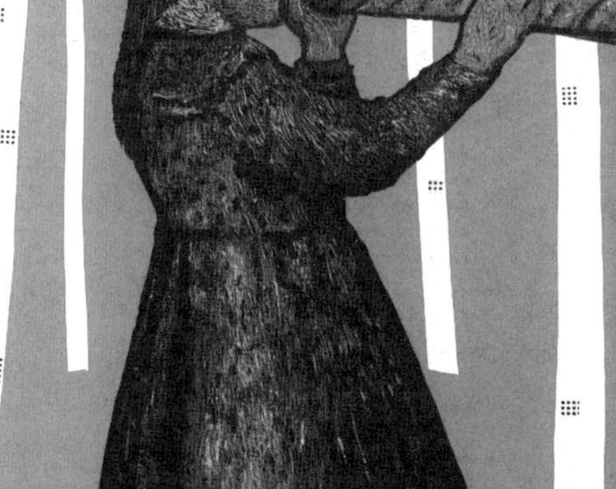

CASEL

ECKER

KE

PAULA
MODERSOHN-BECKER
VON
GUSTAV PAULI

PAULA MODERSOHN-BECKER
HANDZEICHNUNGEN

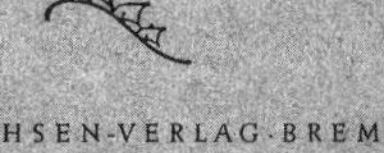

ANGELSACHSEN-VERLAG-BREMEN

PAULA MODERSOHN-BECKER

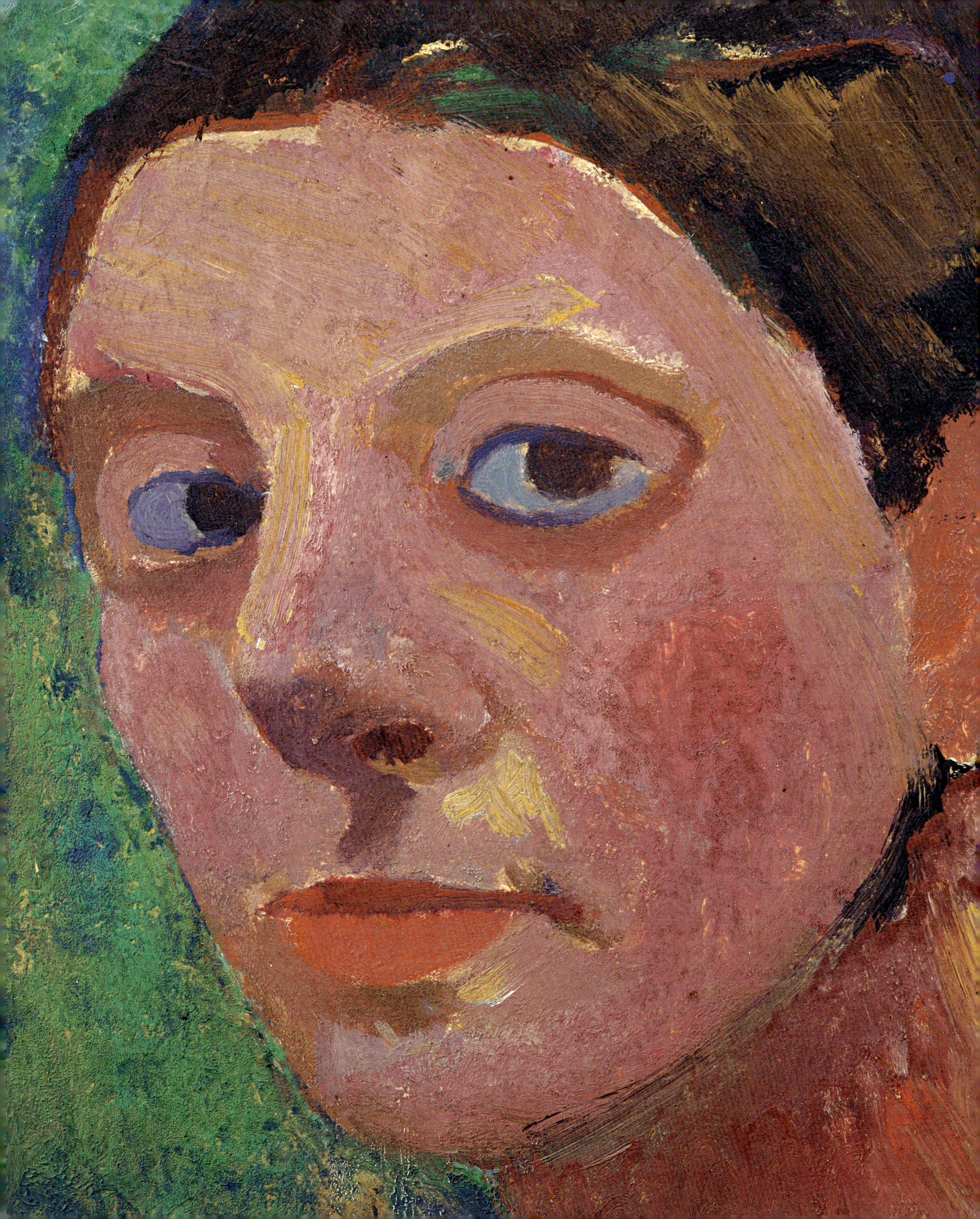

PAULA MODERSOHN-BECKER

EDITED BY INGRID PFEIFFER

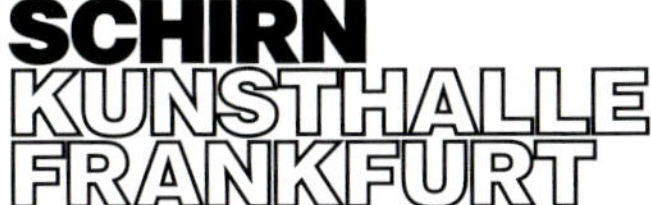

HIRMER

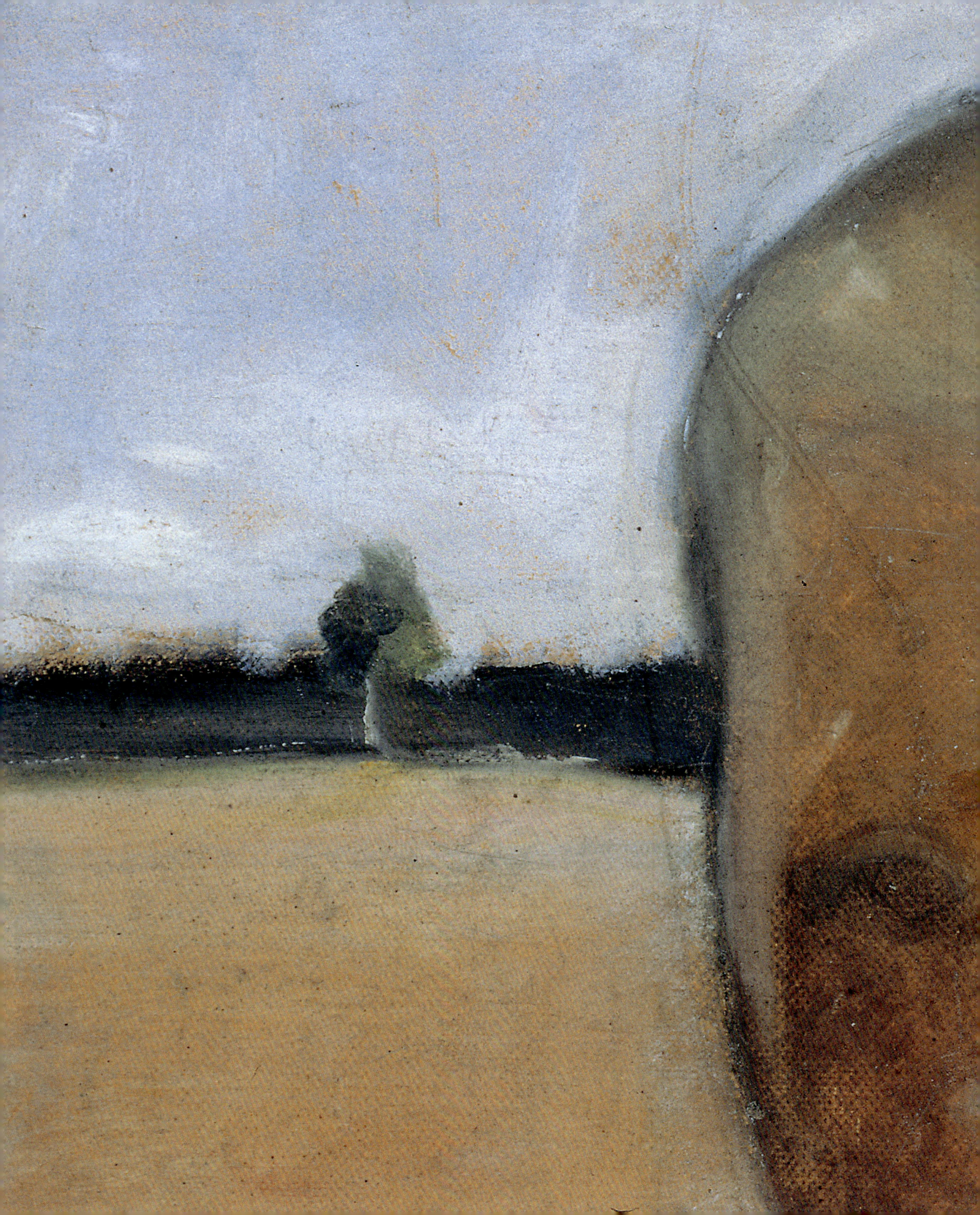

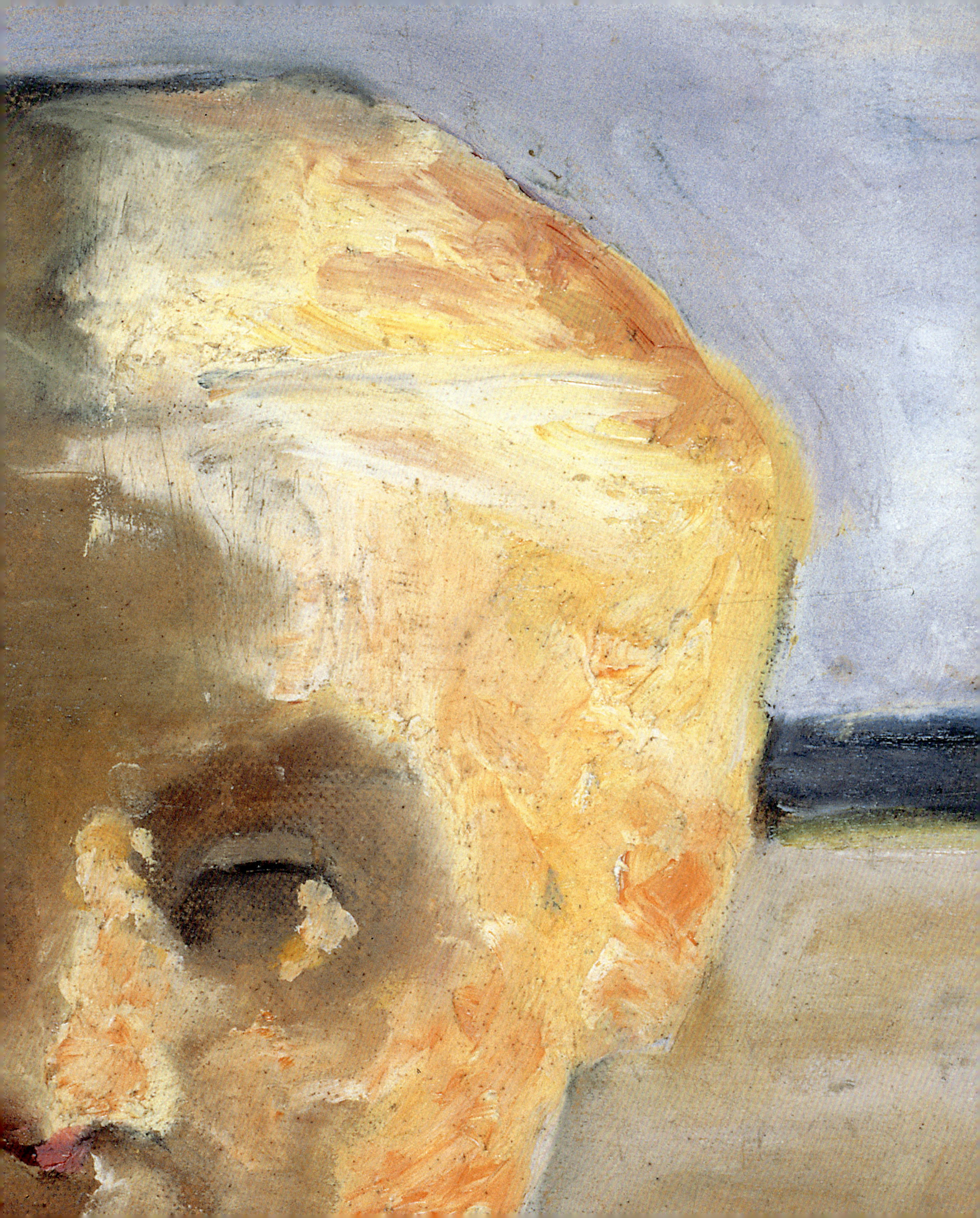

Supported by

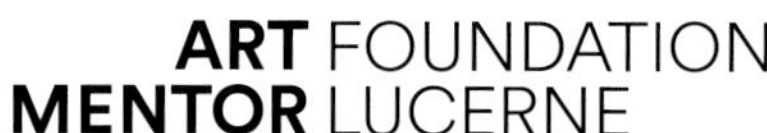

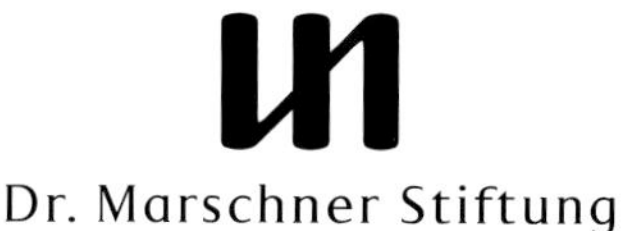

Additional support

Mann Stiftung

WORDS OF GREETING

The works of Paula Modersohn-Becker are famous the world over. With the directness and independence of her artistic expression, she is considered an important pioneer of modern tendencies in Germany. Nevertheless, it is not always easy to find the right approach to her often idiosyncratic work. Paula Modersohn-Becker is worthy of a reappraisal, which the Schirn Kunsthalle Frankfurt dares to undertake in the large, retrospective survey exhibition *Paula Modersohn-Becker*. On the basis of 116 paintings and drawings, the Schirn once again puts a well-known figure of classical modernism up for discussion on a grand scale and scrutinizes the artist in view of her relevance today.

The Dr. Marschner Foundation is pleased to be able to support the Schirn in this ambitious project. We have been closely associated with the Schirn Kunsthalle Frankfurt for a number of years and have already collaborated on various significant projects such as *Yoko Ono*, *Joan Miró*, and *Fantastic Women*. We are particularly proud of the preparation and realization of this magnificent exhibition on Paula Modersohn-Becker, featuring important loans from Europe and the United States. It is not easy to support projects flanked by such adverse circumstances as the Corona pandemic, and yet this support was a matter of course for us. It is important to the Dr. Marschner Foundation to make such an exhibition highlight possible for the public in Frankfurt, as well as for an audience far beyond, and thus to show that we reliably stand behind the cultural scene in our city.

We would like to thank the curator Ingrid Pfeiffer and the entire team of the Schirn Kunsthalle Frankfurt for their outstanding commitment. They deserve our full respect.

Peter Gatzemeier
Executive Board of the Dr. Marschner Foundation

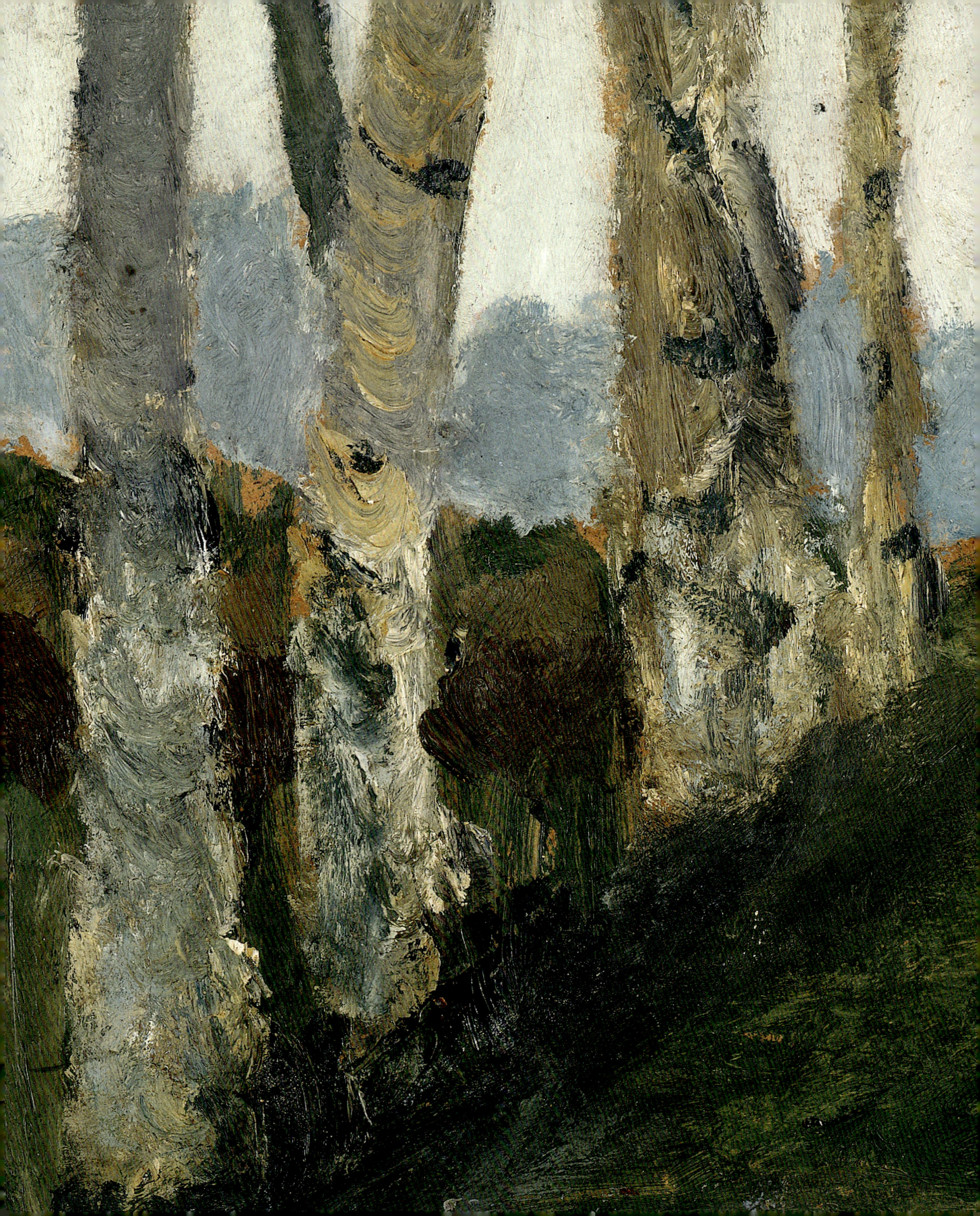

FOREWORD 12
PHILIPP DEMANDT

TIMELESS, DIRECT, PECULIAR–
THOUGHTS ON PAULA MODERSOHN-BECKER 33
INGRID PFEIFFER

ON MOTHERHOOD IN THE WORK OF
PAULA MODERSOHN-BECKER 97
INGE HEROLD

YEARS OF STUDY AND TRAVEL.
PAULA MODERSOHN-BECKER'S STUDIES IN
LONDON, BERLIN, AND PARIS 141
ANNA HAVEMANN

PARALLEL PHENOMENA.
PAULA MODERSOHN-BECKER AND MODERNISM 157
RAINER STAMM

REST IN MOTION.
ON THE POSSIBLE IN THE WORK OF PAULA MODERSOHN-BECKER 181
KARIN SCHICK

PAULA MODERSOHN-BECKER.
A BIOGRAPHY BETWEEN WORPSWEDE AND PARIS 193
SIMONE EWALD AND WOLFGANG WERNER

LIST OF EXHIBITED WORKS 203
BIBLIOGRAPHY 212
IMAGE CREDITS 215
COLOPHON 218

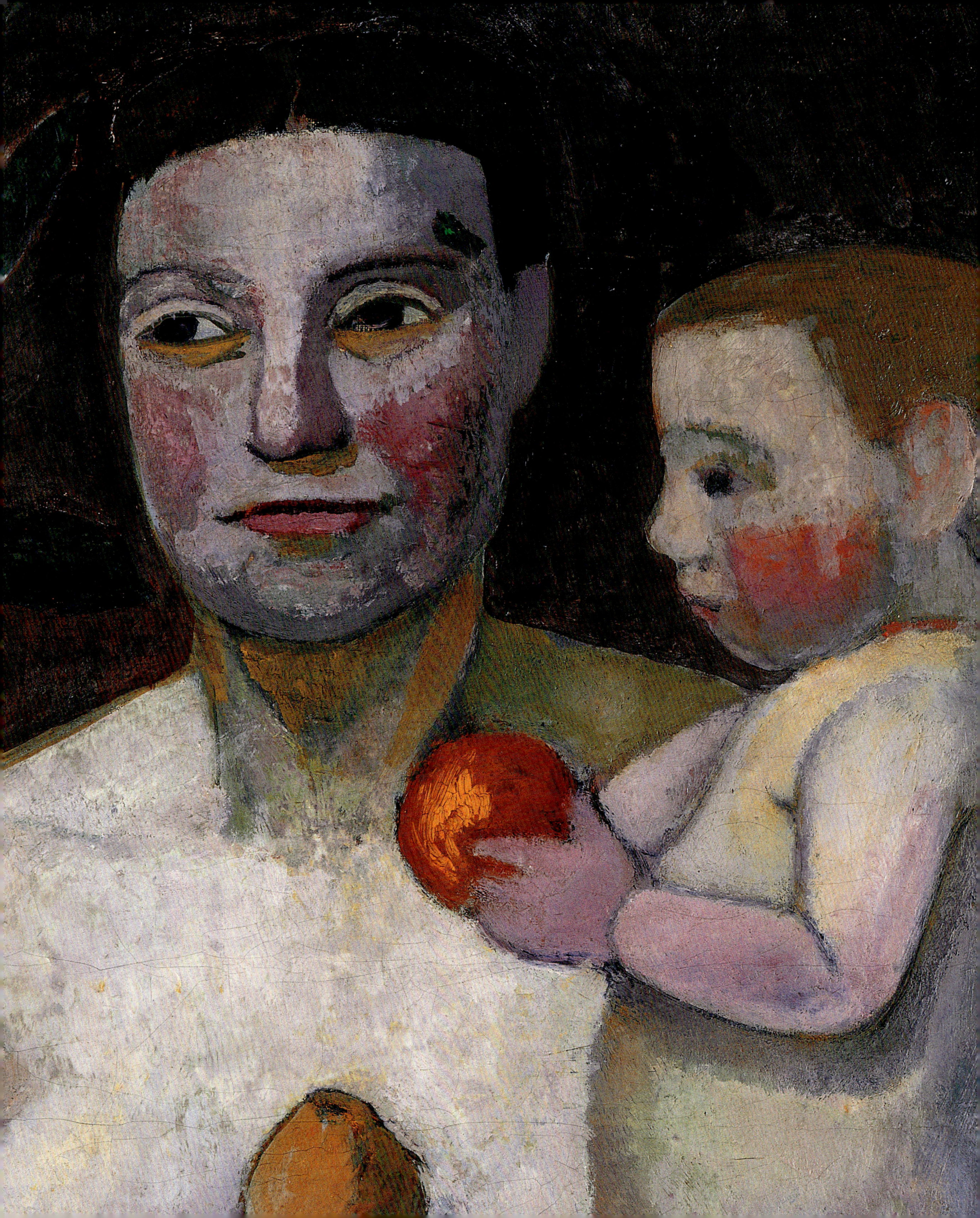

Our special thanks for their generous support go to the museums, institutions, private lenders, and galleries listed below, all of whom contributed to the success of the exhibition:

Albertinum | Galerie Neue Meister, Staatliche Kunstsammlungen Dresden
Detroit Institute of Arts, Gift of Robert H. Tannahill
Galerie Michael Haas, Berlin / Zurich
Hamburger Kunsthalle
Hessisches Landesmuseum Darmstadt
Kallir Research Institute, New York
Kulturstiftung Landkreis Osterholz
Kunsthalle Bremen – Der Kunstverein in Bremen
Kunsthalle zu Kiel
Kunsthalle Mannheim
Kunsthandel Wolfgang Werner, Bremen / Berlin
Kunsthaus Zürich, Zurich
Kunstmuseum Den Haag, The Hague
Landesmuseum für Kunst und Kulturgeschichte Oldenburg
LWL – Museum für Kunst und Kultur / Westfälisches Landesmuseum, Münster
Milwaukee Art Museum, Maurice and Esther Leah Ritz Collection
Museen Böttcherstraße, Paula Modersohn-Becker Museum, Bremen
Museum Ludwig, Cologne / Sammlung Haubrich 1947
Museum Ostwall im Dortmunder U, Dortmund
Museum am Modersohn-Haus, Worpswede, Sammlung Kaufmann
Niedersächsisches Landesmuseum Hannover
Nordfriesland Museum. Nissenhaus, Husum
Paula-Modersohn-Becker-Stiftung, Bremen
Rut- und Klaus-Bahlsen Stiftung
Saarlandmuseum – Moderne Galerie, Saarbrücken / Stiftung Saarländischer Kulturbesitz
Sammlung Sander
Sprengel Museum Hannover
Staatsgalerie Stuttgart
Städel Museum, Frankfurt am Main
Von der Heydt-Museum Wuppertal
Worcester Art Museum, Worcester, MA

As well as all private lenders in Germany and abroad who wish to remain anonymous.

FOREWORD

The last time Paula Modersohn-Becker was honored with an exhibition in Frankfurt am Main was a very long time ago, namely back in 1977 at the Frankfurter Kunstverein. In the meantime, she is now regarded as one of the most important women artists of early classical modernism: Almost every aspect of her extensive oeuvre, which was created in just under ten years, up to 1907, and only became well known after her death, has since been presented and explored in countless solo and group exhibitions. In Germany, however, Modersohn-Becker's work has usually tended to be located in northern Germany, since, during her short life and creative period, she commuted mainly between Worpswede near Bremen and Paris. One of the basic principles of the exhibitions at the Schirn Kunsthalle is to constantly develop different, topical questions for ostensibly all-too-familiar artists. Thus, we believe that Modersohn-Becker's work should once again be considered as a whole, namely as that of a pioneering modern artist and a woman around 1900. Her example can be used to discuss not only individual but also fundamental questions that continue to preoccupy us to this day.

The retrospective exhibition comprising 116 works is divided into thematic rooms with self-portraits and portraits, depictions of children, nudes and depictions of peasants, landscapes from Worpswede and Paris, and still life motifs. Our special selection shows how the artist circled around and varied her often recurring motifs in series and how, from the very beginning, she found her own pictorial solutions that were far ahead of her time. The catalog also deals in depth with individual questions such as her academic training, the mother-child depictions, and the reception of her work.

This ambitious project would never have been possible without a wide range of institutions, as well as individual persons. These include, in particular, the Paula-Modersohn-Becker-Stiftung in Bremen—here, especially Wolfgang Werner and Simone Ewald, who made this exhibition possible in the first place with their unwavering commitment, great expertise, and advice on many detailed questions. In addition, I would like to express my sincere gratitude to Frank Schmidt and the Paula Modersohn-Becker Museum in Bremen and Christoph Grunenberg from the Kunsthalle Bremen for their many years of support in the preparation of the exhibition, as well as for the substantial loans. We would also like to thank Antje Modersohn and Rainer Noeres in Fischerhude for their helpful support. Without all the experts mentioned here, the exhibition would simply not have been possible.

We are also deeply indebted to the numerous private collectors who supported our exhibition: first and foremost, the Sammlung Sander in Darmstadt, the Sammlung Bernhard Kaufmann in Worpswede, as well as Galerie Haas in Berlin and Zurich, and Galerie St. Etienne in New York, and all those who wish to remain anonymous.

The generous grants from the Art Mentor Foundation Lucerne and the Frankfurt-based Dr. Marschner Foundation have helped make the realization of this exhibition possible. Both sponsors support the Schirn in its goal of providing a new perspective on the eventful life and well-known work of Paula Modersohn-Becker. My heartfelt thanks for this outstanding support go to the Board of Trustees and the management of the Art Mentor Foundation Lucerne. I would also like to express my sincere thanks to the Board of Directors of the Dr. Marschner Foundation, Peter Gatzemeier and Hansjörg Koroschetz, as well as the Foundation's Advisory Board, for once again expressing their trust in our work with their commitment. We would also like to thank the Jürgen R. and Eva-Maria Mann Foundation, whose ongoing support has made an additional significant contribution to the quality and scope of the accompanying publication.

I would also like to thank, as always, the City of Frankfurt am Main for its continuous support of our work at the Schirn, in particular and on behalf of all decision-makers, Mayor Peter Feldmann and the Head of the Department of Culture Ina Hartwig.

My special thanks go to Ingrid Pfeiffer, curator at the Schirn Kunsthalle, who has pursued the project with great dedication over many years of work and has driven it forward at all levels. Anna Huber worked with her with great dedication on the realization of both the exhibition and the catalog.

My sincere thanks go to all the authors for their knowledgeable and insightful contributions to this publication: Anna Havemann, Inge Herold, Ingrid Pfeiffer, Karin Schick, and Rainer Stamm. Simone Ewald and Wolfgang Werner also deserve special thanks for compiling the detailed biography. For the careful translation of the texts from German into English, we thank Gérard Goodrow, as well as Vanessa Magson, Olivia Parkes and Susanne Ibisch for their accomplished editing. We would like to thank Hirmer Verlag, especially Kerstin Ludolph and Jutta Allekotte, for their excellent collaboration on the catalog. It was designed with great dedication by Sabine Frohmader. For the creative exhibition design in Frankfurt, we thank John Russo of Studio Heyhey. The successful exhibition architecture was designed by Karsten Weber, Düsseldorf.

Without the dedicated team at the Schirn, this impressive exhibition and accompanying publication would not have been possible. For this, I would like to express my great gratitude to all staff members, especially to the Deputy Director and Head of Exhibitions Esther Schlicht. I would like to thank Karin Grüning and Elke Walter for coordinating the transport, as well as the installation and dismantling of the exhibited works; Christian Teltz and Oliver Taschke for technical support; and Luise Leyer as Assistant to the Head of Exhibitions. Furthermore, my thanks go to Andreas Gundermann and the hanging team. Luise Bachmann, Isabel Reiche, Heike Stumpf, and Angelika Schäfer are to thank for the marketing and the design of the campaign. I would like to thank Johanna Pulz, Julia Bastian, Elisabeth Pallentin, and Clara Nicolay for the press work. I would also like to thank Renate Voget for coordinating and supervising the publication and Anuschka Berthelius for editing the *Schirn Magazin*. For the accompanying educational program, my thanks go to Chantal Eschenfelder with Simone Boscheinen, Laura Heeg, Olga Schaetz, and Anna Haag. For the development and coordination of the events thanks are due to Ute Seiffert and Alena Flemming. I would like to thank Julia Lange, Hannah Ruiz, and Miriam Werner for the coordination and care of our partners and sponsors. I would also like to thank Heike Berndt, Boris Deckelmann, and Hina Ahmad in the administration of the Schirn, as well as Andrea Canthal, Samira Koch, and Marejke Fries for their assistance in numerous matters. Finally, I would like to thank the messenger Stefan Schell, Rosaria La Tona and the building cleaning team, Bettina Beyermann and Vanessa Bernhardt at the reception, as well as all other Schirn employees who were involved in the realization of this comprehensive project.

As an artist, Paula Modersohn-Becker was a pioneer of modernism. With this exhibition and the accompanying catalog, we hope to paint an accurate picture of her extraordinary life and work, and to encourage engagement with her powerful legacy.

Philipp Demandt
Director, Schirn Kunsthalle Frankfurt

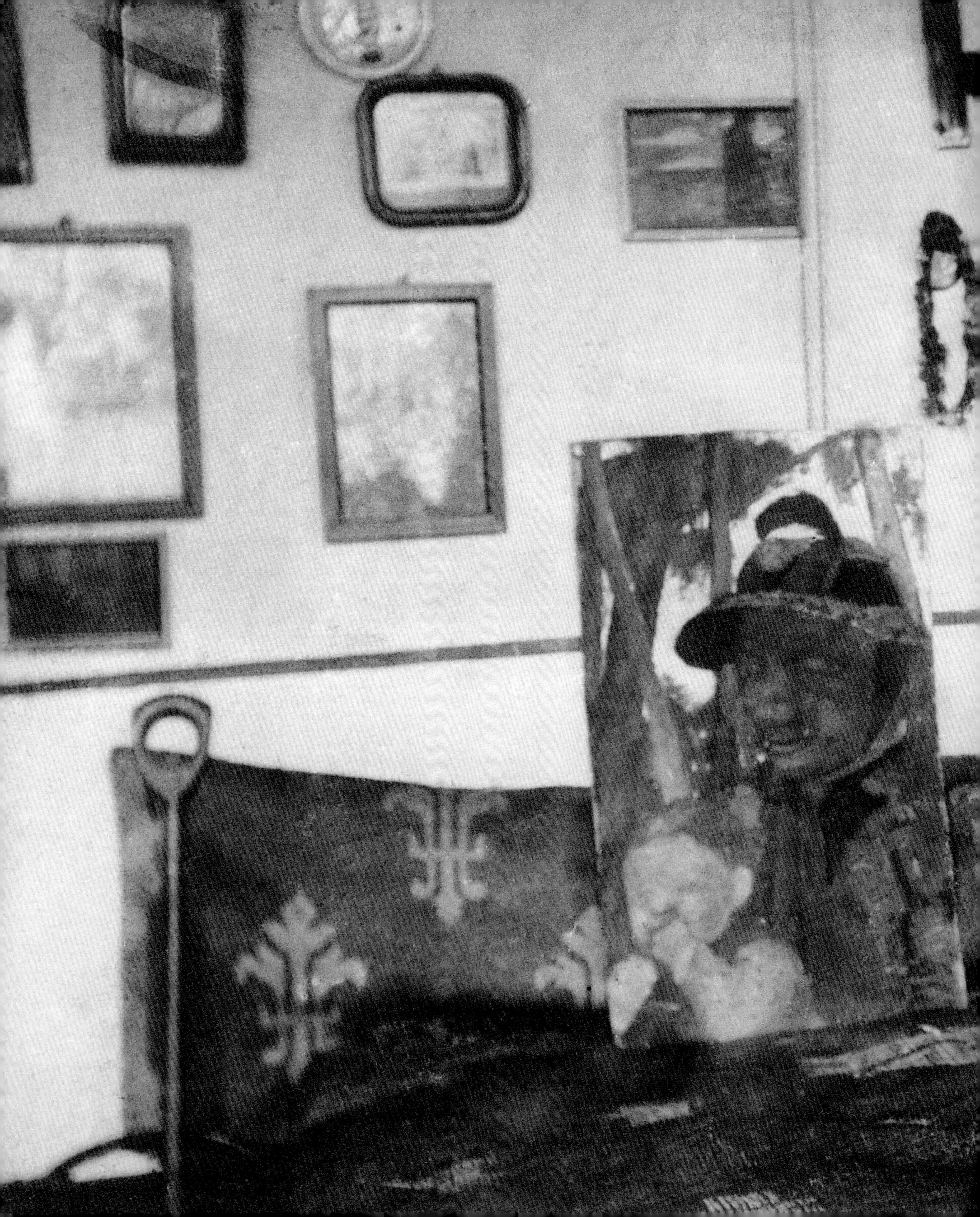

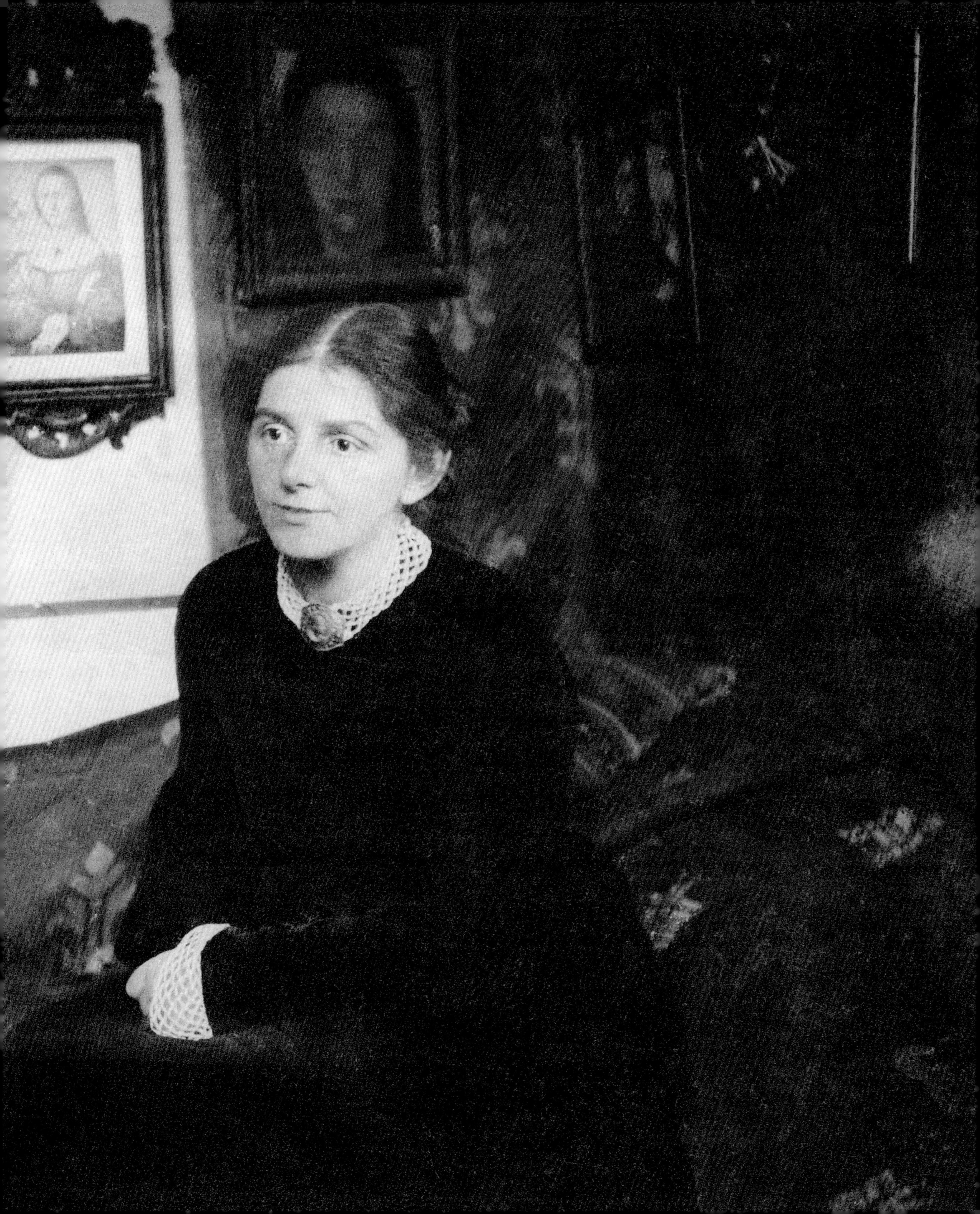

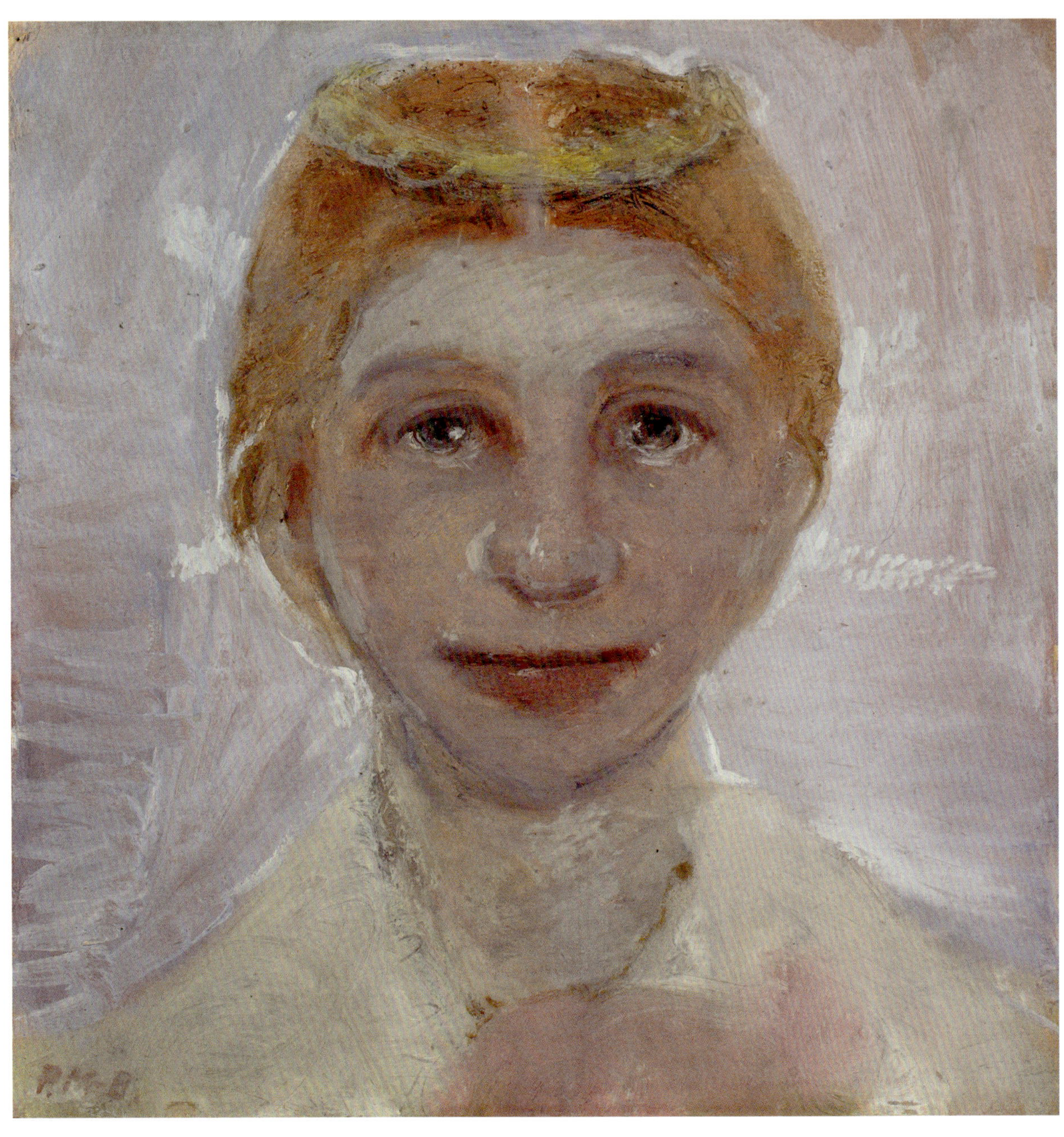

Selbstbildnis mit gelbem Kranz / Self-Portrait with Yellow Wreath, c. 1901

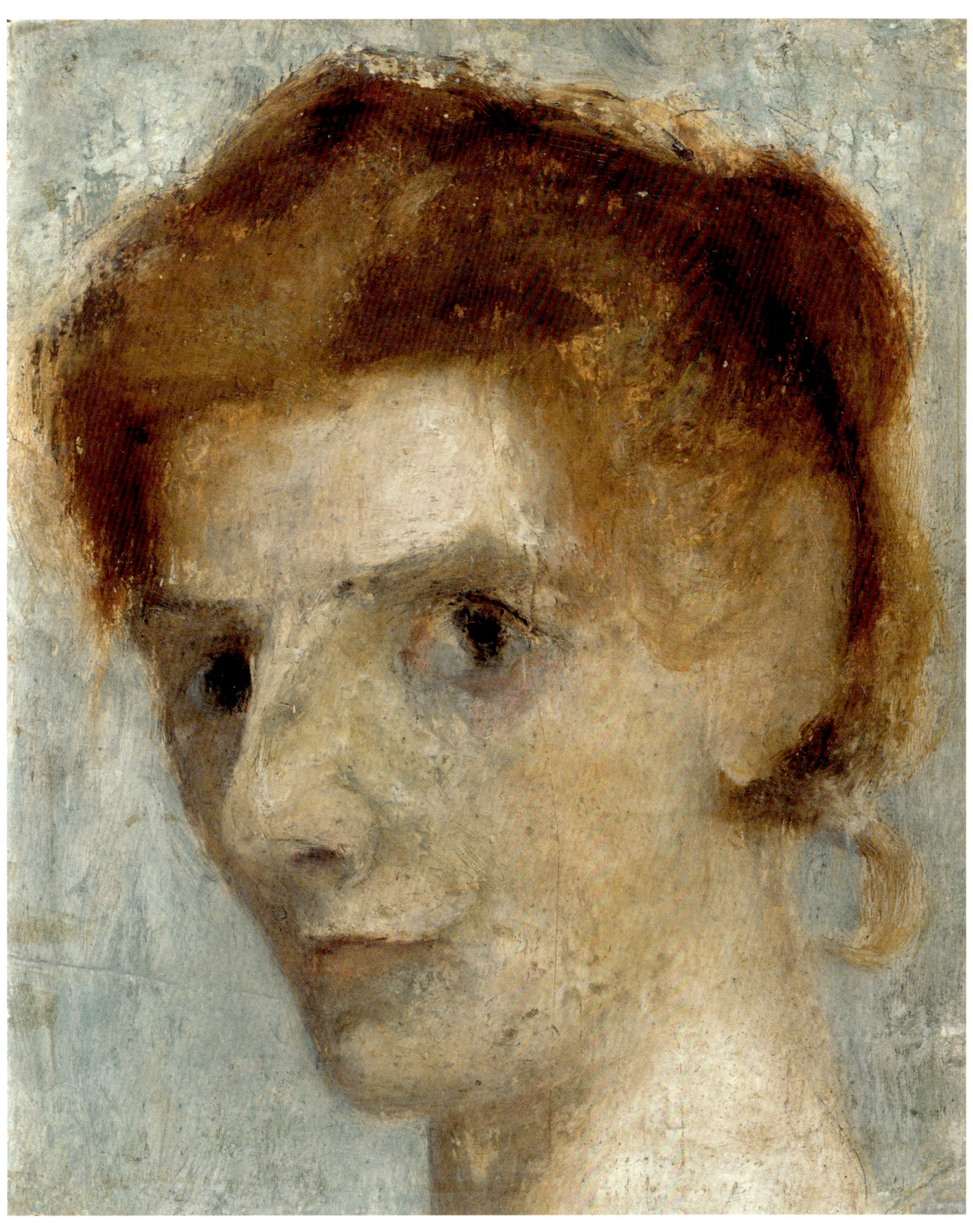

Selbstbildnis / Self-Portrait, c. 1898

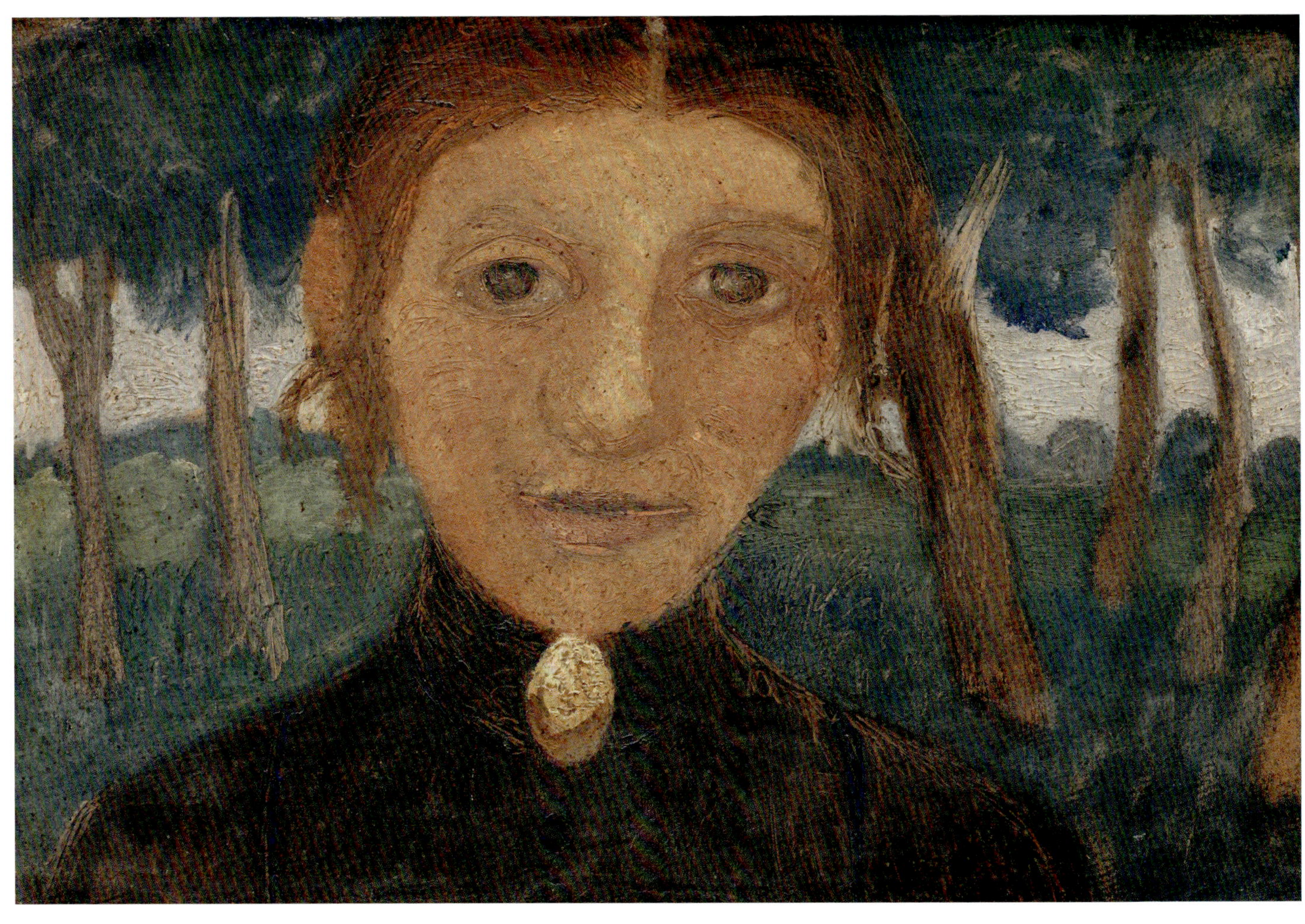

Selbstbildnis vor Landschaft mit Bäumen / Self-Portrait in Front of Landscape with Trees, c. 1903

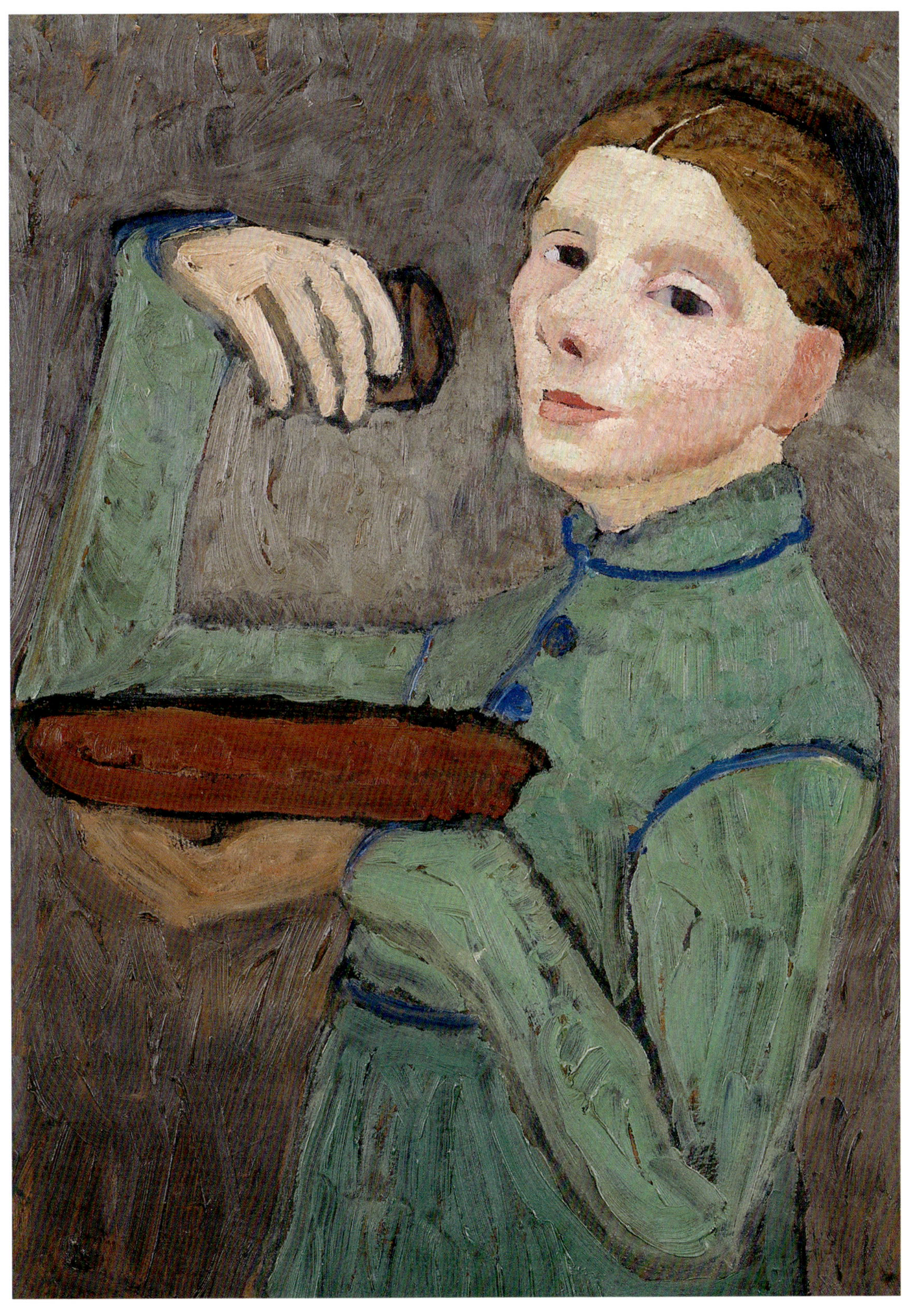

Selbstbildnis, Halbfigur nach links, eine Schale und ein Glas haltend /
Self-Portrait, Half-Length Figure Turned to the Left, with a Bowl and a Glass, c. 1904

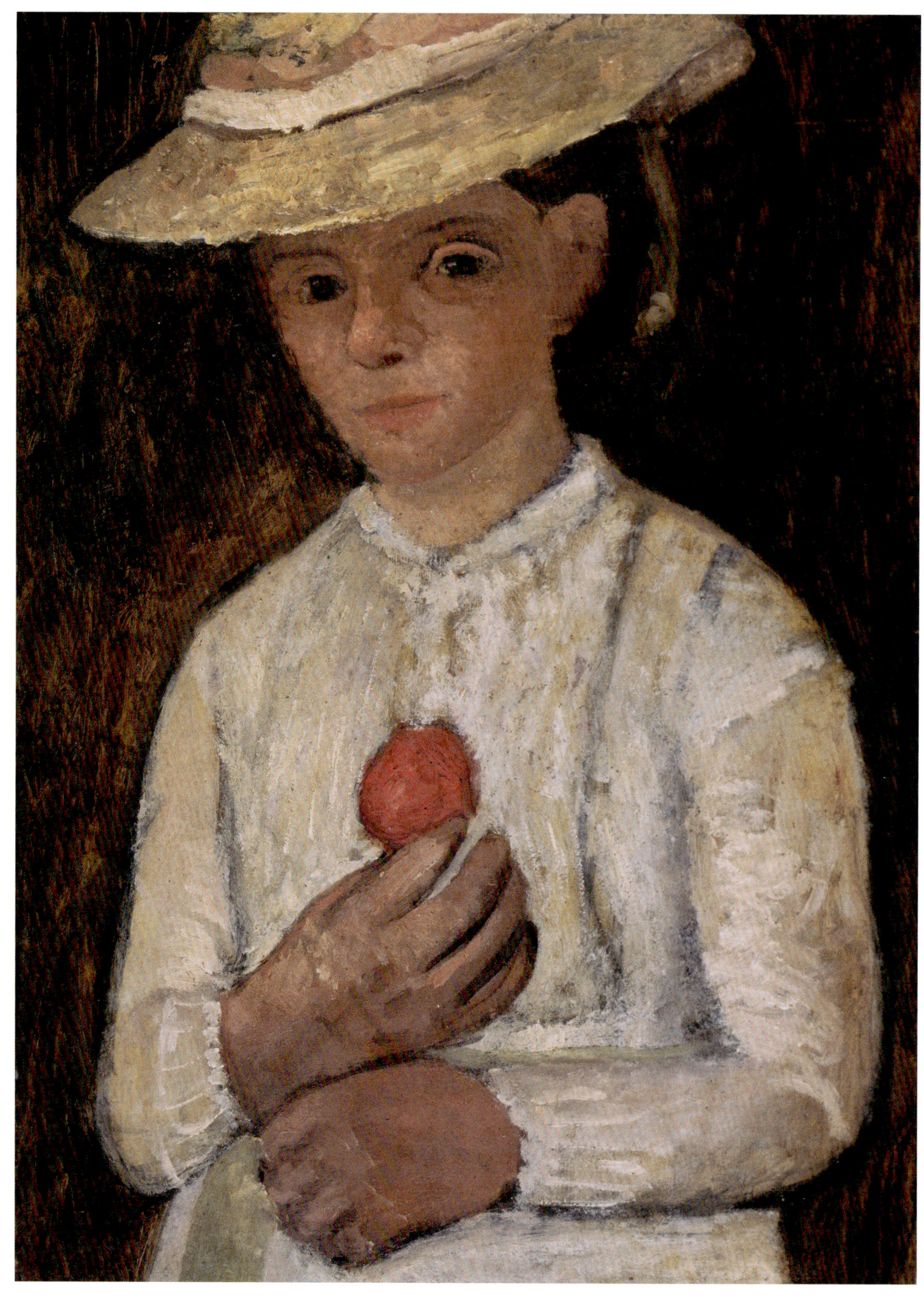

Selbstbildnis mit roter Rose / Self-Portrait with a Red Rose, c. 1905

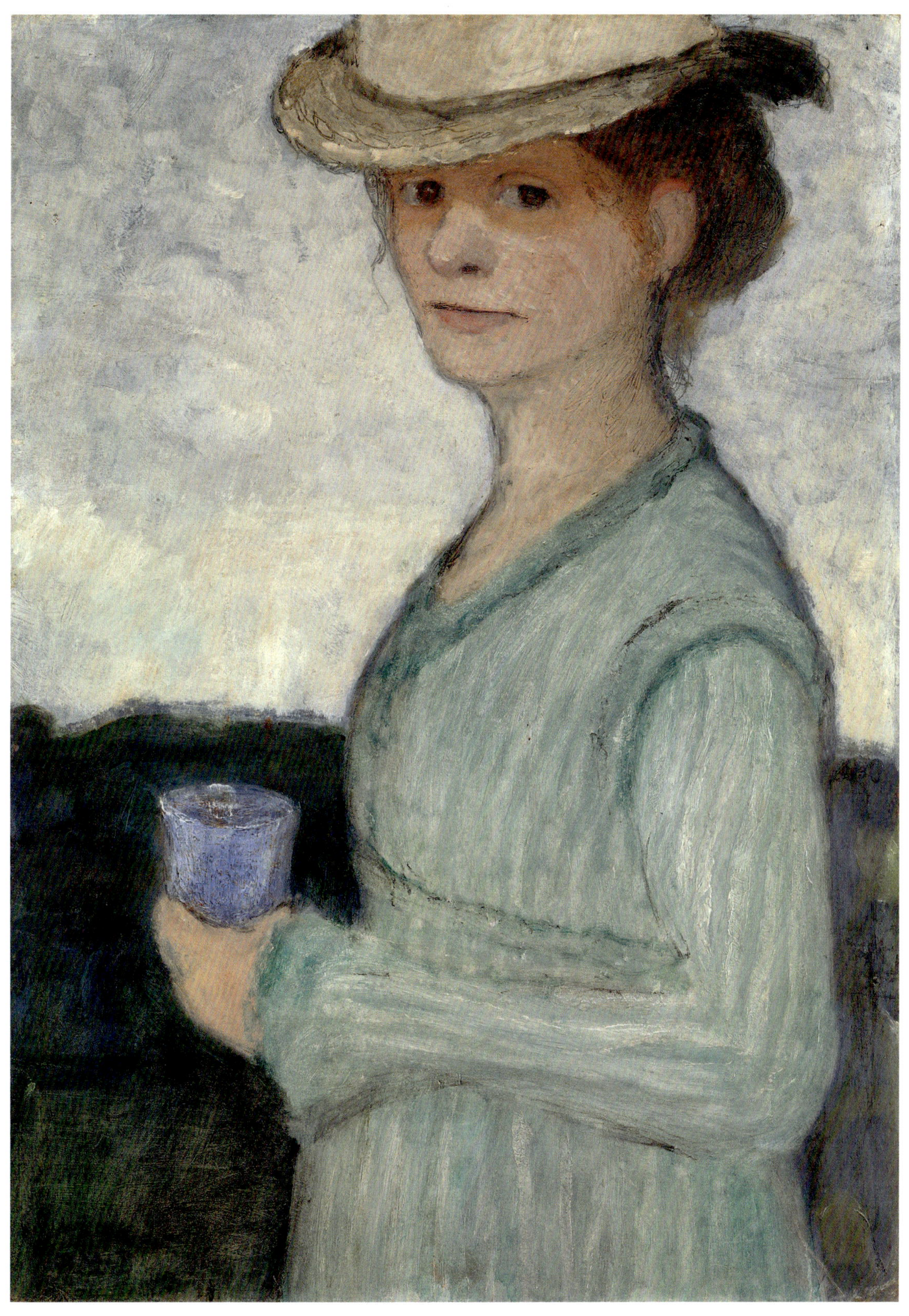

Selbstbildnis mit blauem Glas / Self-Portrait with a Blue Glass, c. 1902

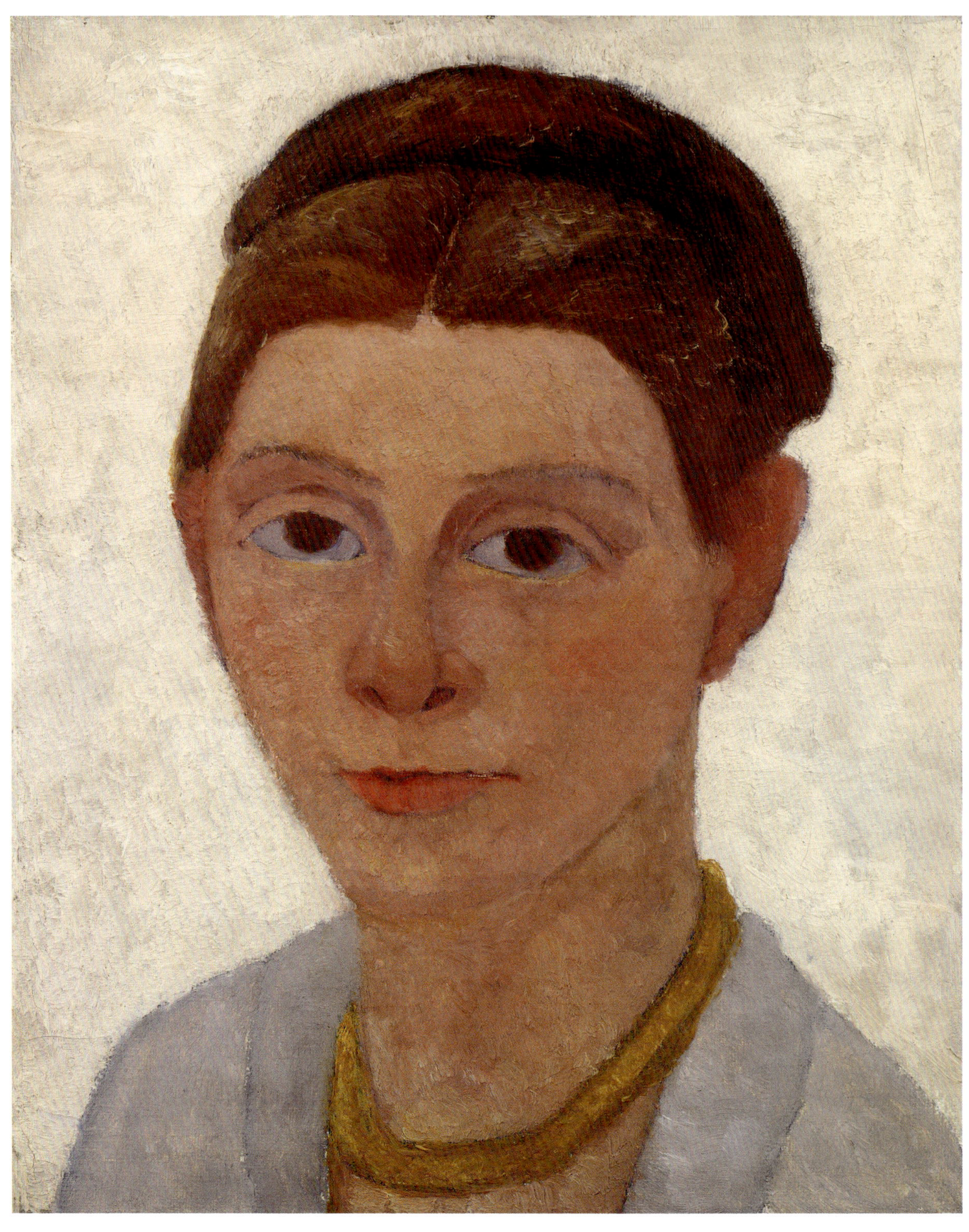

Selbstbildnis mit Bernsteinkette / Self-Portrait with Amber Necklace, c. 1905

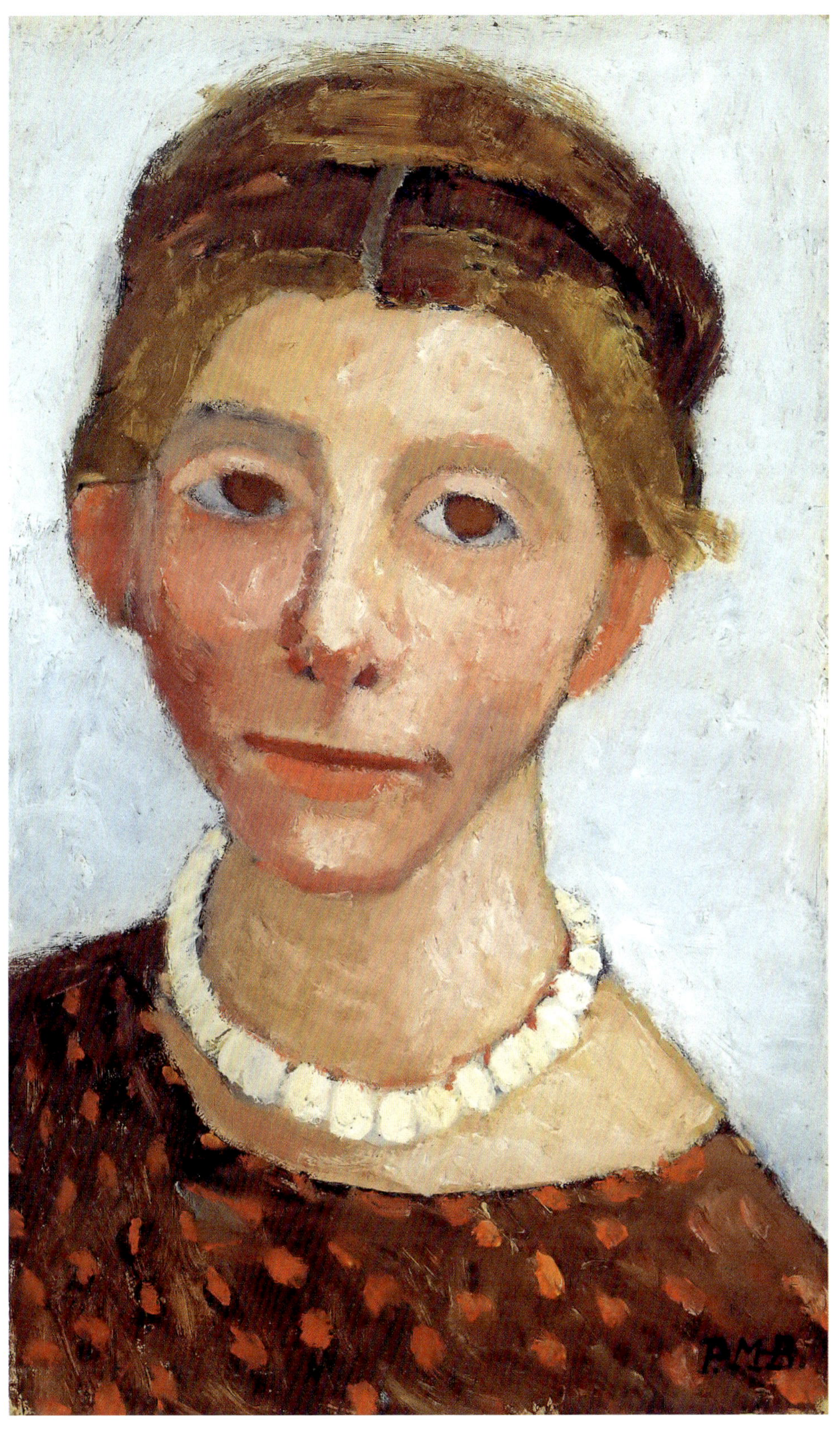

Selbstbildnis mit weißer Perlenkette / Self-Portrait with White Pearl Necklace, 1906

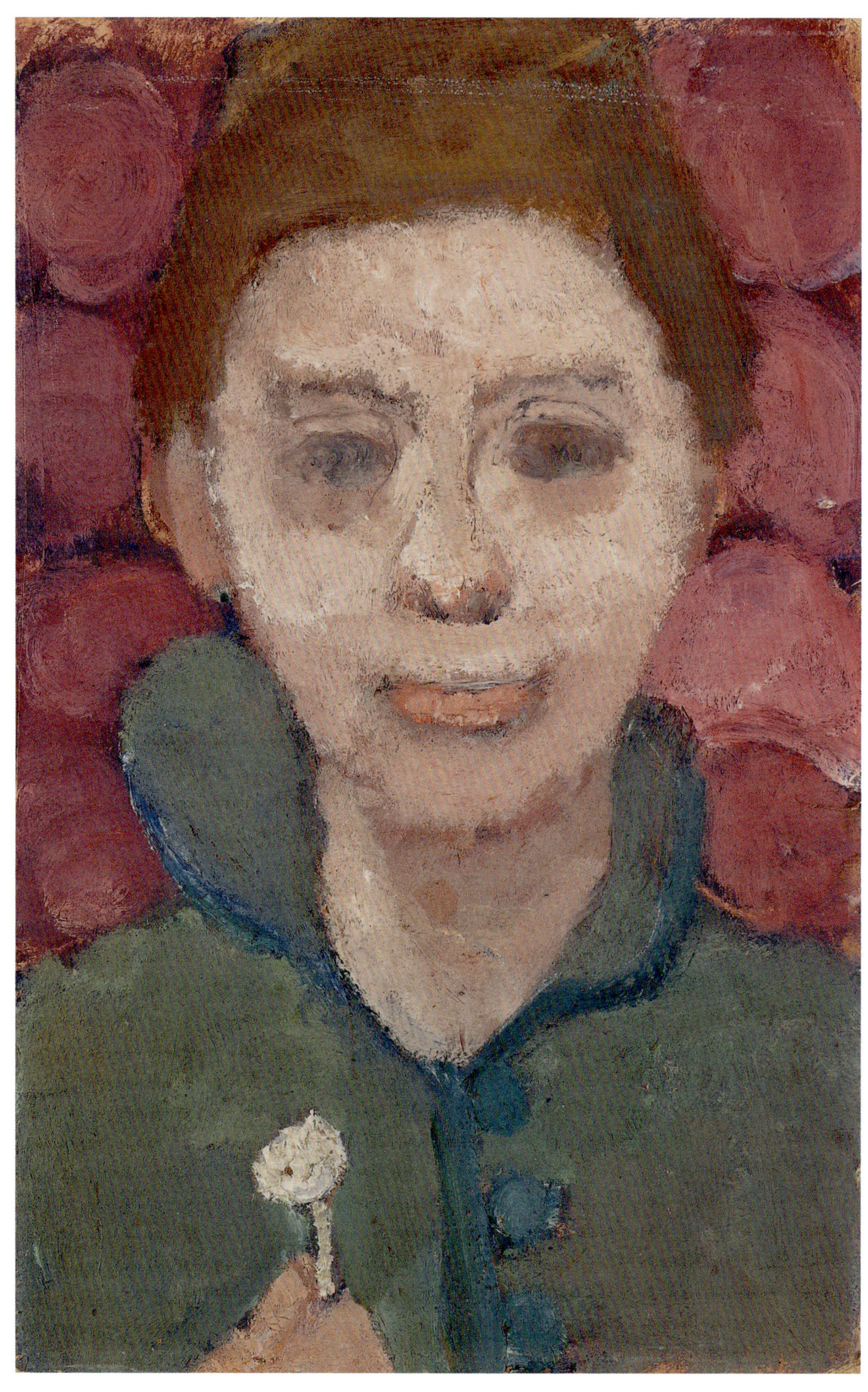

Selbstbildnis mit Blume / Self-Portrait with Flower, 1907

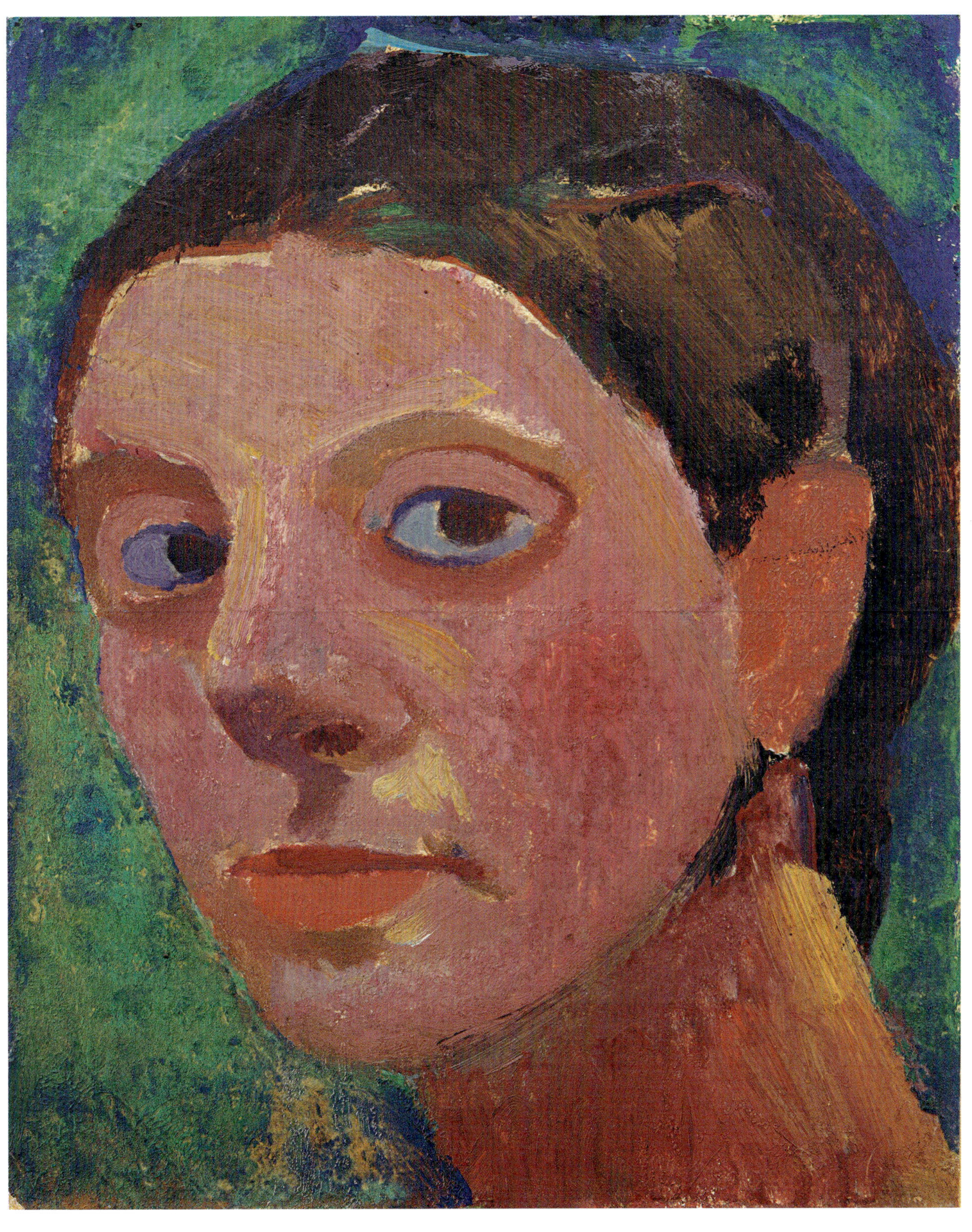

Selbstbildnis nach halblinks / Self-Portrait, Turned to the Left, summer 1906

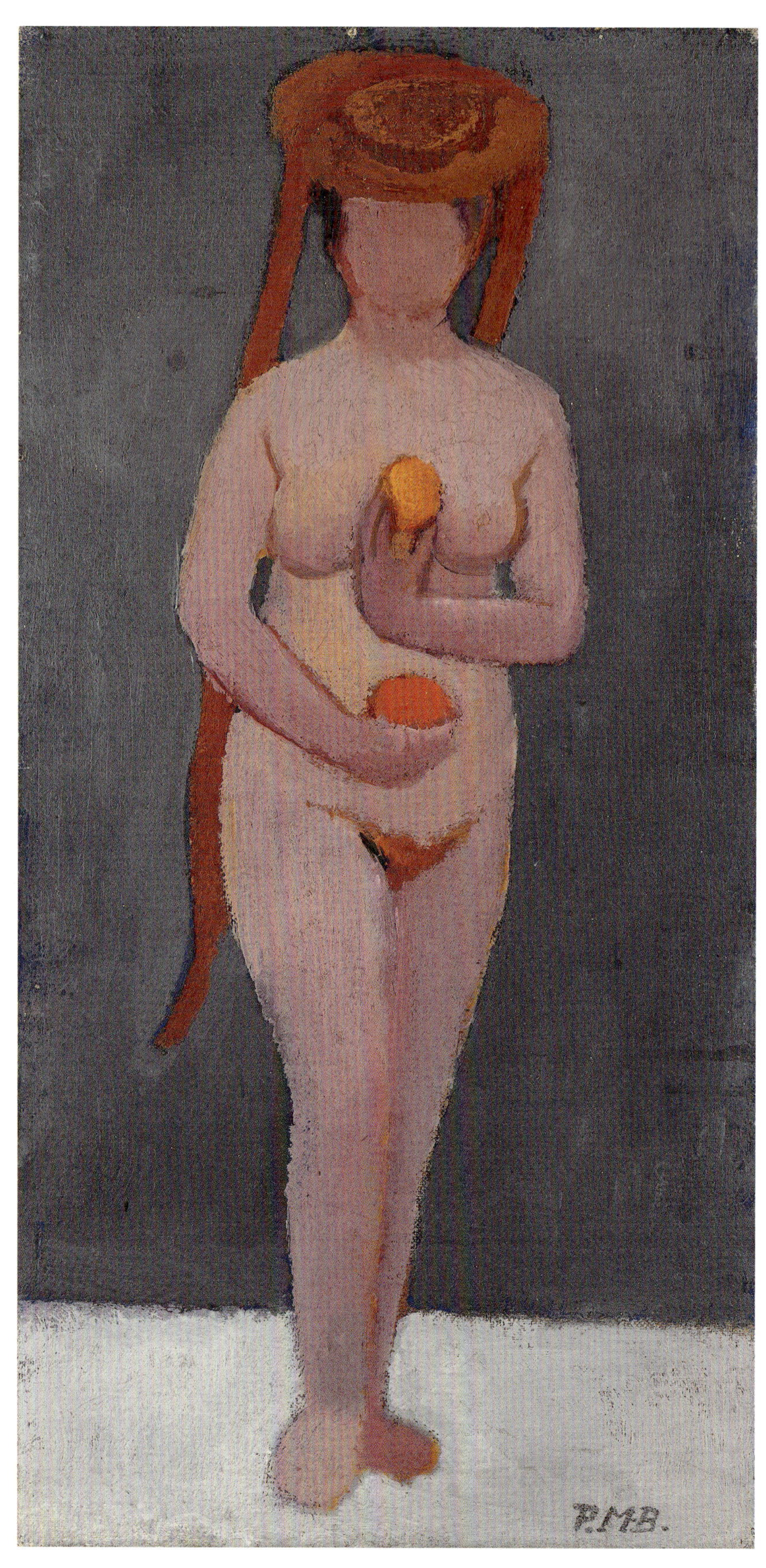

Selbstbildnis als stehender Akt mit Hut /
Self-Portrait as Standing Nude with Hat, summer 1906

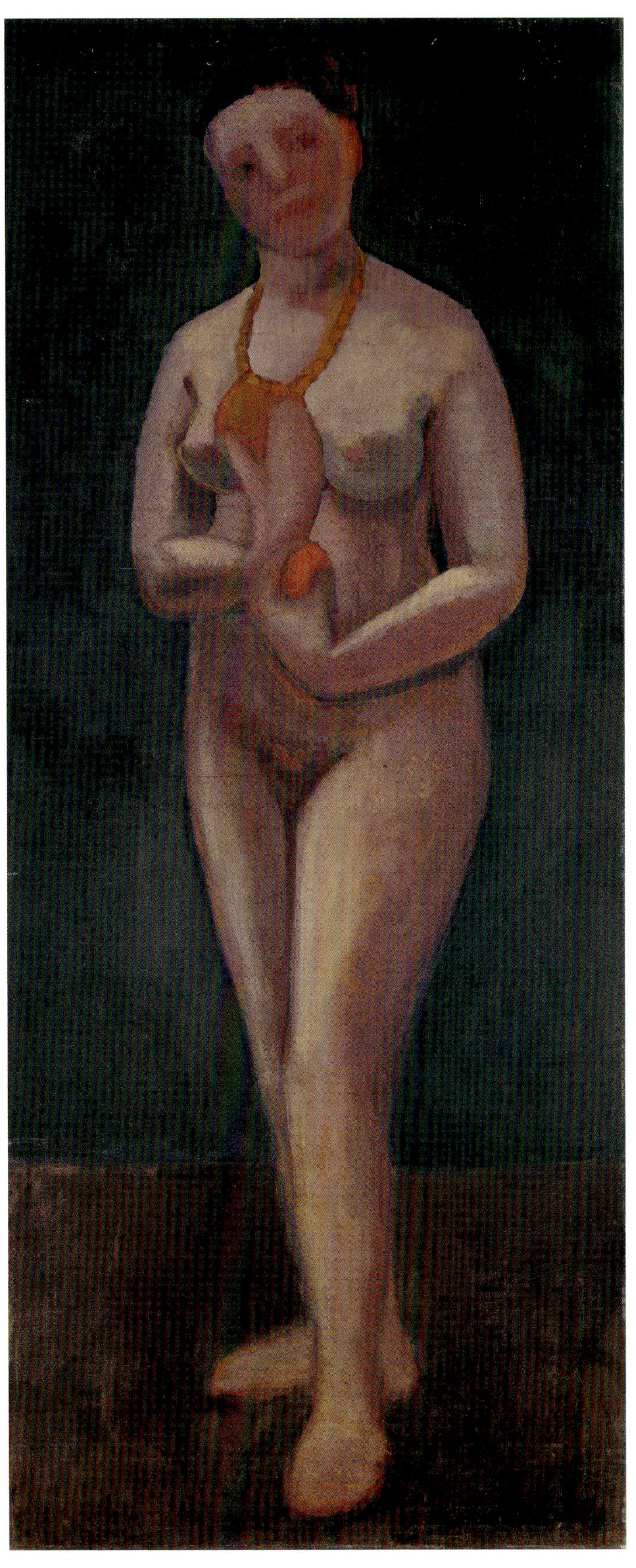

Selbstbildnis als stehender Akt /
Self-Portrait as Standing Nude, summer 1906

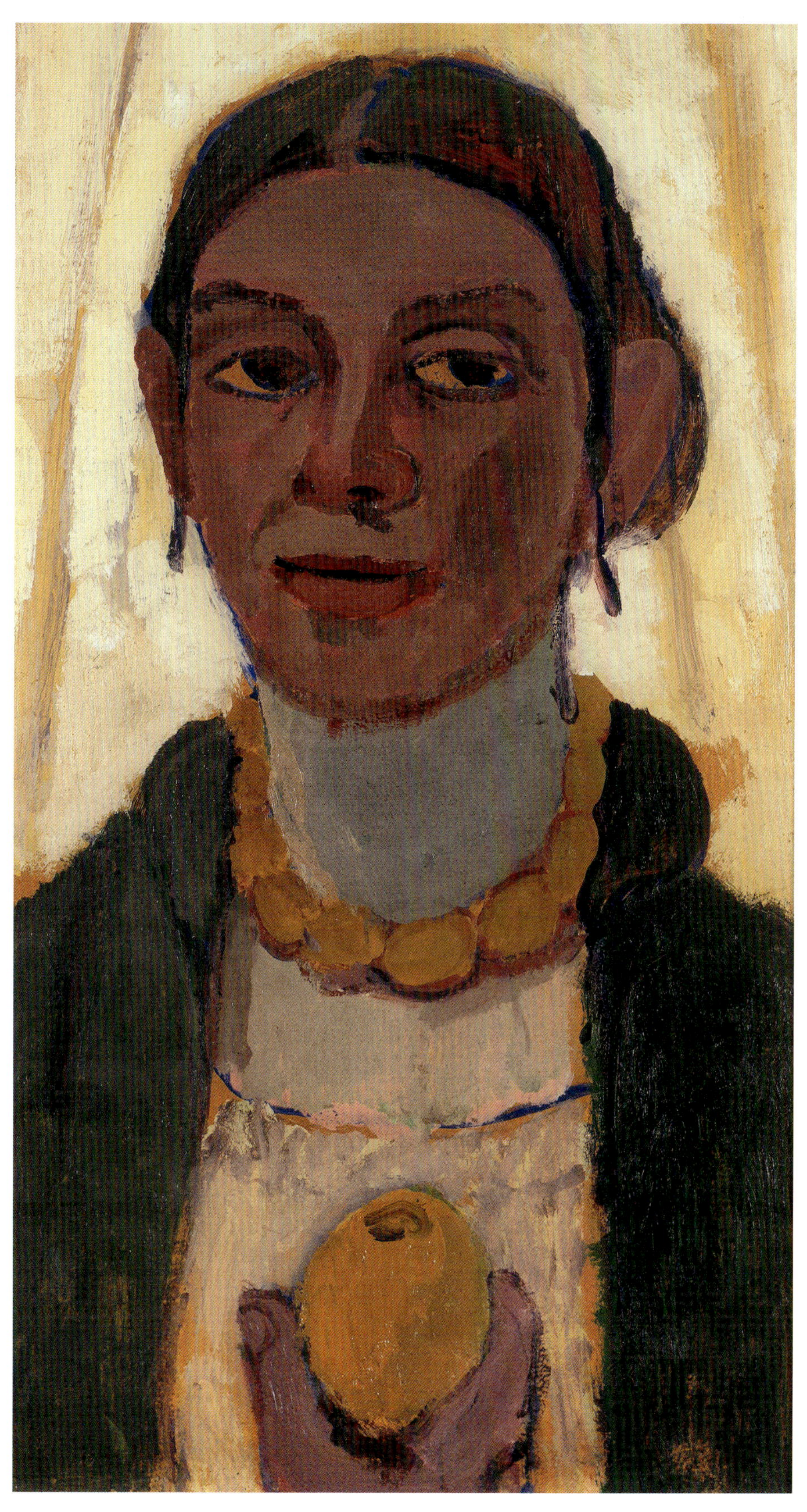

Selbstbildnis mit Zitrone / Self-Portrait with Lemon, 1906/7

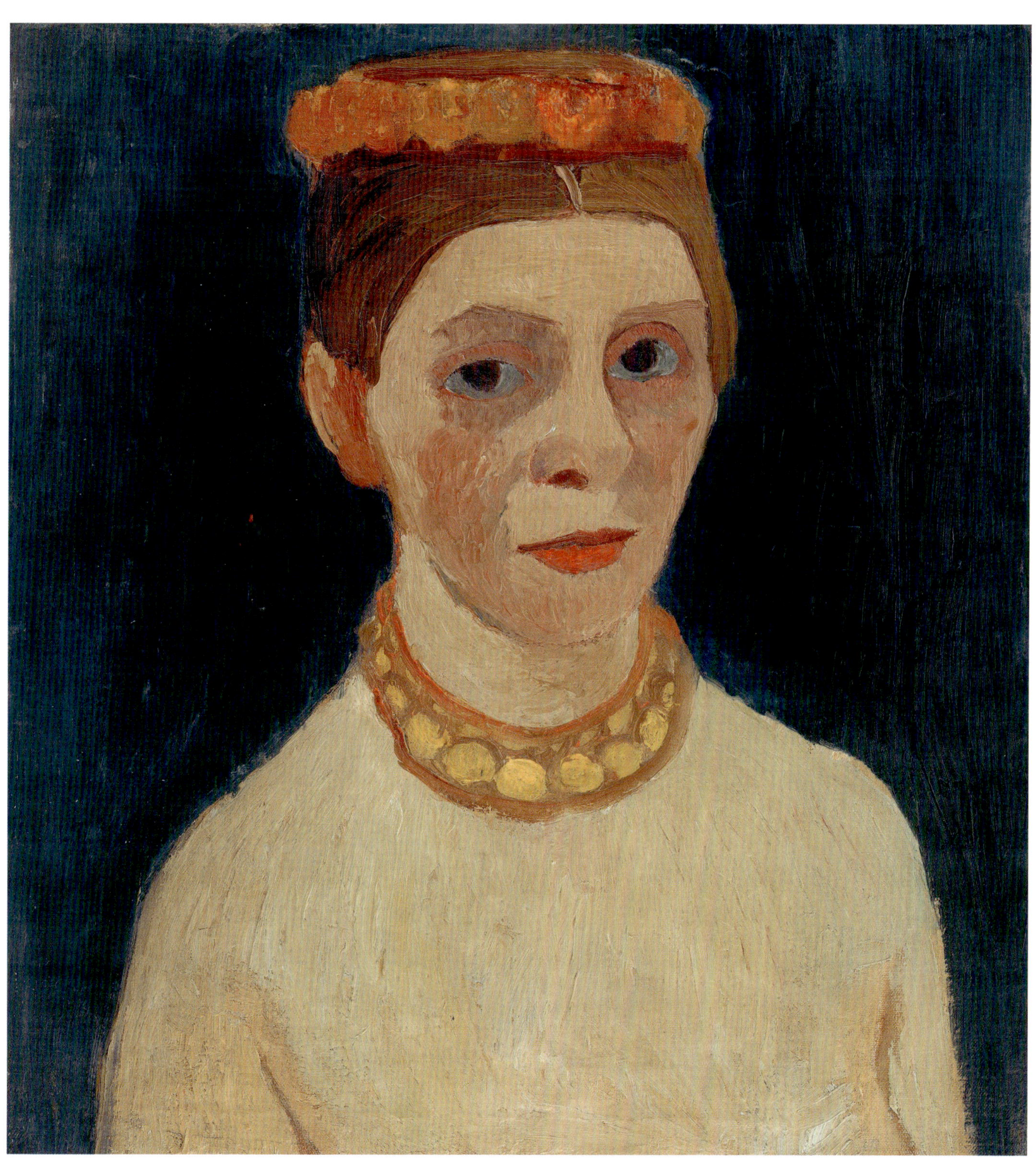

Selbstbildnis mit rotem Blütenkranz und Kette / Self-Portrait with Red Floral Wreath and Necklace, 1906/7

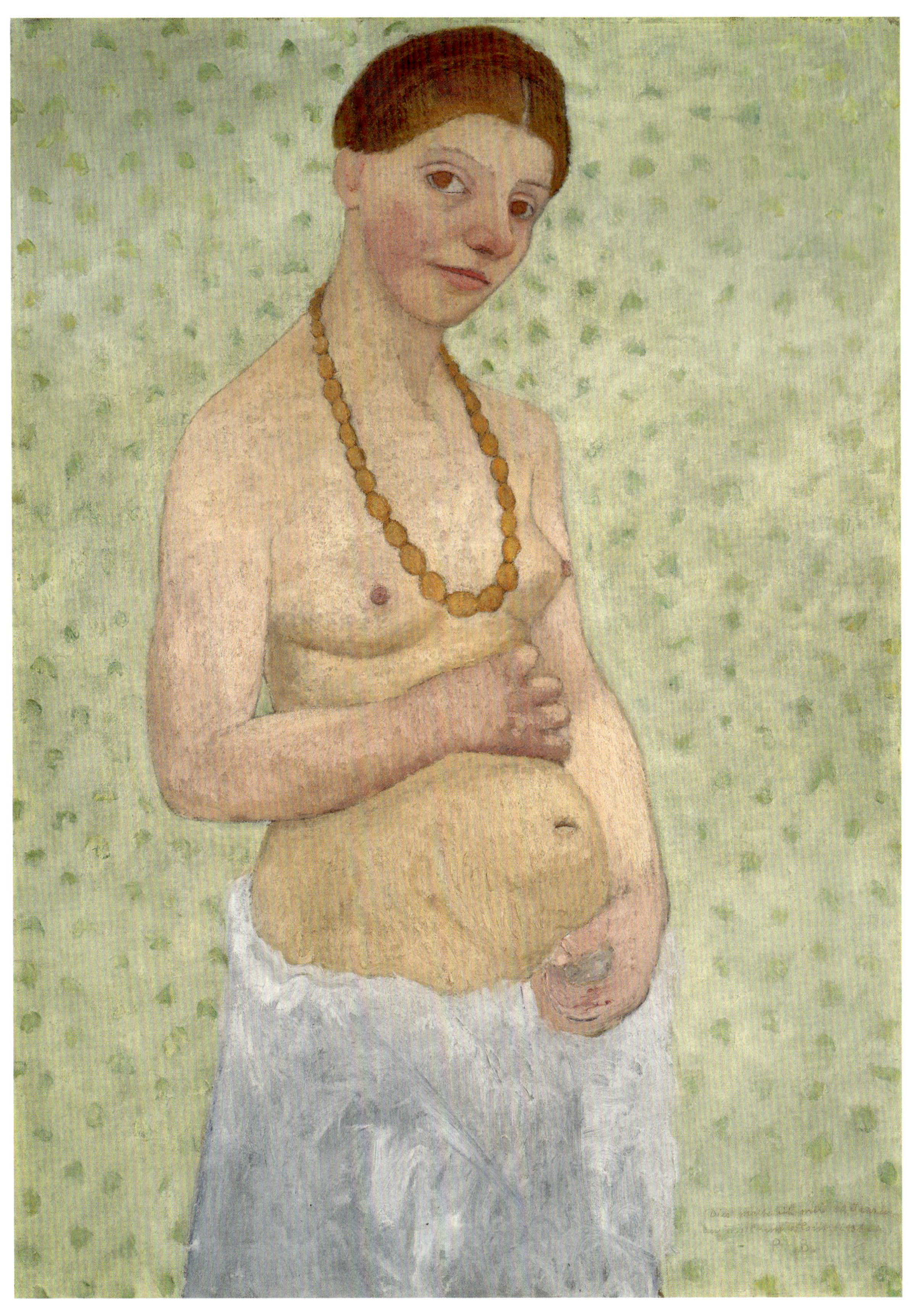

Selbstbildnis am 6. Hochzeitstag / Self-Portrait on the Sixth Wedding Day, May 25, 1906

TIMELESS, DIRECT, PECULIAR—THOUGHTS ON PAULA MODERSOHN-BECKER

INGRID PFEIFFER

"Her judgment in art: independent, peculiar…"[1]

After her premature death in November 1907 at the age of only thirty-one, Paula Modersohn-Becker quickly became a myth, followed by numerous exhibitions and purchases by museums, as well as by a new generation of collectors interested in modern art. Beginning in 1933, the National Socialists confiscated her works from altogether forty German museums; this was followed after World War II and through to today by a steadily increasing international perception of this "exceptional artist." Probably no other woman painter in Germany has been written about more, hardly any other has been honored with more exhibitions—unique also is the fact that an entire museum was dedicated to her in Bremen as early as 1927. During her short life and creative period, she stayed alternately in the Worpswede artists' colony near Bremen and in Paris, where she stayed four times for a total of roughly two years. Alongside this was her marriage to the successful landscape painter Otto Modersohn. There was a great deal of discrepancy between the artist's own high standards and her external success, which was completely lacking during her own lifetime. Today, several of her works are considered veritable "icons" of art history, such as the first nude self-portrait of a woman artist, moreover with implied pregnancy (p. 32)—to this day, a work that has yet to be definitively interpreted.

Today, Modersohn-Becker appears all too familiar, popular, admired—at the same time, however, she is also categorized as a painter of children's portraits, mothers and

1—Otto Modersohn's journal, entry dated December 8, 1900, in: *Paula Modersohn-Becker - Otto Modersohn. Der Briefwechsel*, ed. Antje Modersohn and Wolfgang Werner (Berlin 2017), p. 10 [translated].

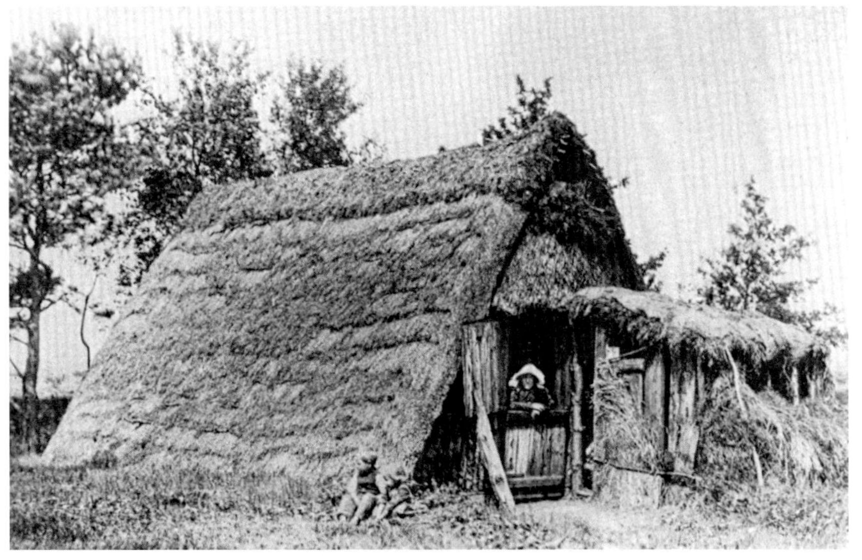

1 Old moor cottage, c. 1900

motherhood, peasants, and the North German landscape. In recent years, the view of her as a "pioneer of modernism" and a pre-Expressionist has dominated. It is the amazing oeuvre of a young woman, with altogether 734 paintings and roughly 1,500 works on paper. But it is also a contradictory oeuvre, which, over the course of more than one hundred years, has become a projection screen for the judgment and prejudice of each respective generation.

Despite—or perhaps even because of—the few years that Modersohn-Becker lived and worked, her work seems like a burning lens directed at the debates, both formal and thematic, not only on art in Germany around 1900 in general, but exemplarily on the art of a woman painter in an extremely difficult era for women. Her motifs are unmistakably feminine, and at the same time rigorous, direct, and at times downright radically different from those of her contemporaries, created in often solitary confrontation with art history as well as the latest trends, which she was able to "absorb" during her stays in Paris between 1900 and 1907.

MEN AND WOMEN ARTISTS IN WORPSWEDE

"It is a strange land. Standing on the small sand hill of Worpswede, one can see it stretched all about [...]. It lies there in all its flatness, almost without a fold, and the roads and creeks run far into the horizon. There begins a sky of indescribable changeability and vastness. It is reflected in every leaf. All things seem to occupy themselves with it; it is everywhere. And everywhere is the sea."[2]
Rainer Maria Rilke

When, from circa 1889 onwards, the Worpswede painters' colony, consisting of Fritz Mackensen, Otto Modersohn, Hans am Ende, Carl Vinnen, and Heinrich Vogeler, settled in the small town on the edge of the former Teufelsmoor (literally the "Devil's Moor"), which had been drained since the eighteenth century, it was their goal to depict the "original" life of the rural population and the expressive landscape in the tradition of the French painters' groups of Pont-Aven and Barbizon. What the artists discovered, however, was a counter-world of peat cutters, farmers, and day laborers—

2—Rainer Maria Rilke, *Worpswede. Fritz Mackensen, Otto Modersohn, Fritz Overbeck, Hans am Ende, Heinrich Vogeler* [1903] (Munich 1987), p. 35 [translated].

people whose lives were marked by hard physical work and a constant struggle for survival. As an escape from the pressures of modern, industrialized life and the hustle and bustle of the big city, the painters idealized rural life and, in a romantic transfiguration of nature, largely blanked out the "realism" of daily life in the village (fig. 1).

In his book about the Worpswede painters' colony, published in 1903, Rainer Maria Rilke described the artists' relationship with the local peasants as a "mystery," pointing out how they perceived "people and things, in silent coexistence, as phenomena of the same atmosphere and as media of colors." "They do not help these people, they do not teach them; they do not better them,"[3] Rilke wrote. In Germany, a whole series of such rural artists' colonies developed in parallel, for example in Dachau or later in Murnau. What they had in common, however, was the proximity to cities such as Bremen or Munich, which was important for the artists, as they offered them exhibition opportunities.[4]

Even before her marriage to Otto Modersohn, Paula Becker had rented a small studio from a farmer, which was later furnished with a glass roof (fig. 2). She was not the only woman artist in the Worpswede painters' colony—several young women chose the colony for their training as painters, since Fritz Mackensen and Otto Modersohn both had good reputations as teachers, and the atmosphere there was lively and liberal. The painter Maria Franck, later wife of Franz Marc and co-founder of the Blaue Reiter, also spent six months in Worpswede in 1905 as a student of Otto Modersohn.[5]

From Modersohn-Becker's circle in Worpswede, Marie Bock (1864–1957) and Ottilie Reylaender (1882–1965) deserve to be mentioned. Modersohn-Becker had taken over Reylaender's studio, and the two of them later participated in the comprehensive Sonderbund exhibition in Cologne in 1912 as two of only four women artists.[6] In this first major avant-garde exhibition in Germany, which took place five years after her death, Modersohn-Becker's major work *Old Peasant Woman* (1907, p. 77) was shown alongside entire rooms of works by Vincent van Gogh and Paul Gauguin.

Many male artists of the era, not only in Worpswede, deliberately chose a wife with artistic training, since they expected them to be particularly understanding and supportive of their work, such as Fritz Overbeck with Hermine Rohte and Heinrich

3—Ibid., pp. 40f. [translated].
4—Ellen Spickernagel, "Worpswede als Mythos. Zu einem Entwurf der Künstlergemeinschaft um 1900," in: *Spiegel der Forschung*, October 1997, p. 22.
5—Marion Ackermann, "Paula Modersohn-Becker und München," in: *Paula Modersohn-Becker 1876–1907. Retrospektive*, ed. Helmut Friedel, exh. cat. Städtische Galerie im Lenbachhaus, Munich (Munich 1997), p. 16.
6—*1912 - Mission Moderne. Die Jahrhundertschau des Sonderbundes*, ed. Barbara Schaefer, exh. cat. Wallraf-Richartz-Museum, Cologne (Cologne 2012), pp. 594, 597.

Vogeler with Martha Schröder. It was common practice for aspiring women artists—even after years of training—to give up painting after marriage in order to devote themselves entirely to the household and to support their artist husband. Otto Modersohn also noted the advantages of a marriage between artists in his journal: "Only an artistically inclined mind can understand an artist [...]. I only want to live with an artistic wife, because my best, my whole, what I have is art."[7]

For Paula Becker, however, giving up painting was out of the question, and Otto Modersohn supported her in this. In the first years of their marriage, the couple still shared many things in common—especially in their landscapes, sketches, and observation of nature—but the age difference of eleven years, their different temperaments, and their pronounced artistic independence led to increasing conflicts. Modersohn increasingly criticized her way of painting people: "Paula hates the conventional, [...] hands like spoons, noses like bulbs, mouths like wounds, expressions like cretins."[8] In addition, she evaded the daily routine of marriage by going to Paris several times and spent one and a half of the six and a half years of their marriage in Paris.

2 Paula Modersohn-Becker's studio on the Brünjes farmstead, 1905

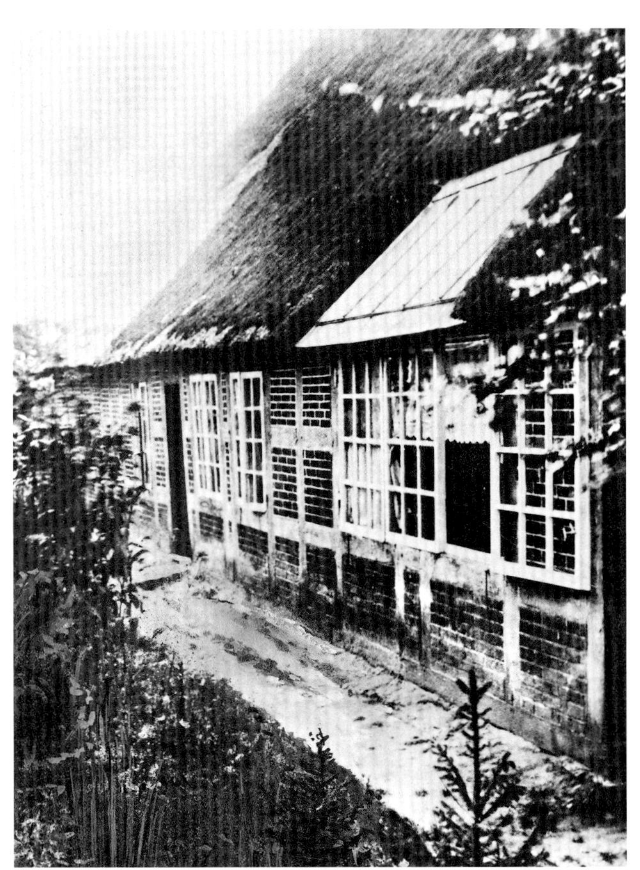

The complexity of such a union of two serious artists (fig. 3) is particularly reflected in the couple's correspondence and in their journal entries; great appreciation alternated with criticism: "This mutual give and take is wonderful. [...] She is a true artist, as there are few of these in the world," wrote Otto Modersohn in 1902, but a short time later: "Egoism, ruthlessness is the modern disease. Nietzsche is the father. [...] Unfortunately, Paula is also very much infected by these modern notions."[9] On the whole, Otto Modersohn was far more tolerant, supportive, and willing to compromise than most artist husbands of the era; but this did not prevent major conflicts between the couple, as well as a prolonged separation.[10]

The sculptor Clara Westhoff (1878–1954; p. 61), Paula Modersohn-Becker's only close friend, also began her training by taking drawing lessons with Mackensen and came to Worpswede as a result. Westhoff and Becker were studio neighbors during their first stay

7—Otto Modersohn's journal, entry dated September 27, 1900, unpublished [translated].
8—Otto Modersohn's journal, entry dated June 15, 1902, in: *Paula Modersohn-Becker in Briefen und Tagebüchern*, ed. Günter Busch and Liselotte von Reinken, revised and expanded by Wolfgang Werner (Frankfurt am Main 2007), p. 379 [translated].
9—Otto Modersohn's journal, entry dated June 28, 1902, in: ibid., p. 381 [translated].
10—Cf. *Paula Modersohn-Becker und Otto Modersohn. Ein Künstlerpaar um 1900*, ed. Heide Grape-Albers, exh. cat. Niedersächsisches Landesmuseum, Hannover, 2007/8 (Munich 2007).

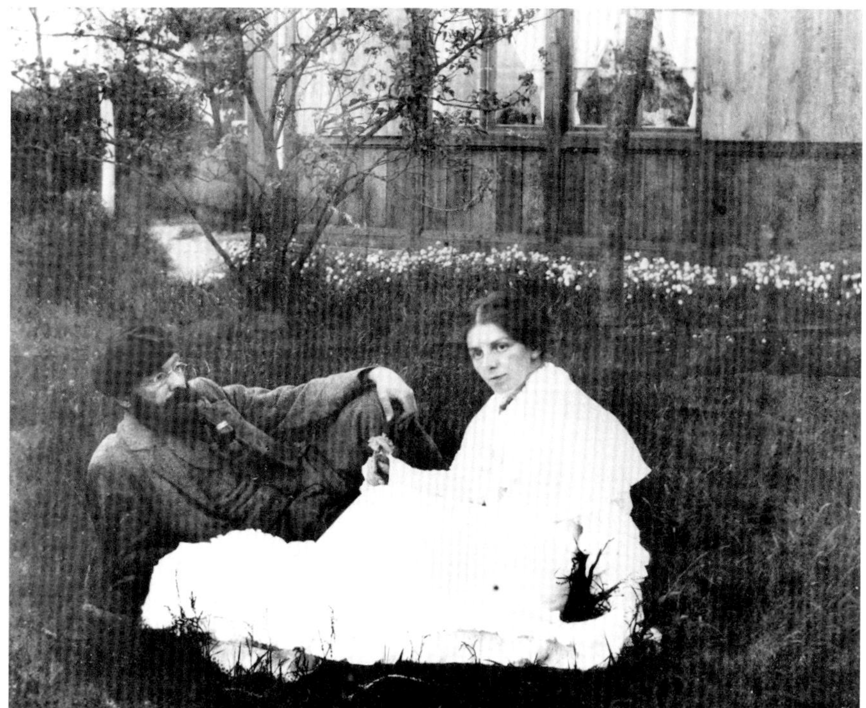

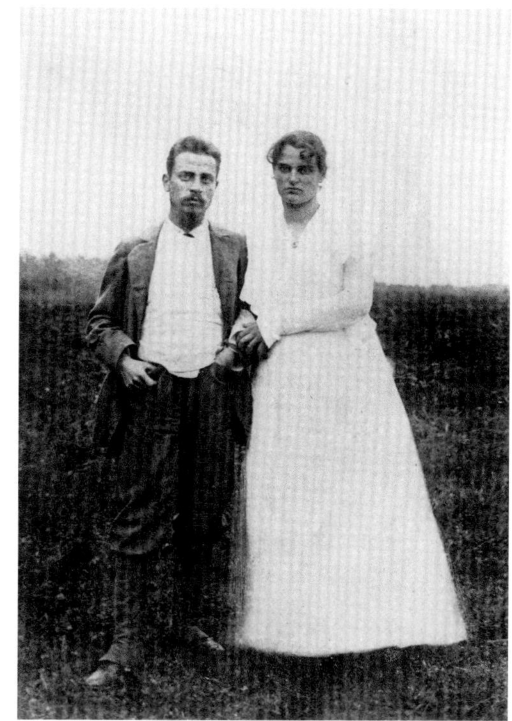

3 Paula and Otto Modersohn in their garden, c. 1904

4 Clara Rilke-Westhoff and Rainer Maria Rilke in Worpswede, 1901

in Paris in 1900. Westhoff did not marry a Worpswede artist, but rather the poet Rainer Maria Rilke (fig. 4), who had attended the festivities at Vogeler's Barkenhoff in the summer of 1900 and had come to know and appreciate both artists. He portrayed the Worpswede artists' community in 1902 in a commissioned work, albeit without mentioning a single woman artist.

Rilke's fascination with Modersohn-Becker as a woman and conversation partner has been described on numerous occasions,[11] but he was only slightly familiar with the artist's work until he met her again around Christmas in 1905 and wrote about her to Karl von der Heydt: "The most remarkable thing was to find Modersohn's wife developing her painting in a way all her own, recklessly and straightforwardly painting things that are very Worpswedish, and yet that no one before her has ever been able to see and paint. And on this very idiosyncratic path, strangely close to van Gogh and his artistic direction."[12] With this assessment and the writing of a "requiem"[13] after her death in November 1907, Rilke was one of the few and important supporters of the artist during her own lifetime.

In the spring of 1906 in Paris, she created a very abstracted portrait of Rilke—cubic, mask-like, and with an open mouth, as if to emphasize his specific medium, namely language (p. 60). As is often the case with Modersohn-Becker's portraits, including her

11—Rainer Stamm, Paula Modersohn-Becker et Rainer Maria Rilke, une amitié des artistes, in: *Paula Modersohn-Becker* (Paris 2016), pp. 144–149.
12—Karl von der Heydt was the cousin of the collector August von der Heydt, who purchased a total of thirty works by the artist; see: *Sammler der ersten Stunde. August von der Heydt entdeckt Paula Modersohn-Becker*, exh. cat. Paula Modersohn-Becker Museum, Bremen, 2017, p. 14 [translated].
13—The requiem was published in 1908 and is printed in full in: Munich 1997 (see note 5), pp. 315–318.

self-portraits, resemblance to the person portrayed played a subordinate role; she strove instead for an "inner" view and created irritations with her painterly experiments. It is thus not surprising that Rilke never spoke about his portrait.[14]

PEASANTS AND WOMEN FROM THE POORHOUSE

"She had a fine sense for everything strange and original."[15]

5 Alte Armenhäuslerin im Garten mit Glaskugel und Mohnblumen / Old Woman from the Poorhouse in the Garden with Glass Globe and Poppies, 1907, oil tempera on cardboard, 96.3 x 80.2 cm, Museen Böttcherstraße, Paula Modersohn-Becker Museum, Bremen

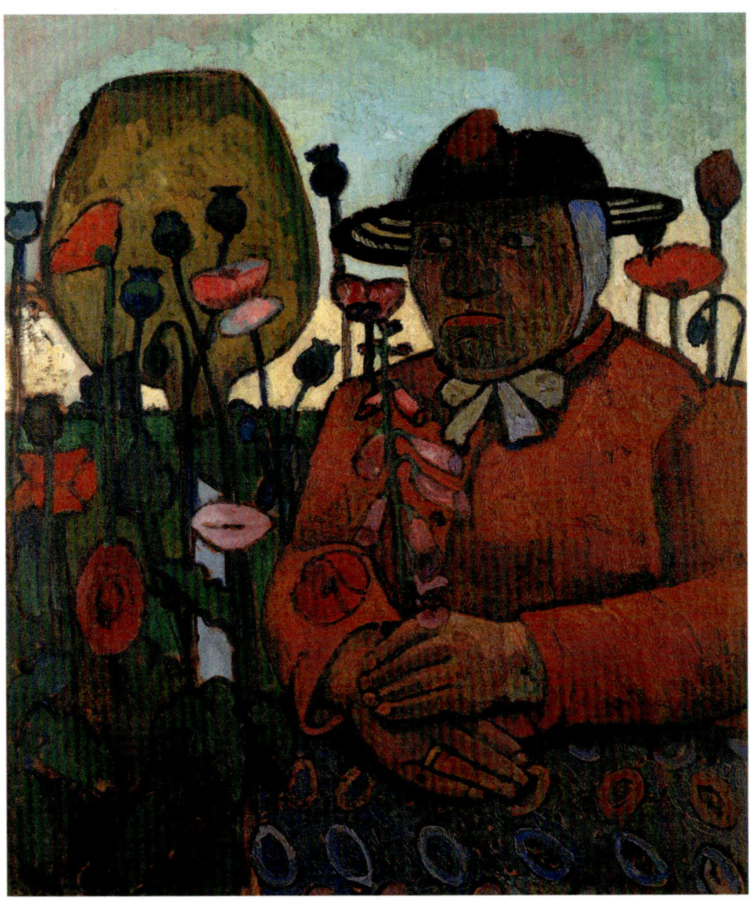

Unlike her teacher Mackensen, Modersohn-Becker usually left out not only the rural surroundings, but also the respective attributes and activities, when she looked for her models among the often elderly farmers and peasants, the women from the poorhouse (pp. 66–77), and the mothers and children. The young painter found her teacher's works too genre-like and missed the "runic" character,[16] the timeless, symbolic aspect, which was to become a central feature of her own work.

The budding artist could not spend much money on models and presumably chose those residents of the village who were satisfied with the low pay and who could manage not to work for a while during the day. As a sheltered young woman who grew up in a bourgeois, urban environment, she accepted the contrast between their worlds, and the injustice inherent in it, as a given. Nevertheless, the choice and quantity of these motifs in her work alone represents a distinctive feature that characterizes her as an artist. The highly varied portraits of the *Armenhäuslerin* (*Old Woman from the Poorhouse*; pp. 74–76), painted between 1903 and 1907, always depict a particular individual, known as "Mother Schröder" or–in the local dialect–*Dreebeen* (Three Legs), because she always had her walking stick with her as a "third leg." Many contemporaries have described how openly, humanely, and unselfconsciously Modersohn-Becker treated her models.[17] Time and again and for years,

14–Brigitte Uhde-Stahl, *Paula Modersohn-Becker* (Stuttgart and Zurich 1989), p. 104.
15–Otto Modersohn, in: *Paula Modersohn-Becker. Ein Buch der Freundschaft* [1932], ed. Rolf Hetsch (Fischerhude 1985), p. 16 [translated].
16–Modersohn-Becker's journal, entry dated December 1, 1902, in: Modersohn / Werner 2017 (see note 1), p. 189 [translated].
17–"Elsbeths Freundin: Annemarie Hosenfeld-Krummacher," in: Hetsch 1985 (see note 15), pp. 49–51.

she drew on the same individuals, especially *Dreebeen*, even in her last, large-format masterpiece, which was painted after her longest stay in Paris and shows the influence of van Gogh's work in its degree of color and abstraction, but moves beyond it in its imaginativeness (fig. 5).[18]

Regardless of the fact that the various depictions of the woman from the poorhouse were of an old woman at the bottom of the social hierarchy—poorhouses were financed by the respective municipality and housed people without families and without any income, often during the last years of their lives—Modersohn-Becker gave the sitter a high degree of dignity and respect. She neither concealed nor glorified her model's age, coarseness, or mental simplicity, she even enhanced them: The woman sits on her chair heavy, static, timeless, with huge hands, and cramped into the picture plane; the angle from below makes her massive body tower before the viewer like a goddess from a distant pre-Christian culture. The series of mostly large-format portraits of the women from the poorhouse is one of Modersohn-Becker's monumental, major work groups.

LANDSCAPES

At her first exhibition, together with Marie Bock at the Kunsthalle Bremen in 1899, the twenty-one-year-old Paula Becker showed a few landscapes created in Worpswede, including *Autumn Landscape at the Weyerberg with Pond* (fig. 6) and several portraits of peasants.[19] The conservative painter Arthur Fitger wrote an extremely scathing review in the local Bremen newspaper,[20] which ultimately encouraged Becker to leave for Paris on New Year's Eve 1899, to "shake off the dust,"[21] and thus leave Bremen and Worpswede behind for the time being.

The lapidary, dark-toned, and sketchy nature of her Worpswede landscapes, which others so heavily criticized, was then also discredited by Carl Vinnen in his reply to Fitger as "immature student work."[22] But instead of changing her style, Modersohn-Becker continued her way of seeing and painting undeterred: In the summer of 1900, she stayed in Worpswede again and painted a few series of birch, moon, and moor landscapes that are remarkably modern from today's perspective (pp. 87–95). Despite all the parallels to works by Otto Modersohn, these paintings already testify to her great sense of autonomy. Her consistent "courage to be austere, unobliging,

18—The painting has been compared several times with van Gogh's *La Berceuse* series from 1889; cf. Anne Buschhoff, in: *Paula Modersohn-Becker und die Kunst in Paris um 1900 - von Cézanne bis Picasso*, ed. Anne Buschhoff and Wulf Herzogenrath, exh. cat. Kunsthalle Bremen, 2007, p. 204.

19—Cf. *"rücksichtslos geradeaus malend." Paula Modersohn-Becker, Marie Bock, Clara Rilke-Westhoff. Die Ausstellung in der Kunsthalle Bremen 1899*, exh. cat. Paula Modersohn-Becker Museum, Bremen, 2003, pp. 22-29.

20—Fitger's attack was directed primarily against the "too modern" acquisition and exhibition policy of the Kunsthalle Bremen and less against the individual women artists; cf. "Frank Laukötter, Galerieleiter als Gralsritter? - Paula Modersohn-Becker und die Direktoren der Kunsthalle Bremen von Gustav Pauli bis Wulf Herzogenrath," in: Bremen 2007 (see note 18), pp. 272-274.

21—Letter to Otto Modersohn, December 30, 1899, in: Busch / Reinken 2007 (see note 8), p. 204 [translated].

22—*Bremer Courier*, December 24, 1899, in: Bremen 2007, pp. 202f. [translated].

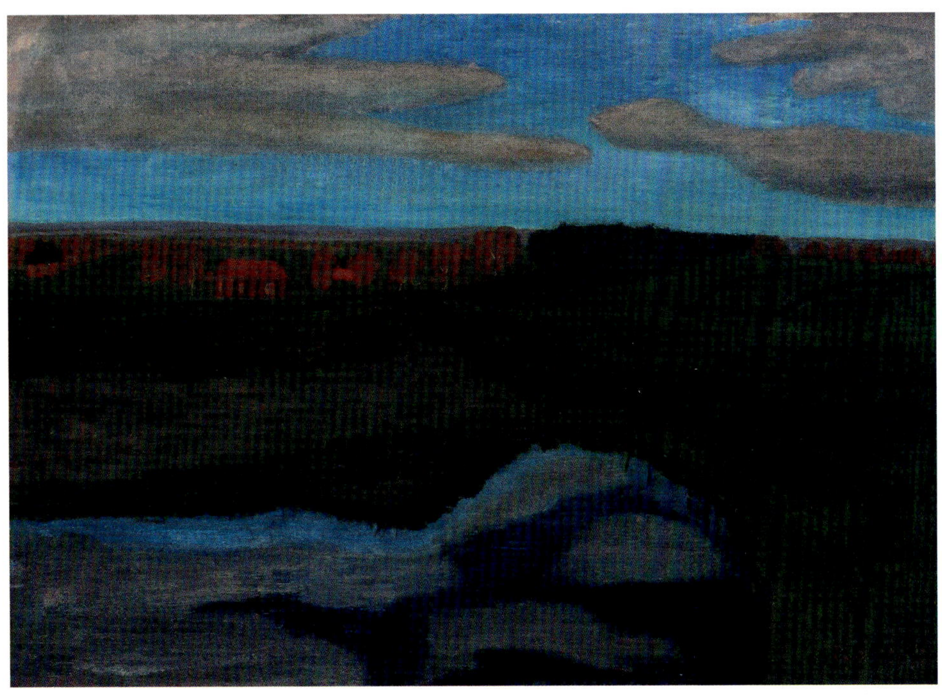

6 Herbstlandschaft am Weyerberg mit Tümpel / Autumn Landscape at the Weyerberg with Pond, c. 1899, oil tempera on canvas, 66 x 90 cm, Private Collection

fierce, and harsh"[23] is evident—as in all other groups of works—in the reduced and abstracted conception of landscape. The paths leading to the horizon, the straight canals through the former moor, and the high sky were the perfect setting for Modersohn-Becker's artistic concept of consolidation and simplification, coupled with a low-contrast coloration, which—especially in the nocturnal moon-scapes (pp. 88, 89)—leads to almost monochrome color surfaces. "I don't think one should think so much about nature when painting, at least not with regard to the conception of the picture," she later wrote.[24]

During the first years of their marriage from 1901 to around 1903, Otto and Paula often painted side by side and shared several preferences, such as the narrow details of birch trees in tall portrait formats (pp. 92–95) reminiscent of Japanese scroll paintings or unspectacular details such as tree trunks or piles of sand (pp. 86, 93). But whereas Otto Modersohn strove for a more romantic, fairy-tale, and mysterious depiction of nature,[25] and the landscape remained the primary subject of representation for him—even if isolated figures appeared in it—Paula Modersohn-Becker formulated very early on that she was interested primarily in the depiction of people. She thus even described the row of birch trees in her paintings as a group of figures: "These are my 'modern women.'"[26]

Parallels can also be drawn with other landscape painters such as Fritz Overbeck in Worpswede and Walter Leistikow, who was particularly popular in Berlin;[27] Modersohn-Becker nevertheless went much further in her rigorous simplification than these painters, dispensing with almost all details such as leaves on the trees, clouds, birds, and other internal structures. The formative influence of Paul Cézanne, which is mentioned time and again,[28] could not yet play a role for Modersohn-Becker in 1899, before her first trip to Paris, and can rather be described as a parallel phenomenon with regard to the early Worpswede landscapes.

23 – Günter Busch, *Paula Modersohn-Becker. Die Landschaften*, exh. cat. Kunsthalle Bremen 1982/83 (Lilienthal 1982), unpaginated.

24 – Modersohn-Becker's journal, entry dated October 1, 1902, in: Modersohn / Werner 2017 (see note 1), p. 182 [translated].

25 – Ernst G. Güse, "Paula Becker & Otto Modersohn. Ein Geben und Nehmen unter Künstlern," in: *Paula Becker & Otto Modersohn. Kunst und Leben*, exh. cat. Paula Modersohn-Becker Museum, Bremen 2018/19, p. 10.

26 – Paula Becker's journal, undated entry, in: Busch / Reinken 2007 (see note 8), p. 128 [translated].

27 – Anne Buschhoff, "'Ich glaube, man müsste beim Bildermalen gar nicht so sehr an die Natur denken, wenigstens nicht bei der Konzeption des Bildes' - Landschaften," in: Bremen 2007 (see note 18), p. 65.

28 – Ibid., p. 66.

The greatest difference between her work and the paintings of other contemporaries, however, is the renunciation of light points and light effects, which makes the landscape formations appear even more abstract. The artist repeatedly described her preferred lackluster coloration as that of cloud-covered skies—a characteristic she also extended to many other motifs. The even light and the matte surface[29] are reminiscent of the works of Édouard Vuillard, whereby Modersohn-Becker found her preferences confirmed here as well, when she visited the studios of the Nabis during her third visit to Paris in 1905. The comparisons between the work of Modersohn-Becker and that of other modern artists, especially in Paris, reveal how little she was actually influenced by others, but conversely sought confirmation of her own ideas—developed for the most part in complete solitude—from them.

STILL LIFES

Static, built, monumental—many of the characteristics that apply to Modersohn-Becker's figure paintings are also characteristic of her more or less seventy still lifes (pp. 170–179), roughly fifty of which were painted between 1905 and 1907.

Already in Worpswede, Modersohn-Becker collected "rare glasses, plates and cups, necklaces and rings, finely colored fabrics and blankets for still lifes, original picture frames, mirrors, candlesticks, books in old bindings,"[30] as Otto Modersohn reported. The painter had a great sense for peasant handicrafts, as well as the structure and texture of materials and surfaces in general. In Paris, in a self-confident gesture, she ordered precious fabrics and objects for viewing purposes, which she draped in her otherwise sparse studio, painted some of them, and later had them picked up again as "unsuitable."[31]

For the French avant-garde around Gustave Courbet, Odilon Redon, Paul Cézanne, and Henri Matisse, which Modersohn-Becker absorbed during her visits to numerous exhibitions and collections, still lifes were a preferred field, an experimental free space for inner pictorial design principles of form and color.[32] Of the Worpswede painters, only Vogeler devoted himself sporadically to the genre; otherwise, it was not a theme. Vogeler was also the only one to buy a still life by Modersohn-Becker during her lifetime.

29 – Cf. Angelica Hoffmeister-zur Nedden, "Zur Maltechnik Modersohn-Beckers," in: *Paula Modersohn-Becker 1896–1907. Werkverzeichnis der Gemälde*, vol. 1, ed. Günter Busch and Wolfgang Werner (Munich 1998), pp. 102–116.
30 – Otto Modersohn, "Erinnerungen an Paula Modersohn-Becker," in: Hetsch 1985 (see note 15), p. 26 [translated].
31 – "Der Freund: Heinrich Vogeler," in: ibid., pp. 36f. [translated].
32 – Anne Buschhoff, "'Der große Stil der Form verlangt auch den großen Stil der Farbe' – Stillleben mit Früchten, Blumenstücke und Figur vor Blumengrund," in: Bremen 2007 (see note 18), p. 192.

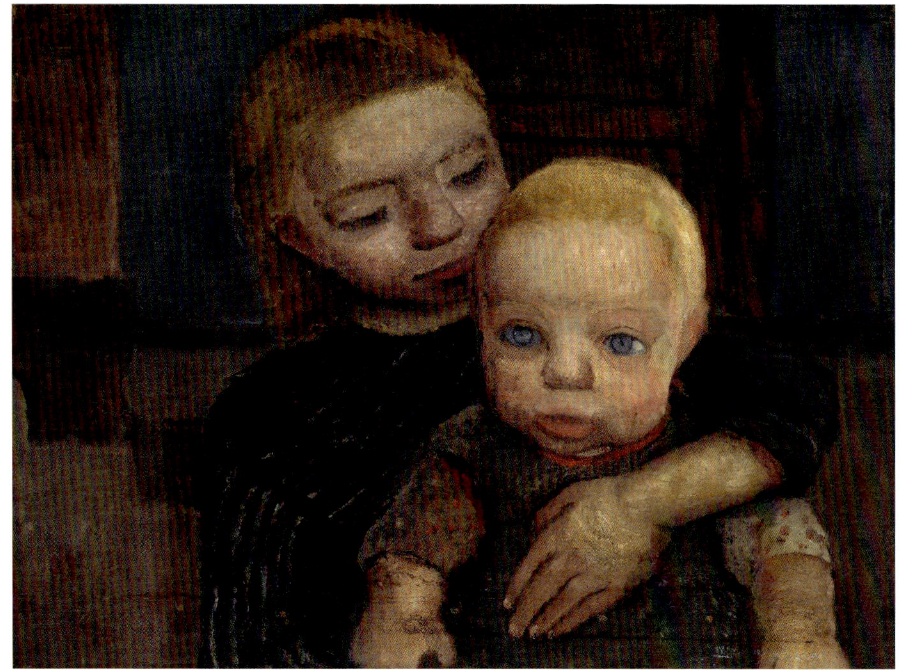

7 Halbfigur eines Mädchens, den Arm um ein Kind gelegt / Half-Length Figure of a Girl with Her Arm around a Child, 1904, oil tempera on canvas, 38 x 50.3 cm, Rut- und Klaus-Bahlsen-Stiftung, Hannover

Like Cézanne, the artist chose a repetitive repertoire of objects for her still lifes, just as she painted several models numerous times over the years and studied them in extensive series. However, apart from a few similarities such as draped fabric, a forward-tipped perspective, and painted fruits such as apples and oranges, Modersohn-Becker's still lifes are very different from Cézanne's. Her aforementioned dense, material style of painting was the opposite, so to speak, of Cézanne's transparent style and reveals the artist's autonomy, which has been described time and again and which characterized her work from the very beginning. The still lifes were among the earliest purchases by museums after her death and initially among the most frequently exhibited works, on the one hand because they took up current modern tendencies and, on the other, featured comparatively neutral and innocuous motifs.

THE STRANGE, MYSTERIOUS CHILD

Paula Modersohn-Becker's intensive preoccupation with portraits of mostly peasant children (fig. 7) constitutes the conclusion and culmination of a major theme in the late nineteenth century, also among contemporaries such as Max Liebermann and Wilhelm Leibl, whom Modersohn-Becker mentioned in her letters, as well as her teacher Fritz Mackensen. The subject was very popular among painters, but consistently intended for a bourgeois audience, and usually presented childhood in the countryside in a highly idealized form: The hard physical labor in the home and on the farm, from which only very young children were exempt, was veiled by an emphasis on the sitter's innocence, cleanliness, and closeness to nature. Since Jean-Jacques Rousseau's writings from the late eighteenth century, the "child of nature" had been stylized into a positive utopia.[33]

Just as the theme had fallen out of fashion in German painting,[34] Modersohn-Becker immersed herself with intensity and psychology in the depiction of children, which

33 – Sonja Grunow, *Kinderbild um 1900*, PhD diss. Karlsruher Institut für Technologie, Karlsruhe 2012 (Münster 2013), pp. 170f.
34 – Ibid., p. 182.

finds no parallel with any other artist. With over 400 pictures of children—mostly girls—children's portraits comprise the majority of works in her oeuvre. This group of works was also a stylistic and thematic field of experimentation throughout the development of her oeuvre: Worpswede and Paris are reflected in equal measure, from one of the earliest works from 1897 (p. 121) until shortly before her death in 1907.

8 Stehender und kniender Mädchenakt vor Mohnblumen II / Kneeling and Standing Girls Nude, Poppies in the Background II, May/June 1906, oil tempera on canvas, 106 x 65 cm, Museum Behnhaus Drägerhaus, Lübeck

With Modersohn-Becker, children are, on the one hand, perceived as autonomous individuals and full members of society; on the other, they are also stylized into symbols, especially in the late work of 1906/7. Their serious faces and gazes, often against an unreal sky, reveal something strange and disconnected (pp. 112–131). They occasionally appear to belong to an alien species. Even an infant in a cradle (p. 108) seems present and intimate due to the close cropping, but retains an autonomy that cannot be compared to any other depictions of children around 1900. The almost universal renunciation of "cuteness" appears particularly radical in this group of the artist's works (fig. 8).

Many of Modersohn-Becker's figure paintings appear at first glance naturalistic or realistic, but symbolic motifs elevate them to a level of the supratemporal and universal. The children—as well as the old women mentioned—seem disconnected: their individuality disappears, facial features blur, become indistinct, and are schematized. With the use of "adjuncts" such as fruits and flowers, tree trunks and animals, they become representatives of a comprehensive mysticism of nature.[35]

In the paintings of her late work (pp. 132–137), which are often reminiscent of cult images, the childlike bodies acquire something unassailable, which is not only due to the accompanying symbols. In 1906/7 in Paris, stylization reached a climax under the impressions of Gauguin's Tahiti motifs. A postcard of a Gauguin motif hung on a wall in Modersohn-Becker's studio.[36] In her own works as well, the predominantly young girls stand or sit in fantastic pictorial spaces like unknown childlike gods from a primordial religion. Thematically, the

35 –"I say God but mean the spirit that flows through nature," the artist wrote in her journal; quoted in: Busch / Reinken 2007 (see note 8), p. 177 [translated].
36 –Bremen 2007 (see note 18), p. 145.

"distant" and alien aspects of the earlier Worpswede children's portraits were continued with different means in the late work. For the group of pictures of children as a whole, the same unmistakable mixture of closeness and distance,[37] naturalism and symbolism, which characterizes the depiction of the women from the poorhouse and several of the portraits and especially the self-portraits, also clearly applies.

SELF-PORTRAITS

"Now that I am free, something can become of me."[38]

"Her smile was shy and superior at the same time," Ottilie Reylaender said of her colleague, noting her "fiery personality."[39] Modersohn-Becker's sister Herma emphasized above all her "extreme individualism."[40] In the numerous photographic portraits of Paula Modersohn-Becker (pp. 192–197), she presents herself as a serious and reserved person in conventional clothing, her head mostly tilted to the side. Only the eyes are large and attentive; one suspects in them a strong and reflected personality. "Paula has more intellectual interests than anyone else," Otto wrote about her.[41]

As a whole, the large group of roughly sixty self-portraits[42] bears little photographic resemblance to the artist; moreover, many works are extremely different in terms of painterly gesture and style. This is also a group that reflects the entire development of Modersohn-Becker's work and was one of her most important fields of experimentation.

Already in one of the first examples from 1897, executed at the age of twenty-one, she has a reserved gaze, but at the same time presents herself frontally and invitingly (fig. 9). Completely filling the pictorial field with a close-up of her face is already her method here. Despite youth and little experience, an ongoing process of self-questioning and communication with the viewer begins. Various artists—from Rembrandt van Rijn and James Ensor to Vincent van Gogh and Frida Kahlo—who at least for a time were seldom in the public eye, created a particularly large number of self-portraits, not only for lack of other models, but also as a conscious act of artistic self-reassurance regarding their own goals. This also seems to have been a major impetus for Modersohn-Becker.

37 –Uwe M. Schneede, "Paula Modersohn-Beckers Weg in die Moderne. Zwischen zwei Künstlergenerationen," in: *Paula Modersohn-Becker. Der Weg in die Moderne*, exh. cat. Bucerius Kunst Forum, Hamburg, 2017, p. 19.
38 –Letter to Martha Vogeler, May 21, 1906, in: Busch / Reinken 2007, p. 542 [translated].
39 –"Die Kollegin. Ottilie Reylaender-Böhme," in: Hetsch 1985 (see note 15), p. 39 [translated].
40 –"Die Schwester: Herma," in: ibid., p. 32 [translated].
41 –Modersohn / Werner (see note 1), p. 252 [translated].
42 –Katharina Henkel, "Zwischen Inszenierung und Wahrheitsanspruch: Selbstporträts der Klassischen Moderne," in: *Ich bin Ich. Paula Modersohn-Becker – Die Selbstbildnisse*, exh. cat. Paula Modersohn-Becker Museum, Bremen, 2019/20, p. 28.

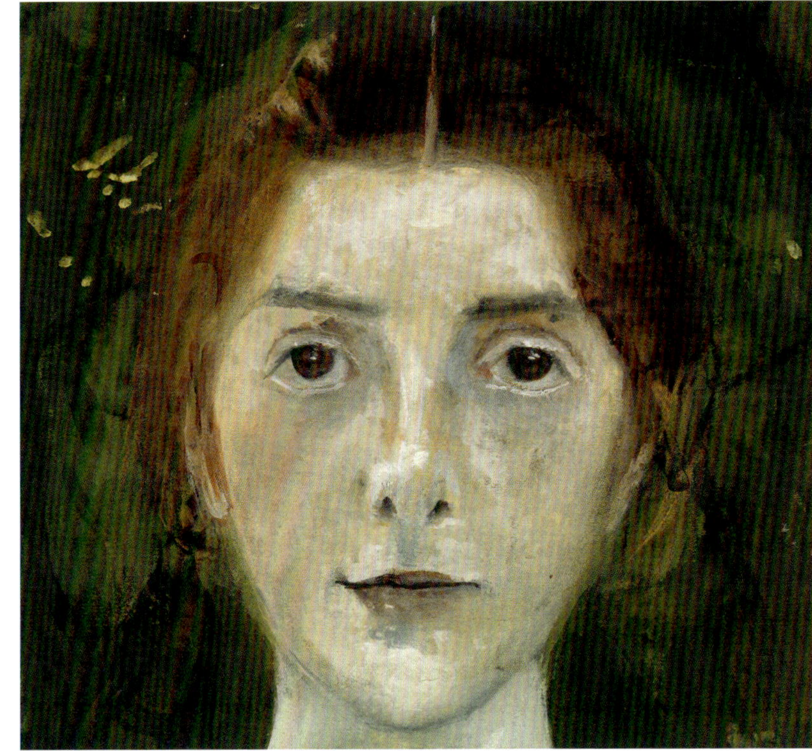

9 Selbstbildnis / Self-Portrait, gouache, 24.5 x 26.5 cm, Paula-Modersohn-Becker-Stiftung, Bremen

Frontality, large eyes, a pearl necklace—during her second stay in Paris in 1903, Modersohn-Becker found a form that suited her aims in the Roman-Egyptian mummy portraits in the Louvre (figs. 10, 11): directness and human closeness, as well as a timeless or supratemporal element, a form of generalization that ideally corresponded to her own aspirations. She also drew on the Egyptian models for her tall portrait formats. Many of the ancient models Modersohn-Becker saw in the Louvre were painted in encaustic: pigments, together with beeswax and resin, form a paste-like mass that was applied with spatulas. This "material" approach must have been of additional interest to Modersohn-Becker, who from circa 1898 onwards and increasingly from 1902 preferred a special, matte tempera technique and in some cases even worked the surface with the brush handle (p. 70).[43]

More than half of the self-portraits were created in Paris in 1906/7, when she was alone, just thirty years old and separated from Otto Modersohn, seeking her way as an artist: "I am becoming something—I am living the most intensely happy time of my life," she wrote from there.[44] Seven of the approximately seventeen self-portraits (pp. 28–32, 48) that were created in her new "freedom" depict the painter half or completely undressed. She often worked on several motifs at the same time.[45] For her time, Paula Modersohn-Becker was astonishingly uninhibited in her relationship to her own body. "I now bathe in the beautiful evening and morning air and take pleasure in my curves and roundness in my full-length mirror," she wrote to Otto from Paris.[46]

In 1901, after only a few months of marriage, the two artists had already practiced "bathing in the air" in their garden in Worpswede, according to the tenets of the *Lebensreform* (Life Reform) movement, which celebrated the "naturalness" of the unclothed body.[47] Together with her sisters Herma and Milly, Paula organized nocturnal nude dances by moonlight, and in such activities lived out her penchant for mystifying the experience of nature.[48] There is a striking similarity between Modersohn-Becker's posture in her few nude photographs, presumably taken by

43 –Cf. Angelica Hoffmeister-zur Nedden, "Kroß, kraus, knusprig. Enkaustik, Tempera und die Maltechnik ägyptischer Mumienporträts im Werk von Paula Modersohn-Becker," in: *Paula Modersohn-Becker und die ägyptischen Mumienporträts*, ed. Rainer Stamm, exh. cat. Paula Modersohn-Becker Museum, Bremen, 2007/8, pp. 96–105.
44 –Letter to Milly Rohland-Becker, Paris, May 1906, in: Busch / Reinken 2007 (see note 8), p. 537 [translated].
45 –Renate Berger, *Paula Modersohn-Becker. Paris – Leben wie im Rausch. Biografie* (Cologne 2007), p. 210.
46 –Letter to Otto Modersohn, March 15, 1905, in: Busch / Reinken 2007 (see note 8), p. 490 [translated].
47 –They also met as a mixed group with the Vogelers for nude bathing and "breakfast in the nude," an allusion to Édouard Manet's famous painting *Le Déjeuner sur l'herbe*. These activities were, however, not approved of by all Worpswede artists; a scandal ensued, further splitting the group. Cf. Doris Hansmann, *Akt und nackt. Der ästhetische Aufbruch um 1900 mit Blick auf die Selbstakte von Paula Modersohn-Becker*, PhD diss. University of Cologne (Weimar 2000), p. 146.
48 –Ibid., p. 148.

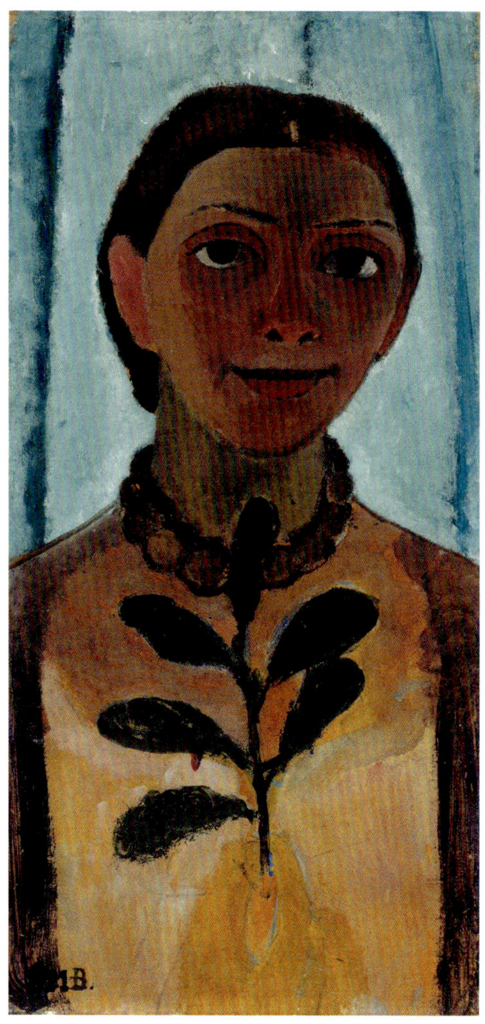

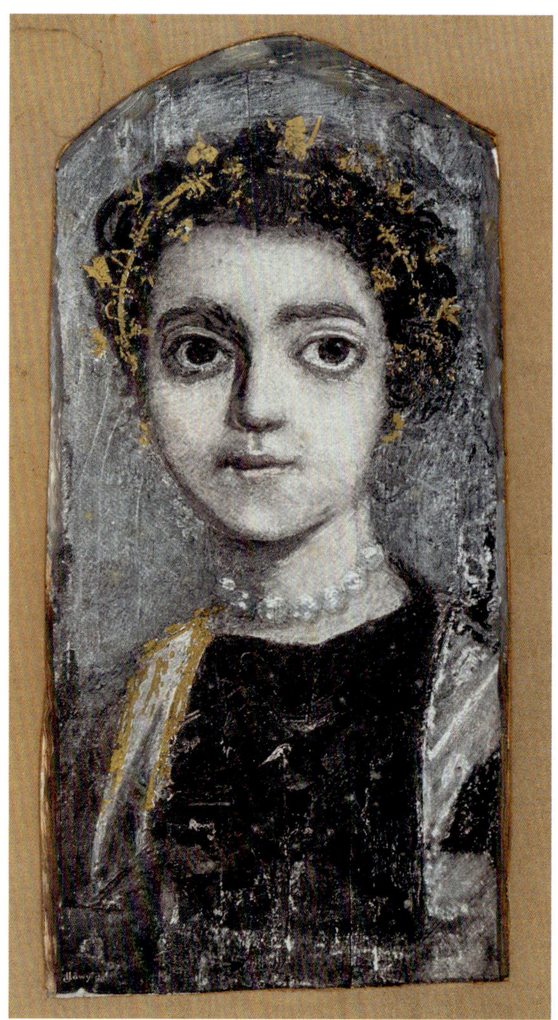

10 Selbstbildnis mit Kamelienzweig / Self-Portrait with Camellia Branch, 1906/7, oil tempera on cardboard, 61.5 x 30.5 cm, Museum Folkwang, Essen

11 Portrait of a Young Woman (detail), c. 100–130 AD, encaustic on wood with gold leaf, 34.2 x 16.4 cm, er-Rubayat (Fayum), Private Collection (on loan to the Archeologic Collection of the University of Erlangen)

her sister Herma (fig. 12),[49] and her painted standing or half-length self-portraits (pp. 28, 29). The pose with closed arms, the contrapposto of the legs, the accessories such as her amber necklace,[50] and the fruits in her hands led—as in the late nudes of children created at the same time—to a stylization and heightening into the symbolic and supratemporal.

The *Self-Portrait as a Half-Length Nude with Amber Necklace II* (fig. 13) thus has the "impression of an archaic goddess";[51] it is for this reason that "matriarchal" references have already been pointed out on many occasions,[52] but without defining them or explaining their derivation more precisely. It is unclear whether the artist knew Johann Jakob Bachofen's book *Das Mutterrecht* (1861, Mother Right);[53] Rilke is said to have reviewed the book in Munich. The idea that matriarchies existed in Early Antique and "primitive" cultures was much discussed in Germany around 1900.[54]

49 – Cf. Simone Ewald, "Über die Rolle von Spiegel und Fotografie in Selbstbildnissen," in: Bremen 2019/20 (see note 42), pp. 18–27.
50 – The amber necklace, a symbol of the North, can be found in ten of the self-portraits; cf. Tine Colstrup, "Venus of Worpswede," in: *Paula Modersohn-Becker*, exh. cat. Louisiana Museum of Modern Art, Humlebaek, 2014/15, pp. 8–19.
51 – Henrike Holsing, "'...die große Wirkung nobler Einfachheit ...' - Der Akt," in: Bremen 2007 (see note 18), pp. 144–157, here p. 149 [translated].
52 – Christa Murken-Altrogge, *Paula Modersohn-Becker. Leben und Werk* (Cologne 1980), p. 16.
53 – Johann Jakob Bachofen, *Das Mutterrecht. Eine Untersuchung über die Gynaikokratie der alten Welt nach ihrer religiösen und rechtlichen Natur* (Stuttgart 1861). See also: idem, *Myth, Religion, and Mother Right: Selected Writings of Johann Jakob Bachofen*, trans. Ralph Manheim (Princeton 1992).

Ideas of a "great goddess" and "Mother Earth" were also popular among the followers of the *Lebensreform* movement.[55] Modersohn-Becker is quoted as saying to Rilke, "To me, God is a 'she,' nature, the bringer, who has and gives life."[56] Doris Hansmann concluded from this that the artist fundamentally pursued "pantheistic-matriarchal ideas" and that she "saw the feminine as an expression of an elementary interpretation of nature."[57]

In this context, the *Self-Portrait on the Sixth Wedding Day* (p. 32) holds a special position among the last nude self-portraits painted in Paris in 1906/7. The artist signed it "P.B." (Paula Becker), thus referring to her new independence; at the same time, she recalled her marriage to Otto Modersohn in the title and the inscription. To this day, this first-ever nude self-portrait of a woman artist is also fascinating for its mysteriousness and contradictory nature: as if standing in front of a mirror, the painter portrays herself very directly, looking at herself and thus at us, with a questioning, scrutinizing gaze, knowing that such a painting had and could have no audience because the three elements—woman artist, nude, and (ostensible) pregnancy—would break all the taboos of her epoch at the same time. The three-quarter self-portrait with all the carefully worked details was, however, too large and too elaborate for a completely private painting.

12 Paula Modersohn-Becker in her studio, Paris 1906, photo: Herma Becker?

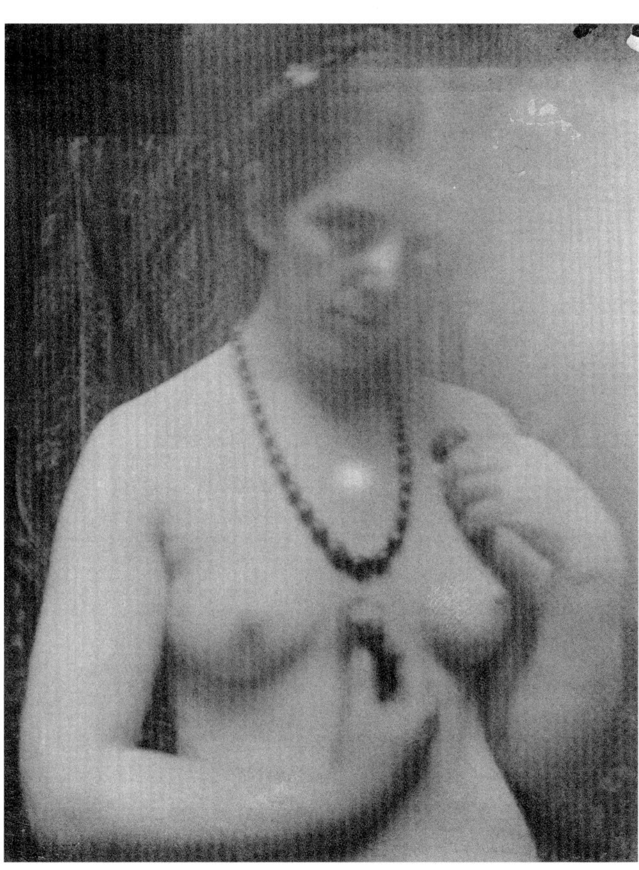

Modersohn-Becker was fully acquainted with all mythological and art-historical precursors, such as the *Venus pudica* of antiquity, who covers her private parts with her hand, while Modersohn-Becker's hand is shaped like a vessel. The curved bellies of Lucas Cranach's depictions of Venus may also be cited, since Modersohn-Becker copied some of these herself in the Louvre.[58] The S-shape of the body refers to medieval images of the Madonna,[59] as well as to Sandro Botticelli's *Birth of Venus*, the epitome of womanhood.

As is often the case with women artists, however, this painting in particular was not interpreted as the complex and allusive work of art that it is. Instead, it was and still is related primarily

54 –Meret Fehlmann, *Die Rede vom Matriarchat. Zur Gebrauchsgeschichte eines Arguments* (Zurich 2011), p. 321.
55 –Ibid., p. 325.
56 –Liselotte von Reinken, *Paula Modersohn-Becker* [1983] (Reinbek 2004), p. 64 [translated].
57 –Doris Hansmann, "'Hier müllert sie im Akte ...' Der Selbstakt zwischen künstlerischer Tradition und Nacktkultur," in: *Paris, Paris! Paula Modersohn-Becker und die Künstlerinnen um 1900*, exh. cat. Paula Modersohn-Becker Museum, Bremen (Stuttgart 2009), p. 116 [translated].
58 –Anne Röver, "Die Nachzeichnungen Paula Modersohn-Beckers," in: *Niederdeutsche Beiträge zur Kunstgeschichte*, no. 16, 1977, pp. 201–214.
59 –Hansmann 2009 (see note 57), p. 112.

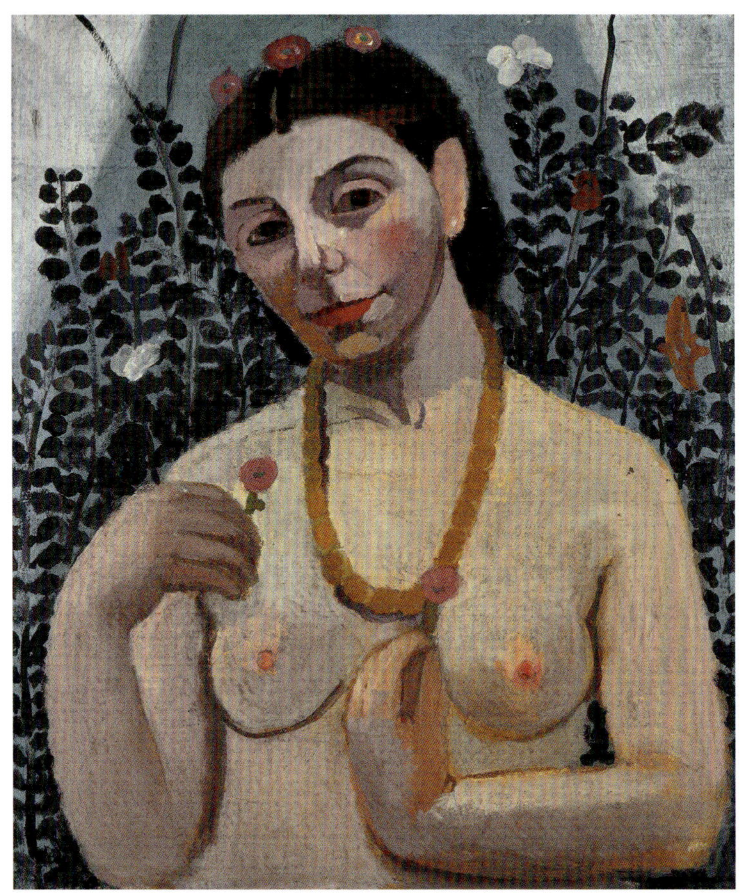

13 Selbstbildnis als Halbakt mit Bernsteinkette II / Self-Portrait as a Half-Length Nude with Amber Necklace II, summer 1906, oil tempera on canvas, 61 x 50 cm, Kunstmuseum Basel

biographically to the artist's unfulfilled desire to have children, her marriage, which had not been consummated in five years because of Otto's "nerves,"[60] and her particular situation alone in Paris. Yet only a month before it was painted, Modersohn-Becker had written to Otto: "I do not want to have a child by you now,"[61] and reaffirmed their separation. Against this background, the interpretation is particularly convincing that Modersohn-Becker presented herself as an artist doubly "potent": she could create art and, at the same time—perhaps in the future—also bring forth new human life. She painted herself in the form of a large vase,[62] a bulbous vessel, self-confident, powerful, and feminine. All religious, mythological precursors were reinterpreted into an extremely daring self-portrayal in a time that, with its moral concepts, was in no way prepared for it.

By way of comparison: in Vienna, also in 1906, Richard Gerstl painted a very restrained portrait of Mathilde Schönberg in a high-necked conventional dress.[63] Ms. Schönberg was pregnant at the time, however, so she had to be placed behind the edge of a table for the painting in such a way that absolutely nothing of her pregnancy could be surmised. This example shows how far ahead of her time Modersohn-Becker actually was. In fact, during her lifetime, it is probable that no one even saw the aforementioned *Self-Portrait on the Sixth Wedding Day*.[64] Many years later, Emil Waldmann, Director of the Bremer Kunsthalle, still called it "offending" and "embarrassing."[65]

I AM I

"And now, I don't even know how I should sign my name. I am not Modersohn, and I am not Paula Becker anymore either. I am I, and I hope to become more and more so. This is probably the ultimate goal of all our struggles."[66]

How Paula Modersohn-Becker thought about herself and others is documented by her extensive correspondence with her husband, family, and friends and was also

60 –In a letter to Rainer Maria Rilke, Clara Westhoff writes about the artist: "She says that for all these five years she has lived unmarried; actually, that the man at whose side she lives was incapable, because of nerves, of completing the sexual act. That she herself had felt and experienced nothing but great disappointment; that he has been less nervous for some time now—but that for her, of course, any approach at this point would be pointless, without meaning—in other words, impossible." Quoted in: Hansmann 2000 (see note 47), p. 318 [translated].
61 –Letter to Otto Modersohn, April 9, 1906, in: Busch / Reinken 2007 (see note 8), p. 528 [translated].
62 –Rainer Stamm, *Ein kurzes intensives Fest. Paula Modersohn-Becker. Eine Biografie* (Stuttgart 2007), p. 203.
63 –Cf. *Richard Gerstl. Retrospective*, ed. Ingrid Pfeiffer and Jill Lloyd in cooperation with Raymond Coffer, exh. cat. Schirn Kunsthalle Frankfurt, Frankfurt am Main and Neue Galerie, New York (Munich 2017).
64 –*Paula Modersohn-Becker. Pionierin der Moderne*, exh. cat. Kunsthalle Krems, 2010, p. 22.
65 –In 1935, Waldmann had to defend the Böttcherstraße Museum against the National Socialists; cf. Busch / Werner, vol. 1 (see note 29), pp. 90f. [translated].
66 –Letter to Rainer Maria Rilke, February 17, 1906, in: Busch / Reinken 2007 (see note 8), p. 520 [translated].

published posthumously in excerpts at an early stage.[67] Her letters and journals contain countless statements about how, for her, working on art took priority over everything else, that she needed "freedom," defended her "egoism," and accepted rejection and disdain. From the very beginning, the young painter was forced to explain and defend herself and her obviously very deviant attitude to those around her: "I feel that everyone is frightened by me," she wrote to her sister Milly in 1899. "And yet I must go on."[68] Many of her statements indicate an unusual ability to assert herself and—packaged in authoritative words—self-confidence as an artist. Explanations of her individual works are seldom found, but rather references to which exhibitions she visited, which literature she preferred to read, and which artists she admired above all others. However, like almost all women artists around 1900, she lacked female role models and the realistic prospect of external success; thus, "a retrospective in her lifetime was completely utopian."[69]

The only woman artist in her close circle comparable to Modersohn-Becker and also ambitious—Clara Rilke-Westhoff—suffered greatly from financial pressure, since neither she nor Rilke could provide enough for a family; she even gave her child to her parents for a longer period in order to be able to make a name for herself independently in Paris. Modersohn-Becker would probably not have been prepared to make such great personal sacrifices; throughout her life, she followed a strategy of appeasing and persuading those around her. Her primary goal was to be able to work as undisturbed as possible.

"To see how far one can go without worrying about public opinion," she wrote in a letter to Otto in 1903, presumably meaning herself, although she did mention Rodin.[70] Since she was never willing to adapt either stylistically or thematically anyway (her father had initially advised her to paint marketable landscapes), there was only one other form of adaptation: as the wife of a well-off artist, but with her own studio and personal freedom. Modersohn-Becker painted and drew almost non-stop, with great self-discipline and a tightly organized daily routine. But she also acted as stepmother to Otto's daughter Elsbeth and was constantly in close contact with her large family.

67 –As early as 1917, although here very much abridged and selected; then in comprehensive form in 1979, edited by Werner Busch and Lieselotte von Reinken (cf. note 8).
68 –Letter to Milly Becker, September 21, 1899, in: Busch / Reinken 2007 (see note 8), p. 196 [translated].
69 –Frank Schmidt, "Zu Selbstdarstellung und Adressat in den Selbstbildnissen von Paula Modersohn-Becker," in: Bremen 2019/20 (see note 42), p. 17 [translated].
70 –Letter to Otto Modersohn, March 3, 1903, in: Modersohn / Werner 2017 (see note 1), p. 227 [translated].

RECEPTION

"No one knows her, and no one appreciates her [...] but that will change."[71]

It is emphasized time and again that Modersohn-Becker created her work in an intermediate phase of art in Germany:[72] too early for Die Brücke, the Blaue Reiter, and the new avant-garde galleries of Herwarth Walden, Wolfgang Gurlitt, Alfred Flechtheim, Paul Cassirer, and Heinrich Thannhauser who, shortly before, during, and after World War I, represented and disseminated the new in art on a grand scale and also inspired an open-minded group of collectors: August von der Heydt in Wuppertal,[73] Carl Ernst Osthaus in Hagen, Herbert von Garvens and Hermann Bahlsen in Hannover, and many others.

14 The Paula Becker-Modersohn Haus on Böttcherstrasse, Bremen, built by Bernhard Hoetger in 1926–27 (partially destroyed during the war), photo: Rudolph Stickelmann

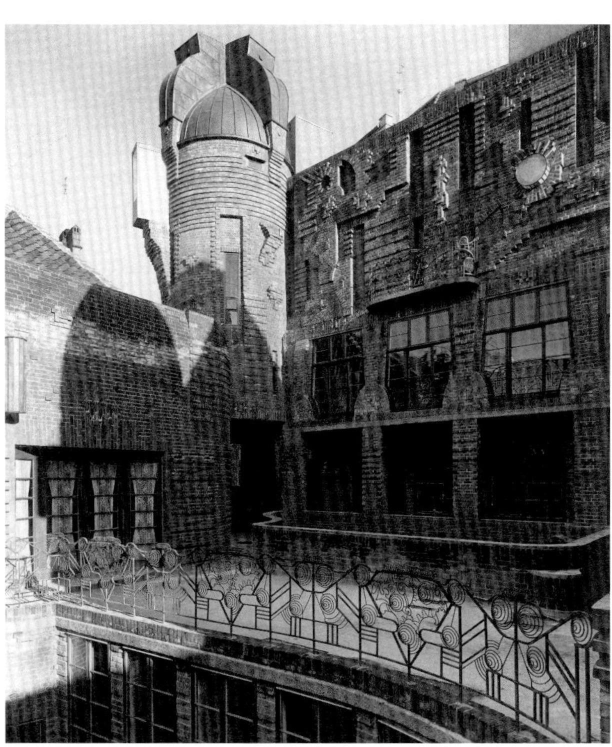

This view largely ignores the fact that, as a woman painter (and artist's wife), Modersohn-Becker could hardly have counted on personal success, both public and above all financial, in her environment at the time. The external perception—even of friends and colleagues—was too far removed from the actual reality of her work. Only after her premature death was it apparently possible, in the absence of the real person, so to speak, to celebrate her work as a "discovery," to stage it, to collect it, to exhibit it, and thus to give rise to the "myth of Paula." At the same time, various critics made the artist, who died at an early age, a projection screen for their own interests.

Among her first supporters was Gustav Pauli (1866–1938), Director of the Kunsthalle Bremen, who exhibited her twice during her lifetime, albeit without success. Immediately after her death, he purchased *Still Life with Yellow Pitcher* (1903/4) for the museum's collection. In 1908, he curated the first memorial exhibition, followed in 1913 by a tour organized by Vogeler in Hagen, Munich, Jena, and Wuppertal. In particular, Pauli's monograph with the publication of the first catalogue raisonné in 1919 (with only 239 numbers compared to the 734 paintings recorded today) contributed to the scholarly reappraisal of her estate. Pauli, who also acquired van Gogh's *Mohnfeld* (Field with Poppies) for the Kunsthalle Bremen in 1911, defended

71—Otto Modersohn's journal, entry dated June 15, 1902, in: ibid., p. 175 [translated].
72—Uwe M. Schneede, "'La grande simplicité de la forme.' La modernité de Paula Modersohn-Becker," in: *Paula Modersohn-Becker*, exh. cat. Musée d'art moderne de la ville de Paris, 2016, pp. 82–87.
73—Between 1909 and 1913, August von der Heydt acquired altogether twenty-eight works by Modersohn-Becker, still the second largest collection ever; cf. Günter Busch, "Einführung in das Werk von Paula Modersohn-Becker," in: Busch / Werner, vol. 1 (see note 29), p. 27.

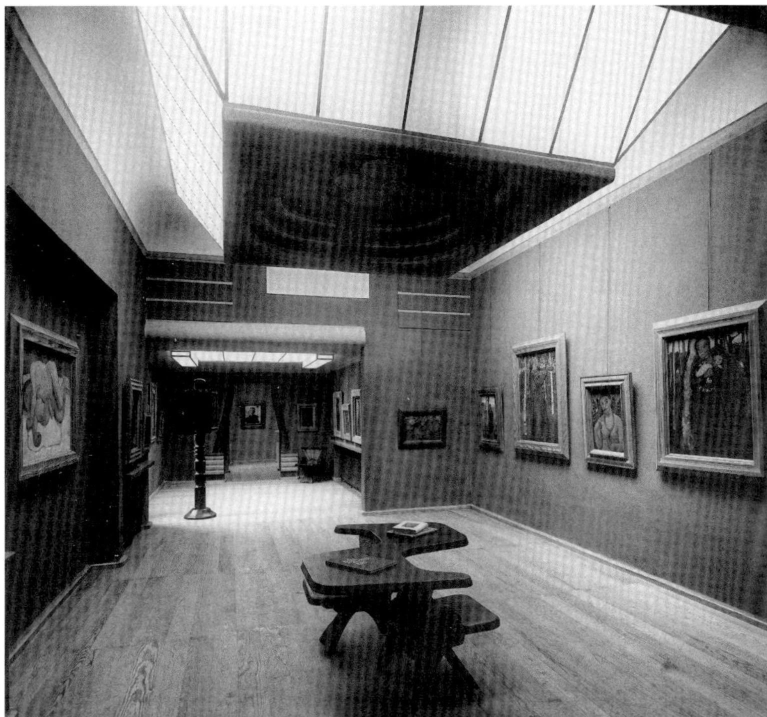

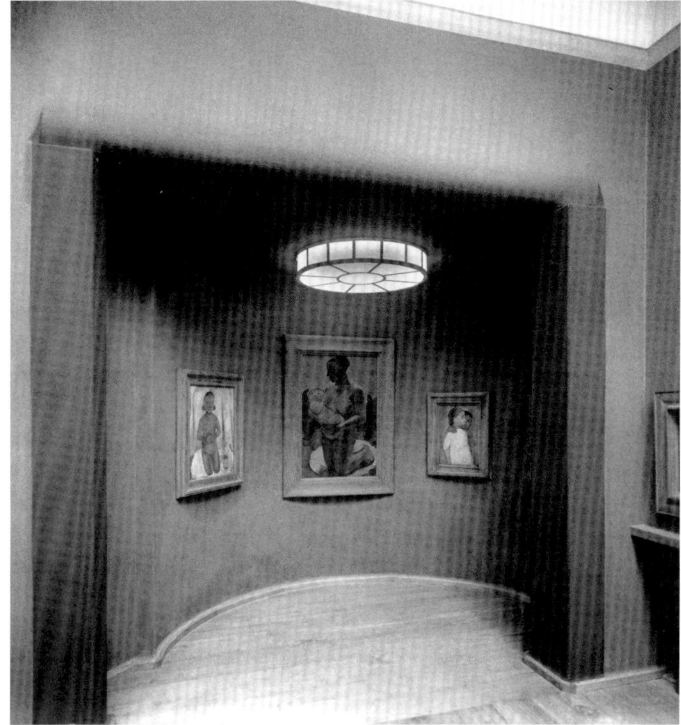

15 The hall on the upper floor of the Paula Becker-Modersohn Haus 1927, photo: Rudolph Stickelmann

16 Skylight alcove in the Paula Becker-Modersohn Haus, 1927, photo: Rudolph Stickelmann

Modersohn-Becker's work against attacks for its "ugliness" and "primitiveness" and related the artist to Expressionism, which in some interpretations was even seen as a contemporary continuation of Gothic and "Nordic" art.[74] A similar discussion took place later in connection with the work of Emil Nolde, as well as with other Expressionists.[75]

Whereas Pauli was enthusiastically committed to "modernism" and Paula Modersohn-Becker, his successor Emil Waldmann (1880–1945) had to defend her work from 1933 onwards against the attacks of the National Socialists. The increased stylization of Modersohn-Becker as an explicitly "Low German" artist with "naturalistic, almost earthy-looking simplicity and inwardness" intensified already in the late 1920s and early 1930s. Some critics, who, on the one hand, held her Worpswede works in high esteem and, on the other, sympathized with National Socialism, attempted to trivialize and suppress the "modern" and Parisian aspects of her works. Evidence for this was above all her depiction of the peasants, whose "essence" and "disposition," allegedly more than in the works of any other artist, captured and characterized that which was unmistakably "German."[76]

When twenty-three paintings, twenty-three drawings, and twenty-two prints[77] by Modersohn-Becker were confiscated from German museums in the 1930s, and her *Self-Portrait with Camellia Branch* (p. 46) was shown in the *Entartete Kunst*

74 – Kai Artinger, *Paula Modersohn-Becker. Der andere Blick*, (Berlin 2008), p. 21.
75 – Cf. *Emil Nolde. Eine deutsche Legende - der Künstler im Nationalsozialismus* (Berlin 2019), pp. 39-65.
76 – Artinger 2008 (see note 74), pp. 27-36 [translated].
77 – Ibid., p. 53.

(Degenerate Art) exhibition in Munich, the then "Paula Becker-Modersohn Haus" (figs. 14–16) was not affected. At that time, the private museum, which was opened in 1927 by the Bremen-based entrepreneur Ludwig Roselius and designed by Bernhard Hoetger as a "Gesamtkunstwerk," contained fifty-nine paintings and fifty-one works on paper by Modersohn-Becker.[78] Roselius, a convinced National Socialist, campaigned for the artist with all his might until the end and was convinced of her uniqueness despite all the criticism.[79]

After World War II, the successful and very broad reappraisal of her work began, and with it the attempt to celebrate her as the embodiment of an unencumbered "modernism in Germany," on a par with Cézanne, Gauguin, van Gogh, and Edvard Munch: "Around 1900, two Frenchmen, a Dutchman, a Norwegian, and a German girl initiated a movement from which the art of our day would emerge," wrote Otto Stelzer in 1958.[80] Accordingly, her works were also shown at the first and third documenta exhibitions in Kassel in 1955 and 1964, respectively. To this day, Modersohn-Becker's early and often radical pictorial inventions are compared to widely respected artists from Cézanne to Picasso.[81] However, it is above all the comparison with works and artifacts of distant cultures, such as mummy portraits, that has contributed to the fundamental understanding of her thinking and her specific interest in the "great simplicity of form."[82]

Beyond that, however, Modersohn-Becker's oeuvre, as has been shown here, appears even more complex and contradictory and cannot be thought of without her specifically "feminine" themes, her mysticism of nature, and her matriarchal counterworld. The timeless or rather "supratemporal" aspect of many of her works seems like a common thread and was presumably also a kind of demarcation mechanism from her immediate surroundings. By citing distant cultures and long-past art movements, the artist created a sphere of "distance" in terms of both content and form that allowed her a great deal of freedom. Time and again, one is surprised by her intellectual independence and the courage to paint things in great solitude that were practically impossible to exhibit, because they would have overwhelmed her environment. It is not only thematically that her mother-and-child motifs[83] provoke various critics to this day, as does her at times disobliging painting style, which anticipates Art Brut. The work remains a projection surface for each new generation and their taboos and values; in this respect, the discussion about Paula Modersohn-Becker is far from over.

78 –Ibid., p. 41.
79 –Gisela Götte, "Der Sammler und Mäzen Ludwig Roselius," in: *Tausche Cranach gegen Monet / Tausche Monet gegen Modersohn-Becker*, exh. cat. Paula Modersohn-Becker Museum / Arp Museum Bahnhof Rolandseck, 2021-22, pp. 10-15.
80 –Otto Stelzer, *Paula Modersohn* (Berlin 1958), p. 7 [translated].
81 –Cf. Rainer Stamm in the present catalog, pp. 156-163.
82 –Modersohn-Becker's journal, February 25, 1903, in: Modersohn / Werner 2017 (see note 1), p. 216 [translated].
83 –Cf. Inge Herold in the present catalog, pp. 97-103.

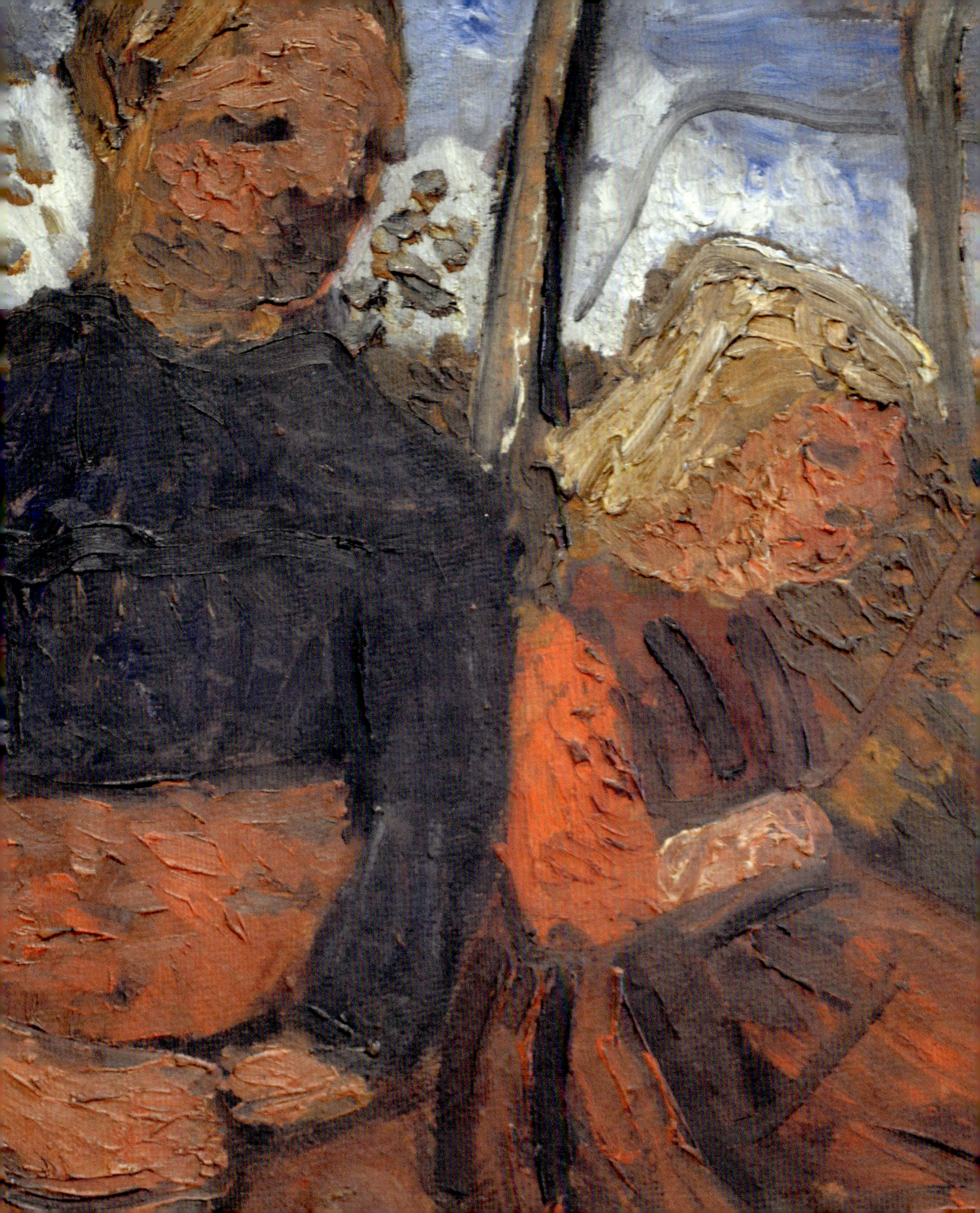

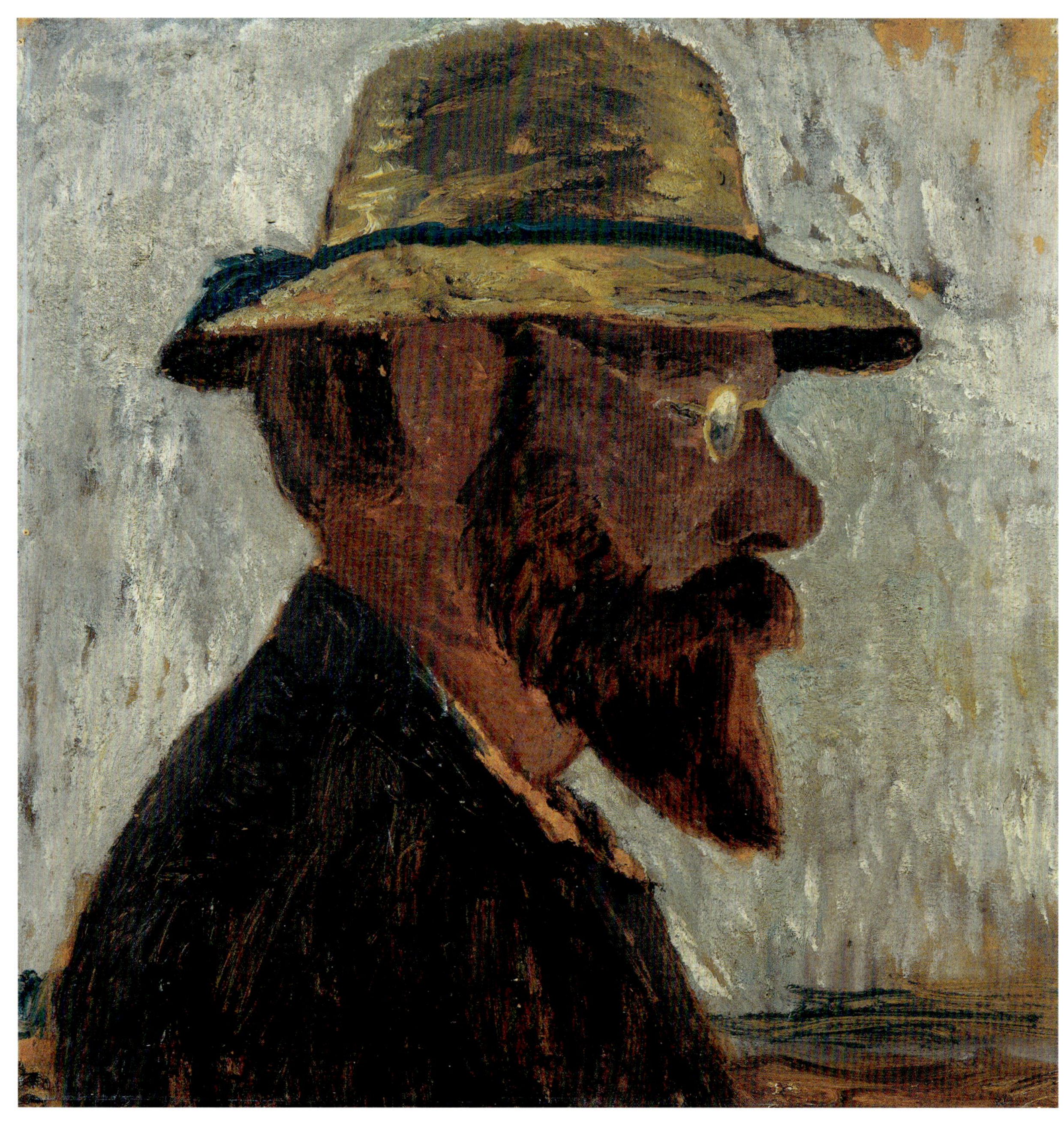

Otto Modersohn mit Strohhut im Profil nach rechts / Otto Modersohn with Straw Hat in Right-Headed Profile, c. 1905

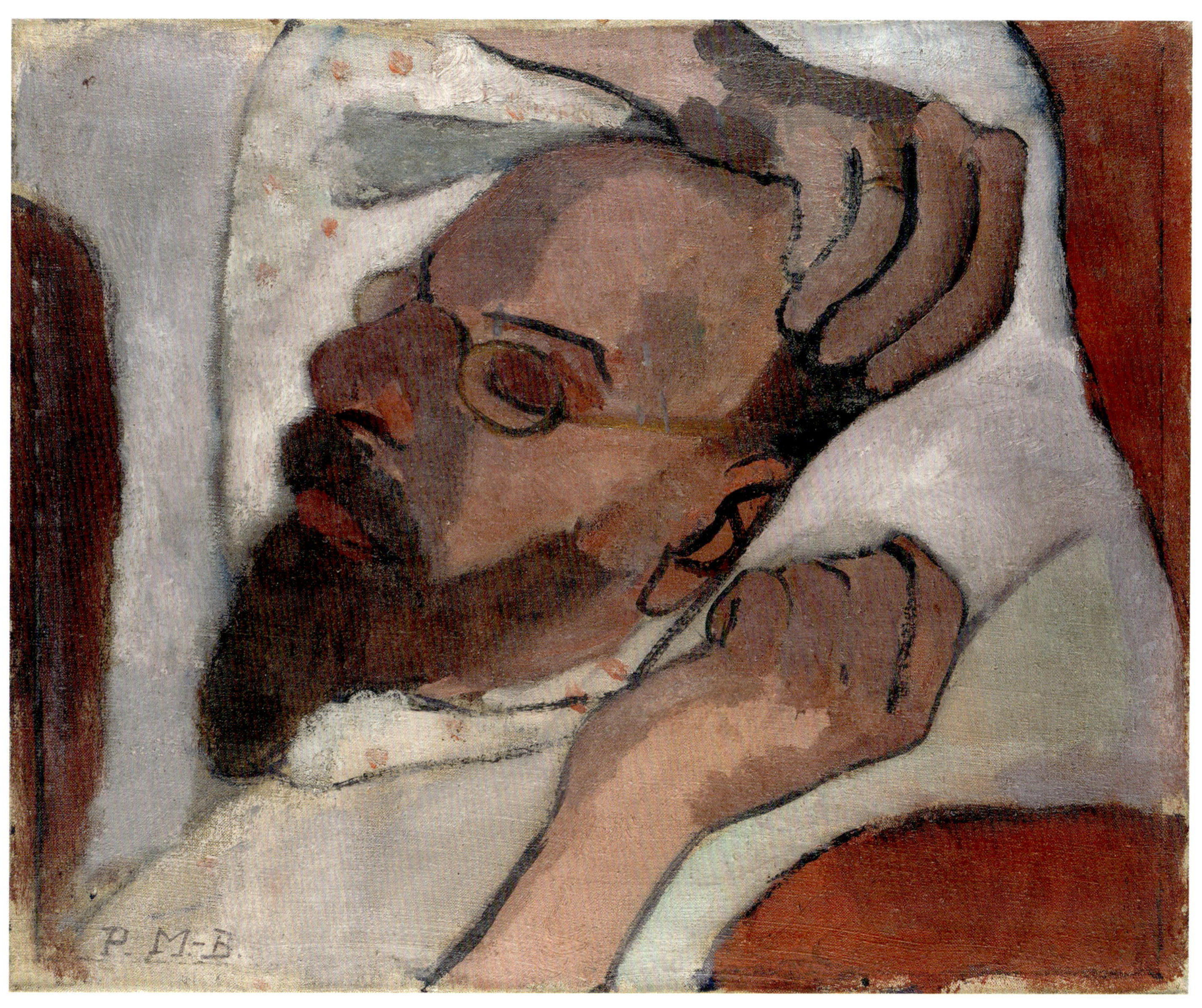

Otto Modersohn schlafend / Otto Modersohn Sleeping, winter 1906/7

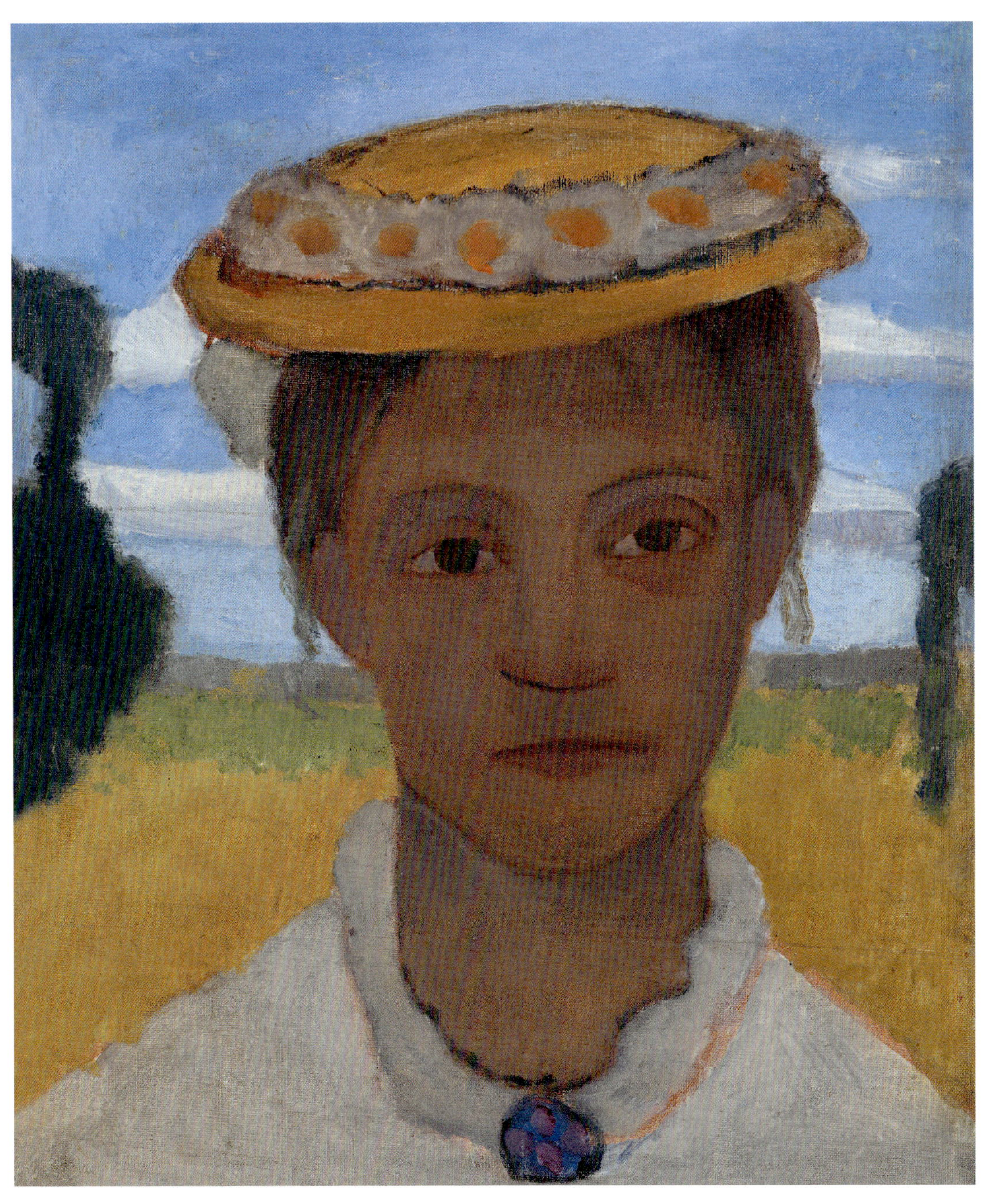

Kopf der Schwester Herma mit Marienblümchenkranz auf dem Hut /
The Artist's Sister Herma with a Wreath of Daisies on Her Hat, c. 1901

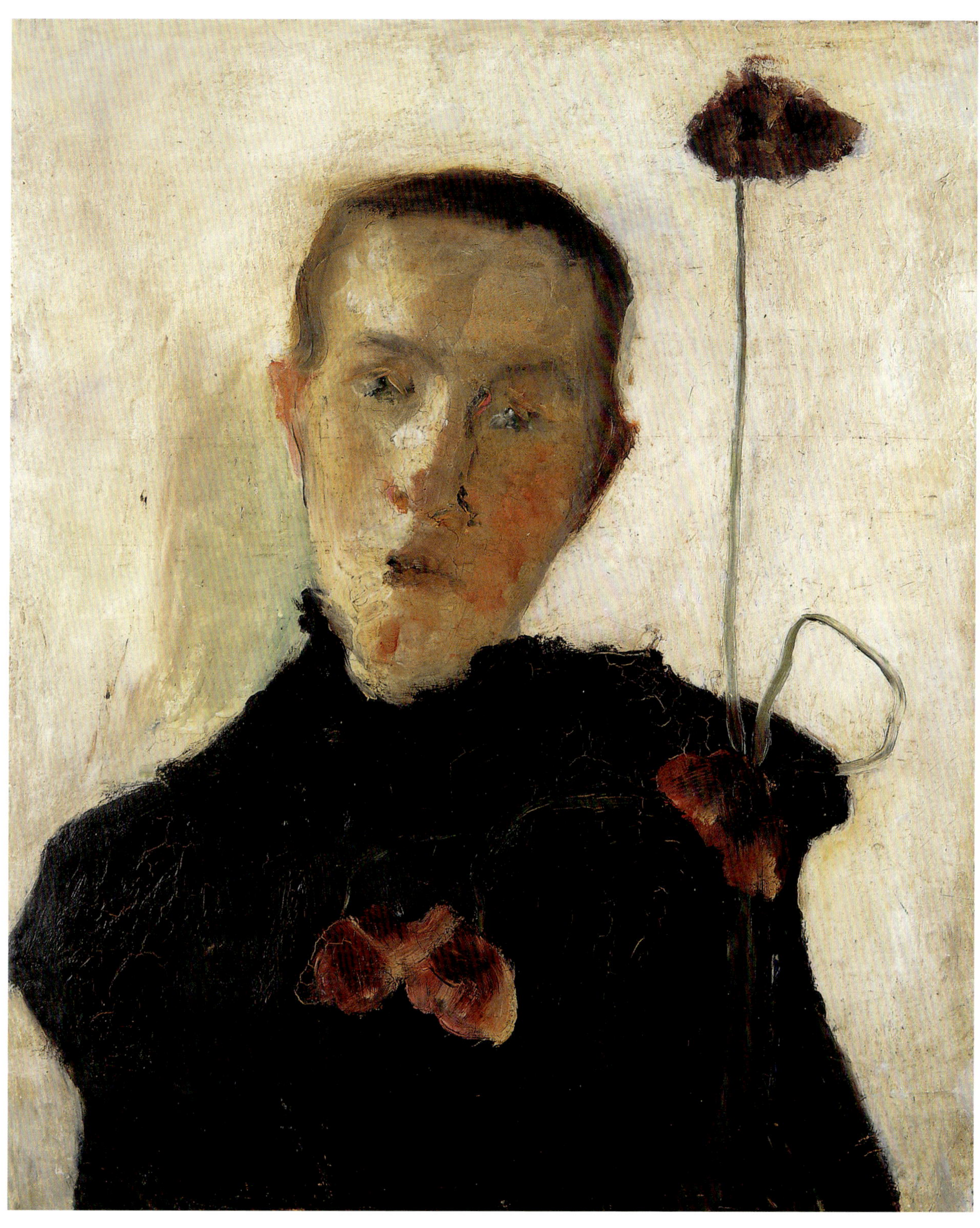

Brustbild einer Frau mit Mohnblumen / Woman with Poppies, c. 1898

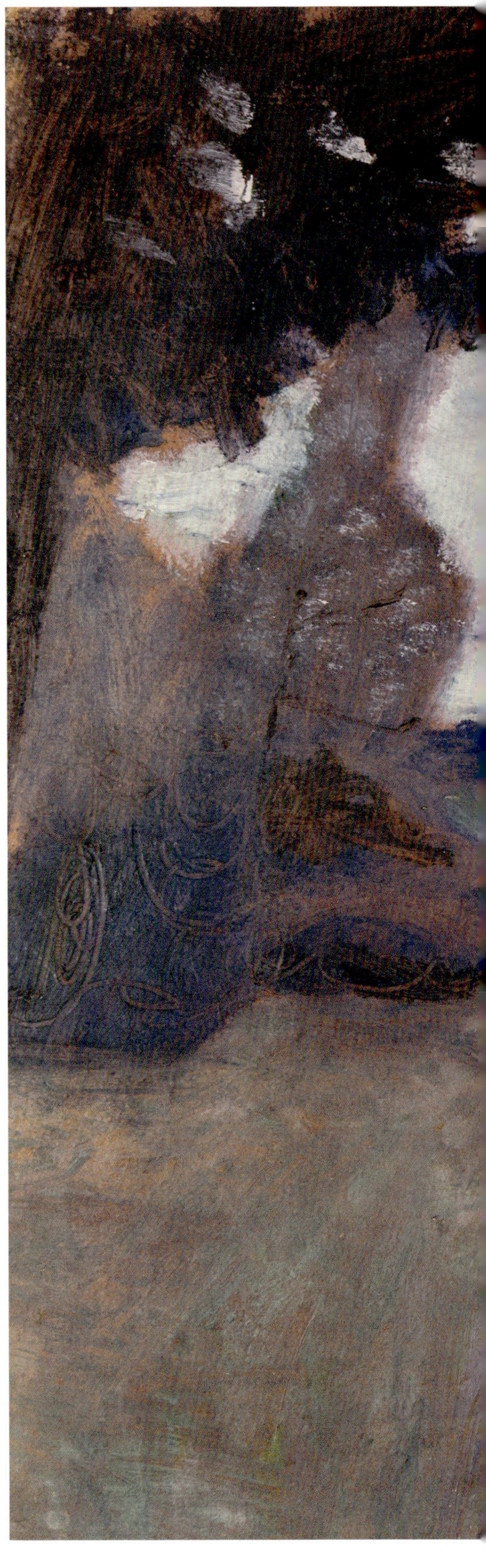

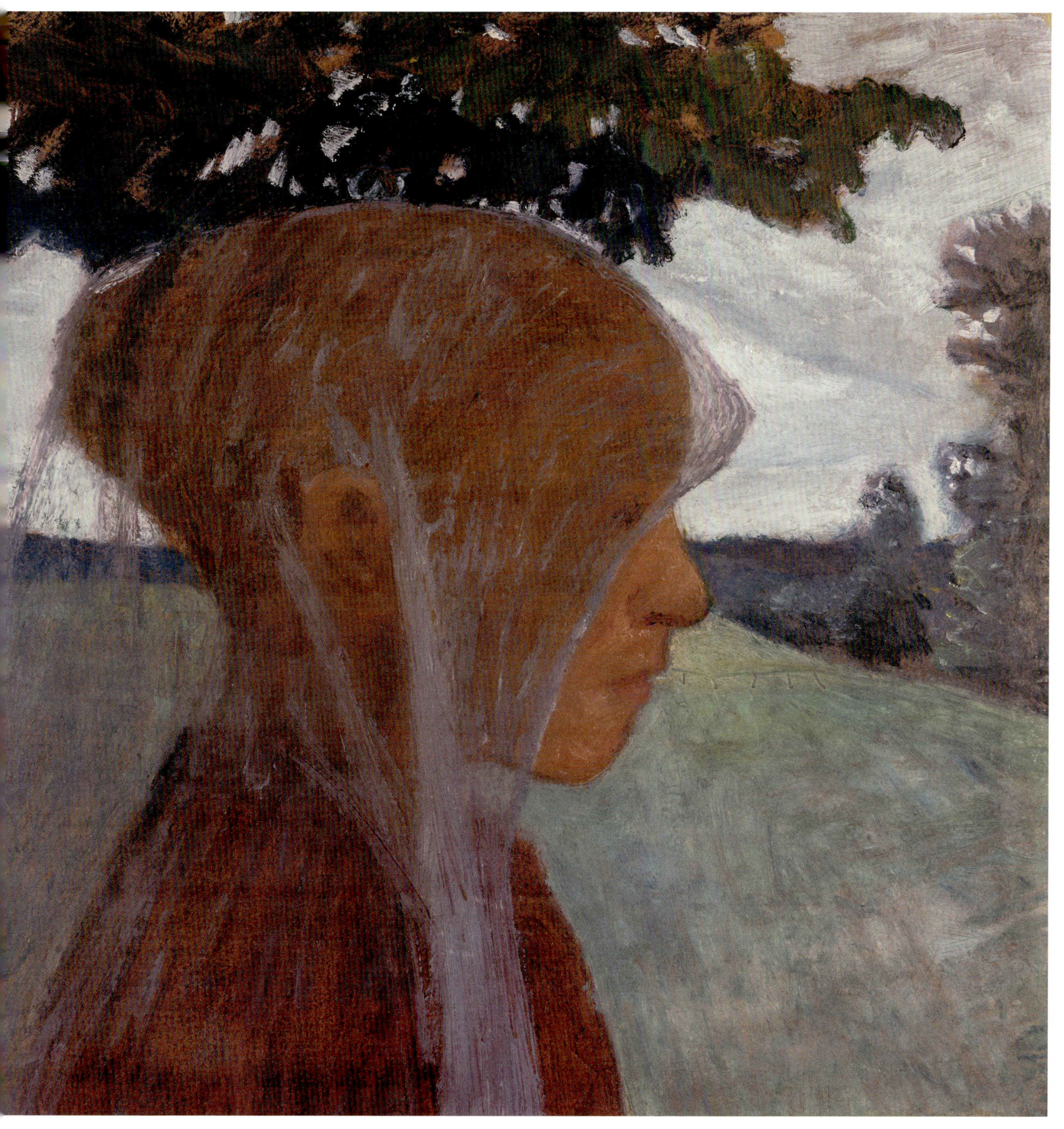

Brustbild eines Mädchens mit Schleier nach rechts gewandt vor Landschaft /
Half-Length Portrait of a Girl with a Veil Turning to the Right in Front of a Landscape, c. 1901

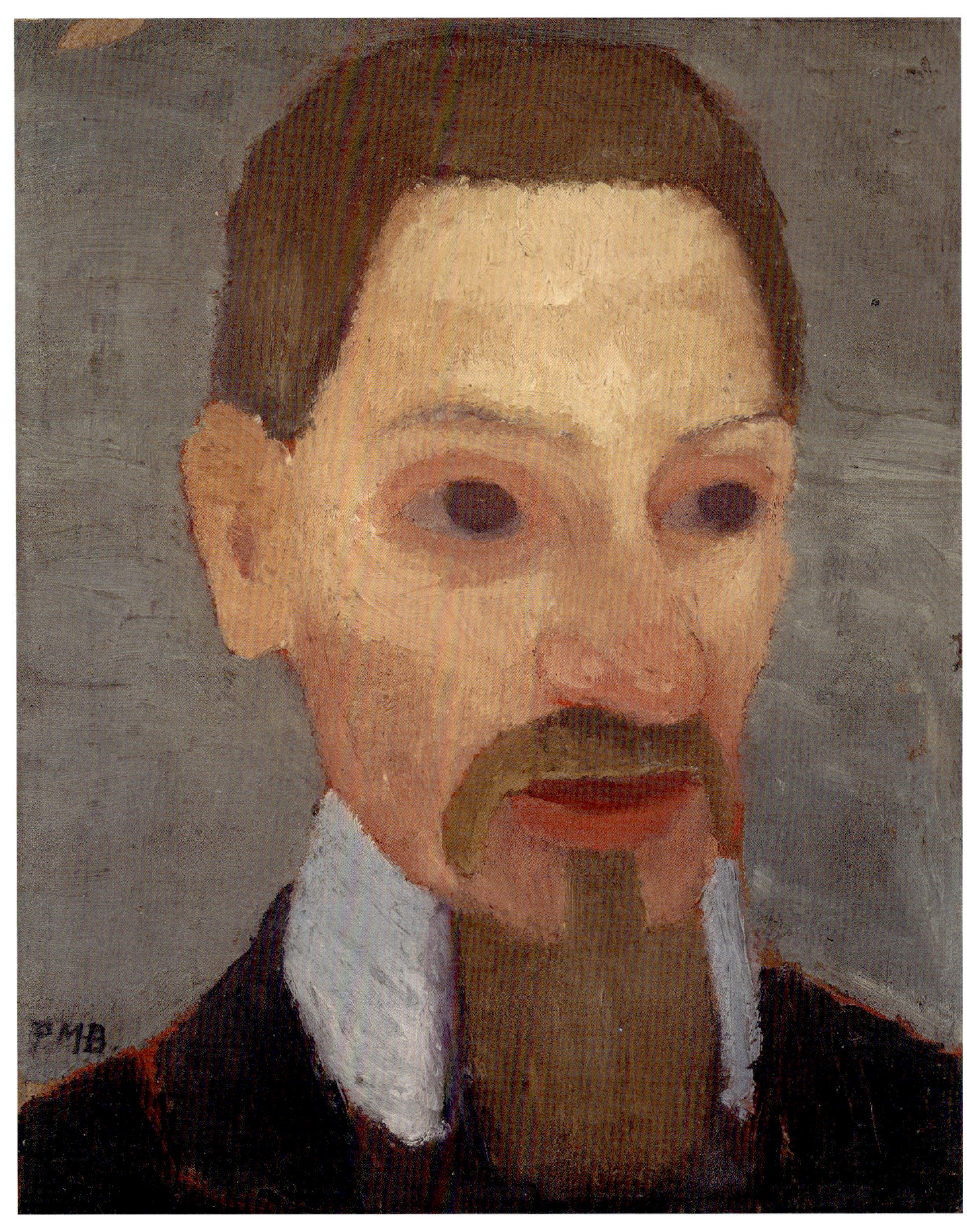

Bildnis Rainer Maria Rilke / Portrait of Rainer Maria Rilke, May/June 1906

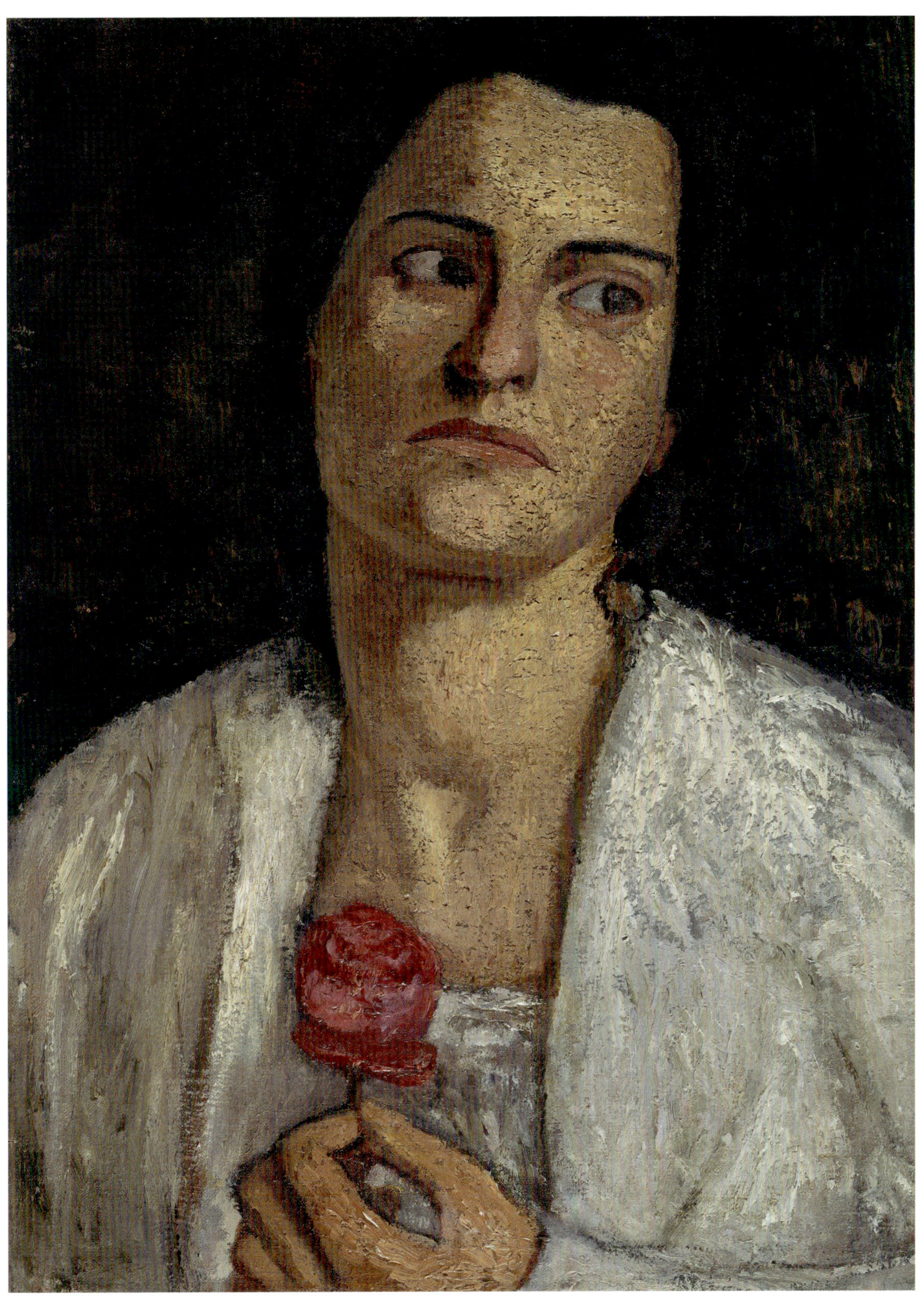

Die Bildhauerin Clara Rilke-Westhoff / The Sculptress Clara Rilke-Westhoff, November 1905

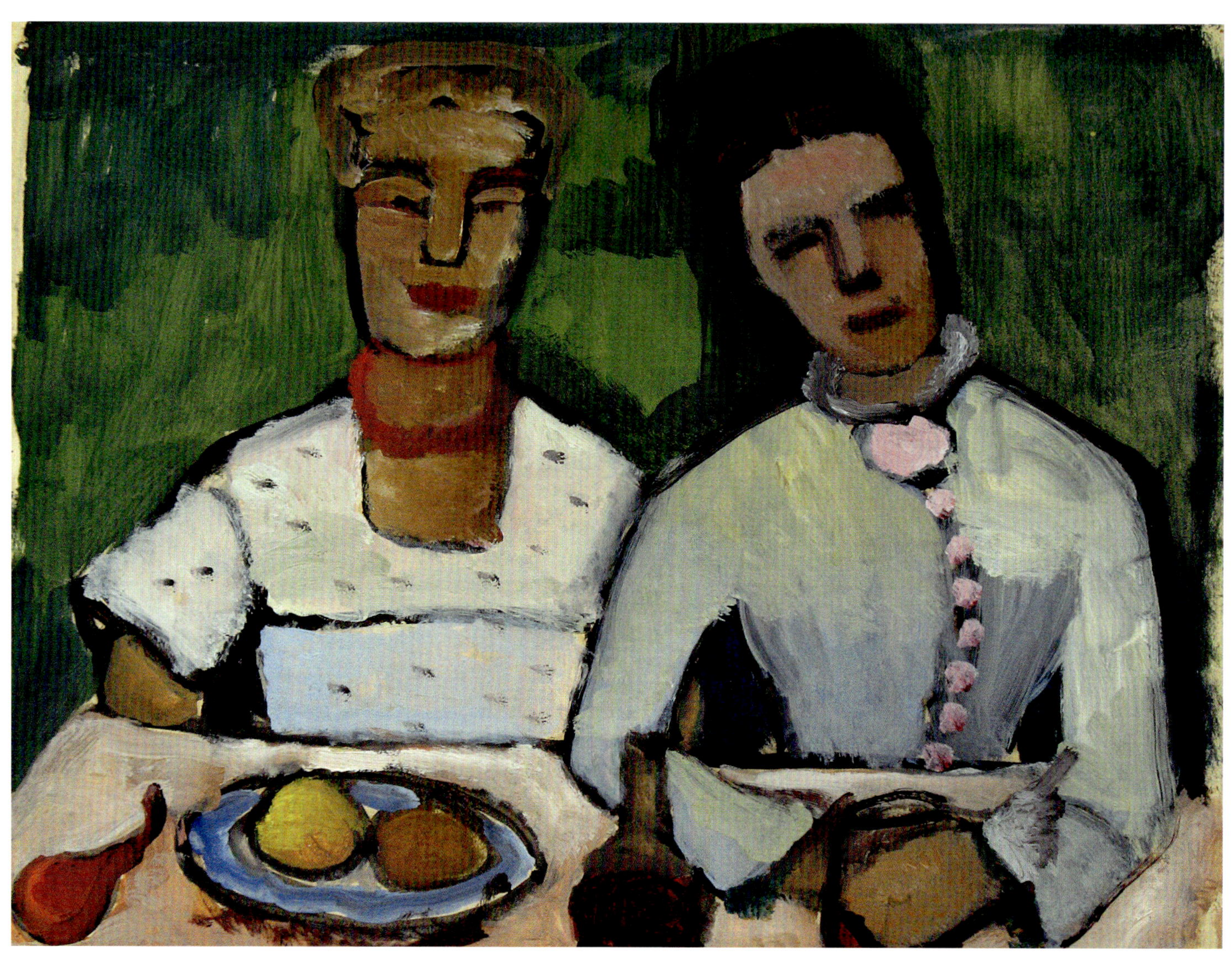

Bildnis Lee Hoetger und Clara Haken / Portrait of Lee Hoetger and Clara Haken, July/August 1906

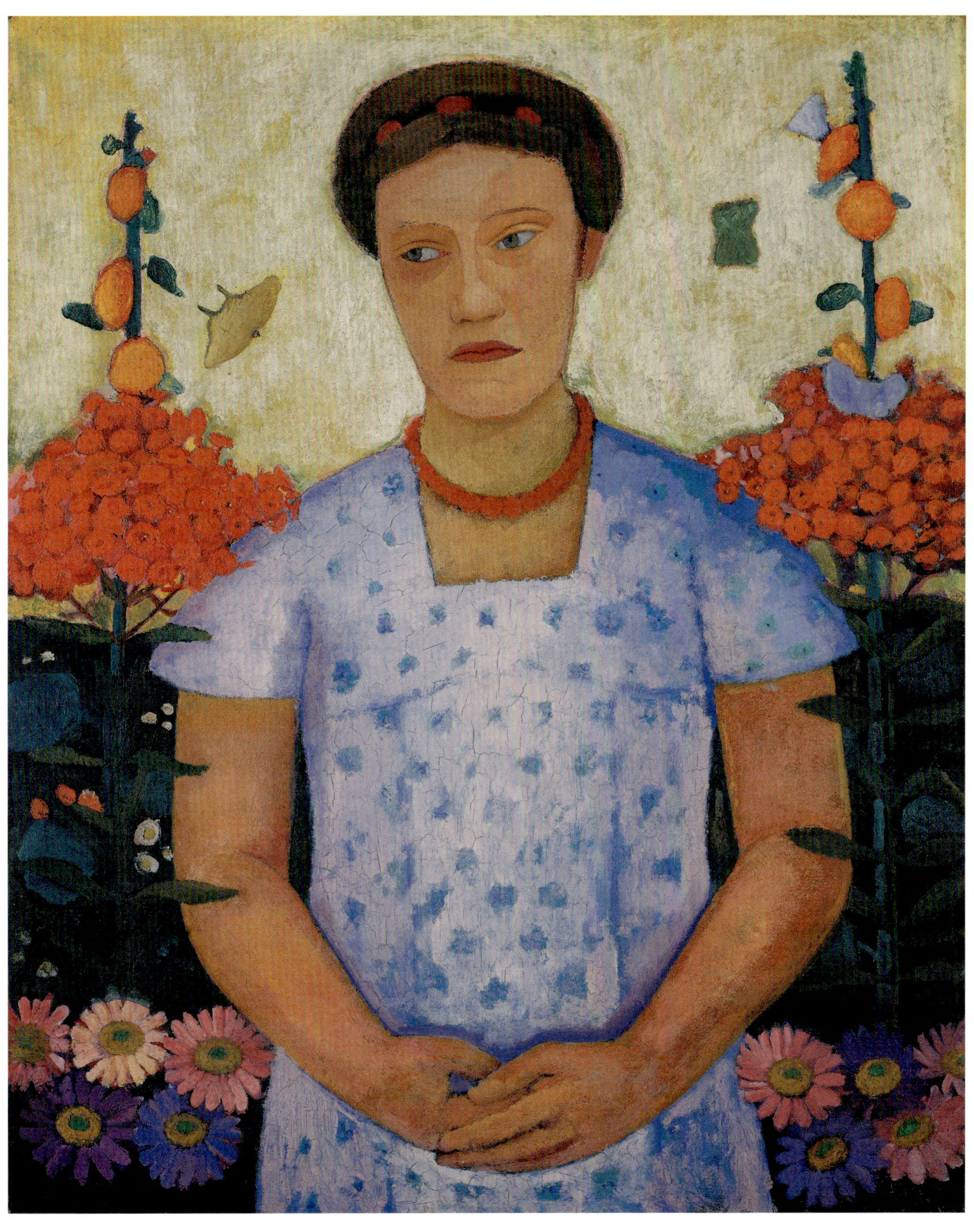

Bildnis Lee Hoetger vor Blumengrund / Lee Hoetger in Front of a Floral Background, August 1906

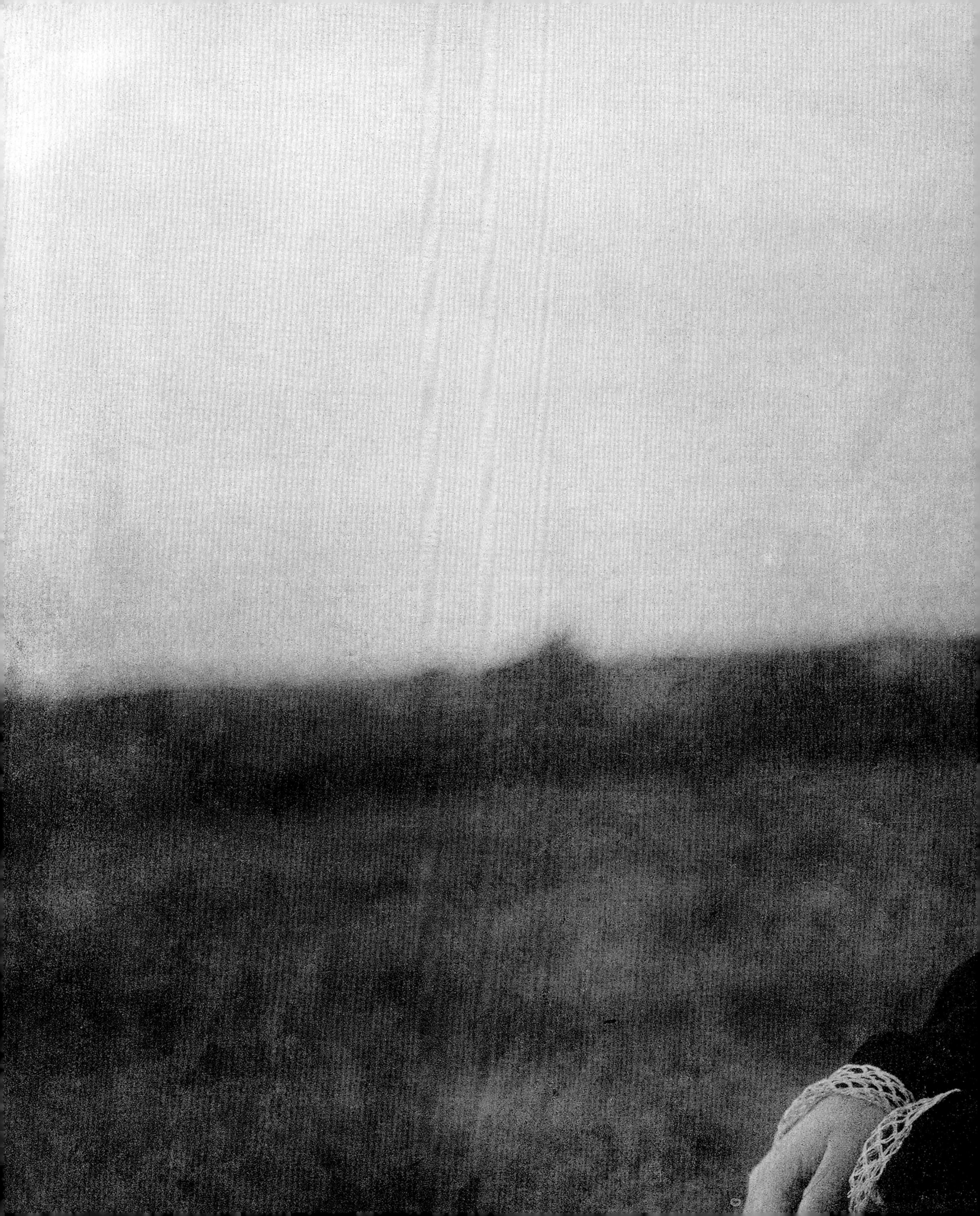

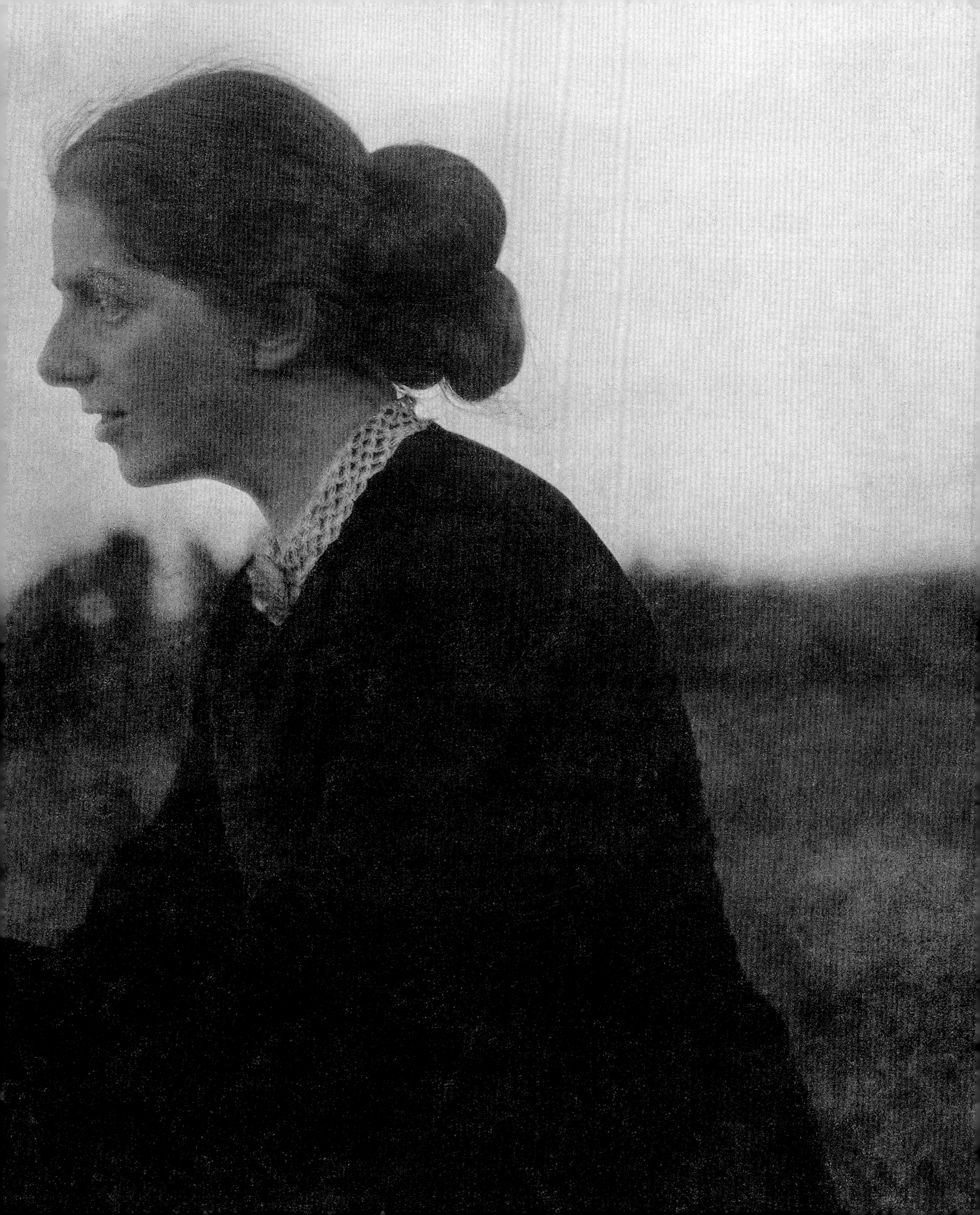

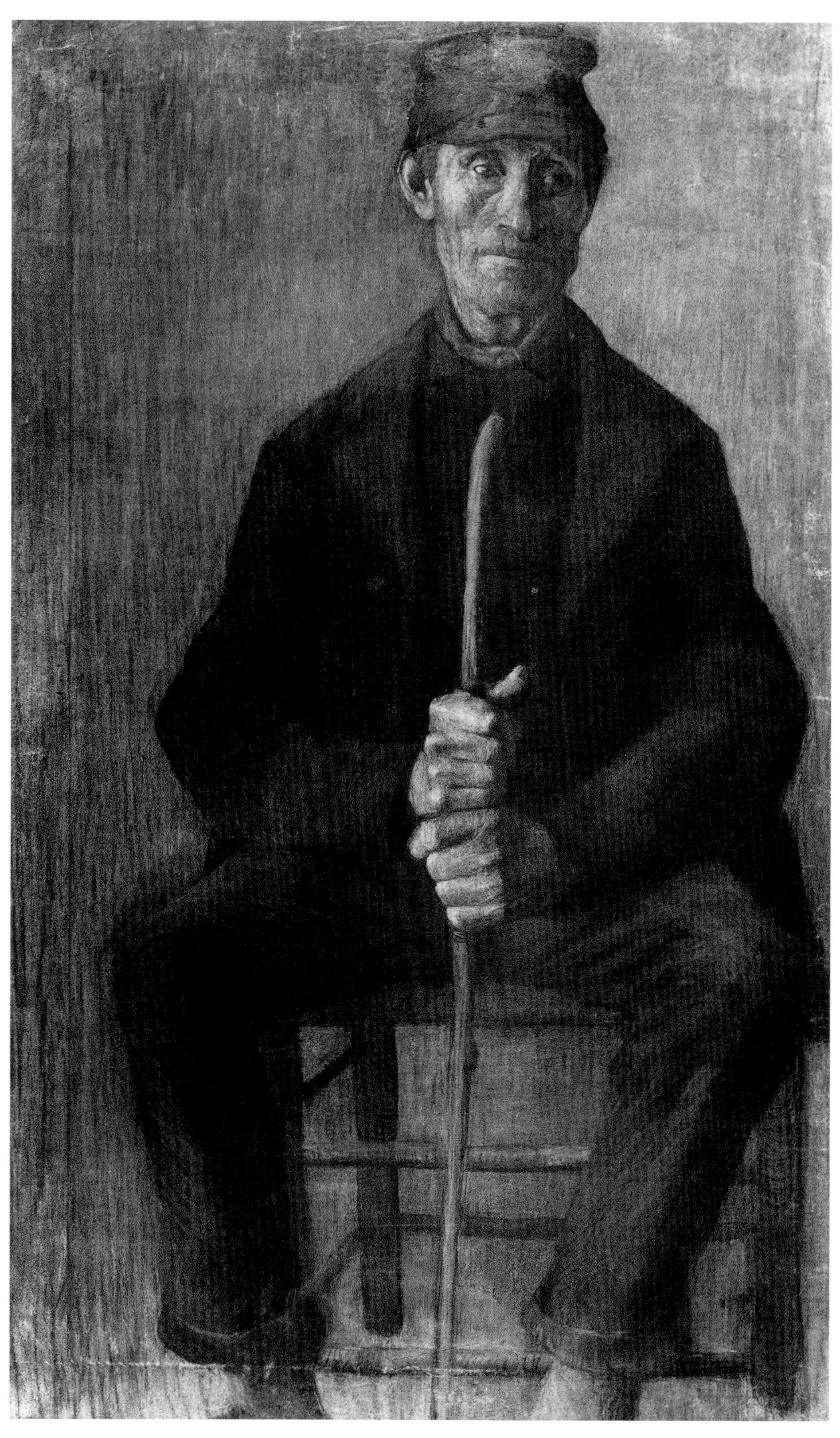

Alter Bauer / Old Peasant Man, 1899

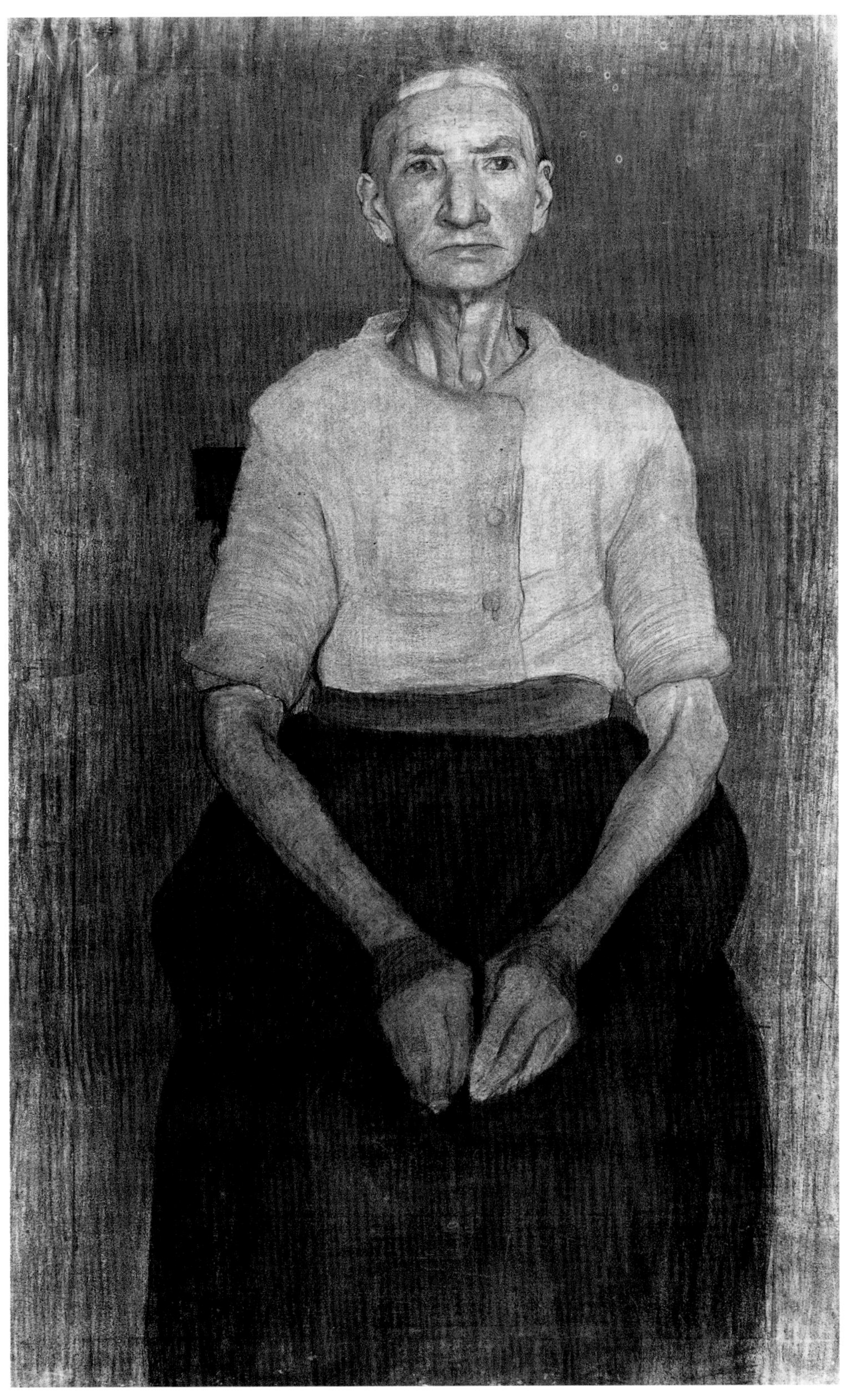

Alte Bäuerin / Old Peasant Woman, 1899

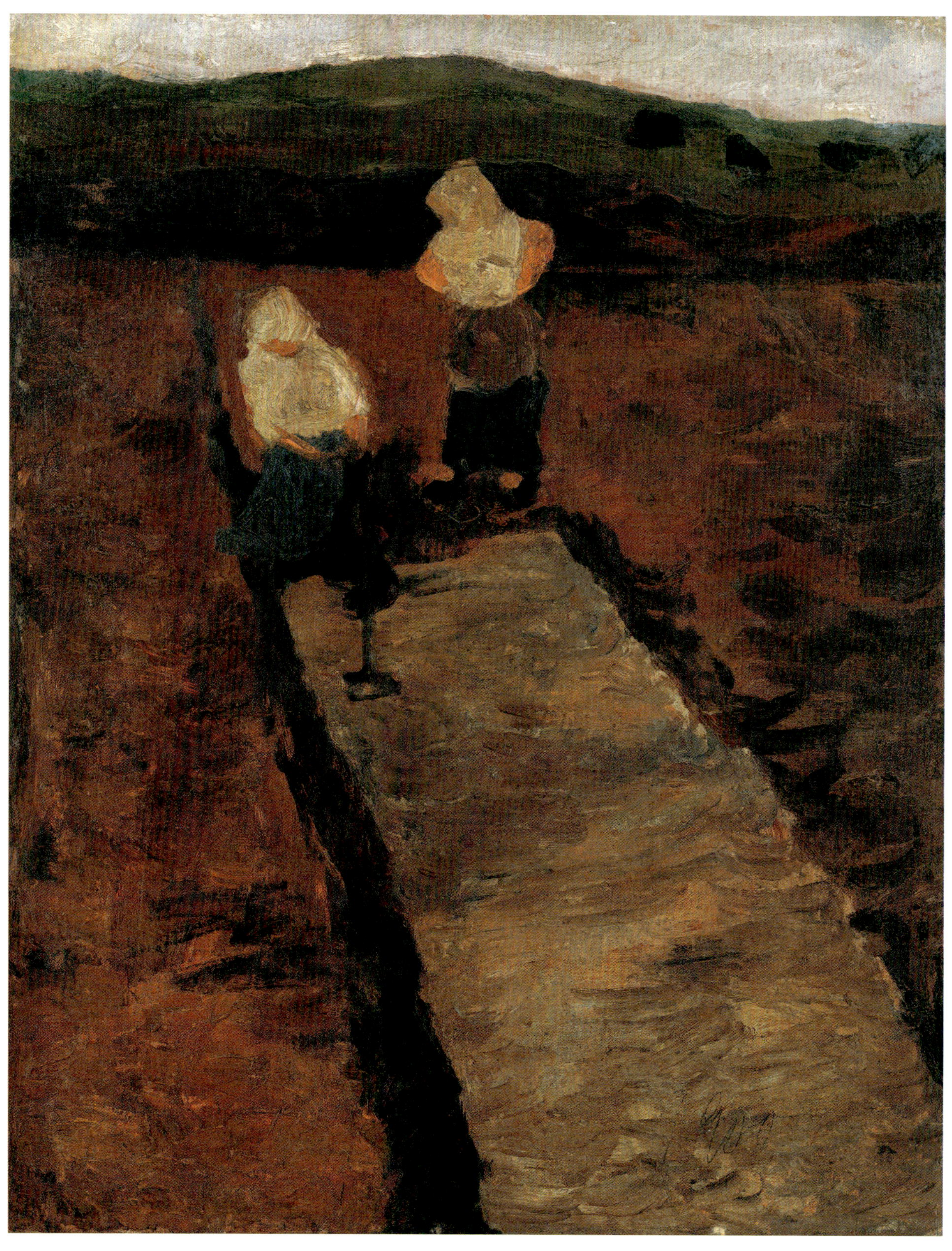

Zwei Bäuerinnen beim Torfstechen / Two Peasant Women Cutting Peat, 1900

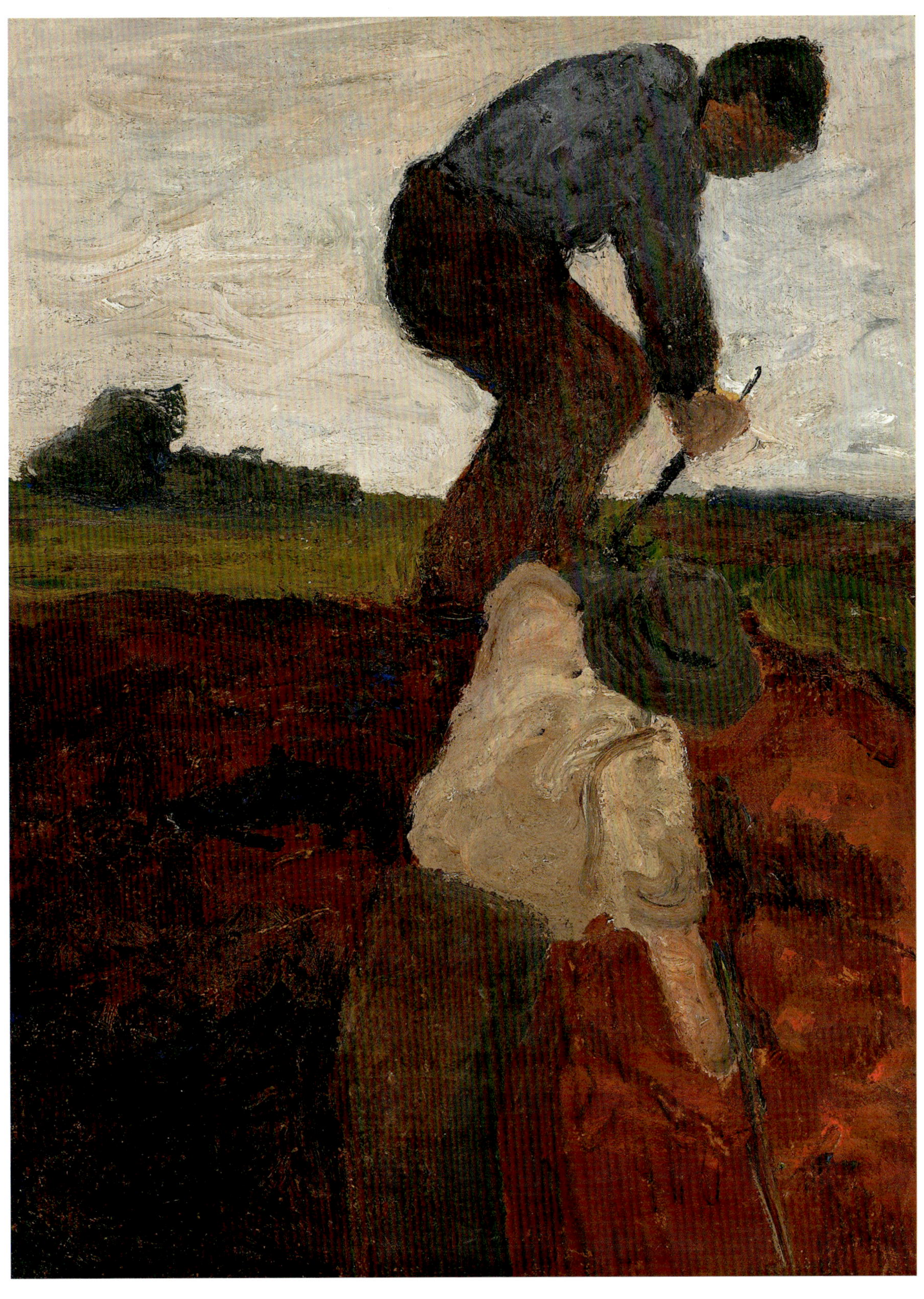

Zwei Männer beim Torfstechen / Two Men Cutting Peat, 1900

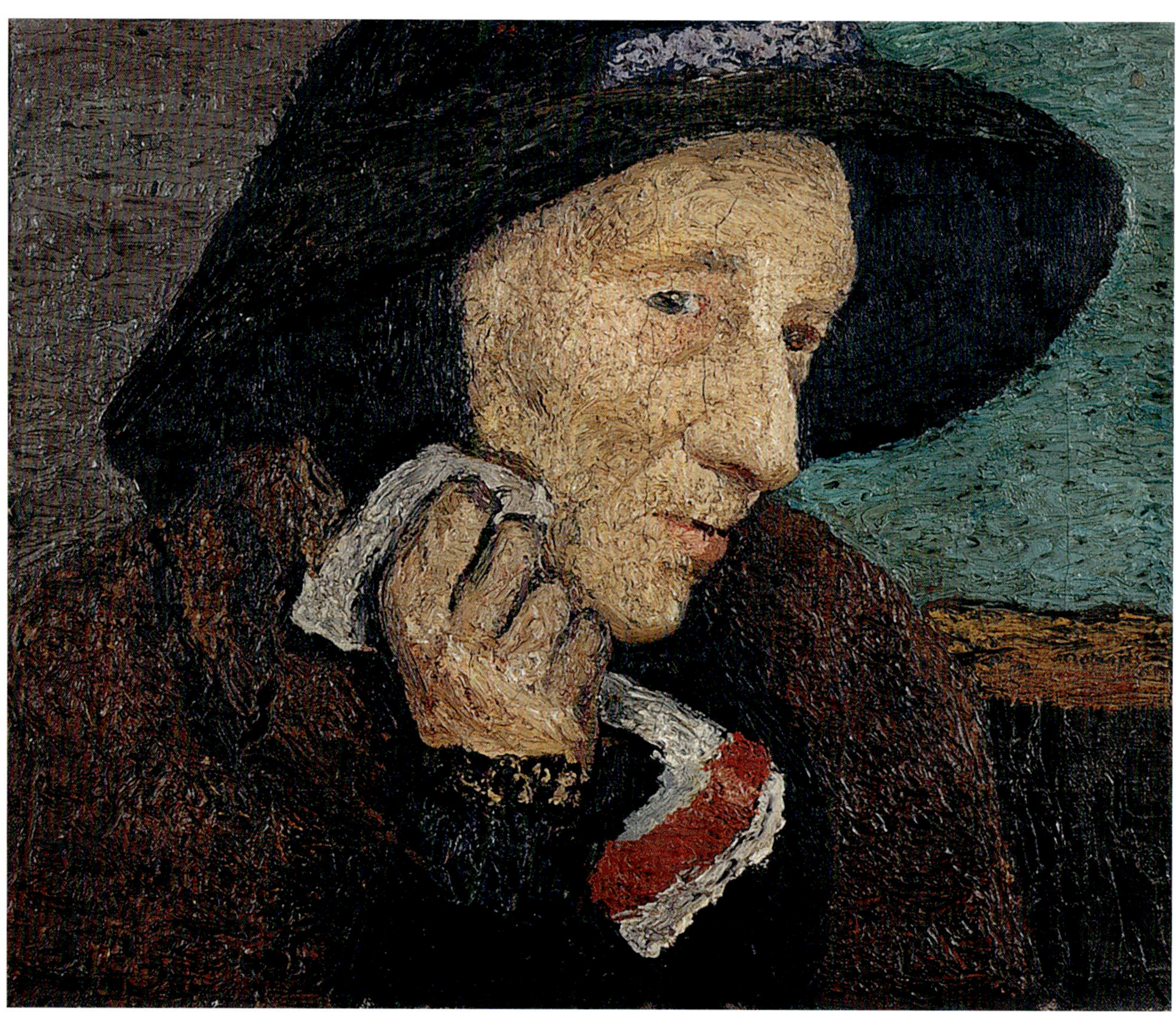

Alte Frau mit schwarzem Strohhut / Old Woman in a Black Straw Hat, c. 1905

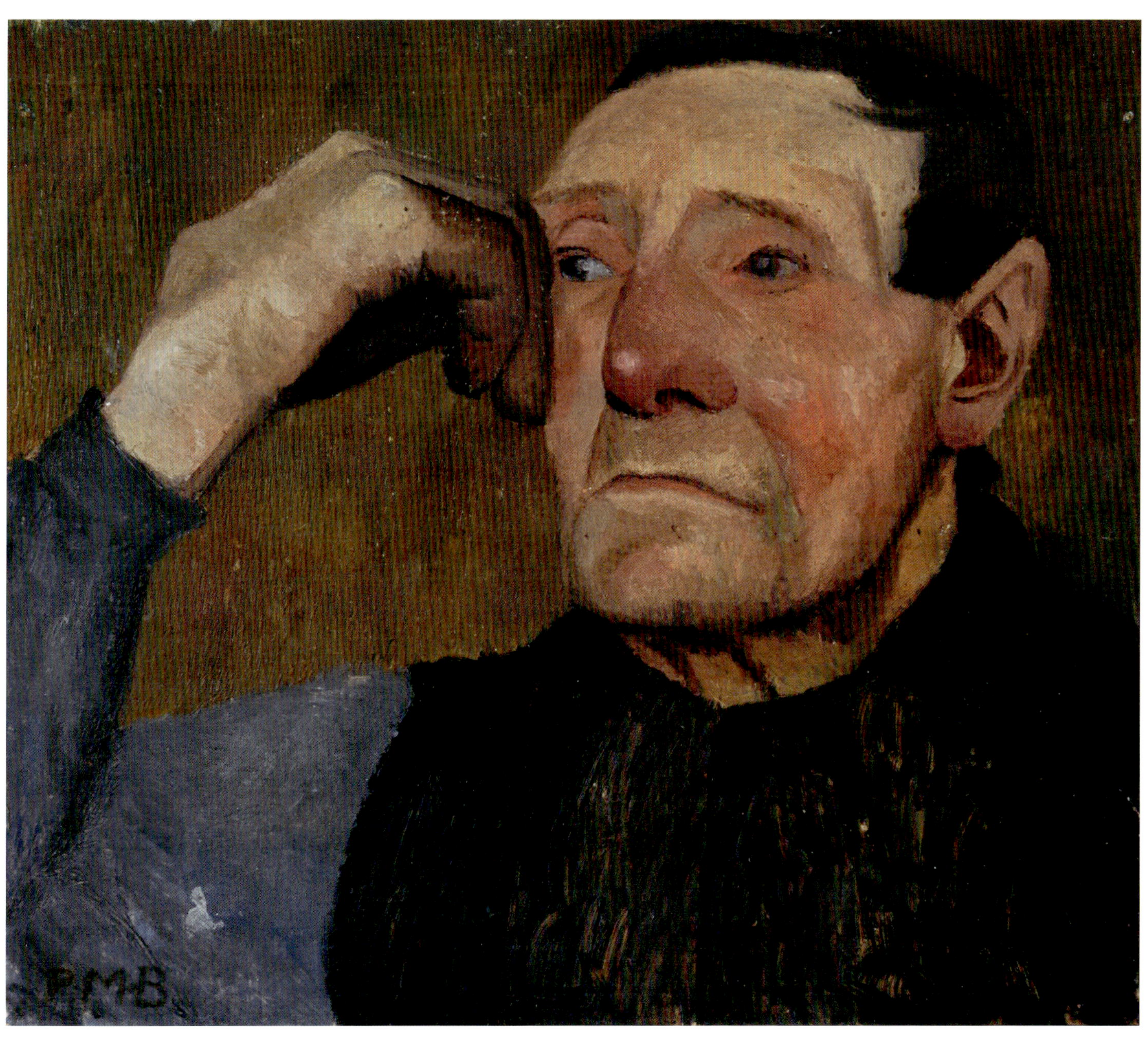

Brustbild eines Bauern, den Kopf auf die rechte Hand gestützt /
Half-Length Portrait of a Peasant, His Head Resting on His Right Hand, c. 1903

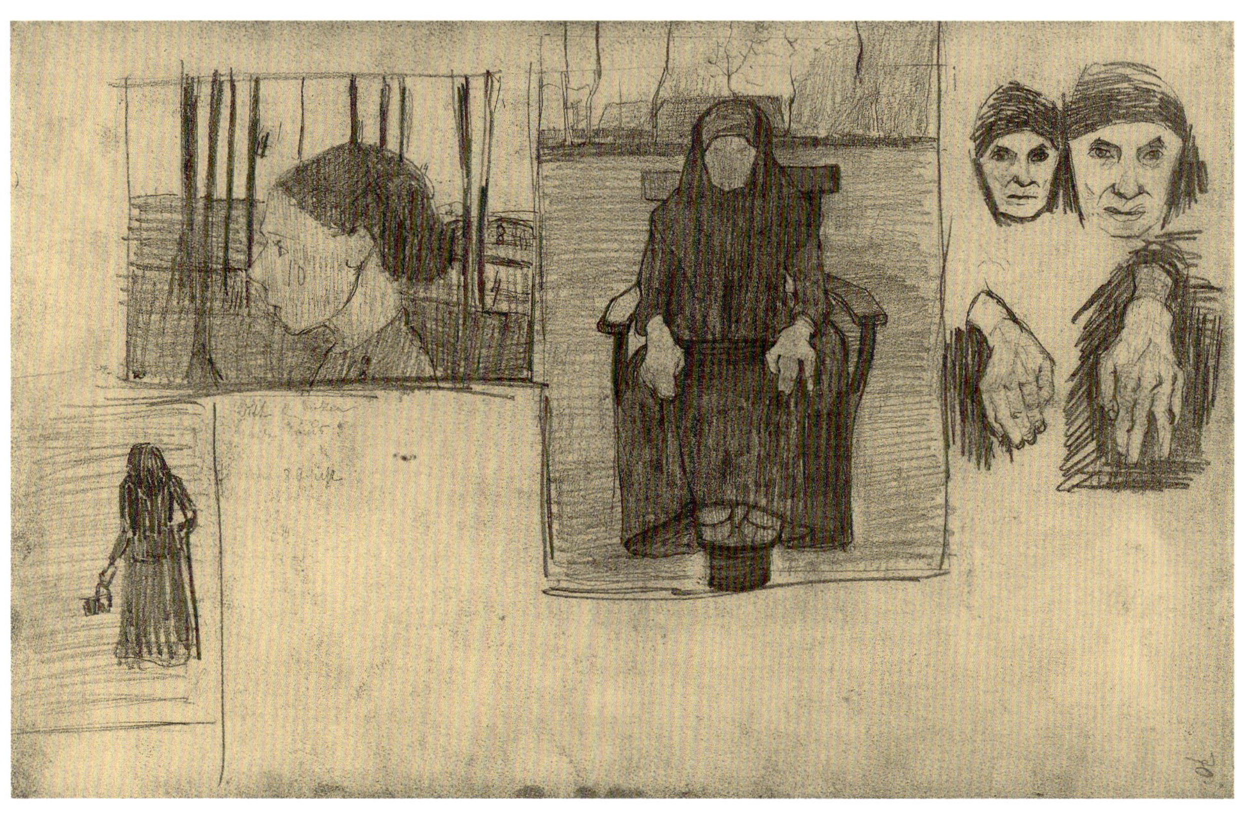

Skizzenblatt mit Kompositionsskizze für *Sitzende Alte* / Composition sketch for *Seated Old Woman*, 1899

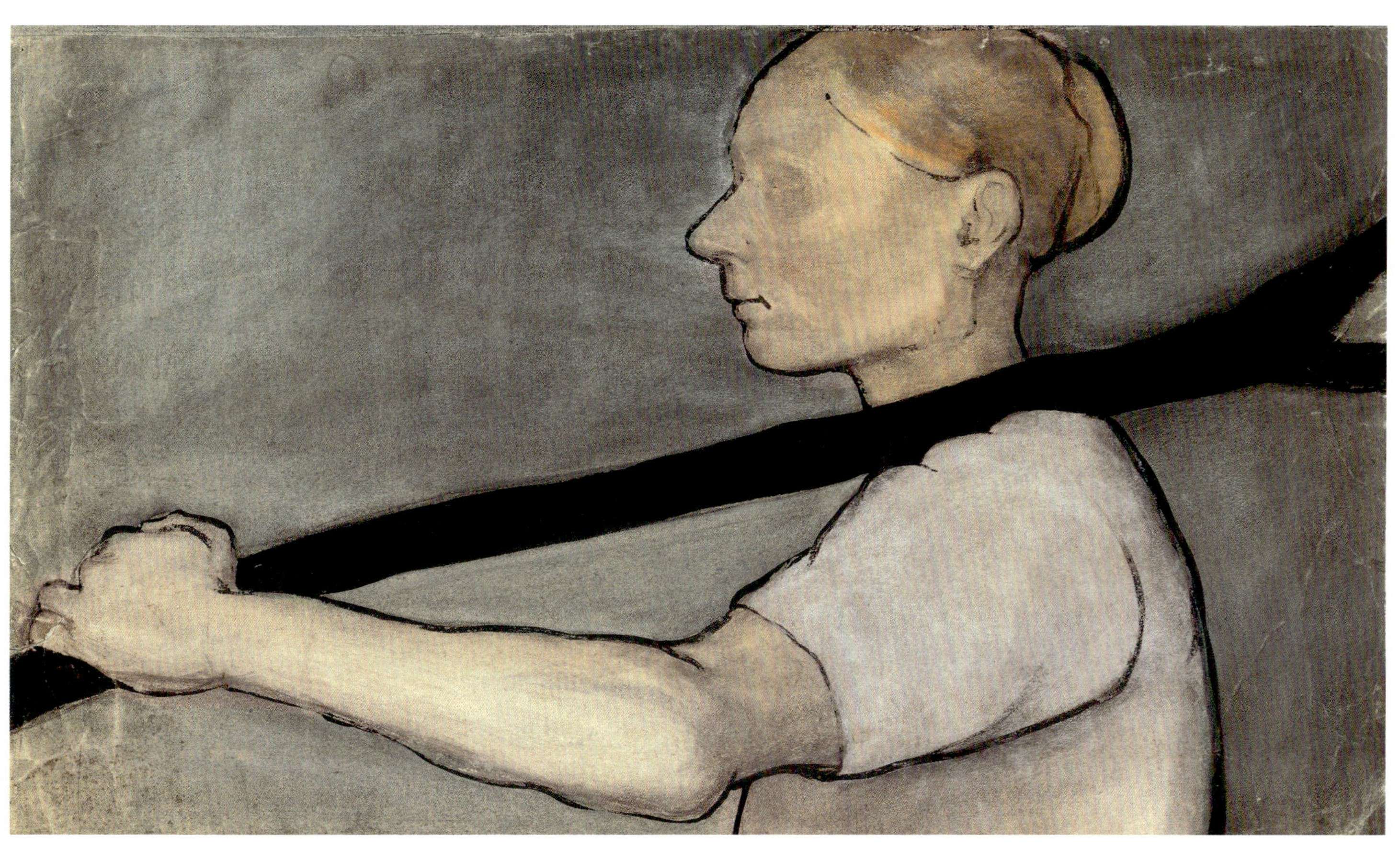

Bäuerin, eine Astgabel tragend / Peasant Woman Carrying a Branch Fork, c. 1898/99

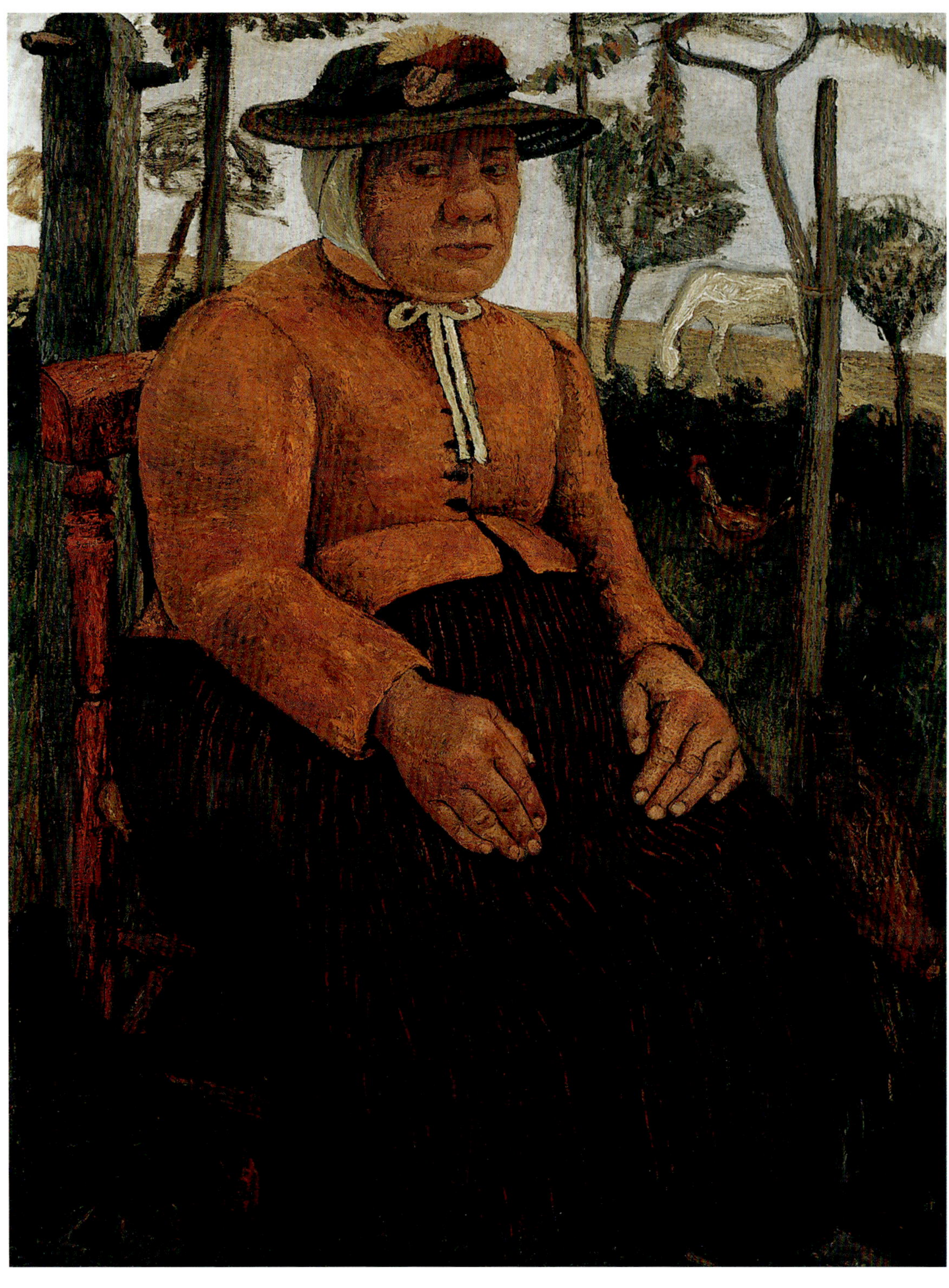

Alte Armenhäuslerin / Old Pauper, c. 1905

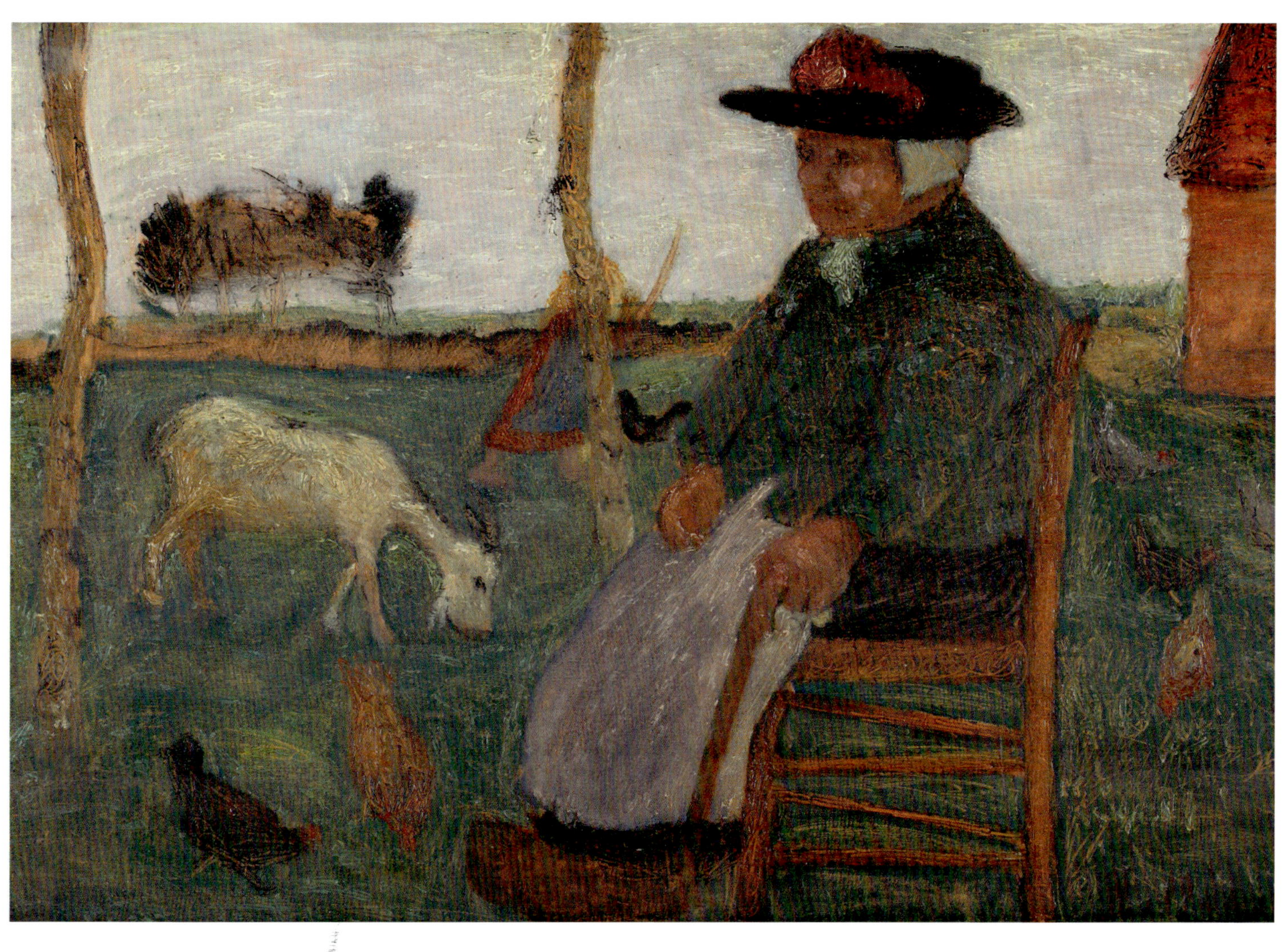

Dreebeen mit Ziege und Hühnern / Old Peasant Woman with Goat and Chickens, 1902

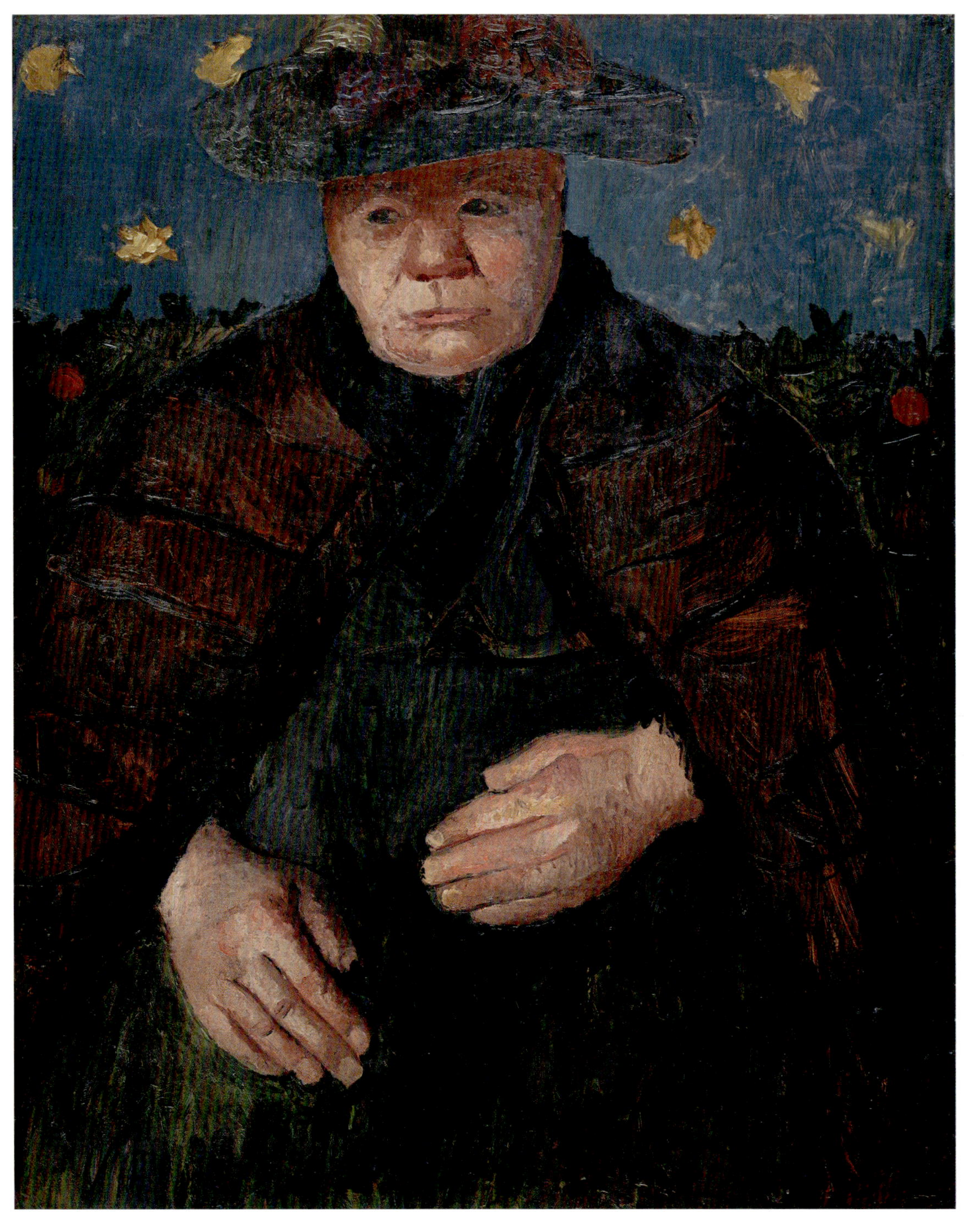

Armenhäuserin / Woman from the Poorhouse, 1906

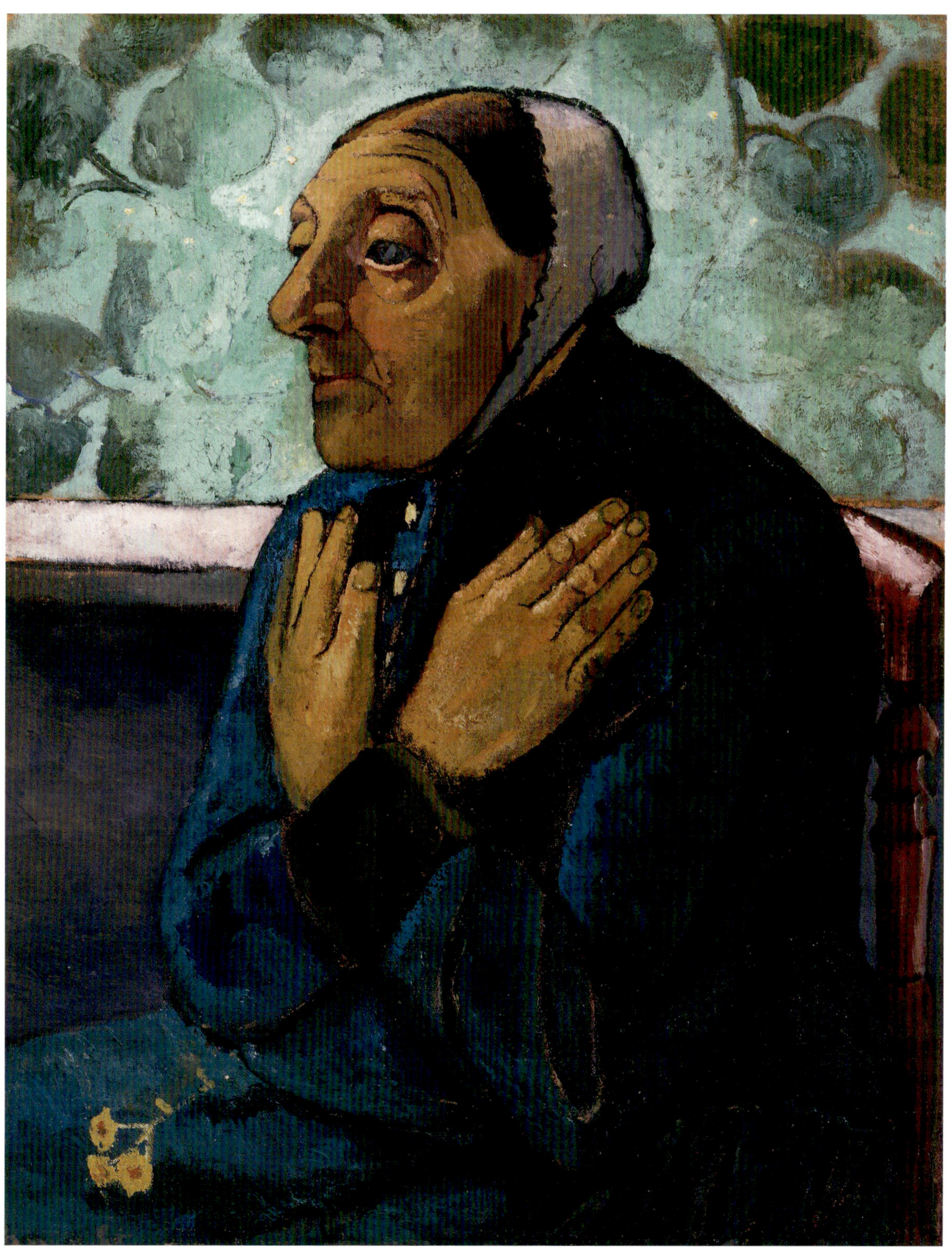

Alte Bäuerin mit auf der Brust gekreuzten Händen / Old Peasant Woman, 1907

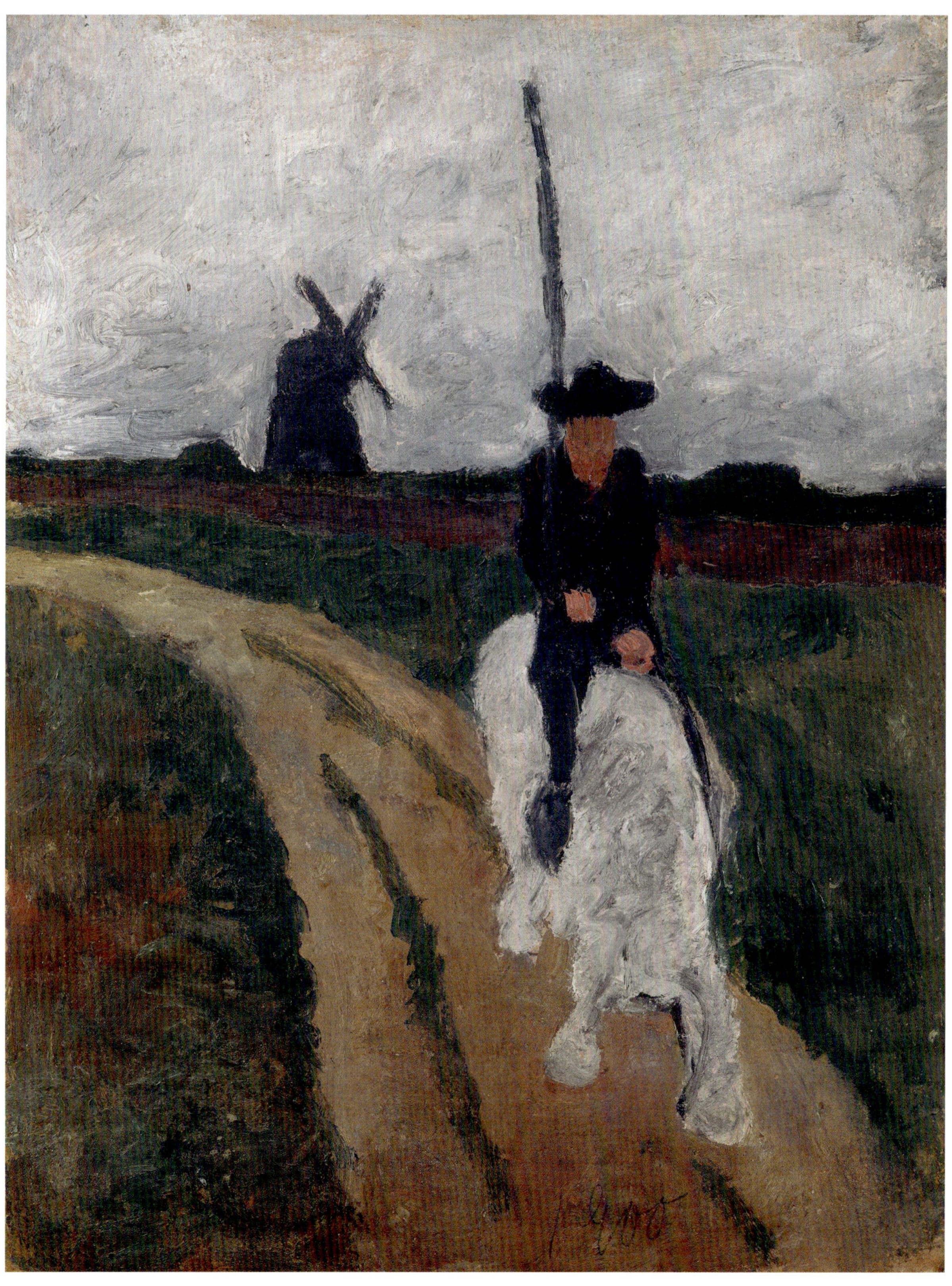

Don Quichote / Don Quixote, 1900

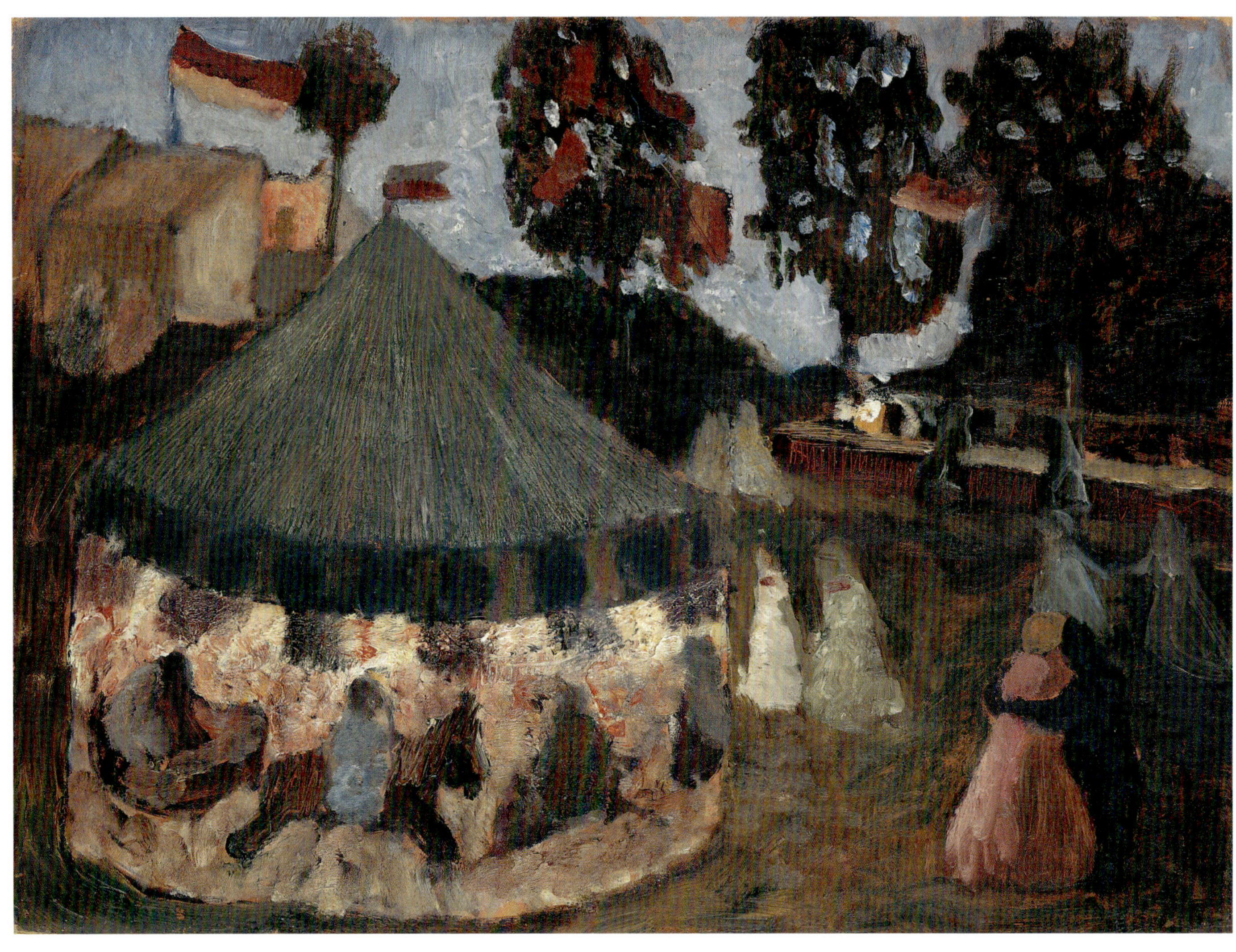

Schützenfest mit Karussell II / Festival with Carousel II, 1904

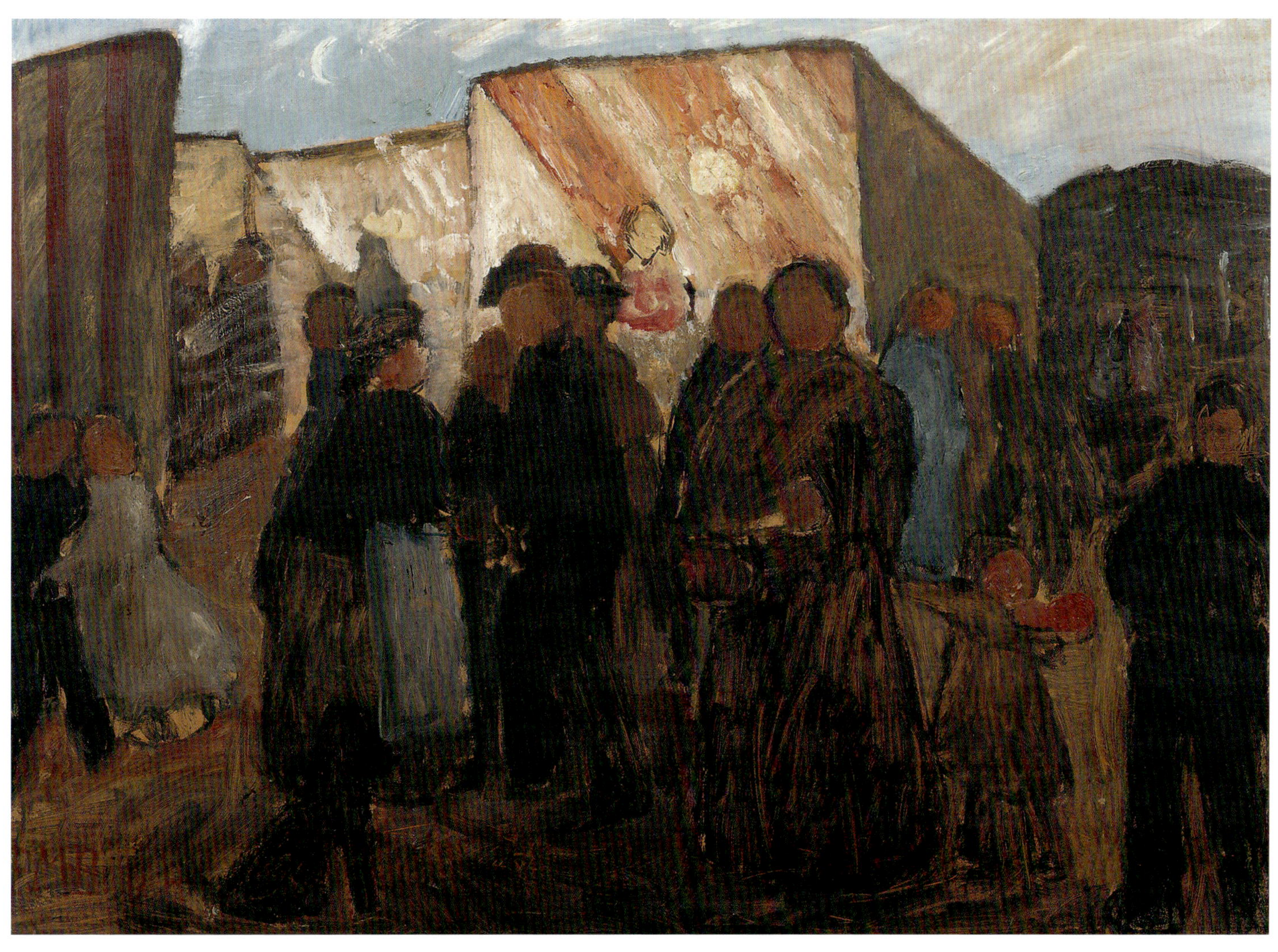

Schützenfest in Worpswede I / Festival in Worpswede I, 1904

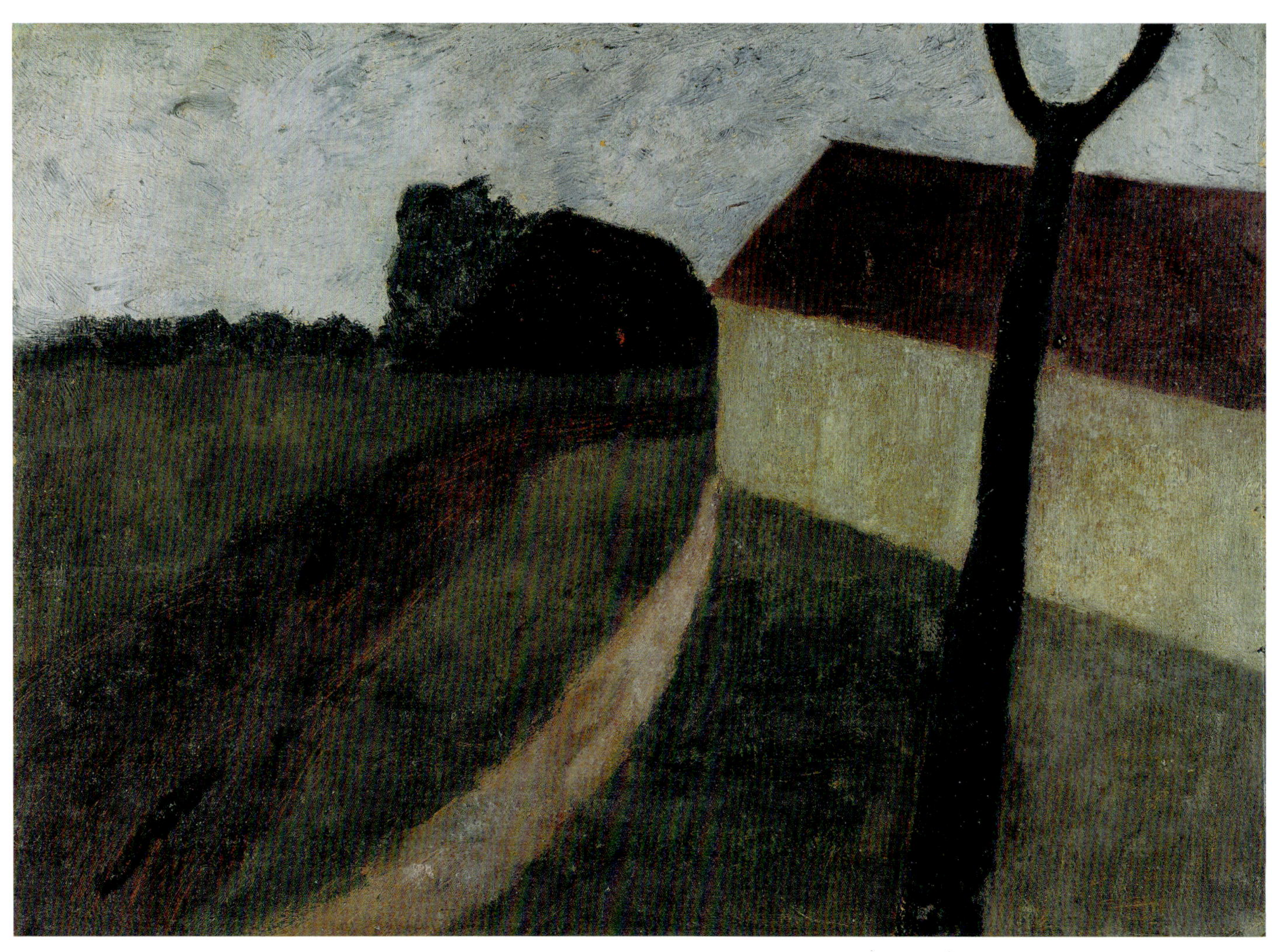

Dämmerungslandschaft mit Haus und Astgabel / Landscape in Twilight with House and Branch Fork, c. 1900

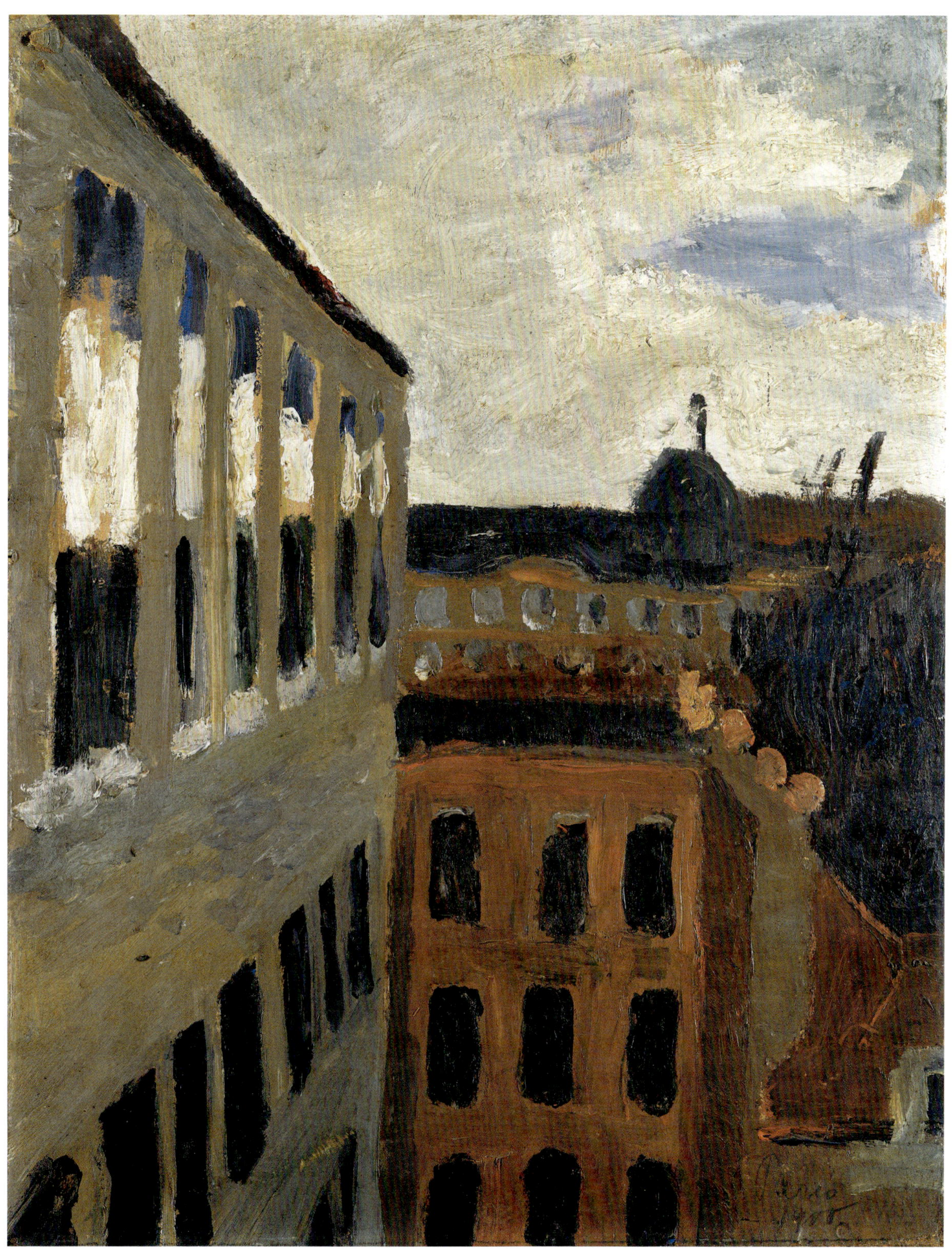

Blick aus dem Atelierfenster der Künstlerin in Paris / View from the Window of the Artist's Studio in Paris, 1900

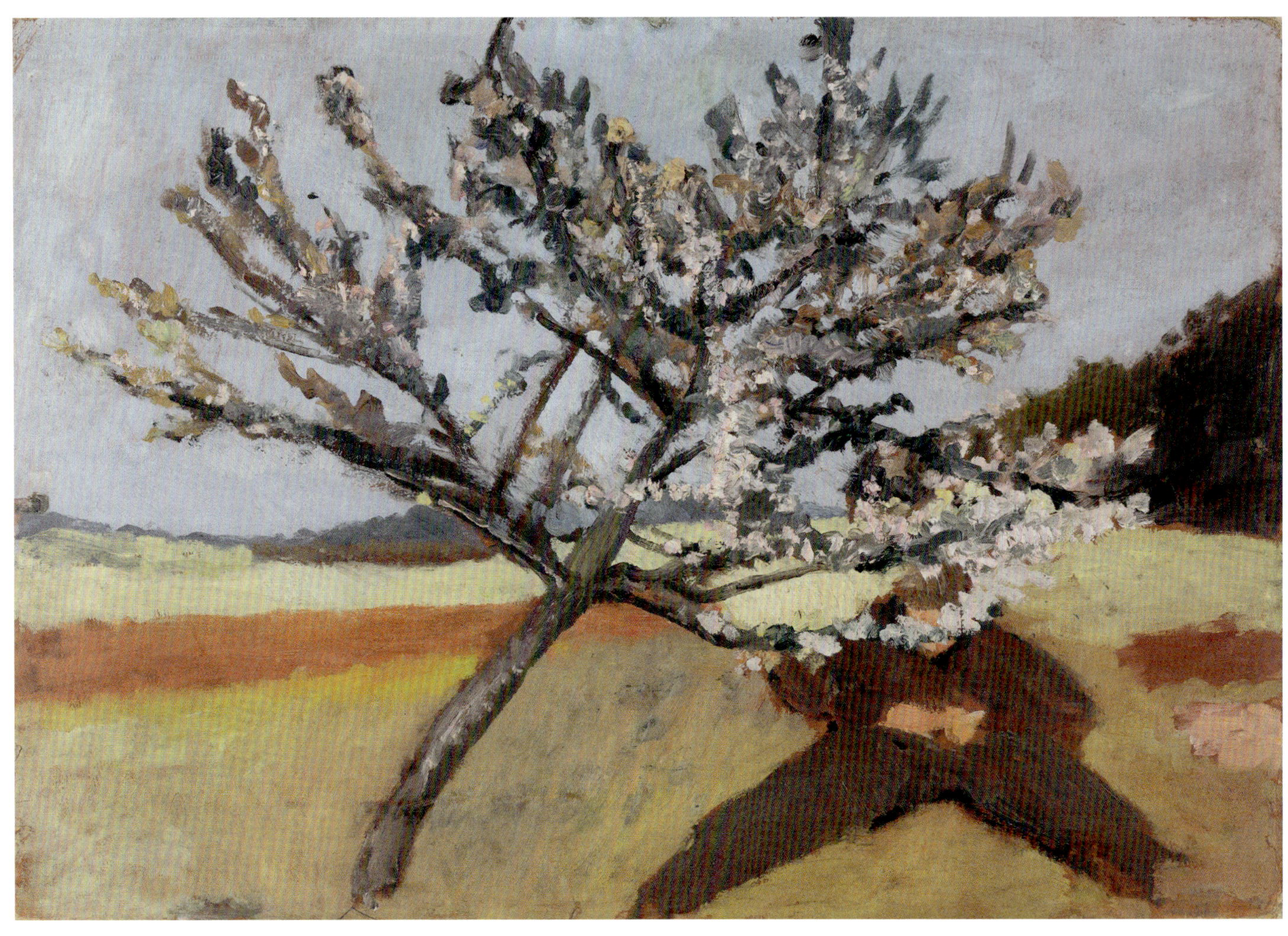

Liegender Mann unter blühendem Baum / Man Lying under a Blossoming Tree, 1903

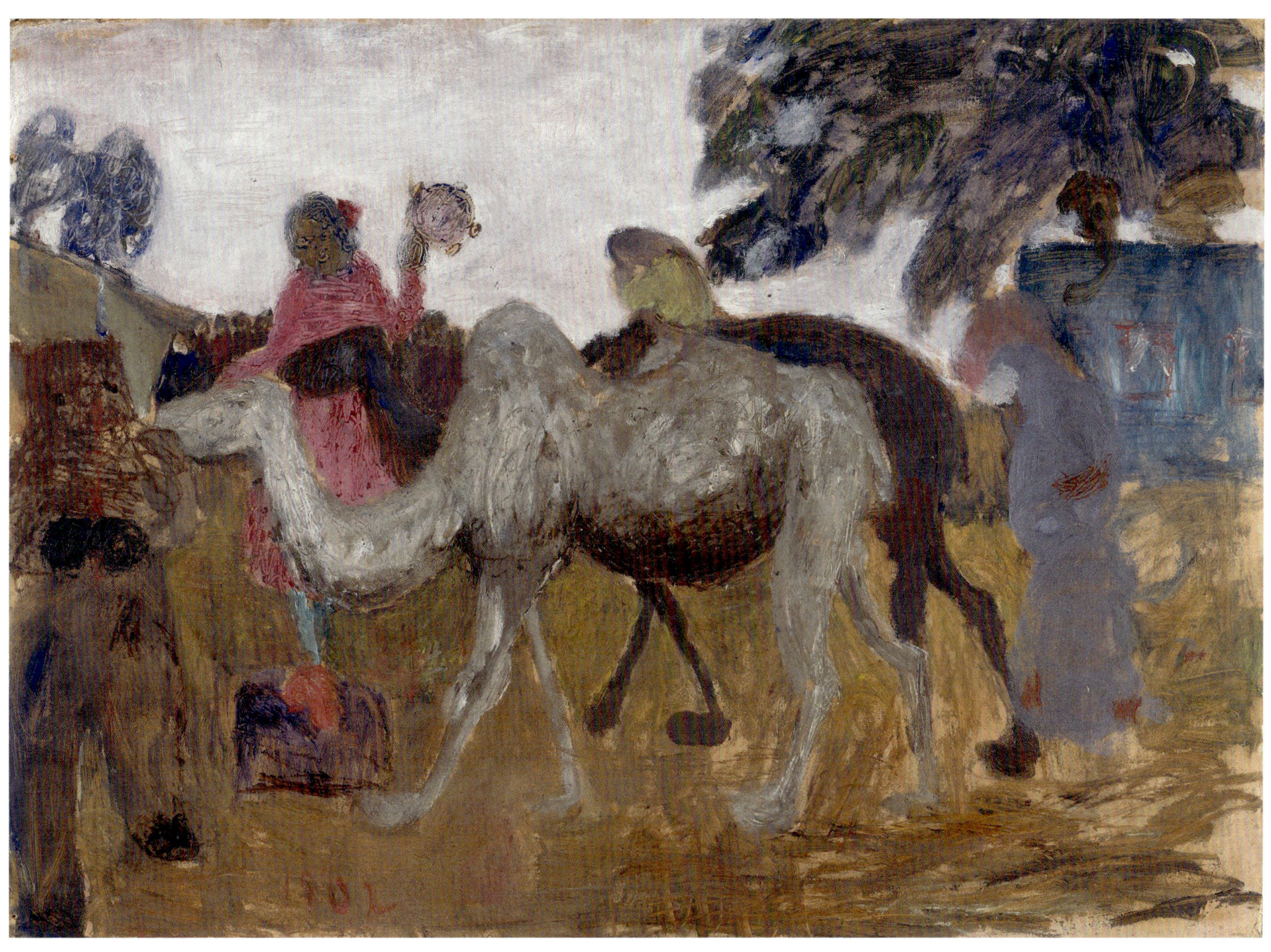

Jahrmarkt am Weyerberg / Funfair at the Weyerberg, 1902

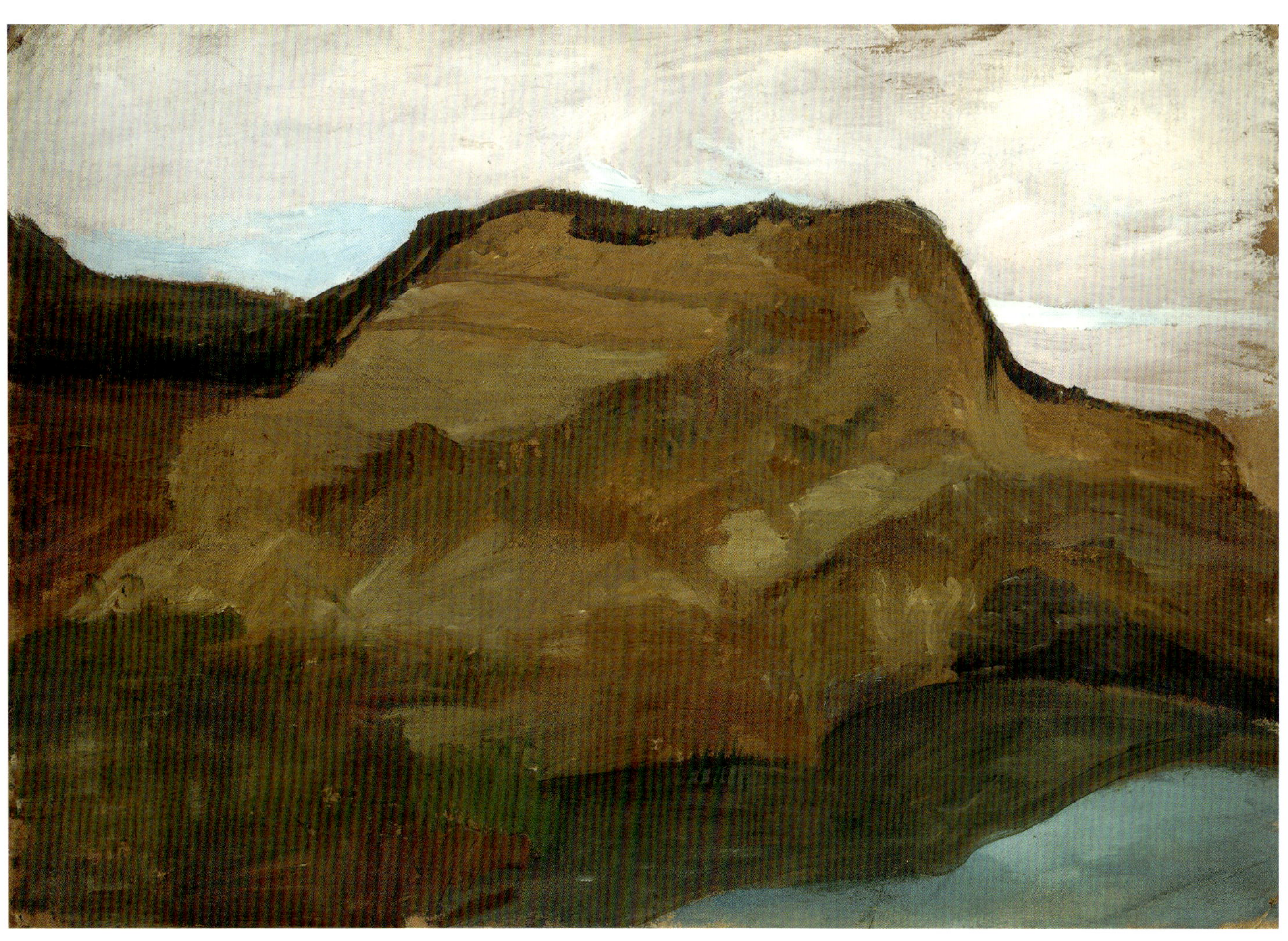

Sandkuhle / Sand Pit, 1901

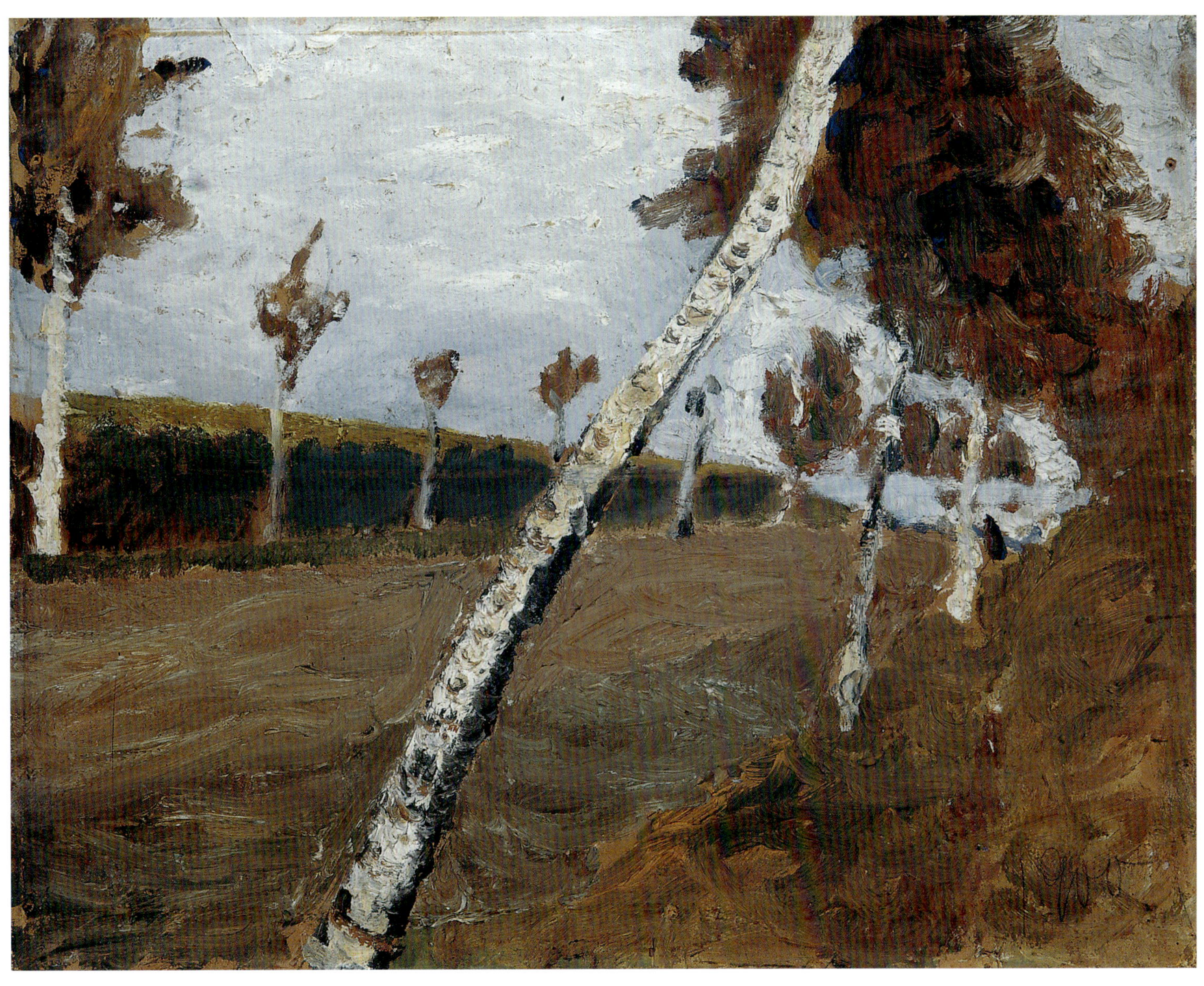

Birkenallee im Herbst / Birch Avenue in Autumn, 1900

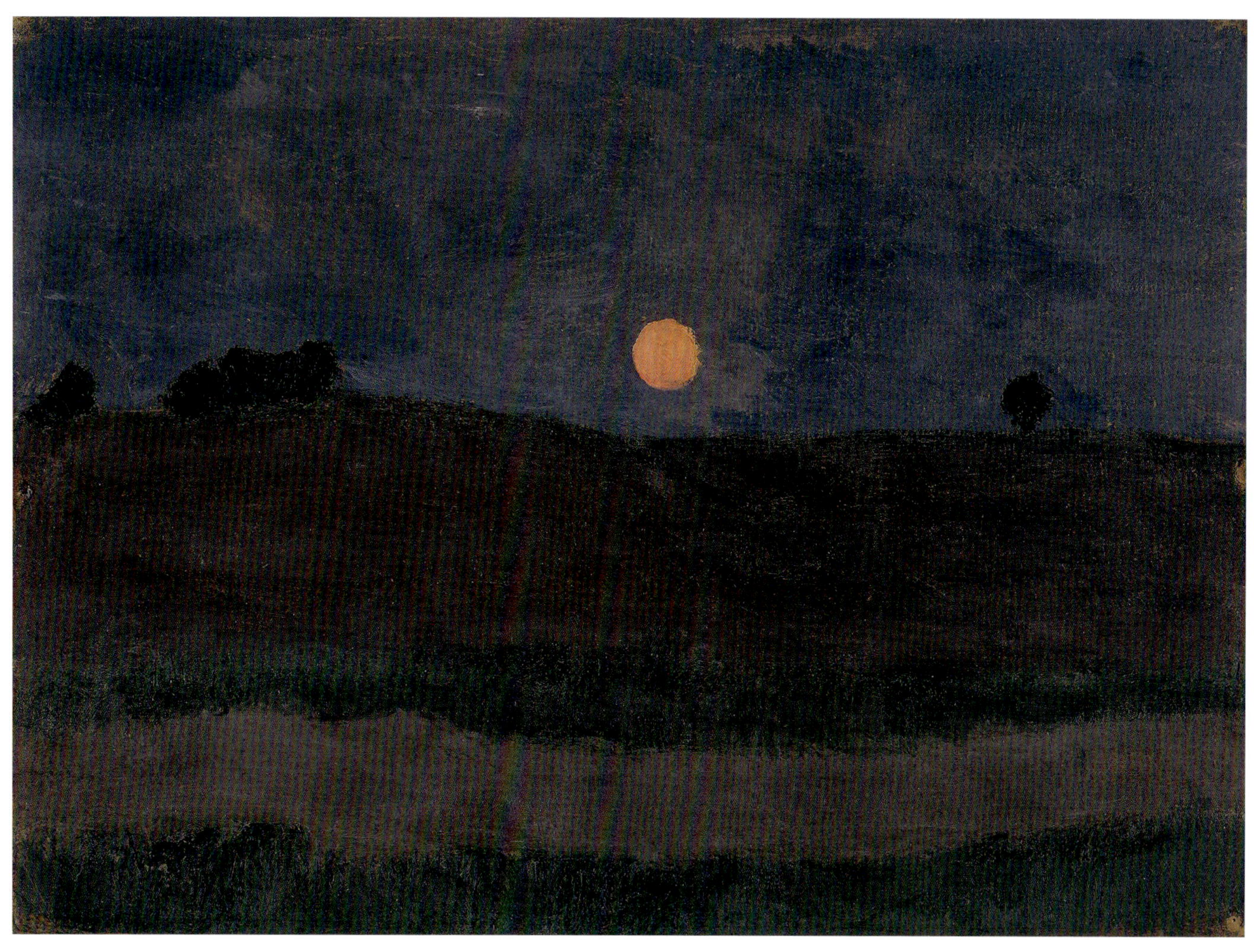

Mond über Landschaft / Moon over Landscape, 1900

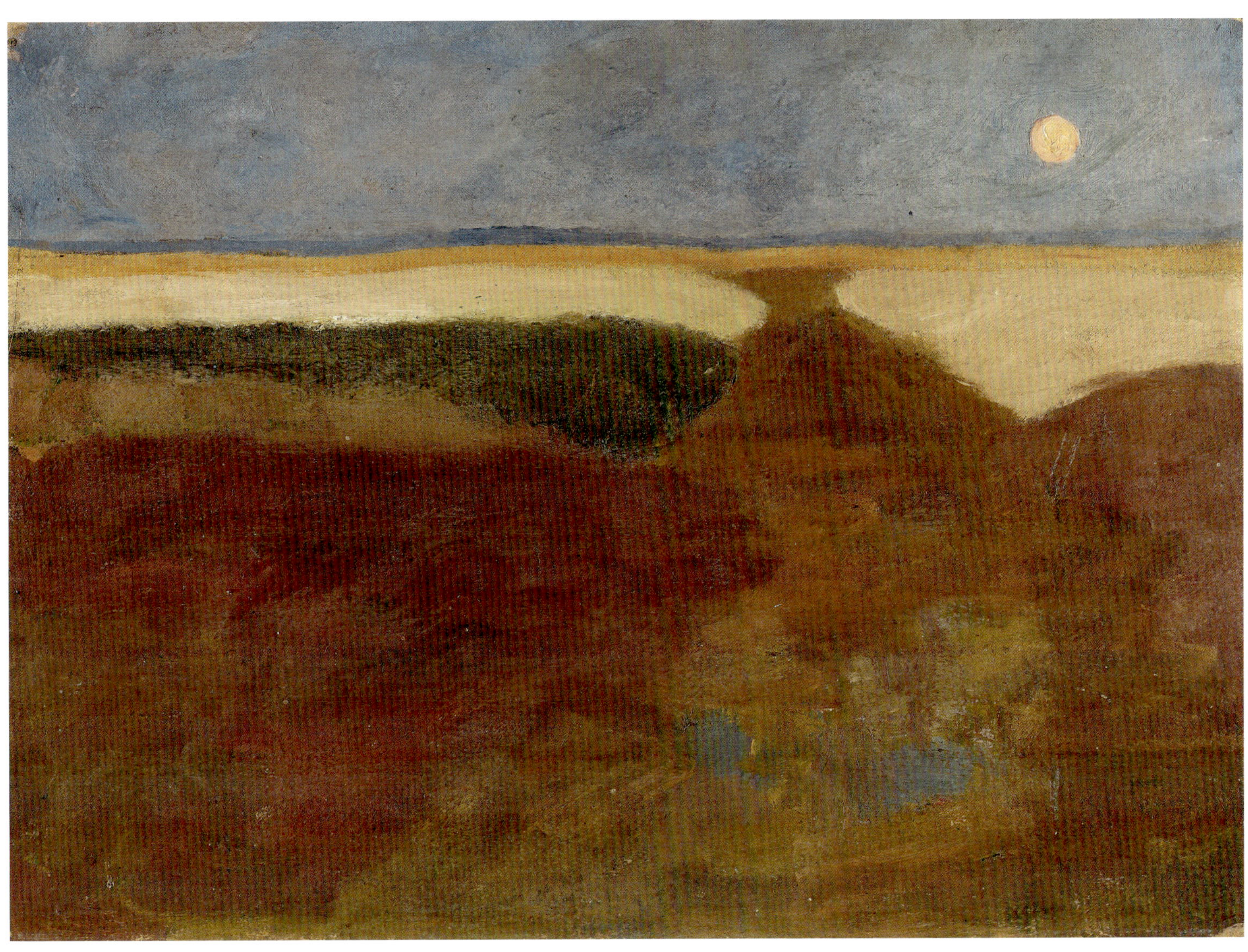

Mond über Feldern / Moon over Fields, 1900

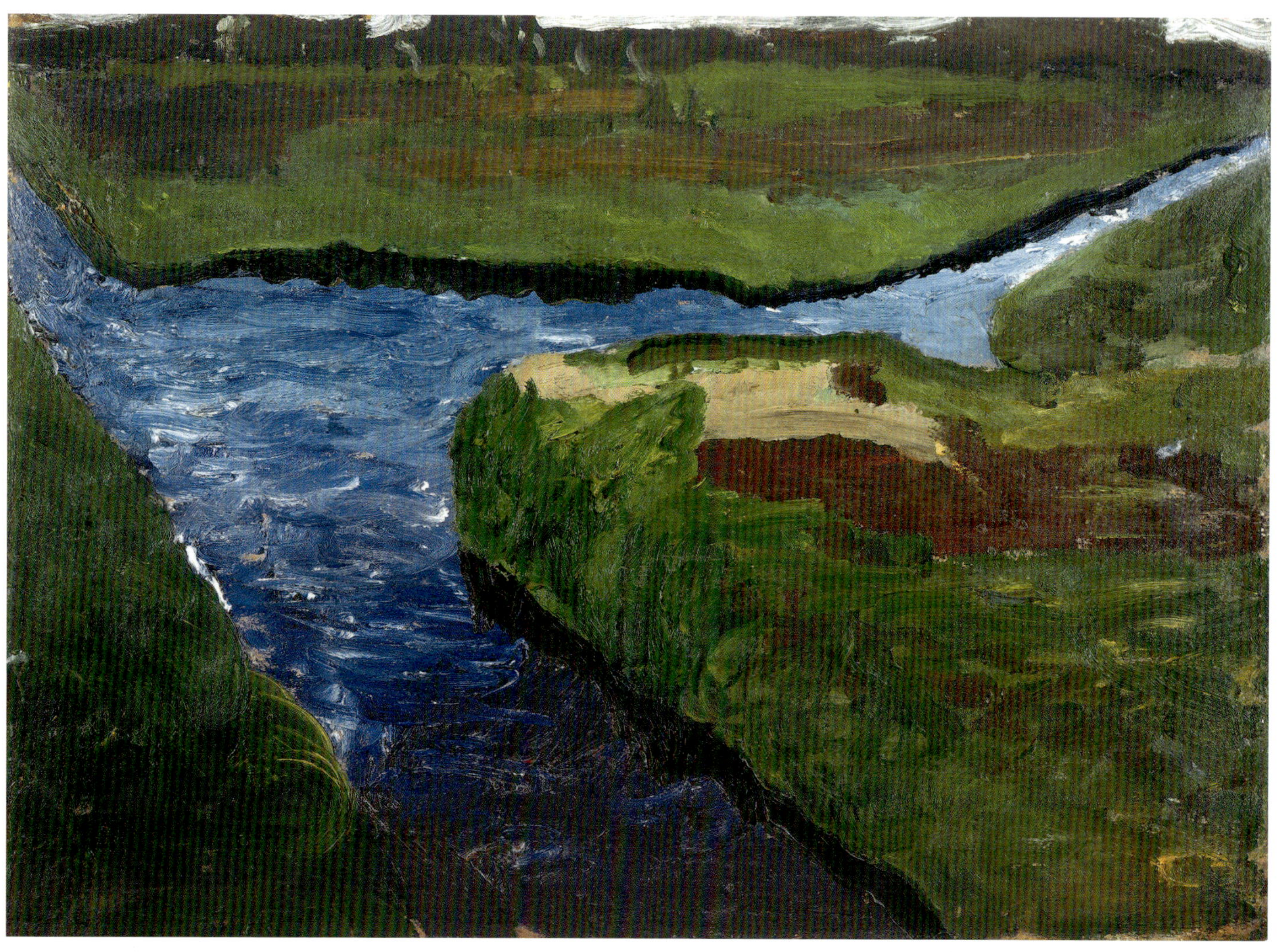

Moorgraben / Moor Ditch, 1900

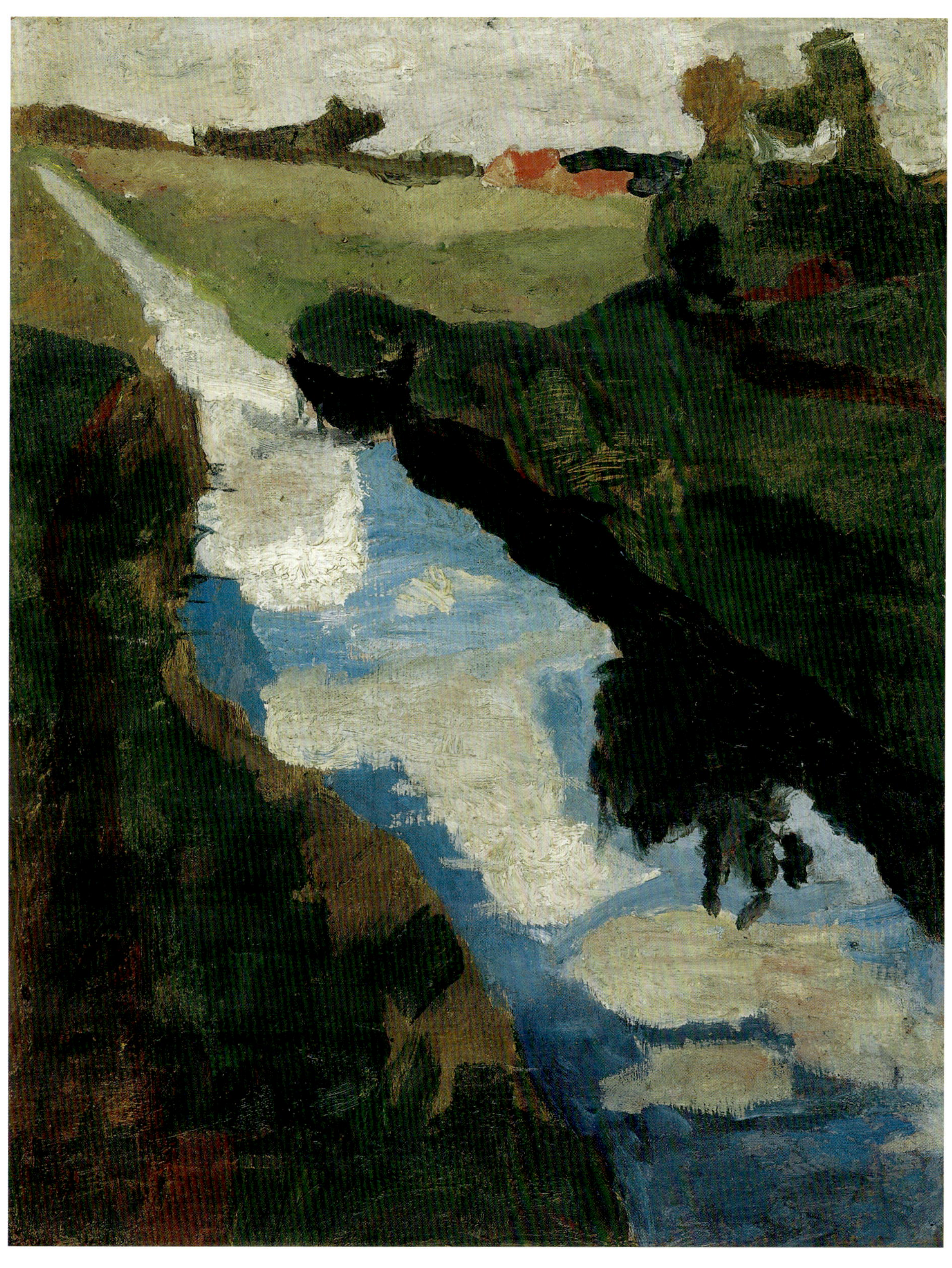

Moorgraben / Moor Ditch, c. 1900

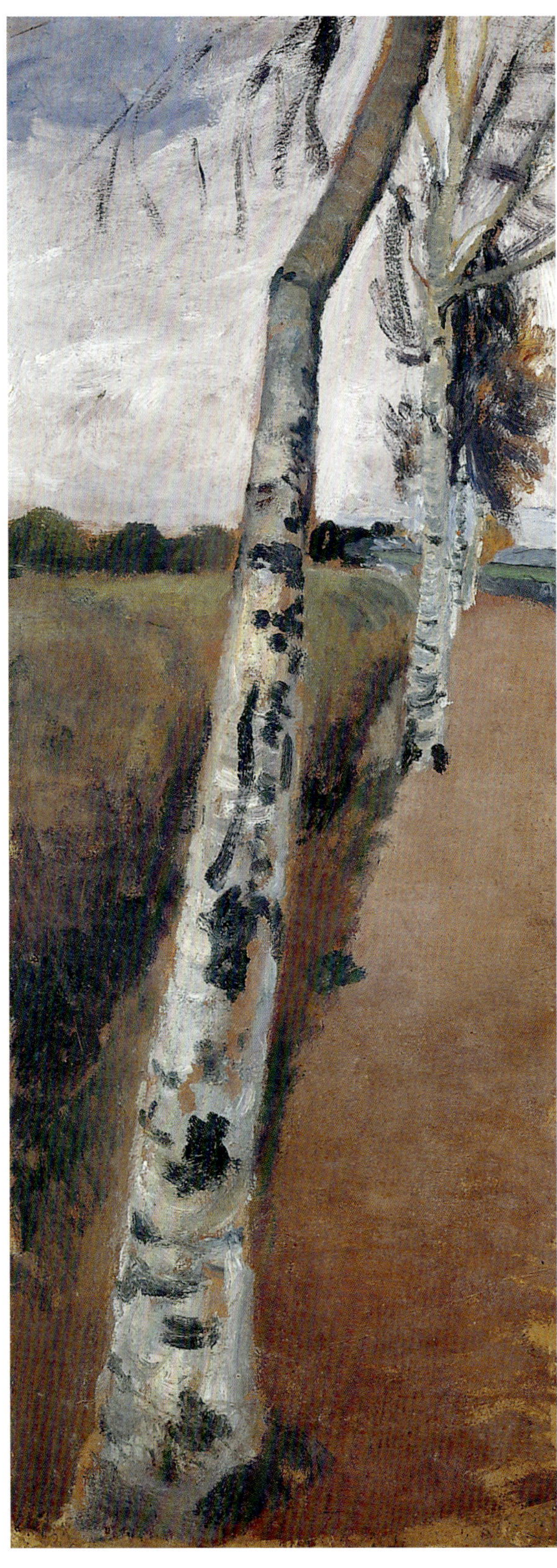

Weg mit Birken / Path with Birch Trees, 1900

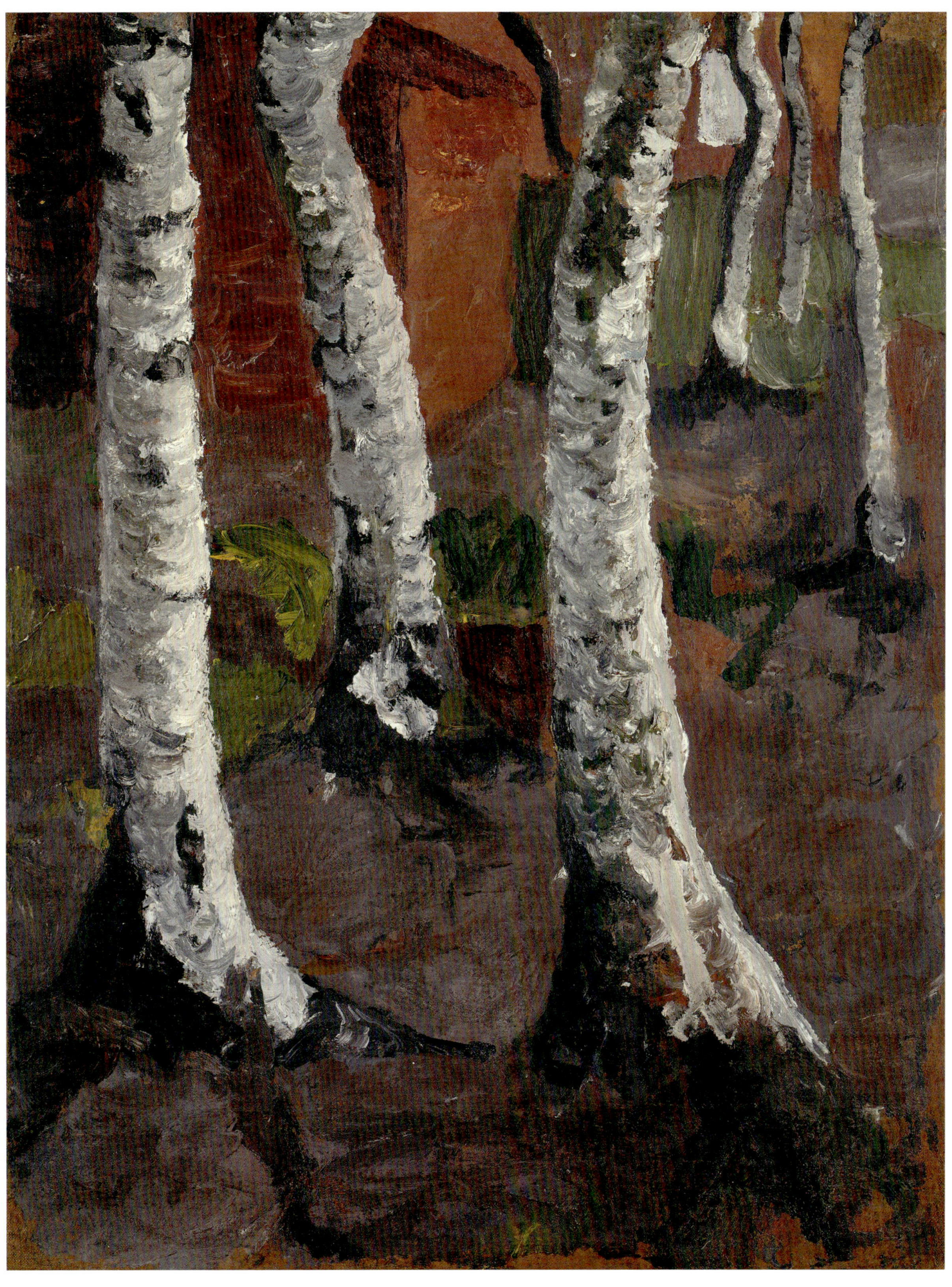

Birkenstämme vor roter Hauswand / Birch Trunks in Front of a Red House Wall, c. 1901

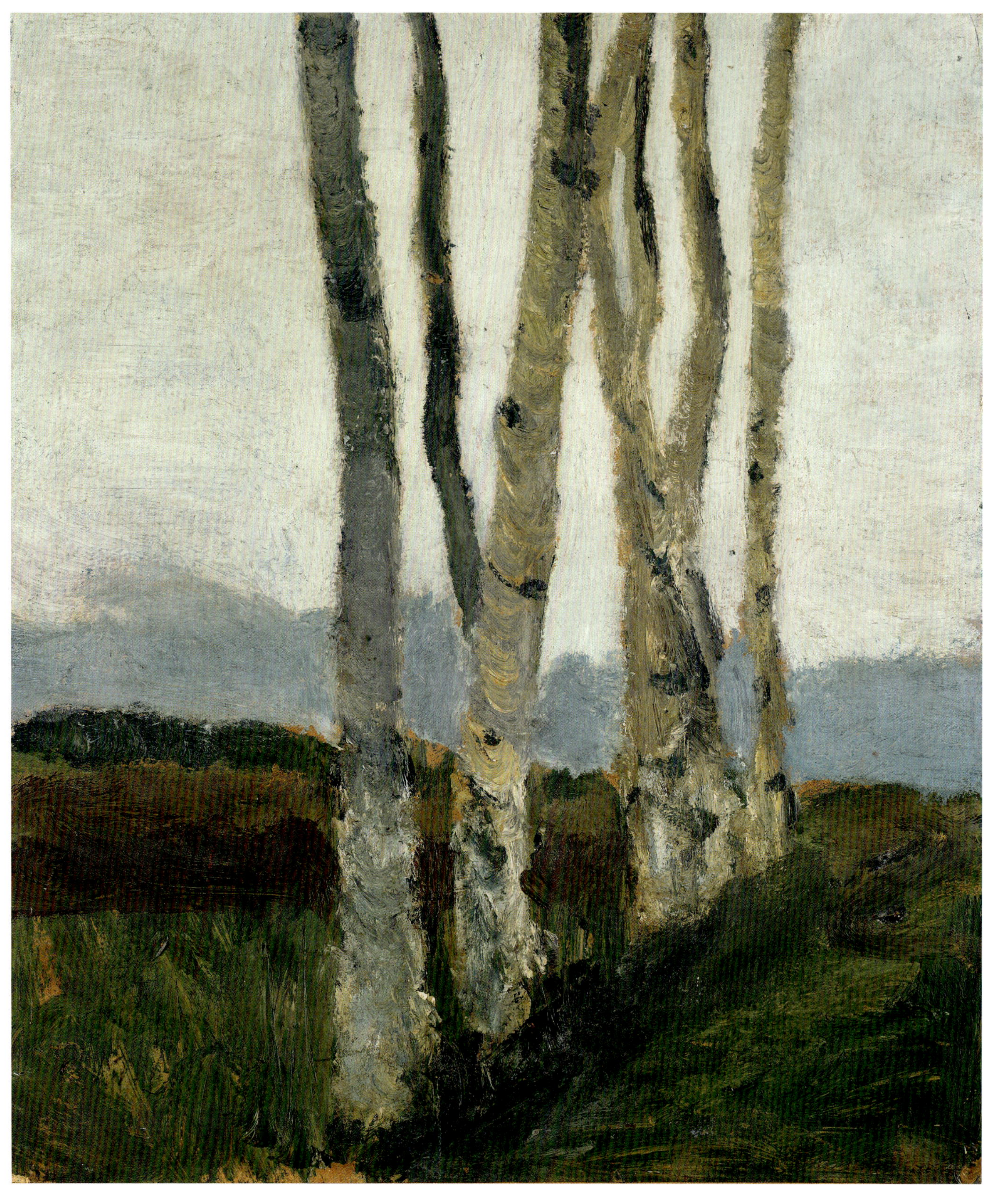

Birkenstämme / Birch Trunks, 1900

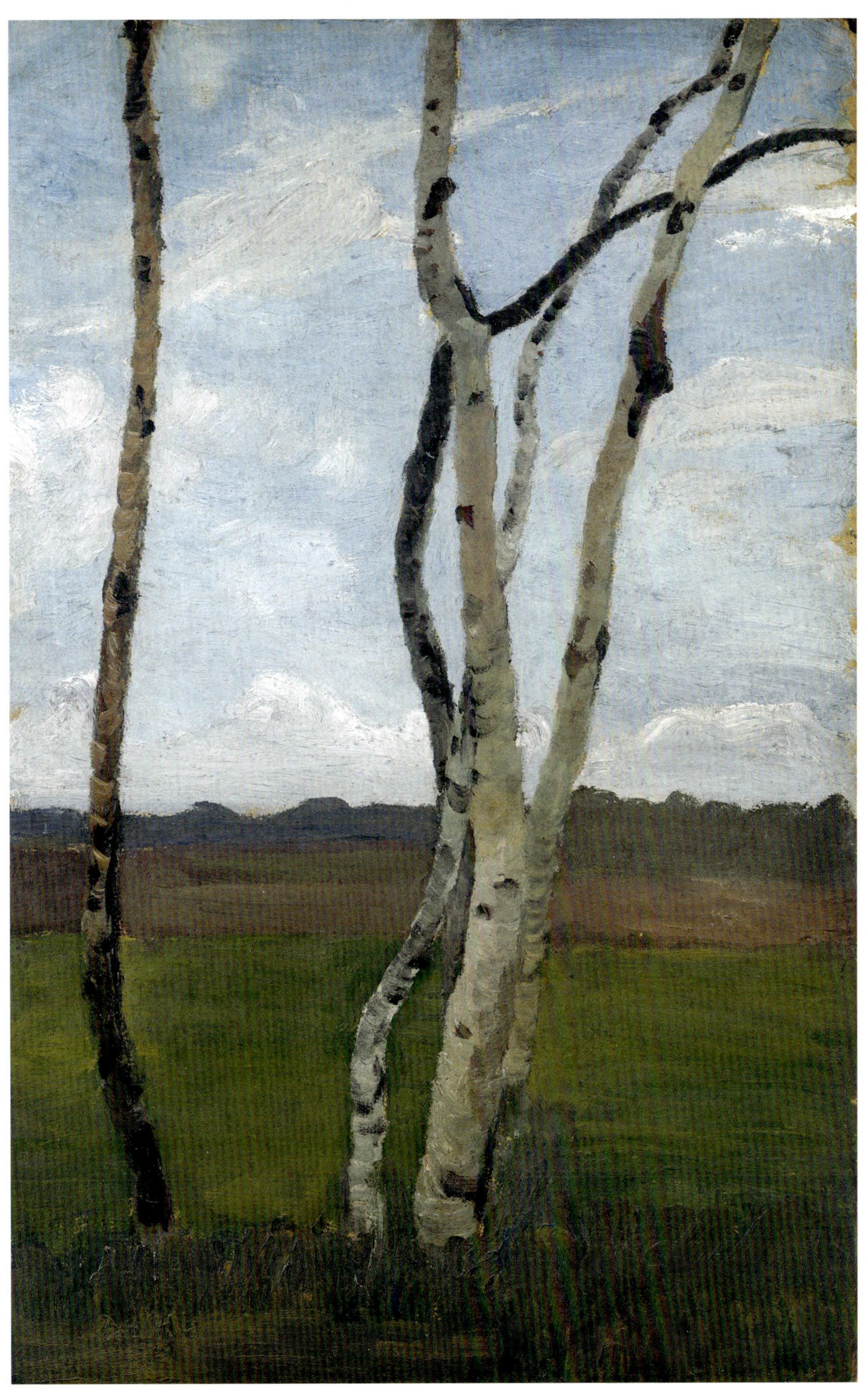

Birkenstämme vor Landschaft / Birch Trunks in Front of a Landscape, c. 1901

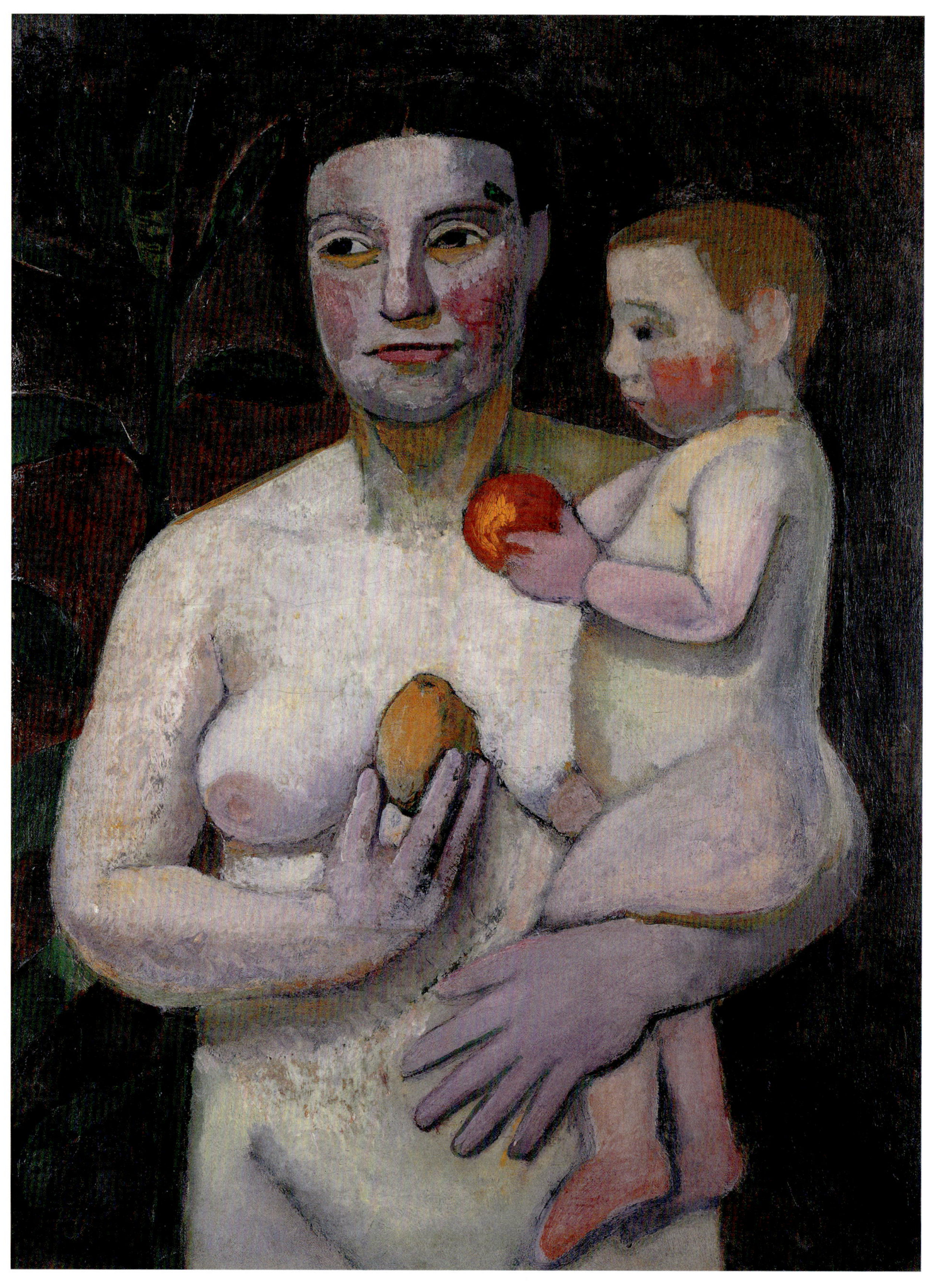

Mutter mit Kind auf dem Arm, Halbakt II / Mother with Child in Her Arms, Half-Length Nude II, autumn 1906

ON MOTHERHOOD IN THE WORK OF PAULA MODERSOHN-BECKER

INGE HEROLD

Although they are not numerous, Paula Modersohn-Becker's depictions of mothers and their children enjoy great popularity. This is due not least of all to the artist's fate: her early death in childbirth in 1907. On the one hand, the accompanying emotionalizing mixture of artistic and biographical aspects made it difficult to take an unbiased look at this group of works; on the other hand, her works on the theme of motherhood *in particular* were initially appropriated by ideological concepts of folk origin and then classified as "degenerate" in the 1930s.[1]

Stylized as a female icon of modernism, the mother-child depictions finally came into the focus of feminist art historiography in the 1980s and 1990s. Rosemary Betterton, for example, emphasized that Modersohn-Becker had resolved "the conflict between her hard-earned identity as a professional artist and the ideological conception of motherhood as a vocation for women."[2] According to the author, her "glorification of primitive motherliness" stemmed from a pantheistic understanding of nature and had no real socially oriented impetus.

In fact, in contrast to Käthe Kollwitz, for example, Modersohn-Becker was far removed from the workers' and women's movements due to her conservative, bourgeois background and her identification with the naturalism of the Worpswede artists' colony, despite the fact that she repeatedly depicted less privileged people from the peasant milieu. "Women's emancipation is very unattractive and unpleasant in these tumultuous

1—Cf. Kai Artinger, *Paula Modersohn-Becker. Der andere Blick* (Berlin 2009). See also: Milena Schicketanz, "'Entartete Kunst' - Das Schicksal der Werke von Paula Modersohn-Becker," in: *Paula Modersohn-Becker 1876-1907. Werkverzeichnis der Gemälde*, vol. 1, ed. Günter Busch and Wolfgang Werner (Munich 1998), pp. 83-101.

2—Rosemary Betterton, "Die Darstellung des Mütterlichen. Der weibliche Akt im Werk deutscher Künstlerinnen um die Jahrhundertwende," in: *Profession ohne Tradition. 125 Jahre Verein der Berliner Künstlerinnen*, exh. cat. Berlinische Galerie, Berlin (Berlin 1992), pp. 89-103, here p. 90 [translated].

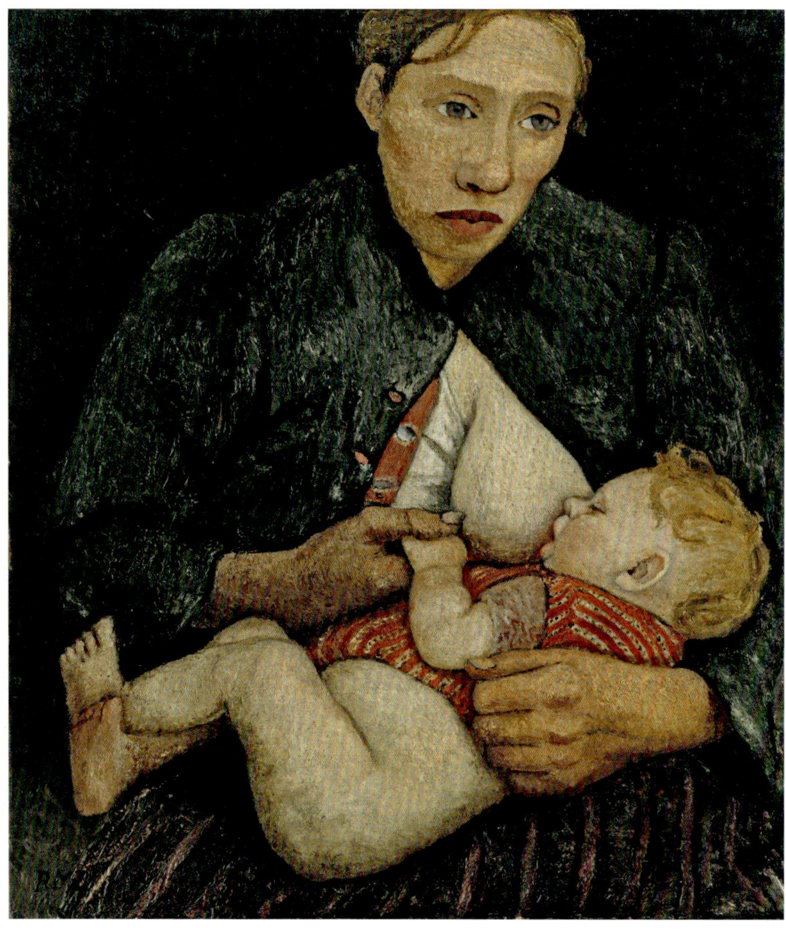

1 Stillende Mutter / Breastfeeding Mother, c. 1903, oil tempera on canvas, 70 x 58.8 cm, Niedersächsisches Landesmuseum Hannover

crowds," Modersohn-Becker wrote in a letter in 1901.[3] Her image of women, which was only moderately progressive despite all her efforts to become independent as an artist, leaned much more toward the maternalistic theories of the Swede Ellen Key, whom Modersohn-Becker had met in Paris in 1905.[4]

Her own statements on the topic of motherhood revolve on the one hand around her desire to have children and on the other hand bear witness to her imaginative world, which was characterized by mystification, but also focused on purely artistic aspects. One of the artist's key messages to Otto Modersohn at Christmas 1900 was: "And then, you know, it's really a festivity for women, because of this proclamation of maternity which, of course, continues to live on in every woman. It's all so sacred. It's a mystery, [...] I defer to it where I encounter it. I kneel before it in humility. That and death, that is my religion."[5] As early as 1898, she had recorded in her diary: "I've made a drawing of a young mother with her child at her breast [...]. A sweet woman, an image of charity [...]. And the woman simply gave her life and youth and strength to the child, not knowing that she was actually a heroine."[6] In December 1898, she then noted: "A bristling blonde woman, a natural beauty. [...] Her sensuality reminds me of that of the great Mother Nature with her full breasts [...]. She had to be drawn as a mother. That is her only true purpose in life [...]. The whole thing has something grand about it, in both form and color."[7] The visual charms of the model apparently seemed to have been of greater importance to the artist than the startling fact that she had served four weeks in prison for child abuse.

The hope for a child of her own, the marriage with Otto Modersohn—marked by ups and downs, with him withdrawing from her sexually—the separation and finally the reconciliation of the couple, which resulted in the pregnancy, is sufficiently known and depicted through letters, journal entries, and testimonies of contemporaries.[8] The tension between family life and radical artistic self-realization, ultimately also between two contrasting environments—Worpswede and Paris—came to a

3—Paula Modersohn-Becker (Berlin) in a letter to Otto Modersohn (Worpswede), dated January 31, 1901, quoted in: Artinger 2009 (see note 1), p. 104 [translated].
4—Cf. Ellen Key, *Das Jahrhundert des Kindes* (Berlin 1902). While Key called for comprehensive protective measures for the child-rearing woman, she also believed that a woman's natural place was in the home, and her only vocation was that of motherhood.
5—Letter dated December 25, 1900, in: Günter Busch und Liselotte von Reinken, *Paula Modersohn-Becker in Briefen und Tagebüchern* (Frankfurt am Main 1979), p. 253 [translated].
6—Journal entry dated October 29, 1898, in: ibid., p. 140 [translated].
7—Journal entries dated December 15 and 16, 1898, in: ibid., p. 148 [translated].
8—Cf. Artinger 2009 (see note 1), pp. 105ff.; Anne Buschhoff, "'Bei intimster Beobachtung die größte Einfachheit anstreben' - Kinderbilder und frühe Darstellungen von Mutter und Kind," in: *Paula Modersohn-Becker und die Kunst in Paris um 1900 - Von Cézanne bis Picasso*, exh. cat. Kunsthalle Bremen (Munich 2007), pp. 108ff.; Marina Bohlmann-Modersohn, *Paula Modersohn-Becker. Eine Biografie mit Briefen* (Munich 2007), pp. 251ff.

resolution in the spring of 1907. Modersohn-Becker justified herself to Clara Rilke-Westhoff, stating that she was "not the sort of woman to stand alone in life."[9] By then, however, Modersohn-Becker had set milestones in the depiction of mothers and their children within four years. Few women artists before her had worked on the motif so systematically. Mary Cassatt, who lived in Paris from 1874 onwards, is particularly worthy of mention here. Her paintings depict intimate scenes between mothers and their children but exclude negative aspects such as poverty or loss.[10]

Paula Modersohn-Becker's catalogue raisonné includes only twenty-three paintings with the mother-child motif. The first was created in 1902, the last in the fall of 1906, while the more intensive examination in drawings began as early as around 1898.[11] Remarkably, there are also numerous depictions in which girls assume caring poses. Even if this is due to the reality of life in rural Worpswede, where older children performed maternal duties and were also readily available as models, it nevertheless reflects Modersohn-Becker's specific interest: the depiction of a close bond between two people, the closest of which she regarded as the relationship between a mother and her child. She herself also took the perspective of the—adult—child. The letters to her mother, with whom she had a close relationship and who always greatly supported her, bear impressive witness to this. In January 1906, she wrote: "I lay my head in your lap, in the womb from which I came forth, and thank you for my life."[12]

Outstanding among the series of mother-child depictions are first of all the paintings created between 1902 and 1905 with the motif of the breastfeeding mother, which, in terms of iconography, follows the Christian image of the *Virgo Lactans* or the mode of presentation of classical Madonna paintings. In the works of Modersohn-Becker, the female protagonists are depicted full-format in half or three-quarter view, and in each case different moods, settings, and formal solutions are tried out: in the interior or—in an exploration of related motifs by Modersohn-Becker's teacher Fritz Mackensen—transposed into the Worpswede landscape, which functions here as a mood carrier. The compositions are carefully balanced, built up from interlocking and interrelated elements and directional sequences. This is exemplified by the painting of the nursing mother from around 1903 with its effective arrangement of lines and forms and contrasts of light and dark (fig. 1). Although the physical relationship between the mother and her child is close, the woman seems exhausted and full of worries, performing the life-giving act without emotional involvement.

9—Letter to Clara Rilke-Westhoff, dated November 17, 1906, in: Busch / Reinken 1979 (see note 5), p. 463.
10—Cf. *Impressionistinnen. Berthe Morisot, Mary Cassatt, Eva Gonzalès, Marie Bracquemond*, ed. Ingrid Pfeiffer and Max Hollein, exh. cat. Schirn Kunsthalle Frankfurt, Frankfurt am Main and Fine Arts Museums of San Francisco (Ostfildern 2008).
11—For more on the paintings, see the catalogue raisonné: Busch / Werner (see note 1), vol. 2.
12—Letter to her mother, dated January 19, 1906, in: Busch / Reinken 1979 (see note 5), p. 431 [translated].

In 1906, a caesura occurred in the design of the motifs: The interpretations that still adhered to realism were now followed by the nude depictions of mothers and children striving for simplification and monumentalization. They are also to be seen against the background of her specific modern body consciousness, for Paula Modersohn-Becker was one of the first protagonists of a practiced nude culture that went hand in hand with a mystification of the experience of nature, in which the naked body became the bearer of a pantheistic and matriarchal world of ideas.[13]

2 Mutter mit Kind an der Brust, Halbakt / Half-Length Nude of a Mother with Child at Her Breast, May/June 1906, oil tempera on cardboard, 74.5 x 52 cm, Von der Heydt-Museum Wuppertal

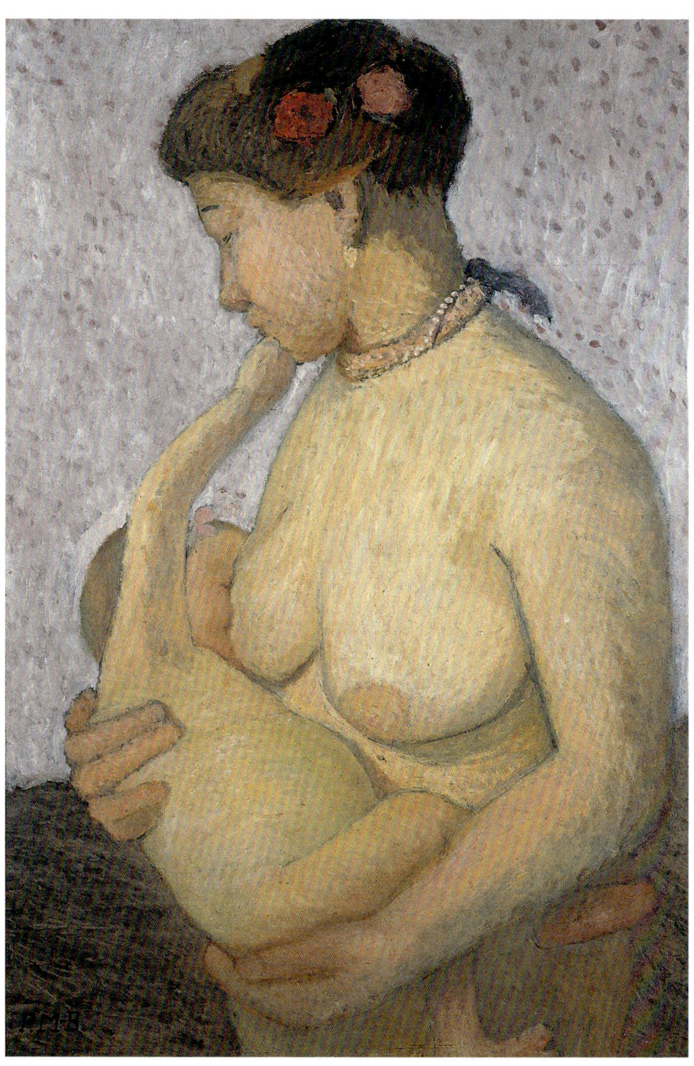

The representation of naked mothers had derived until the nineteenth century from ancient and Christian iconography and was considered a symbol of charity (Latin: *caritas*). As a naked, breastfeeding mother, she has been a personification of Christian philanthropy since the Renaissance, for example in the work of Lucas Cranach the Elder. The semi-nude probably painted in May/June 1906 is Modersohn-Becker's first attempt to focus on nudity in order to show the symbiotic connection between a mother and her child (fig. 2).[14] The decoratively speckled background and the hair ornaments and necklace of the woman—a professional model—attest to the sphere of influence of France; this also clearly sets the interpretation apart from the Worpswede paintings. Once again, circular composition lines visualize the close relationship between the mother and her child.

The artist takes a step away from this still realistic conception in the depiction of a seated mother with a child on her lap (p. 105). Here, she is obviously trying out new formal means in the reduction of the palette to brown tones and in the two-dimensional linear rendering of the bodies. Modersohn-Becker heightens the symbiosis of mother and child both compositionally and in terms of content: The girl, whose body remains enclosed within the contour of the mother, seems like her double. The use of color also makes them identical. The only iconographically charged splash of color is the orange, which the child holds in the same way that Christ holds the globe.

13 —Cf. the dissertation by Doris Hansmann, *Akt und nackt. Der ästhetische Aufbruch um 1900 mit Blick auf die Selbstakte von Paula Modersohn-Becker* (Weimar 2000).

14 —The painting is possibly a first version of the full-length painting *Kniende Mutter mit Kind an der Brust / Kneeling Mother with Child at Her Breast* (fig. 3) which was then trimmed by the artist; cf. Busch / Werner (see note 1), p. 478.

Somewhat later, probably in the fall of 1906, she worked on another new compositional idea in various versions (p. 96).[15] The strong bodies of mother and child are colored in light flesh tones and are sparingly modeled and contoured in a restrained Fauvist manner with yellow and orange tones. The strict frontal and profile view of the two, together with the stylizing reduction, is reminiscent of iconic statuary. And the exemplary gesture of the two fruits, which in the case of the mother is placed exactly between the breasts—as also in Modersohn-Becker's nude self-portraits painted from photographs (pp. 28, 29)—supports the anti-naturalistic and at once archaic character.

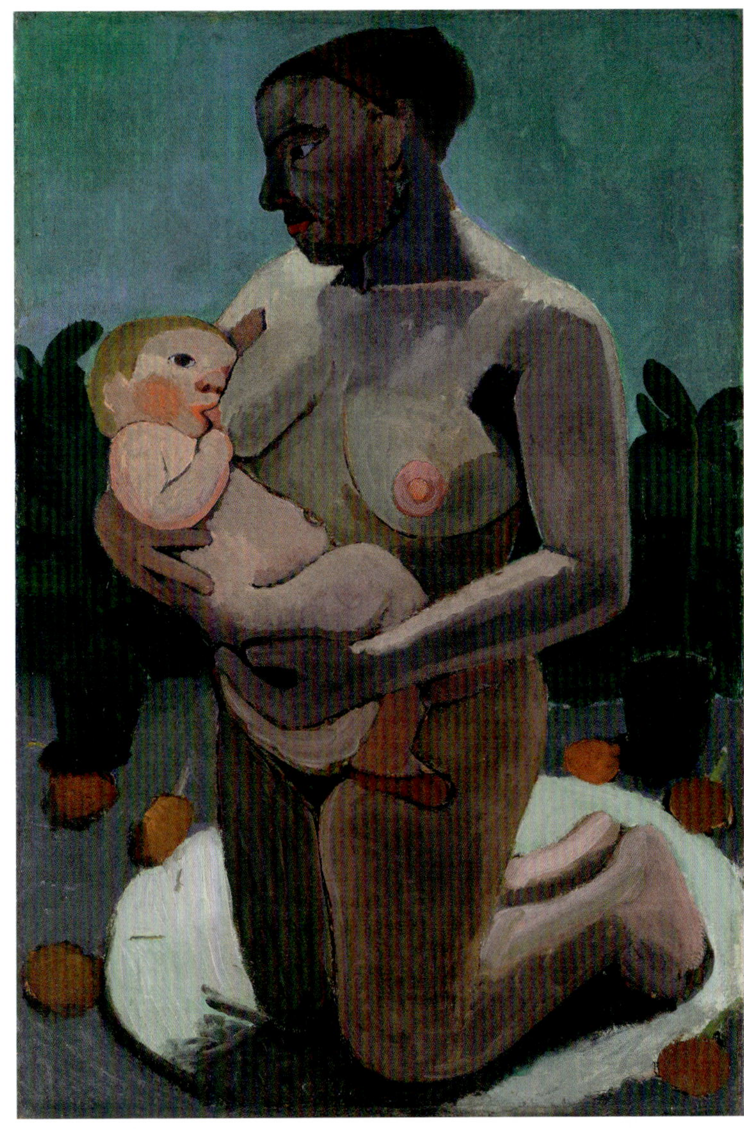

3 Kniende Mutter mit Kind an der Brust / Kneeling Mother with Child at Her Breast, autumn 1906, oil tempera on canvas, 113 x 74 cm, Nationalgalerie, Staatliche Museen zu Berlin, Preußischer Kulturbesitz

Modersohn-Becker developed another variant by introducing the posture of kneeling, presumably already tried out in *Kneeling Mother with Child at Her Breast* (fig. 3) and, once again, she clarifies the idea by means of a series of drawings (p. 107). In its abstracting monumentality, which has an almost sacral effect, the painting is considered one of the artist's main works. Carl Georg Heise, who had acquired it early on for his own collection, saw in the painting the consummate "path from likeness to allegory."[16] After seeing it in the artist's Parisian studio in 1906, Heinrich Vogeler declared it to be the "archetype of motherhood."[17] Not to be overlooked as a point of reference is, on the one hand, Henri Rousseau, whom Modersohn-Becker had met personally during a visit in 1906, but also the art of Paul Gauguin, whom she held in high esteem, whose works she had studied in Paris in April 1905 and at the Salon d'Automne of 1906, and with whom she shared the idea of a paradisiacal primordial state, within which nudity is a matter of course. The woman's head is marked by coarse facial features and an almost mask-like shadowing reminiscent of non-European sculpture. Potted plants and fruits emphasize the aspect of nature and fertility. The woman kneels on a light, circular ground—an element frequently used by Modersohn-Becker, which has a focusing effect both formally and in terms of content. The dominant circular form, which reappears in the breast, heads, and fruits, thus becomes the symbolic form of the composition which underscores

15—Regarding the first version, cf. Busch / Werner 691 (see note 1).
16—Carl Georg Heise, *Paula Modersohn-Becker. Mutter und Kind,* early summer 1906, Private Collection, (Stuttgart 1961), p. 6 [translated].
17—See: Rainer Stamm, *"Ein kurzes intensives Fest." Paula Modersohn-Becker. Eine Biographie* (Stuttgart 2007), p. 223 [translated].

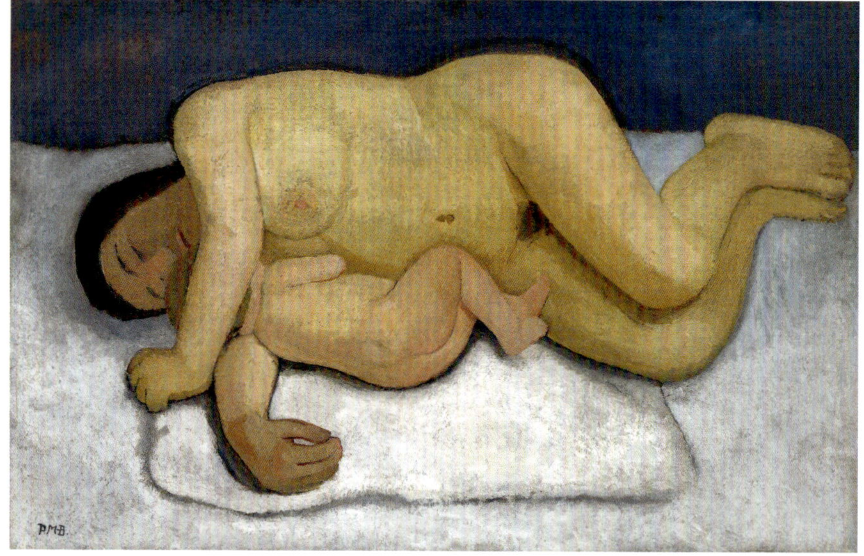

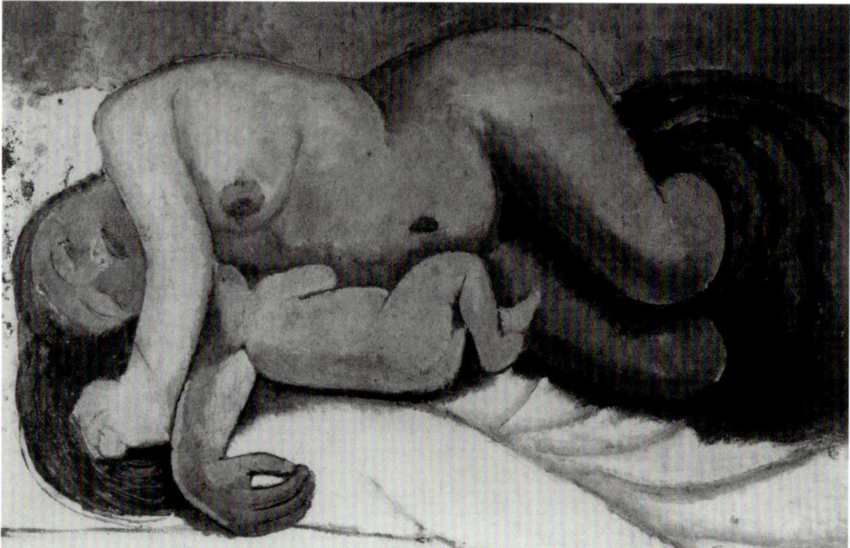

4 Liegende Mutter mit Kind II / Reclining Mother with Child II, summer 1906, oil tempera on canvas, 82.5 x 124.7 cm, Museen Böttcherstraße, Paula Modersohn-Becker Museum, Bremen

5 Liegende Mutter mit Kind III / Reclining Mother with Child III, summer/autumn 1906, oil tempera on cardboard, 77 x 122 cm, destroyed in World War II (formerly in the Paula Becker-Modersohn Haus, Bremen)

the meaning. The kneeling posture is also interesting on a thematic level as a gesture of humility and submission, as well as an expression of religious veneration or a posture of blessing, prayer, and meditation.

Already in the summer of 1906, the artist had dealt with another posture, namely that of lying down; and here as well, she came up with a completely new solution. She played through the situation in several drawings after the living model. The variant with the closed outline form was then implemented in three painting versions (figs. 4, 5).[18] The first and the third version were destroyed during the war, the latter is at least documented by a photograph: The mother's open hair, a shawl at her feet, and her curvier body contour make her appear more decorative and narrative. In the second version, owned by Clara Rilke-Westhoff until 1927, Modersohn-Becker's approach is far more radical and the proximity to Gauguin becomes even clearer.[19] However, Modersohn-Becker dispenses with props from or details of nature. Despite all the reduction, the depiction is extremely three-dimensional and has an almost sculptural character. In closed outline, the figures stand out from the ground; against the blue background, the woman's body appears like a landscape formation. If the theme here is the close symbiosis of mother and child, the feeling of security and protection, these thoughts contrast with the complete exposure of the two naked figures. At the same time, by lying on the ground, her connection to the mythical "Mother Earth" is emphasized. Whereas the previously described picture is about the almost cultic idealization of being a mother, Modersohn-Becker now focuses on a self-referential, archaic-animalistic creatureliness. She juxtaposes the two modes of representation, breastfeeding and presentation, with the aspect of serene passivity, of devotion withdrawn from the

18 – Cf. *Freie Hansestadt Bremen Böttcherstraße, Liegende Mutter mit Kind von Paula Modersohn-Becker, ed. Kulturstiftung der Länder, Bremen 1989, text by Gisela Götte;* Busch / Werner 565, 657, 658 (see note 1).
19 – Cf. Henrike Holsing, "'… die große Wirkung nobler Einfachheit' – Der Akt," in: exh. cat. Bremen 2007, p. 152.

world. Grace, eroticism, but also shame are faded out, just as individual characteristics are avoided.

Finally, Modersohn-Becker expanded the variety of representational possibilities by the concentrated, fragmented view of the motif, as shown in the small painting *Infant with Its Mother's Hand*, c. 1903 acquired by Rainer Maria Rilke (p. 104): an effective result of a correction, for the artist had cut the motif out of a painting that originally still showed the mother and another child.[20] The portrait-like, brightly colored double image of mother and child from the early summer of 1906 is also distinguished by its tight cropping (fig. 6). It is free of exaggeration and idealization and is instead characterized by a sense of cheerful serenity. The open gaze of the two is directed at the viewers, and the parallel offset heads with dark hair lend the depiction an extremely lively expression.

6 Mutter und Kind / Mother with Child, early summer 1906, oil tempera on cardboard, 42.5 x 30 cm, Private Collection

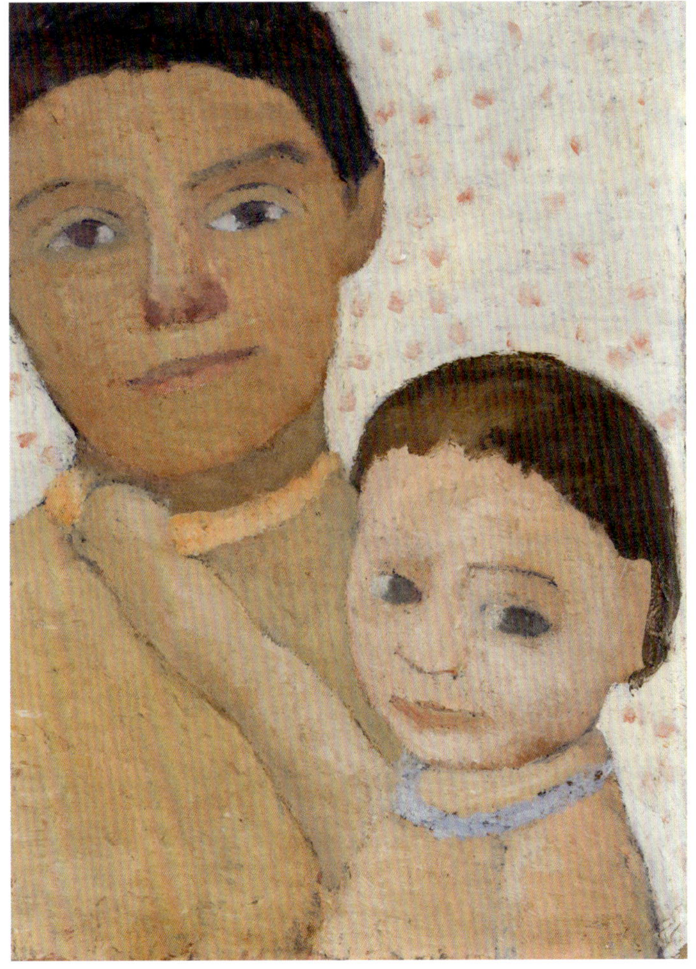

Modersohn-Becker's interpretations of the mother-child motif are of an irritating ambivalence: She undoubtedly found completely new modes of representation, approached the subject systematically, tested variants, and worked out a radically simplified, expressive pictorial language that was grounded in both the tradition of older art and a preoccupation with the contemporary avant-garde. In contrast to this modern formal language is her biographically conditioned, predominantly idealizing, exaggerated image of the mother, which lacks an obvious critical-social component. The artist lived and worked in a time of upheaval. This is also reflected in her works, which tell of aspects such as femininity and sexuality, self-determination and dependence, identity and role, and thus of themes and areas of conflict that are still being discussed today.

20 –Cf. Buschhoff 2007, p. 110.

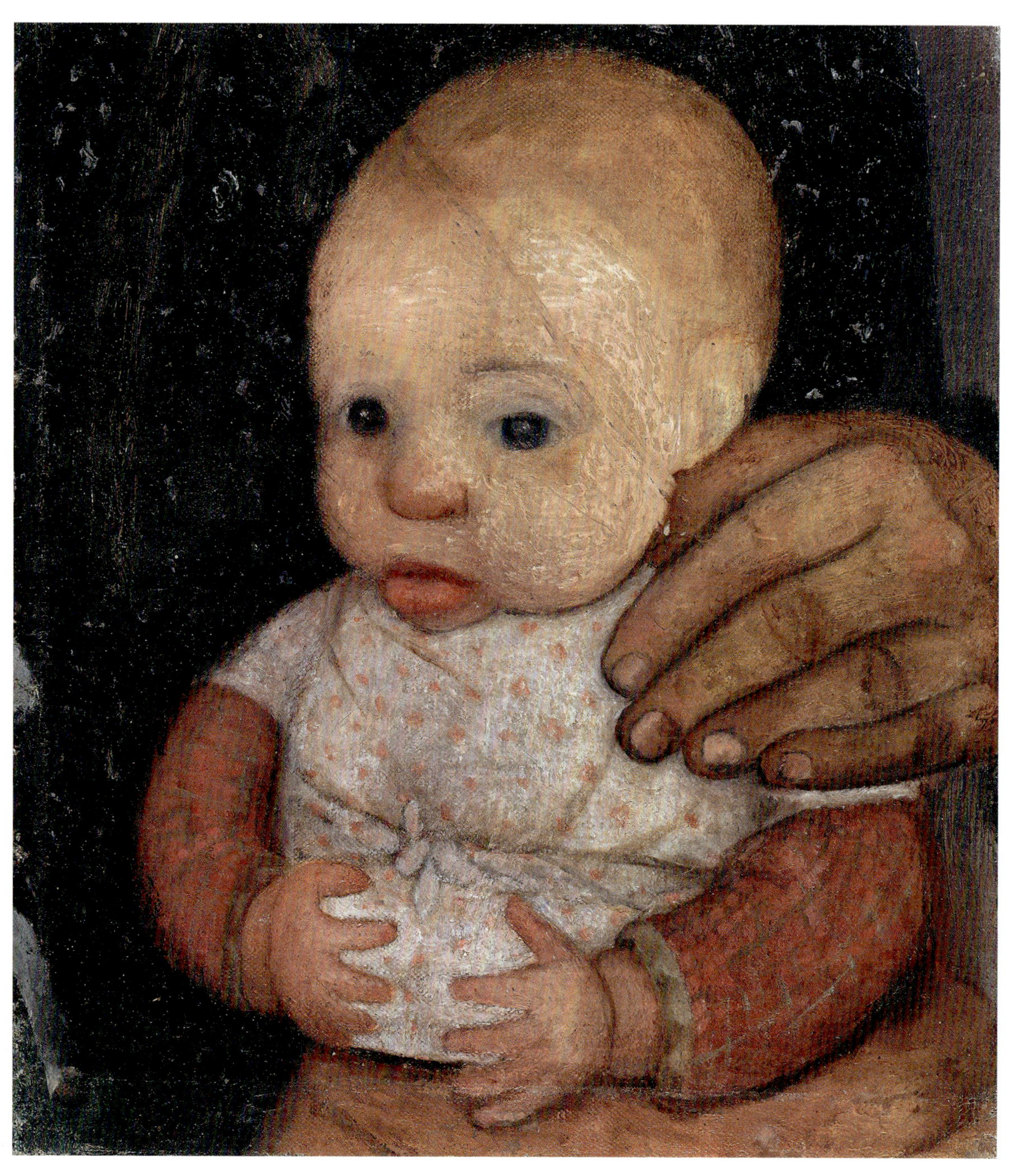

Säugling mit der Hand der Mutter / Infant with Its Mother's Hand, c. 1903

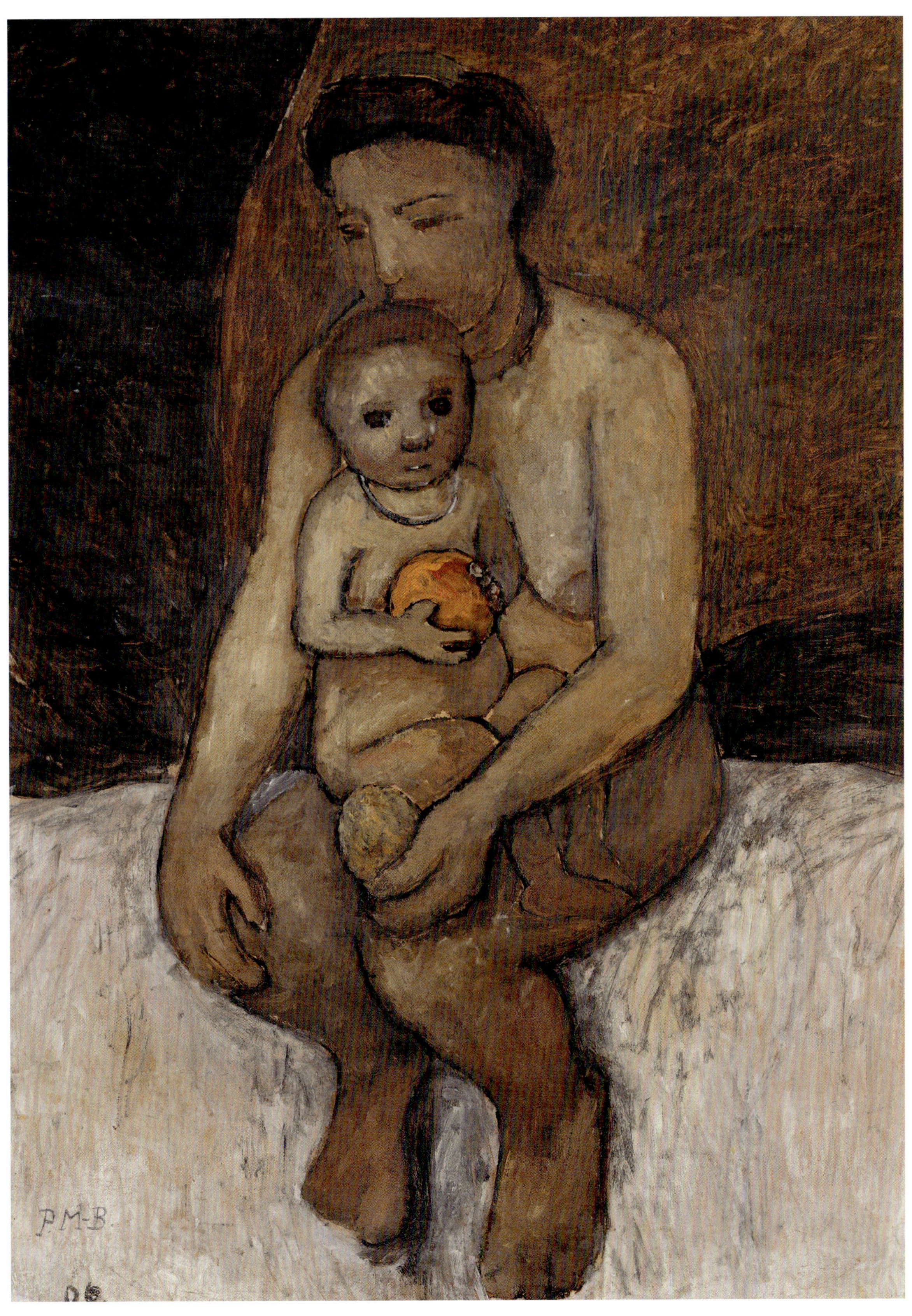

Mutter und Kind / Mother and Child, May/June 1906

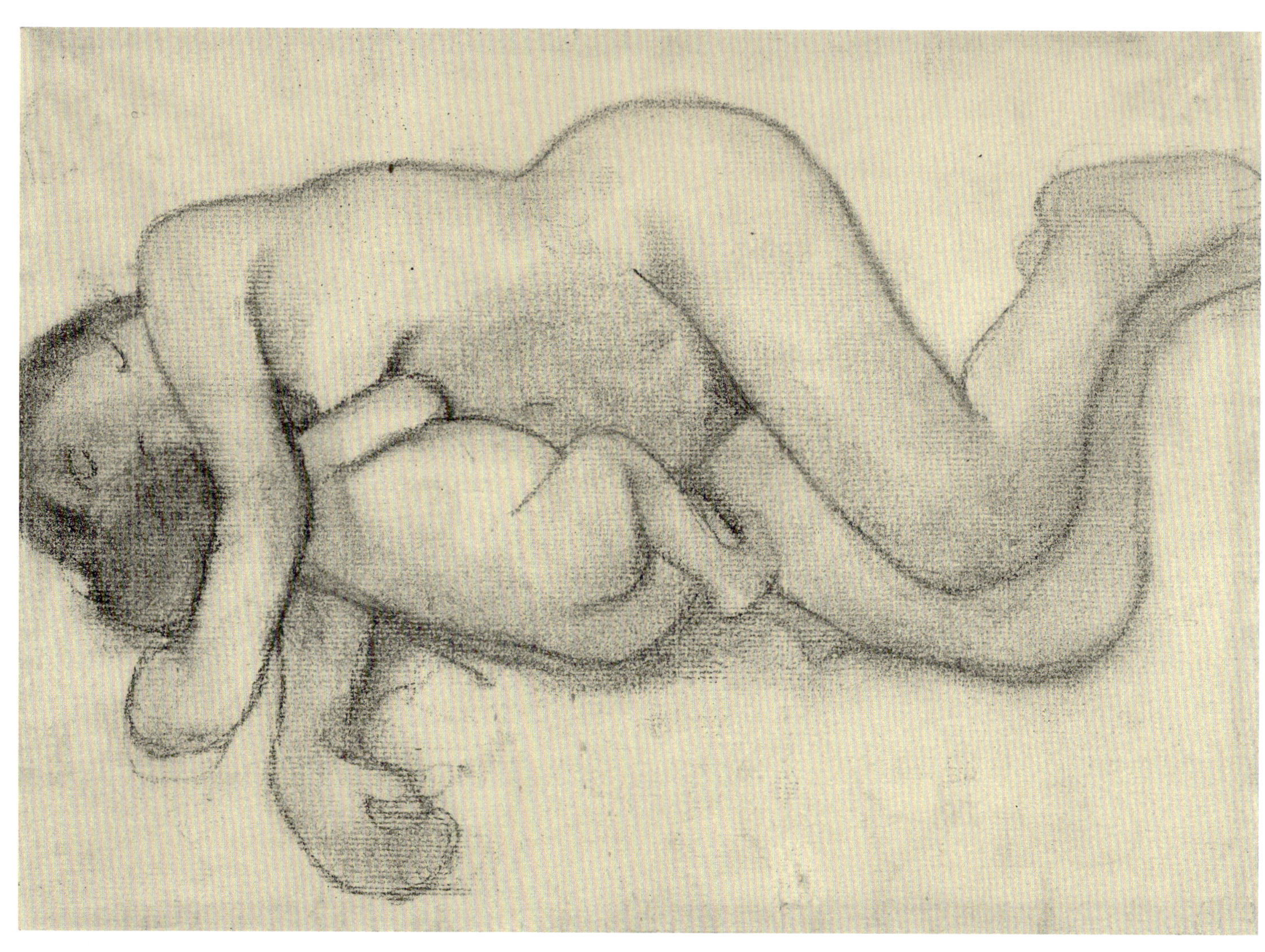

Liegende Mutter mit Kind / Reclining Mother with Child, 1906

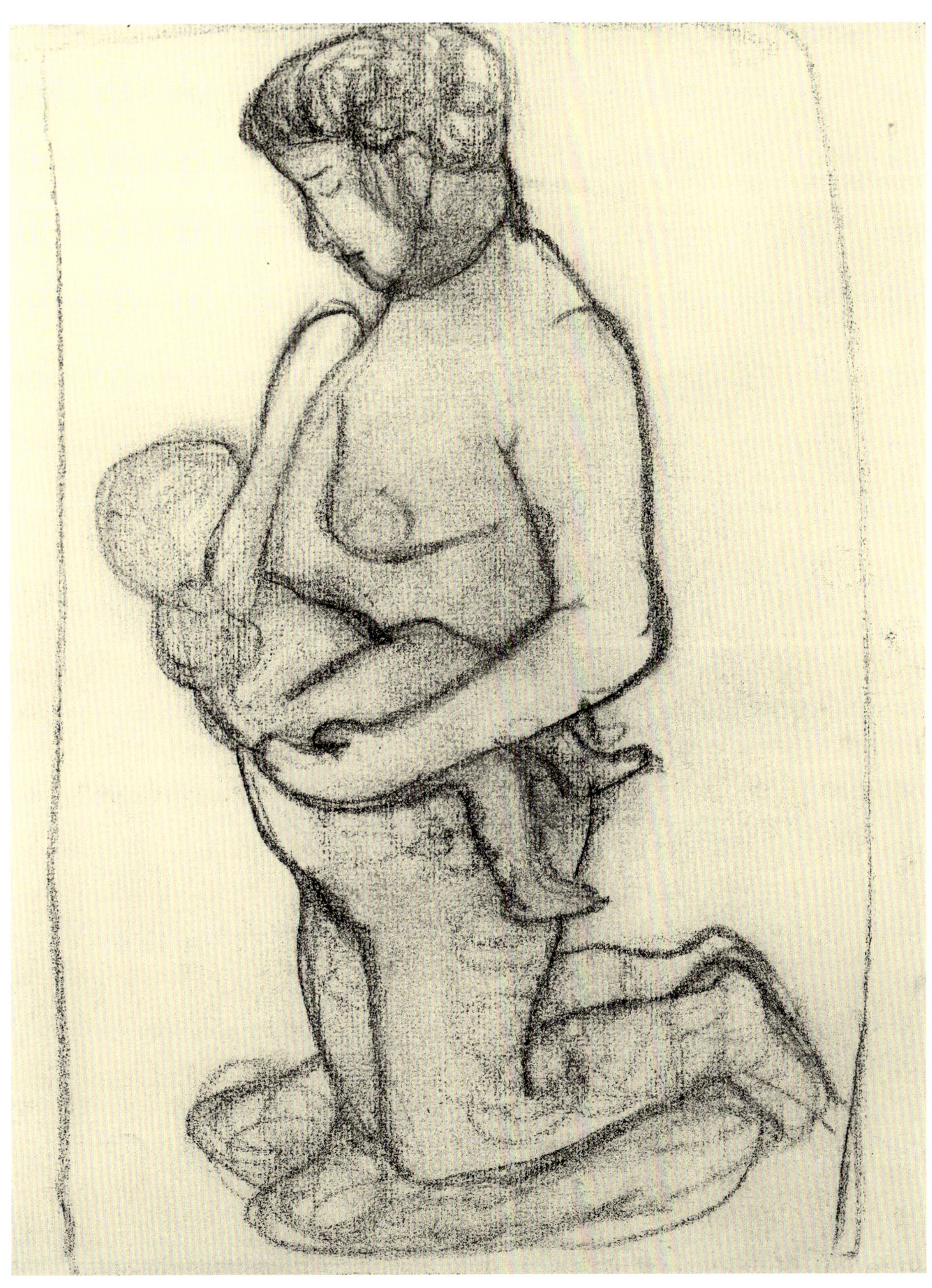

Kniender Frauenakt mit Kind / Kneeling Female Nude with Child, c. 1906

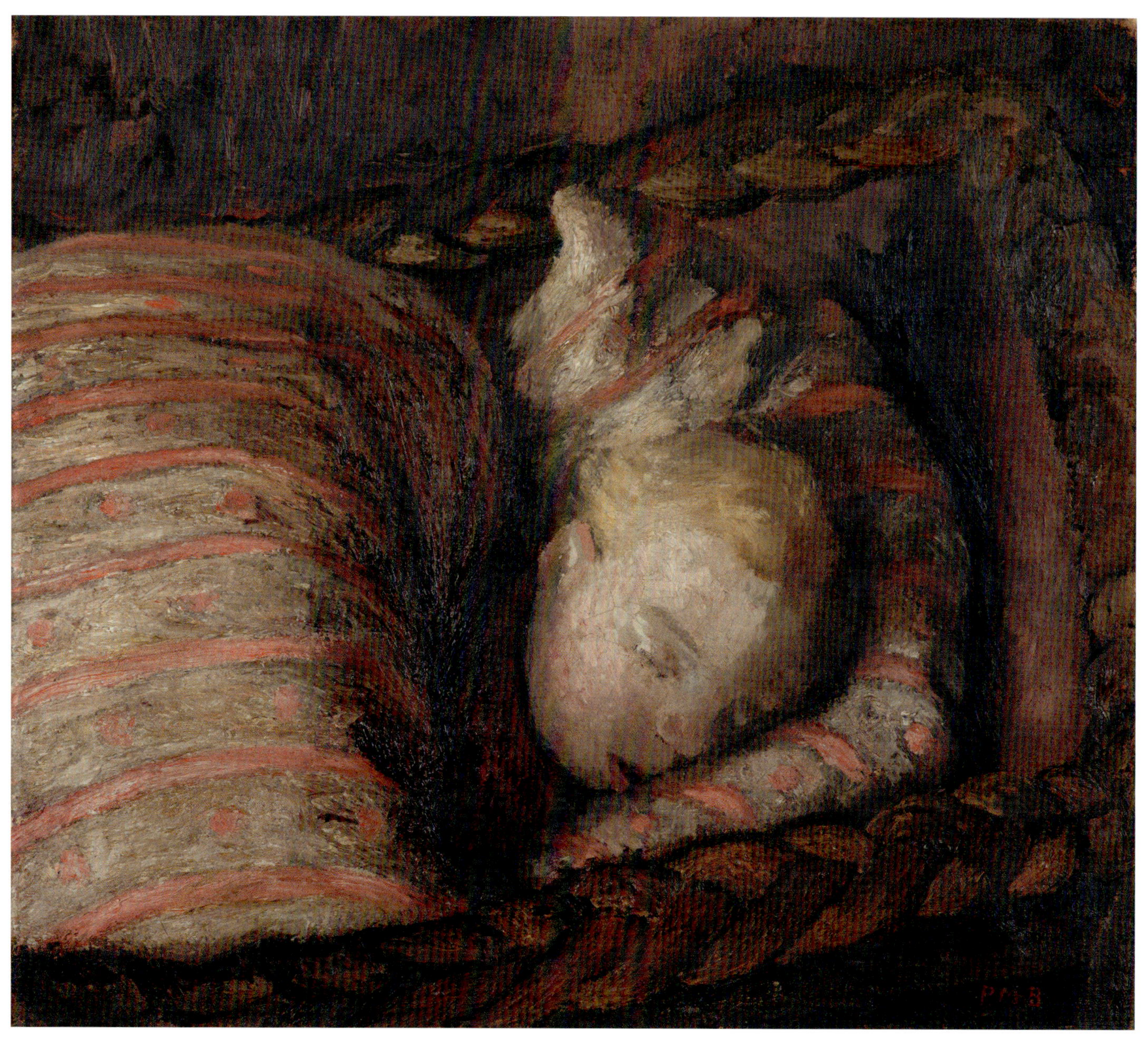

Kind in der Wiege / Child in Cradle, c. 1904

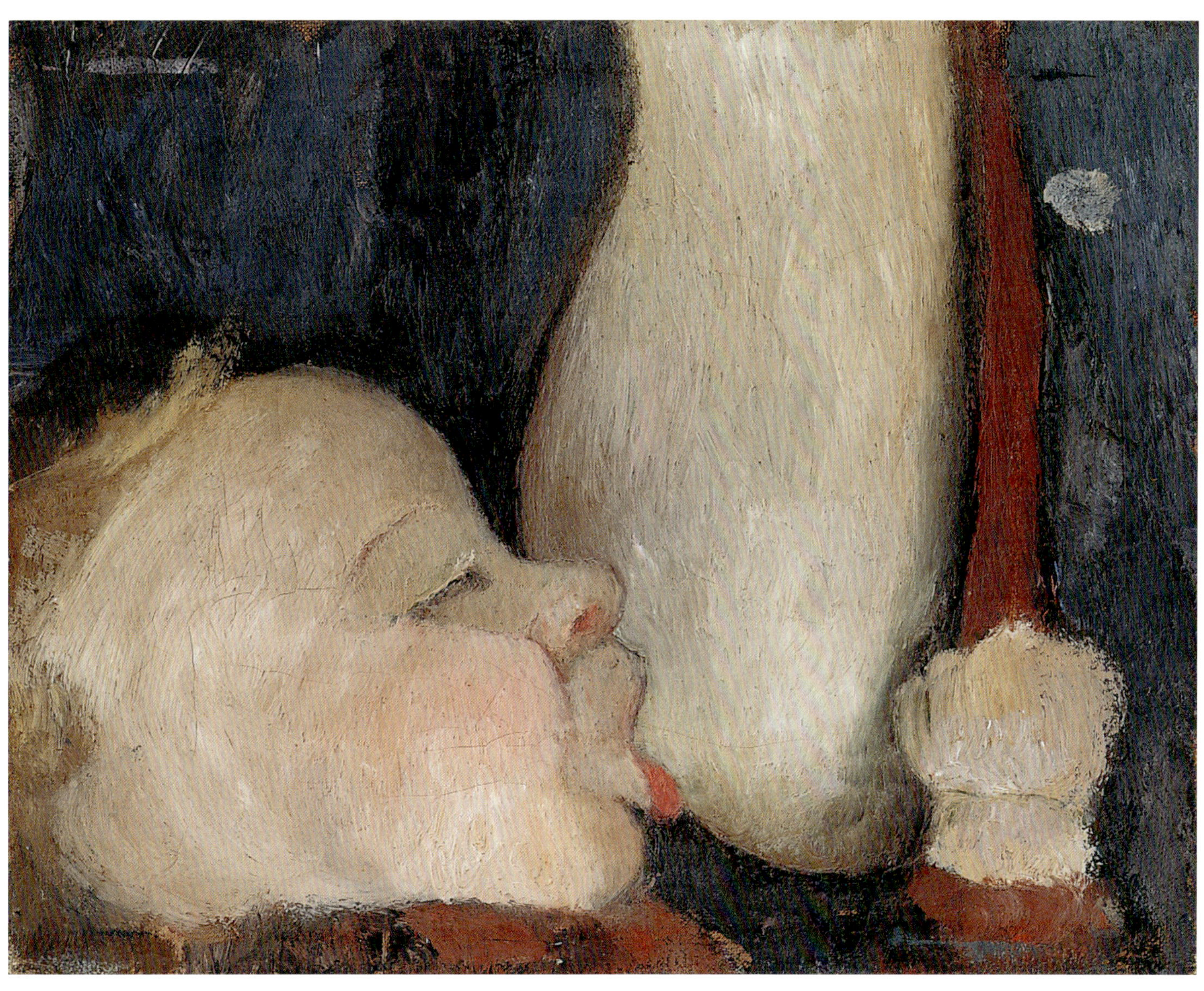

Kind an der Mutterbrust / Infant, Breastfeeding, c. 1904

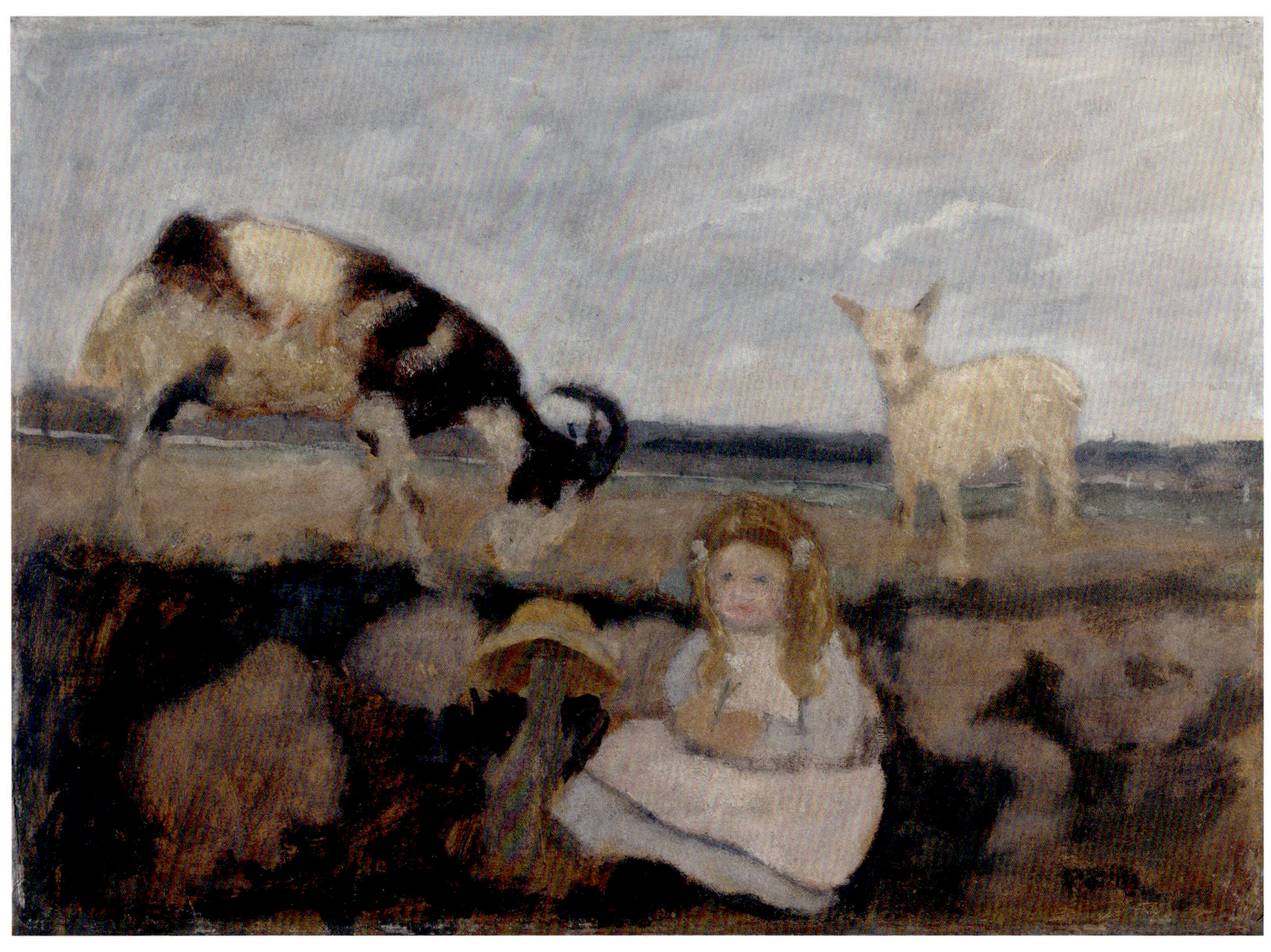

Elsbeth mit Ziegen / Elsbeth with Goats, c. 1902

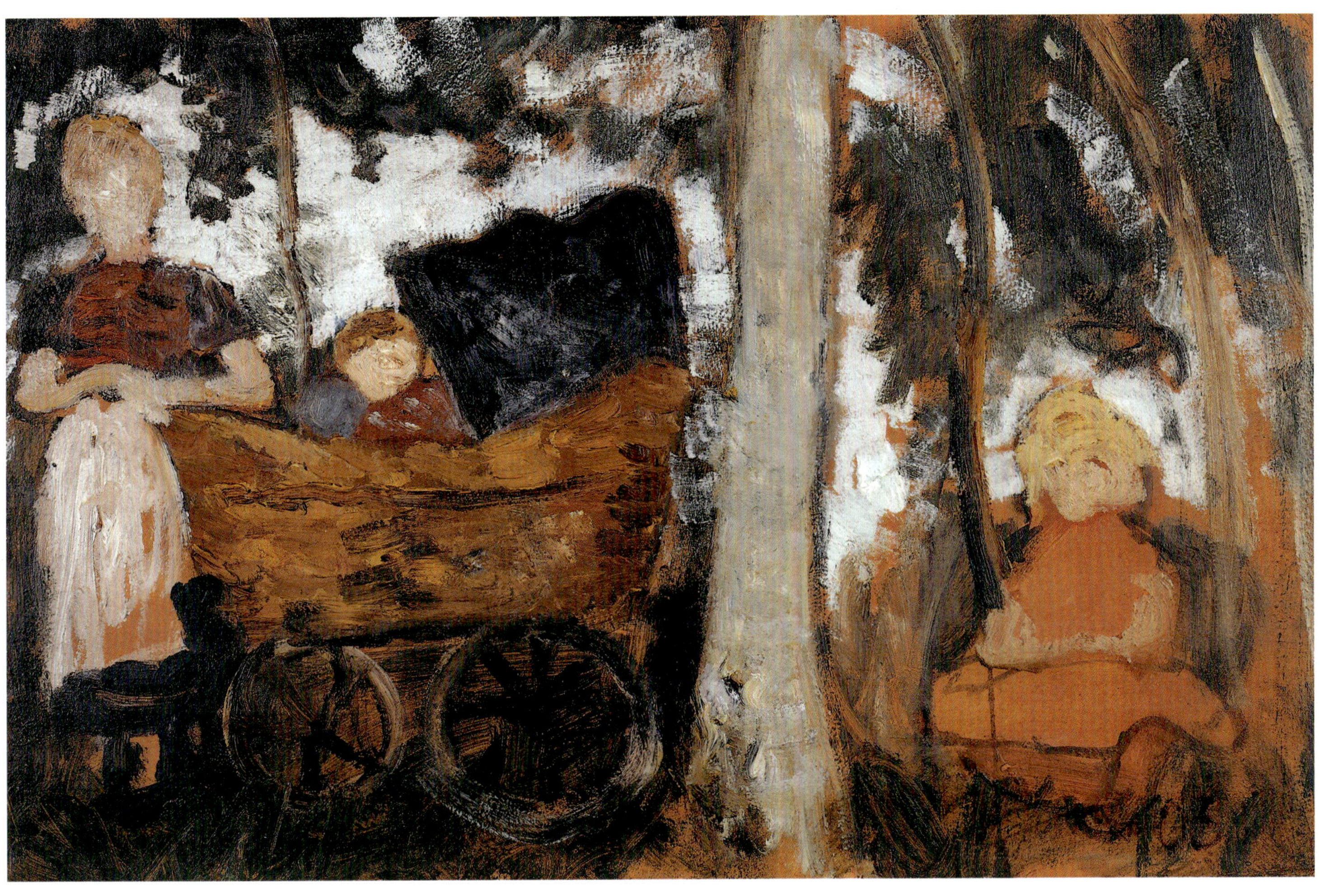

Kinderwagen mit Kindern unter Bäumen / Stroller with Children Under Trees, 1905

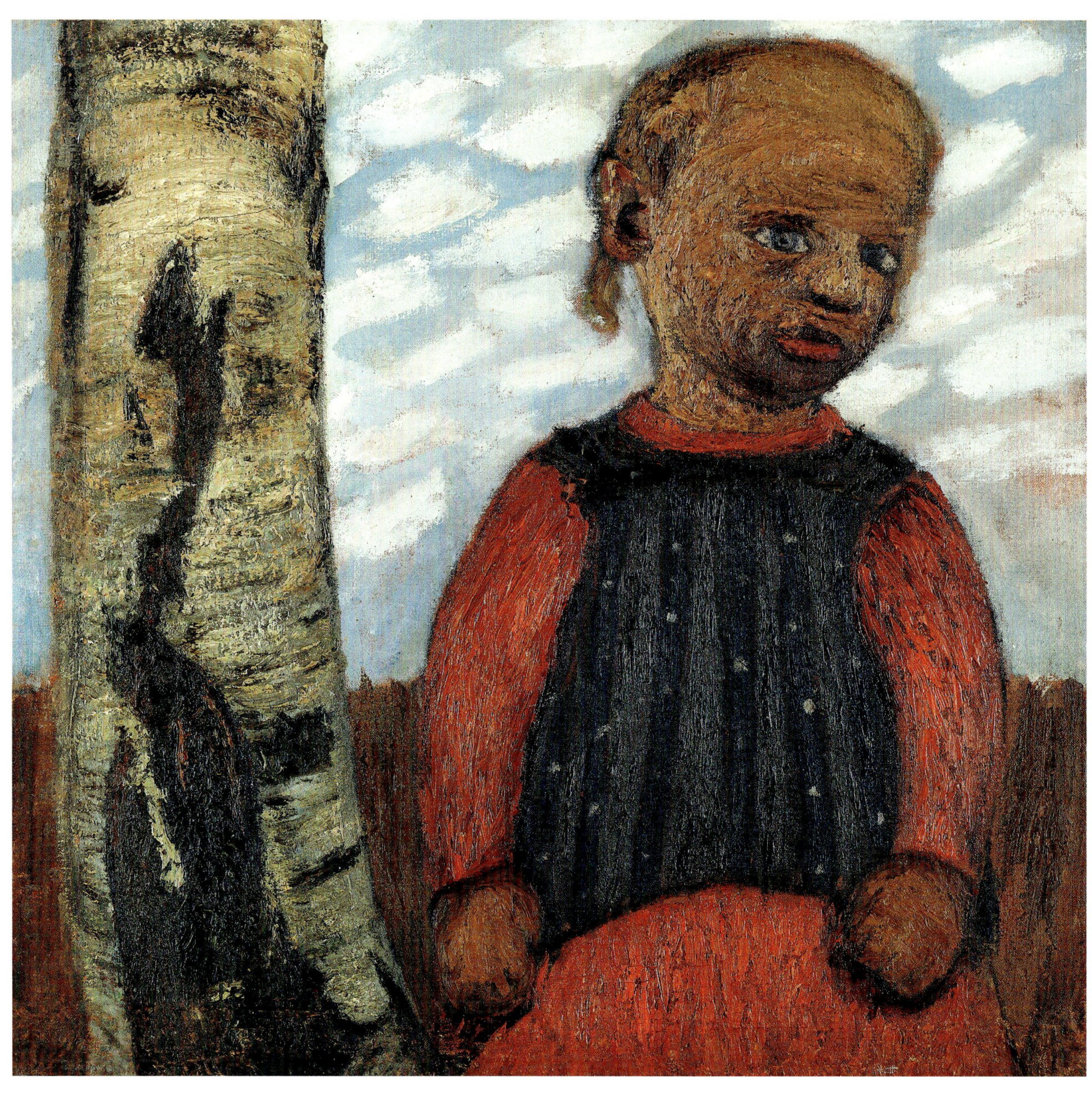

Mädchen in rotem Kleid am Baumstamm vor Wolkenhimmel /
Girl in a Red Dress by a Tree Trunk in Front of a Background of a Cloudy Sky c. 1905

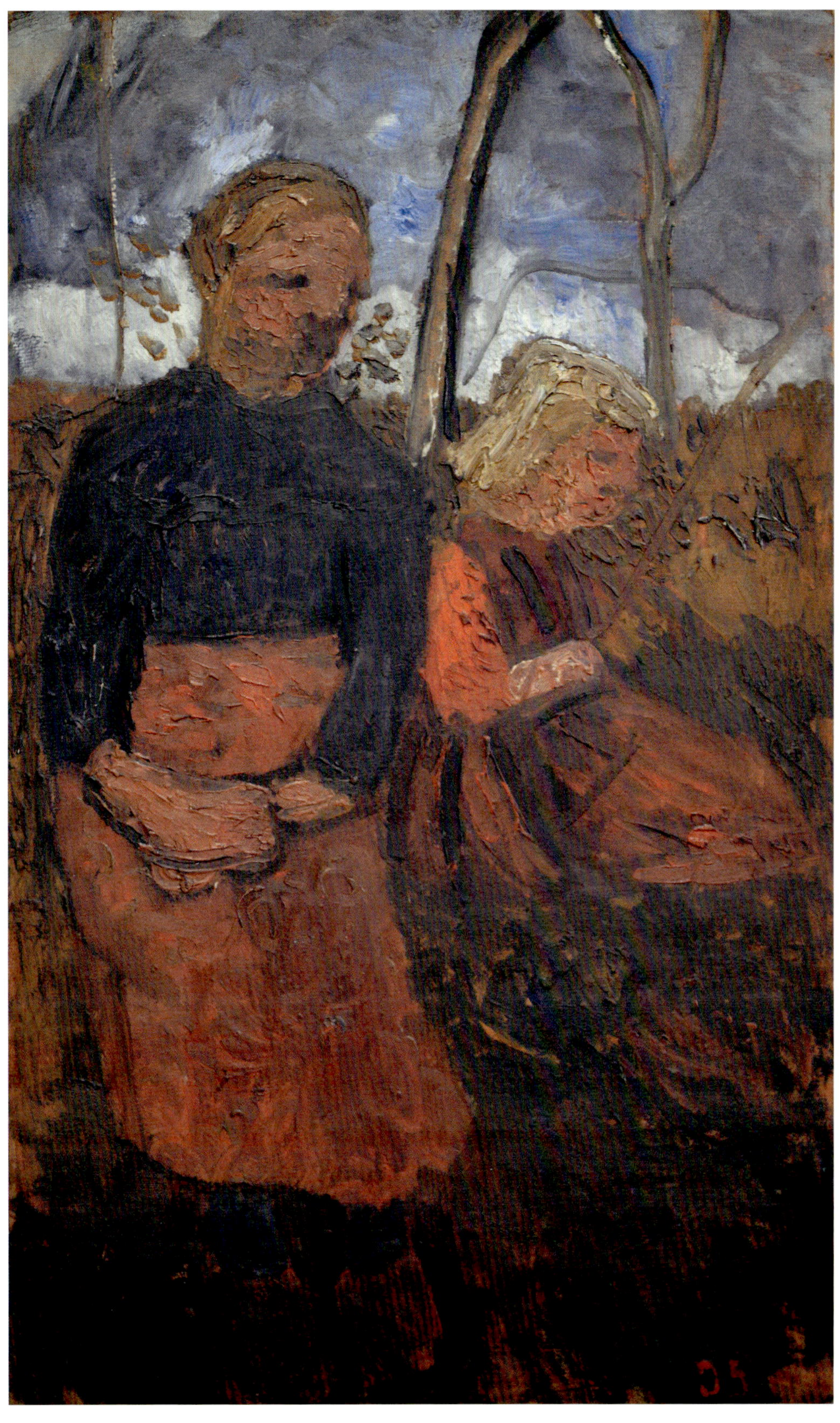

Zwei sitzende Mädchen in der Landschaft / Two Girls Sitting in Landscape, 1905

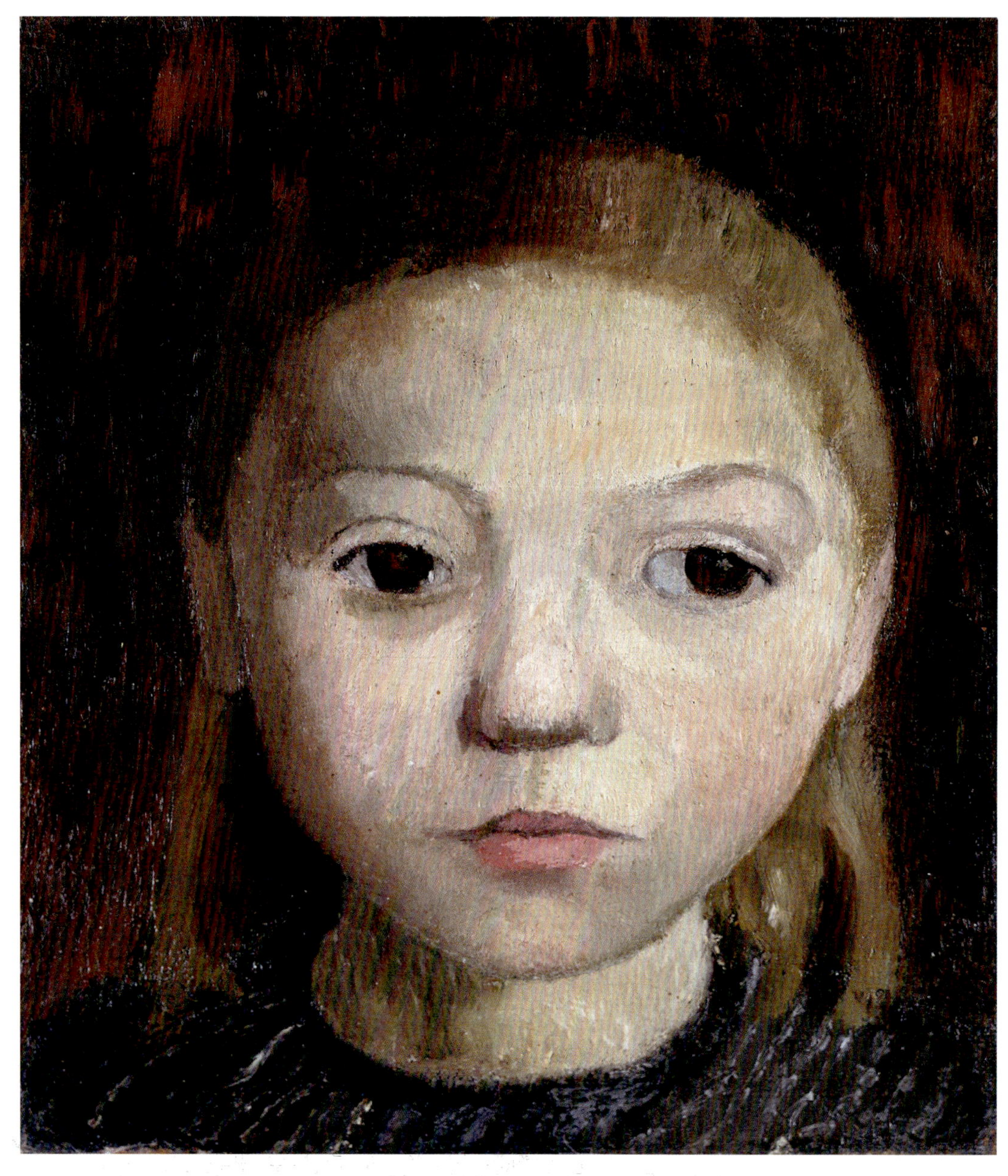

Mädchenkopf / Head of a Girl, c. 1905

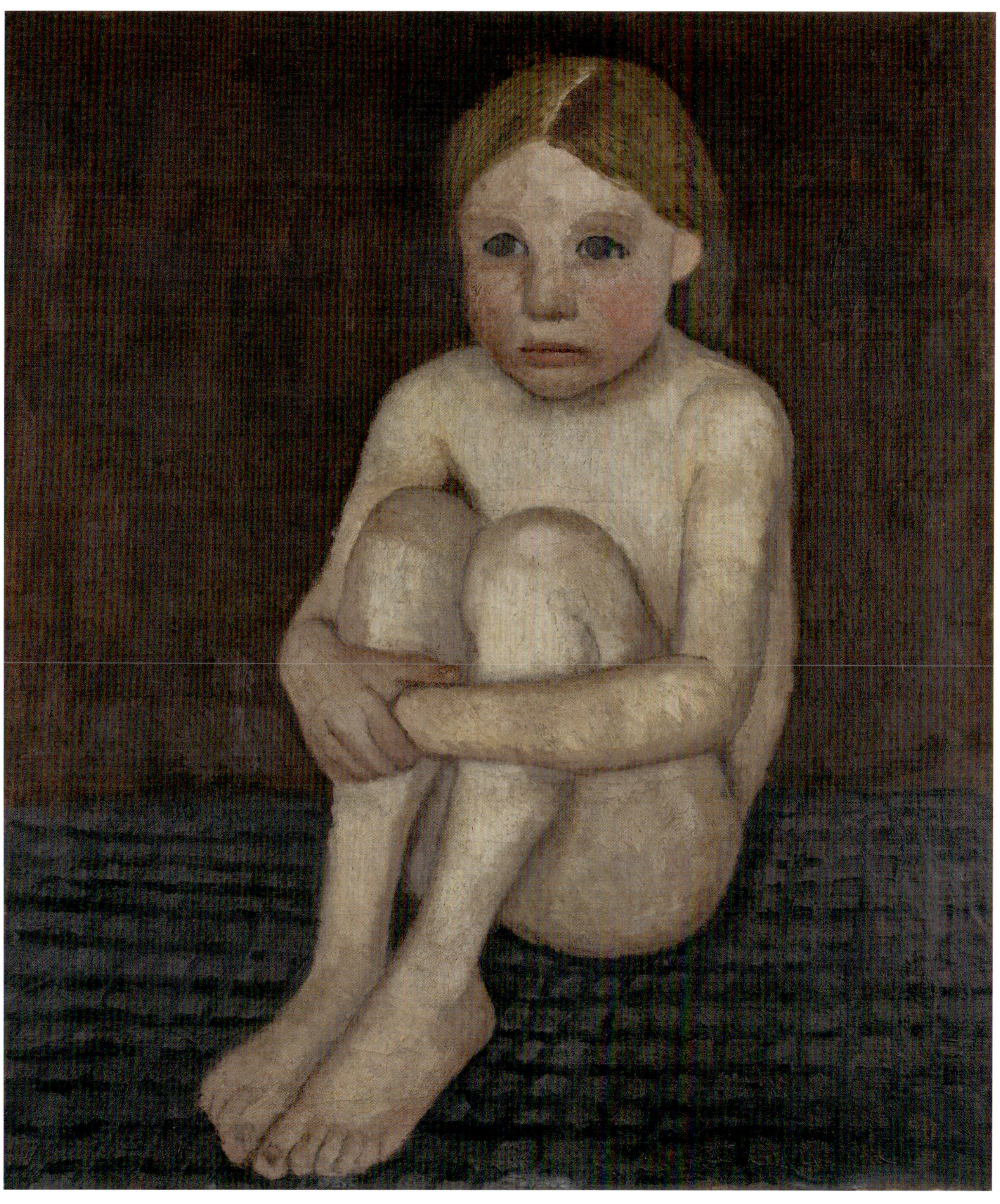

Sitzender Mädchenakt mit angezogenen Beinen I / Seated Girl Nude, Her Legs Pulled Up I, c. 1904

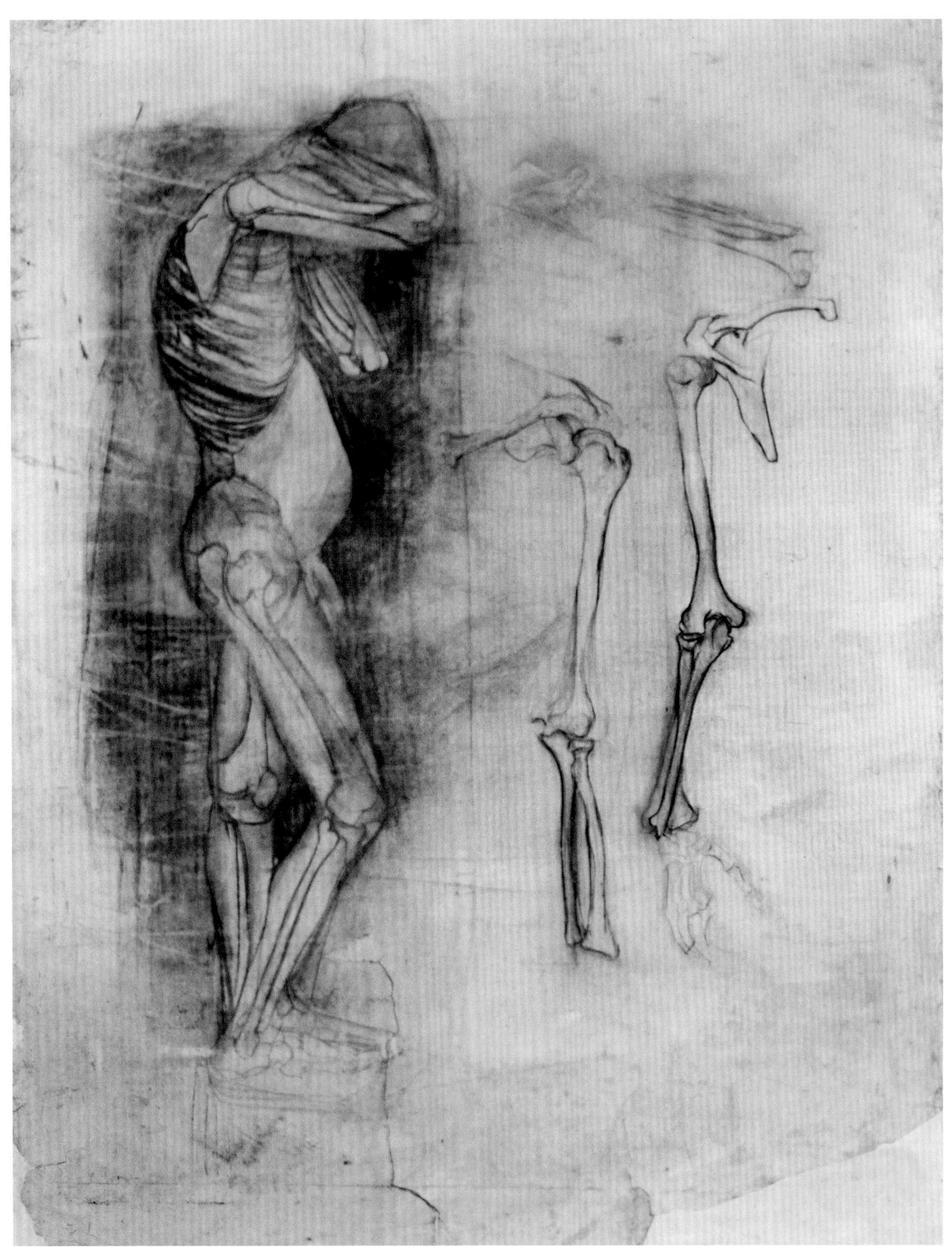

Stehender Kinderakt mit eingezeichnetem Skelett sowie Knochenstudien /
Standing Child Nude with the Skeleton Drawn in and Bone Studies, June 1899

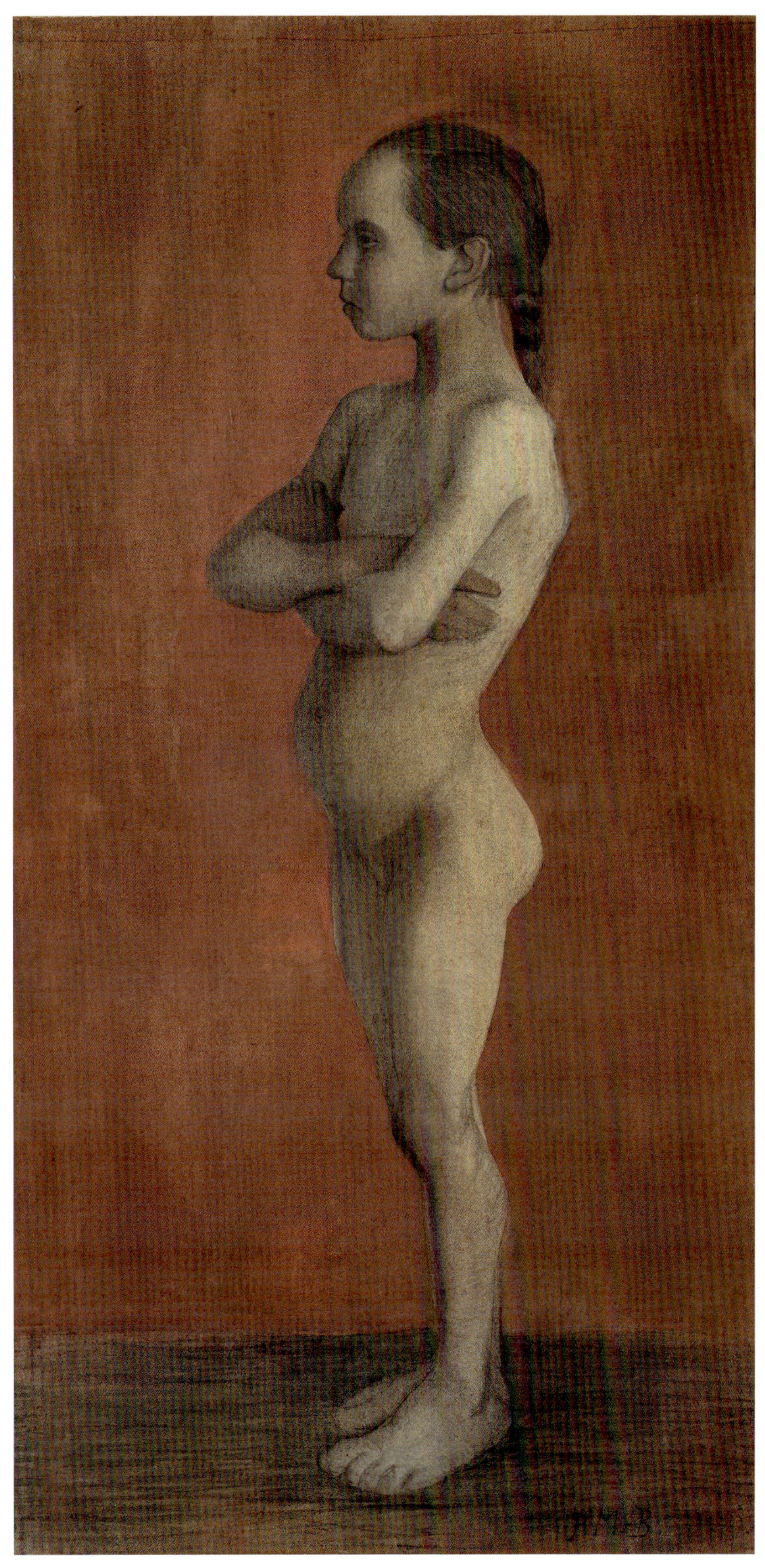

Stehender Mädchenakt nach links, mit verschränkten Armen /
Standing Girl Nude, Turned Left with Crossed Arms, c. 1899

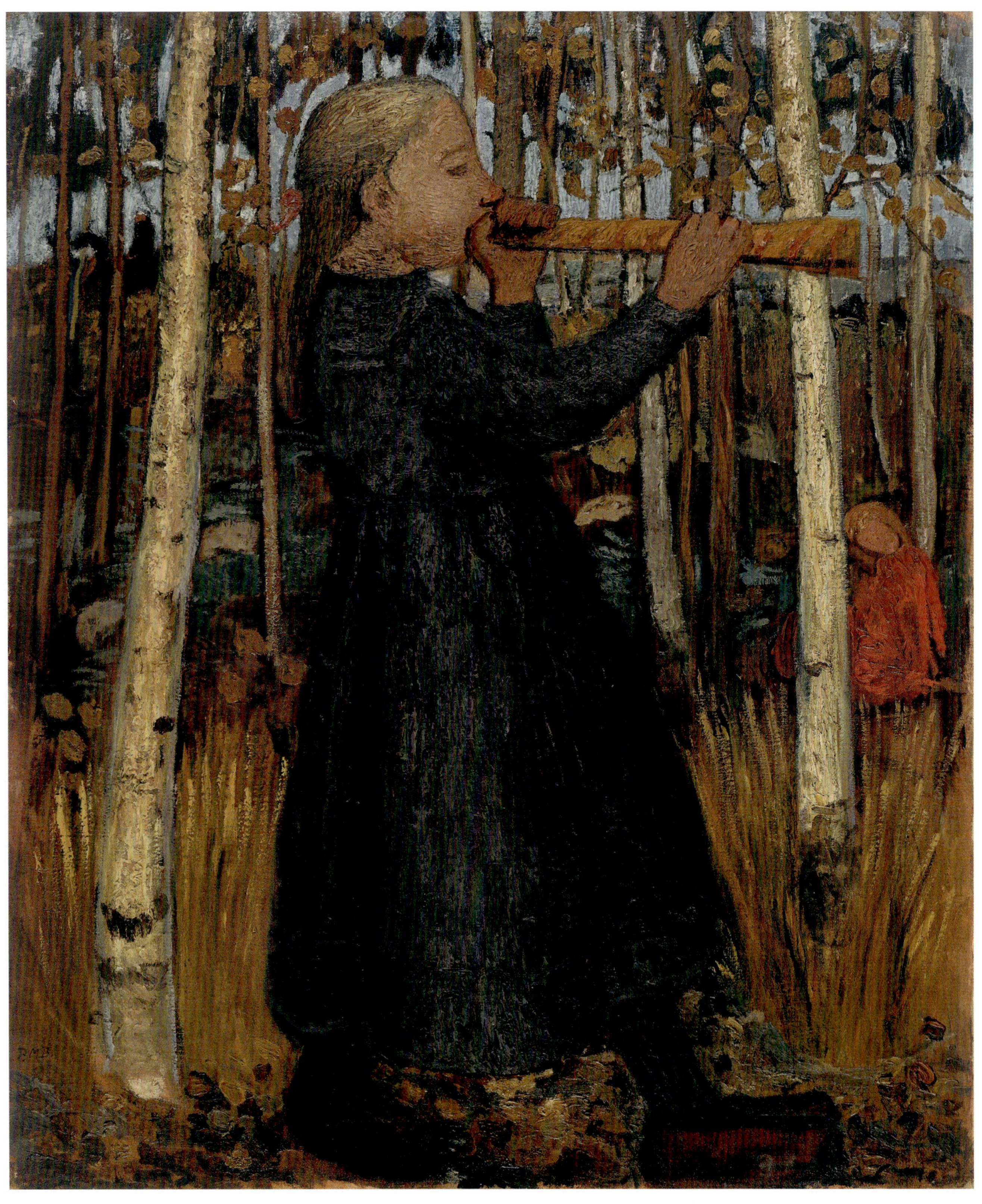

Flöte blasendes Mädchen im Birkenwald / Girl Blowing a Flute in the Birch Forest, 1905

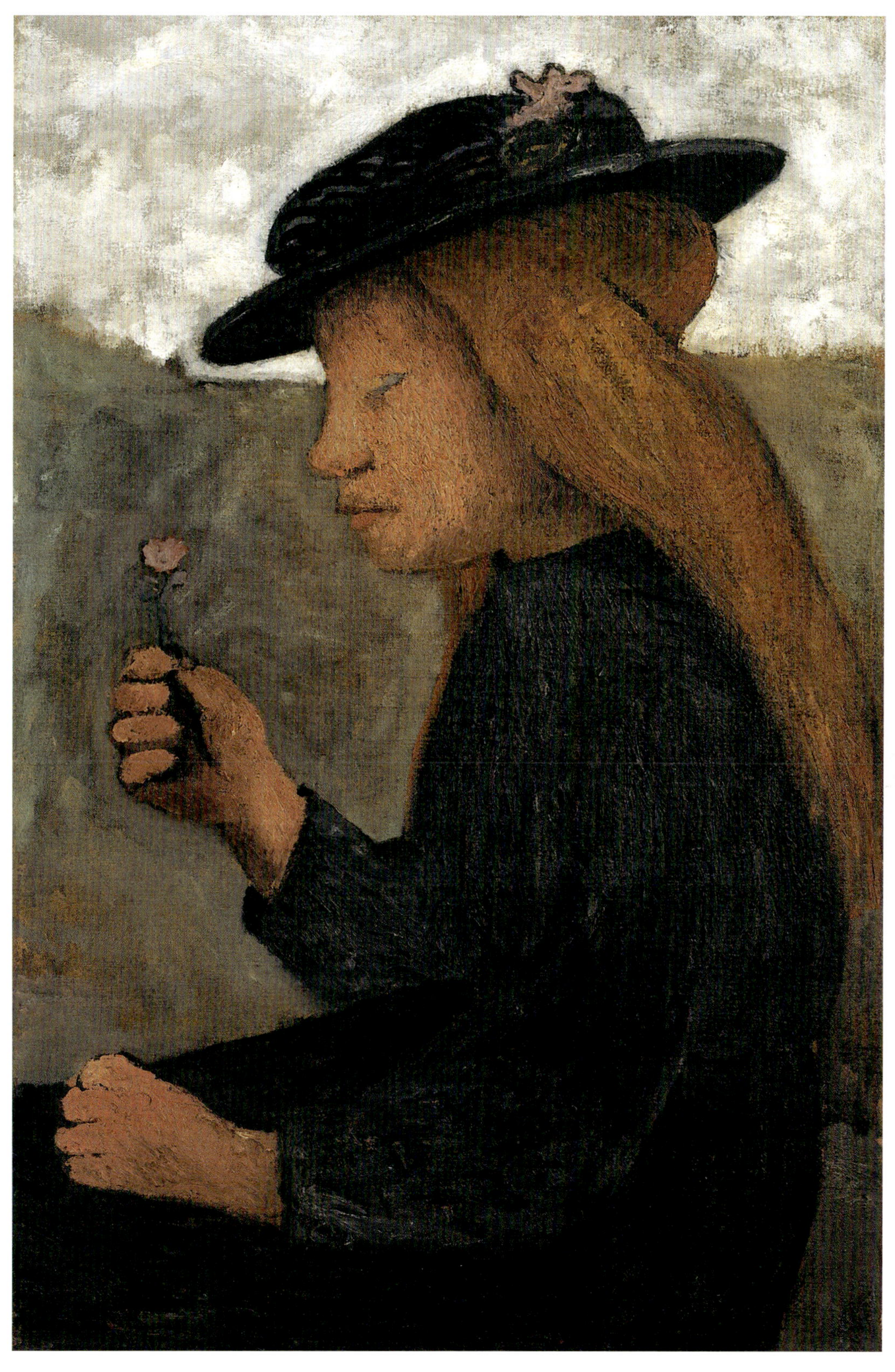

Sitzendes Mädchen mit schwarzem Hut und Blume in der rechten Hand / Seated Girl with a Black Hat and a Flower in Her Right Hand, c. 1903

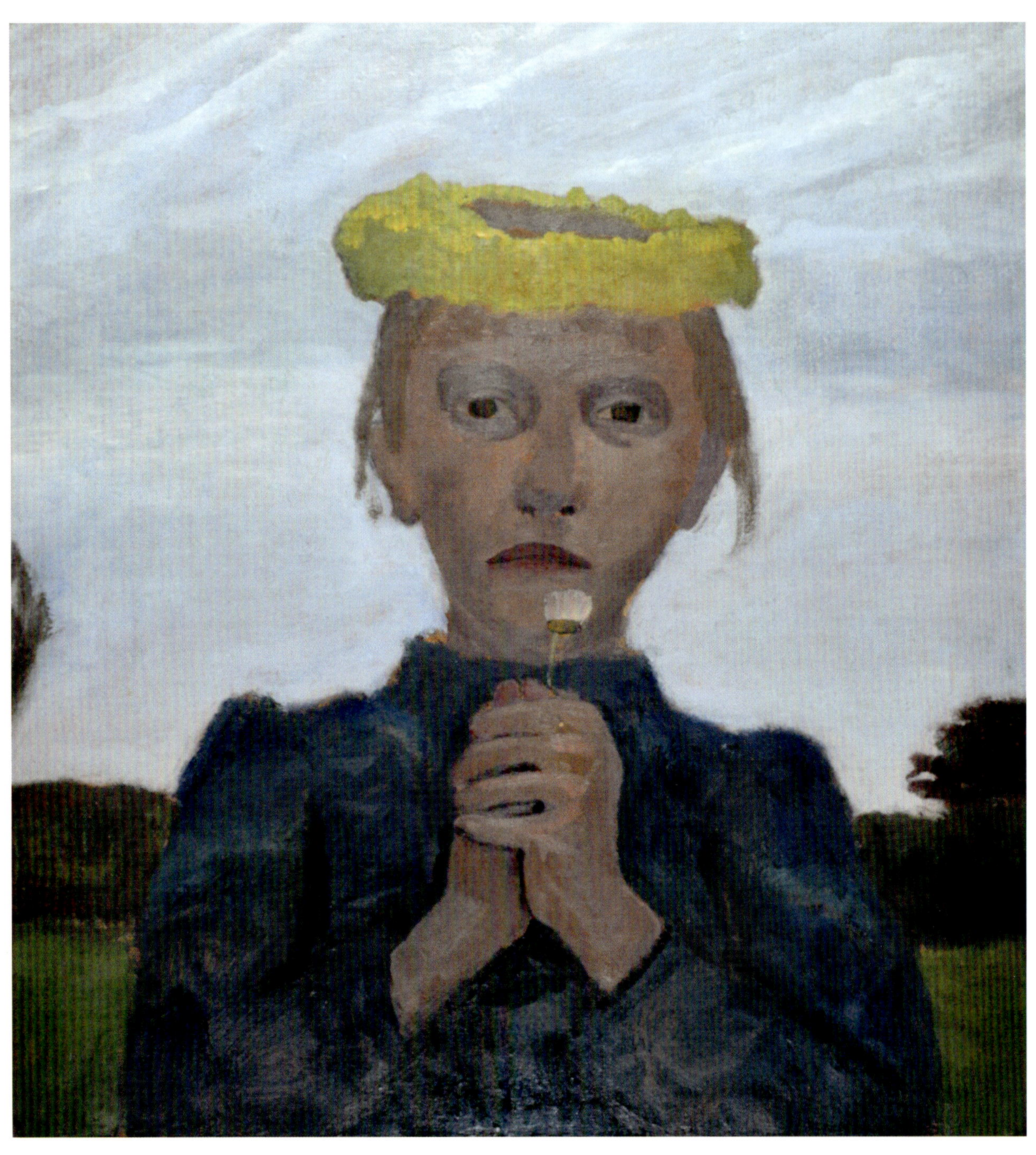

Brustbild eines Mädchens mit Kranz und Gänseblume in den Händen / Girl with Yellow Wreath and Daisy, c. 1901

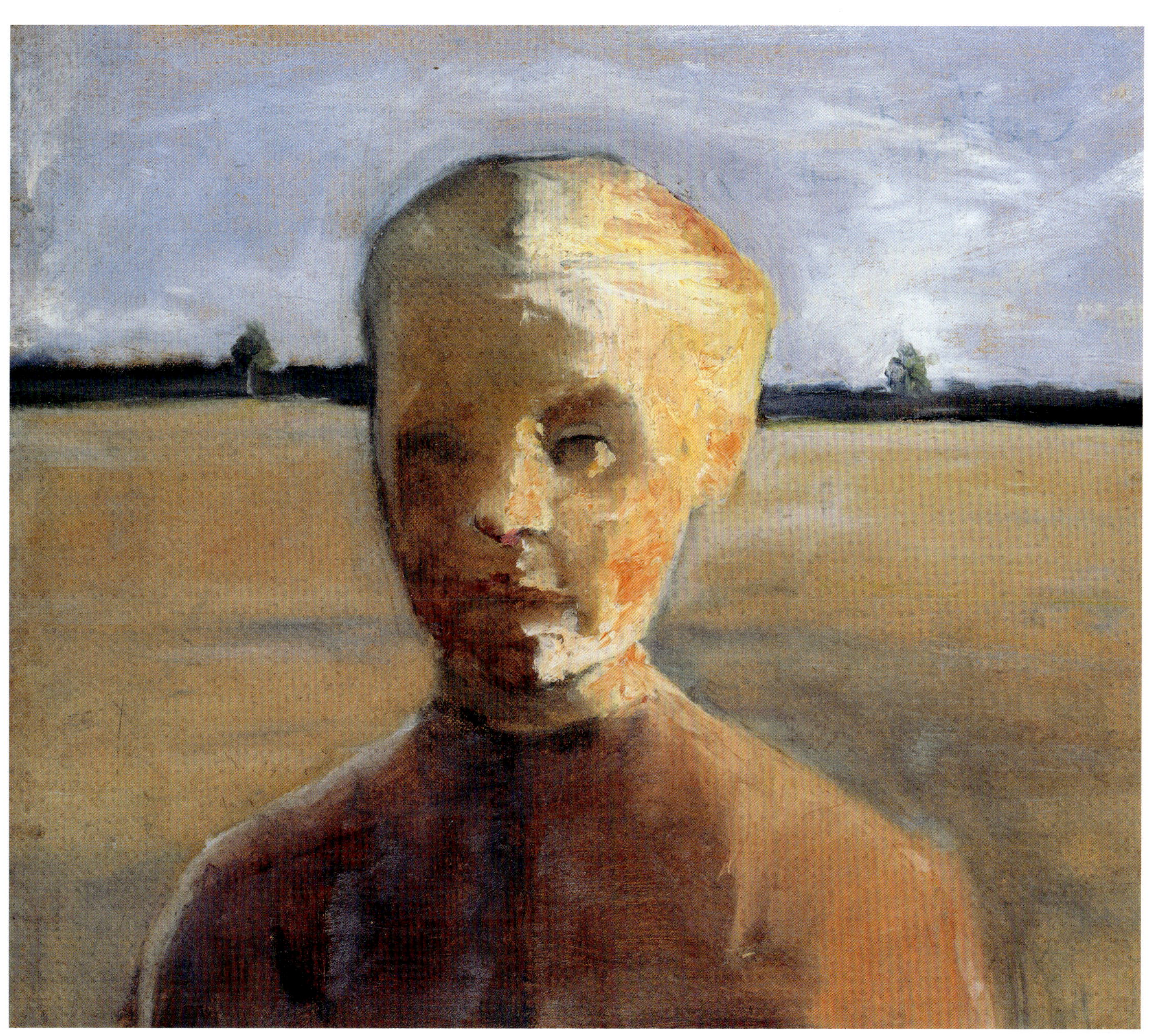

Brustbild eines Mädchens in der Sonne vor weiter Landschaft / Half-Length Portrait of a Girl in the Sun in Front of a Wide Landscape, 1897

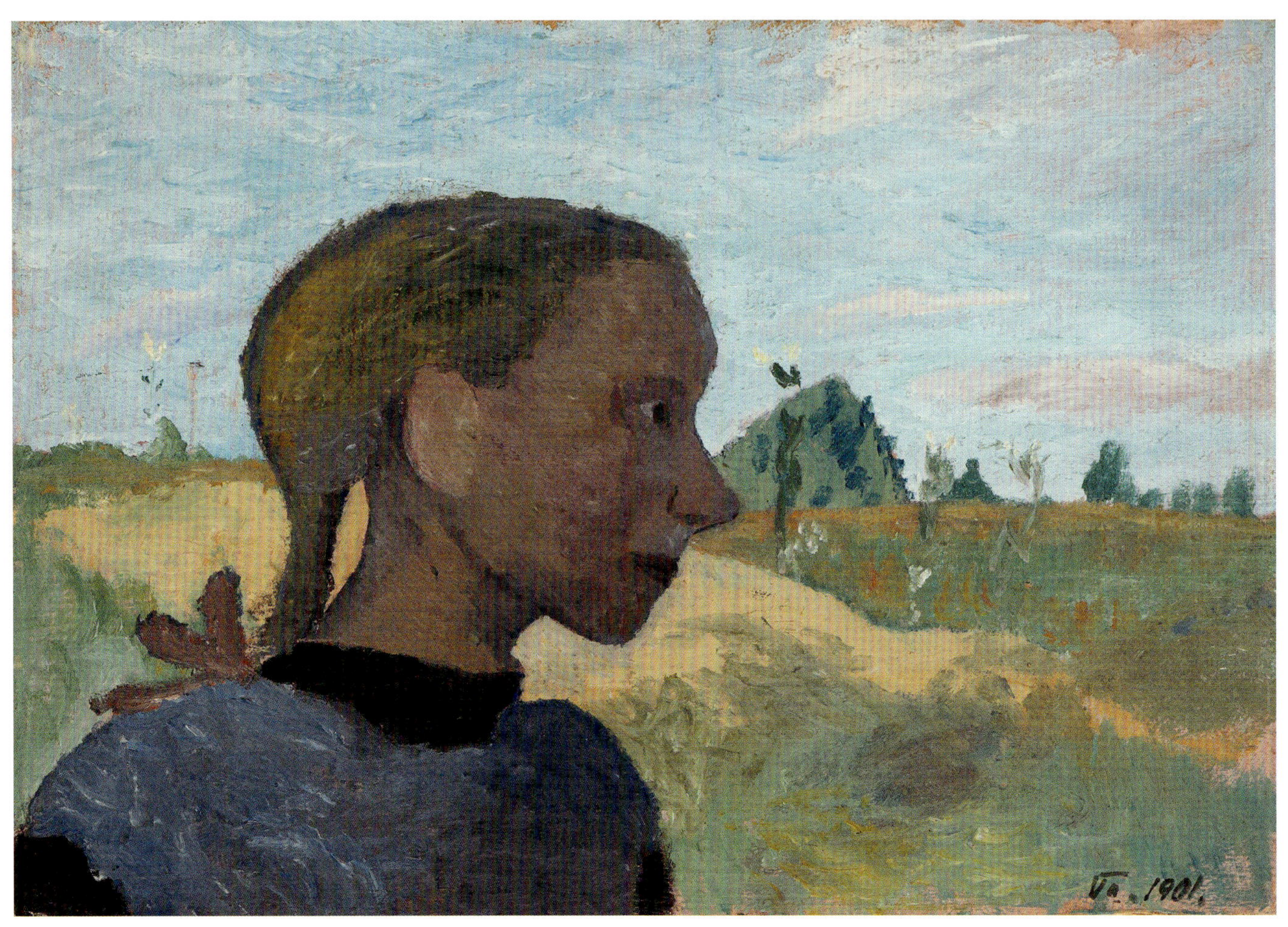

Mädchenbildnis / Portrait of a Girl, 1901

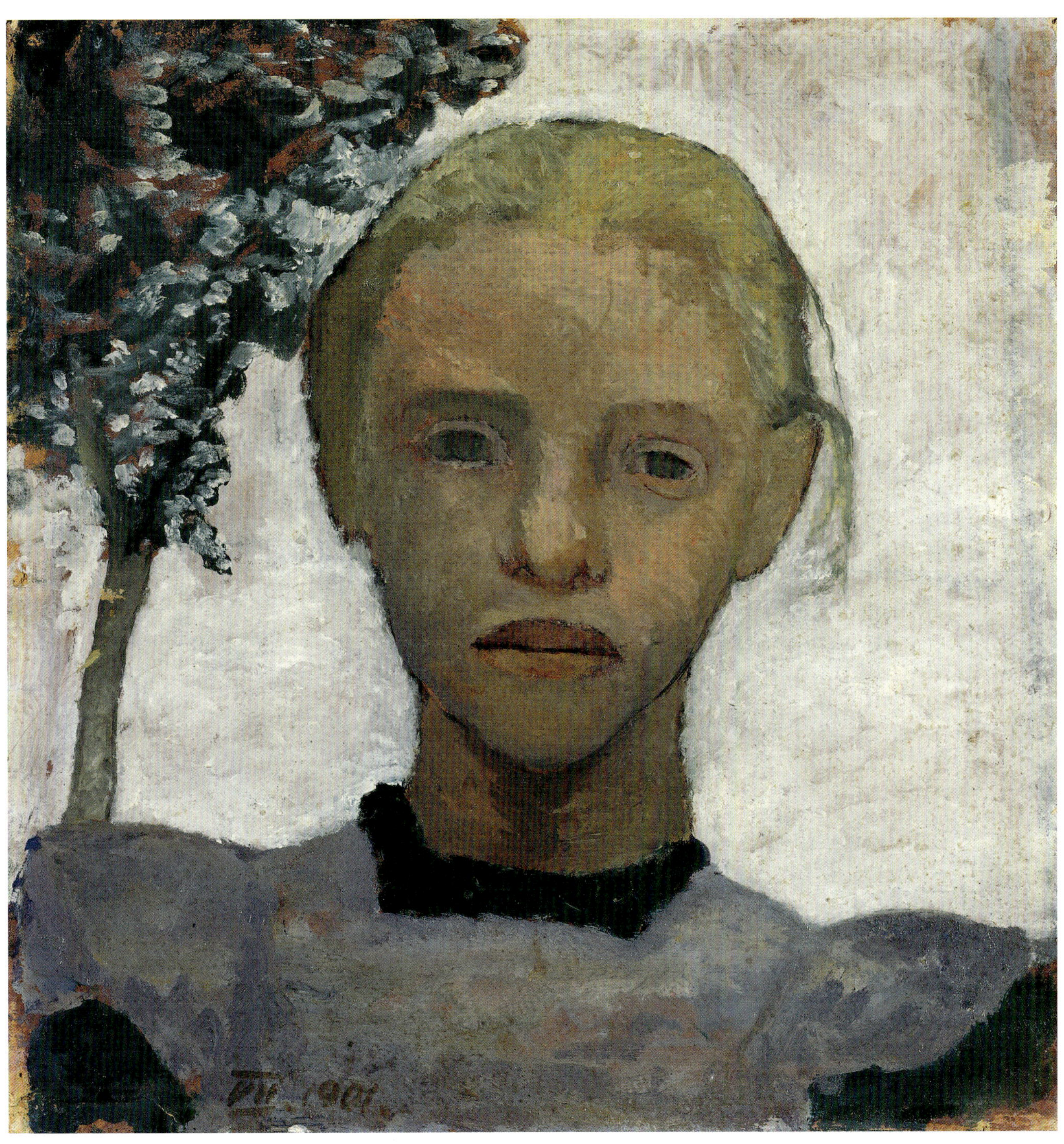

Mädchenkopf / Head of a Girl, 1901

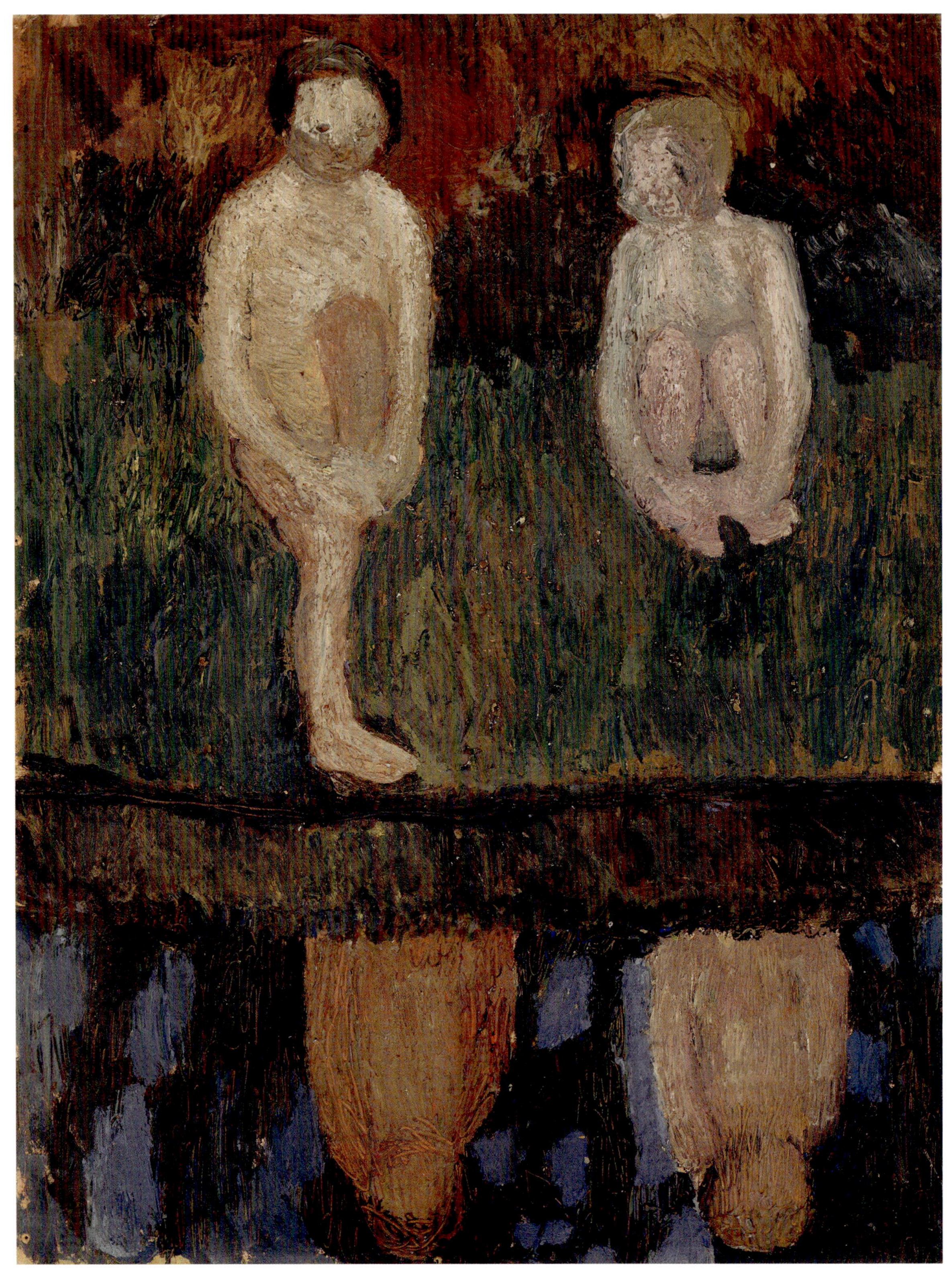

Zwei nackte Jungen am Ufer hockend I / Two Naked Boys Squatting on the Shore I, c. 1902

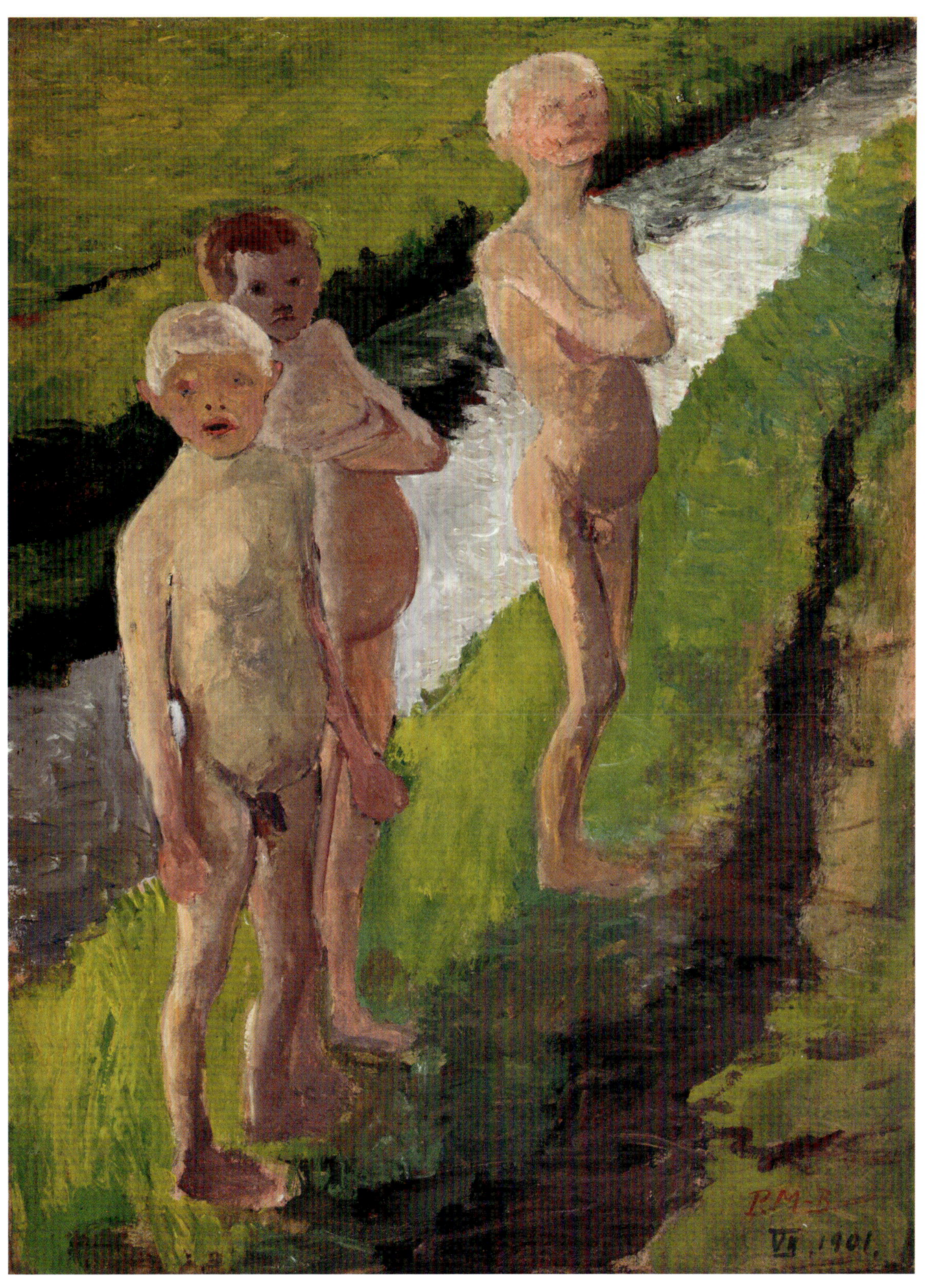

Drei badende Jungen am Kanal / Three Boys Bathing by a Canal, 1901

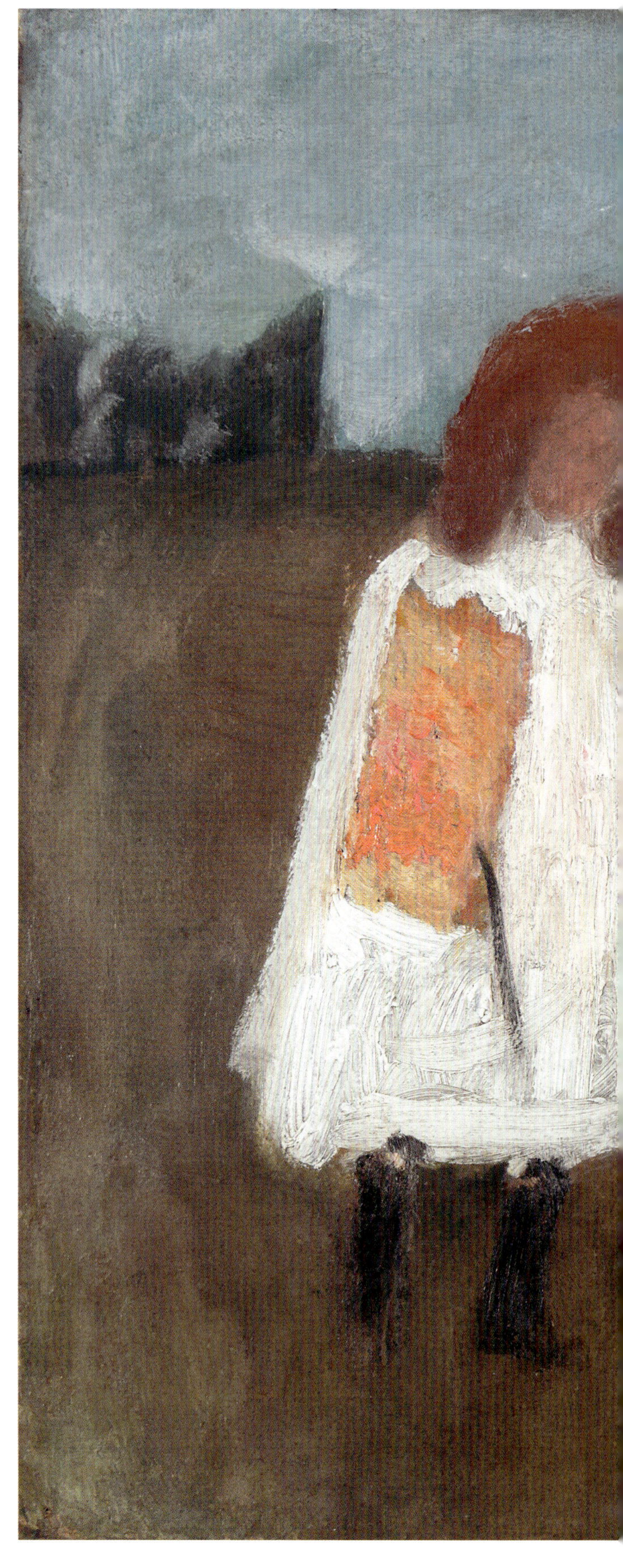

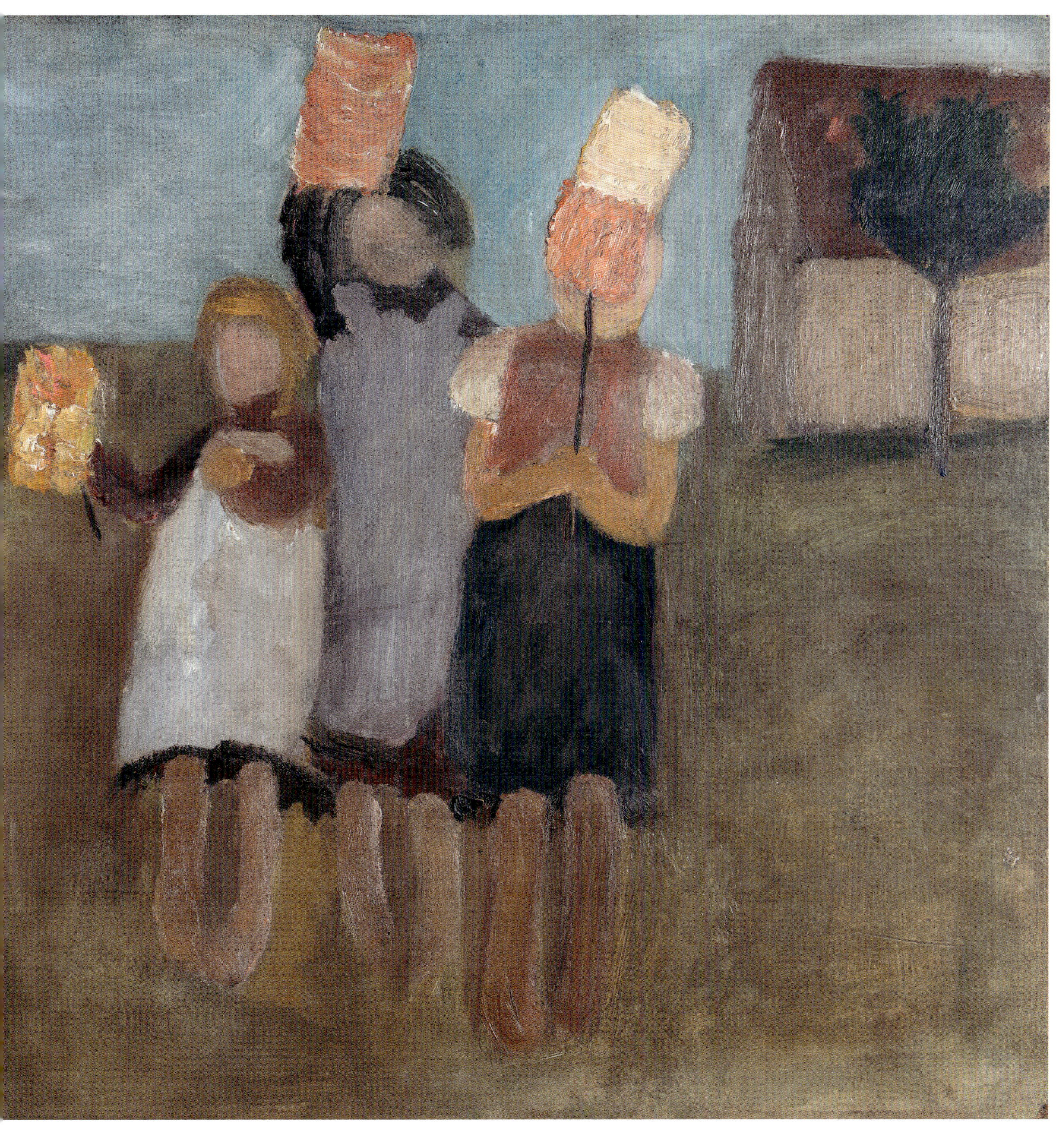

Kinder mit Laternen vor Haus / Children with Lanterns in Front of a House, c. 1901

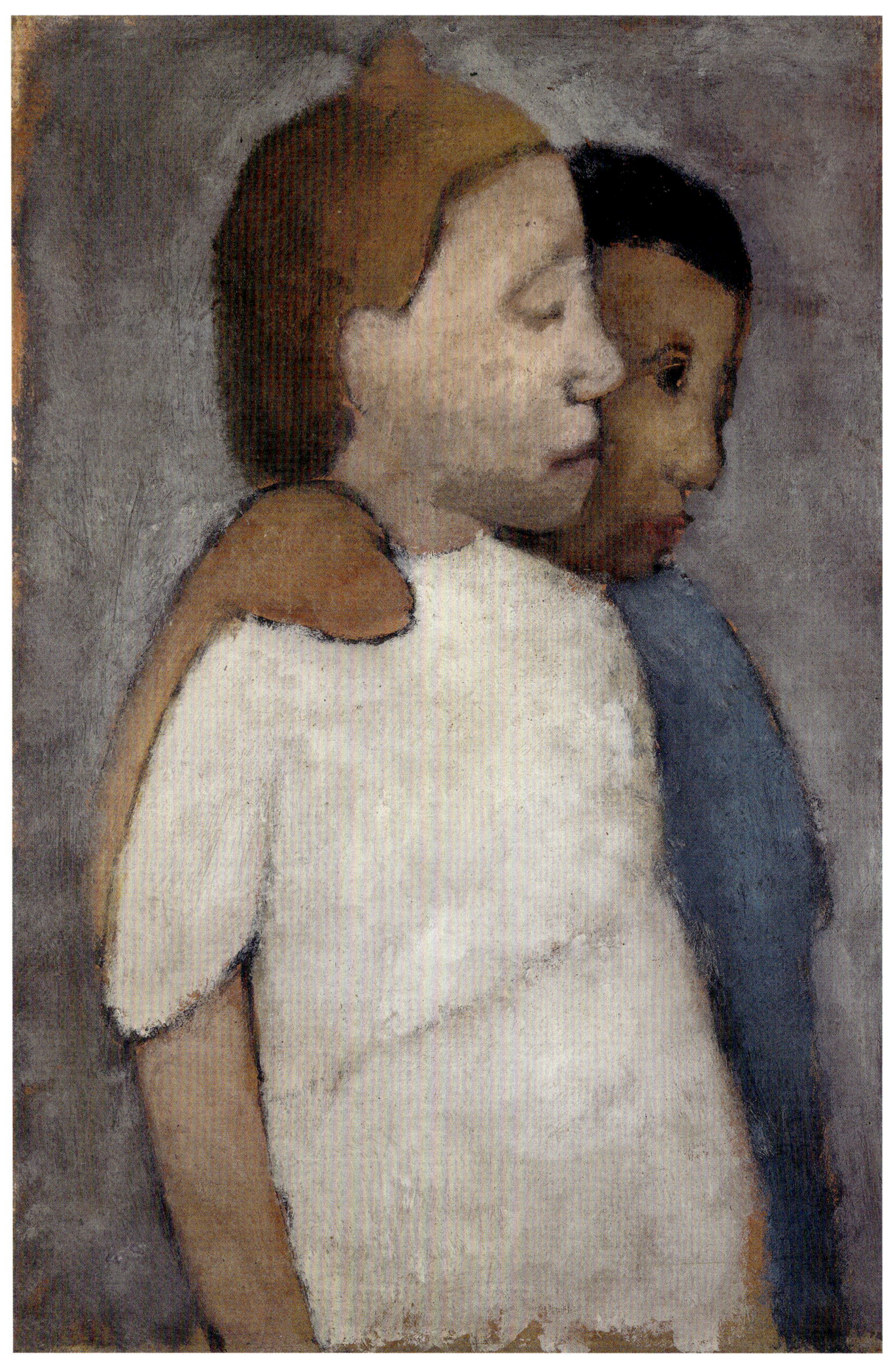

Zwei Mädchen in weißem und blauem Kleid / Two Girls in White and Blue Dresses, May/June 1906

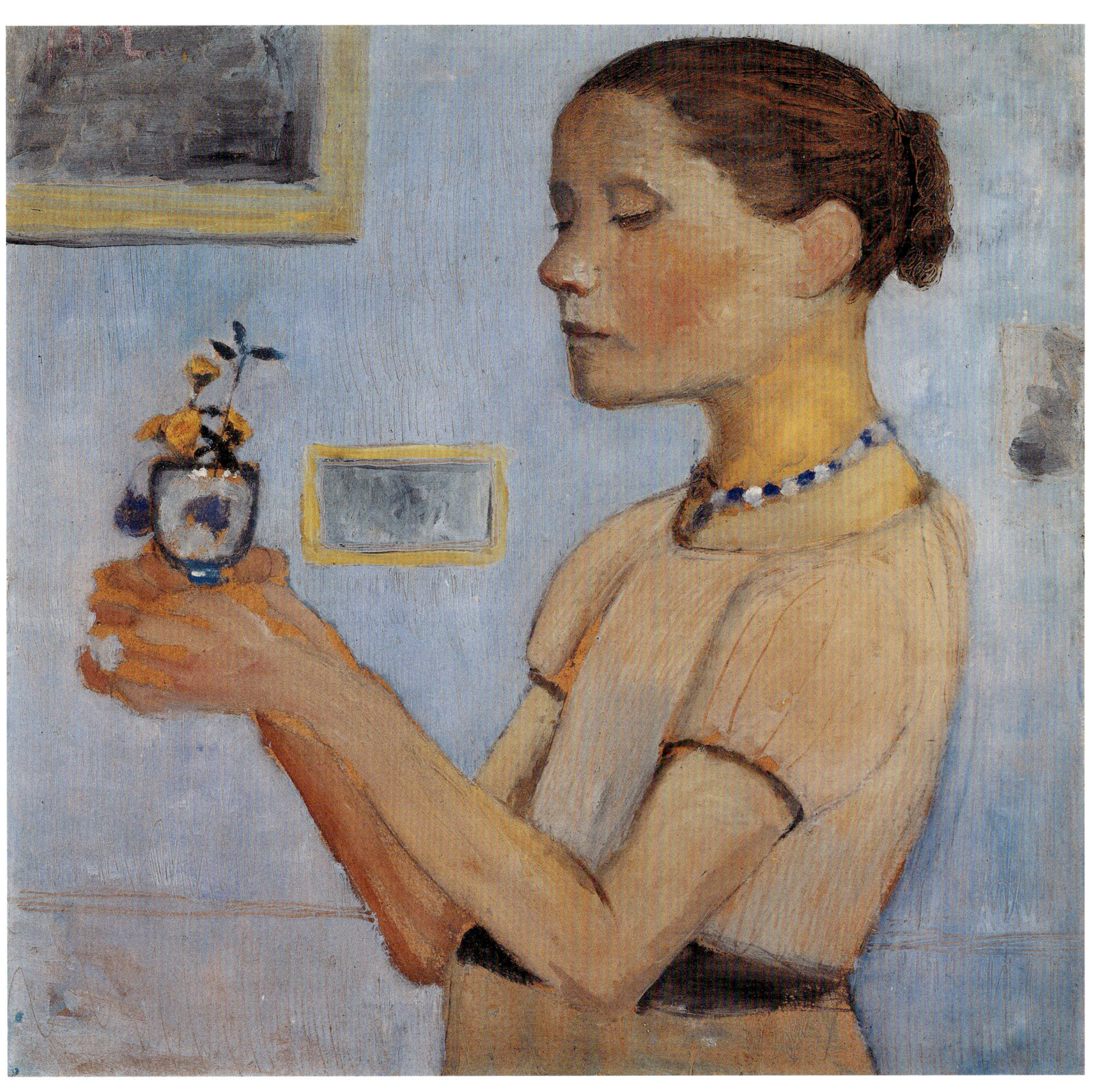

Junges Mädchen mit gelben Blumen im Glas / Young Girl with Yellow Flowers in a Glass, 1902

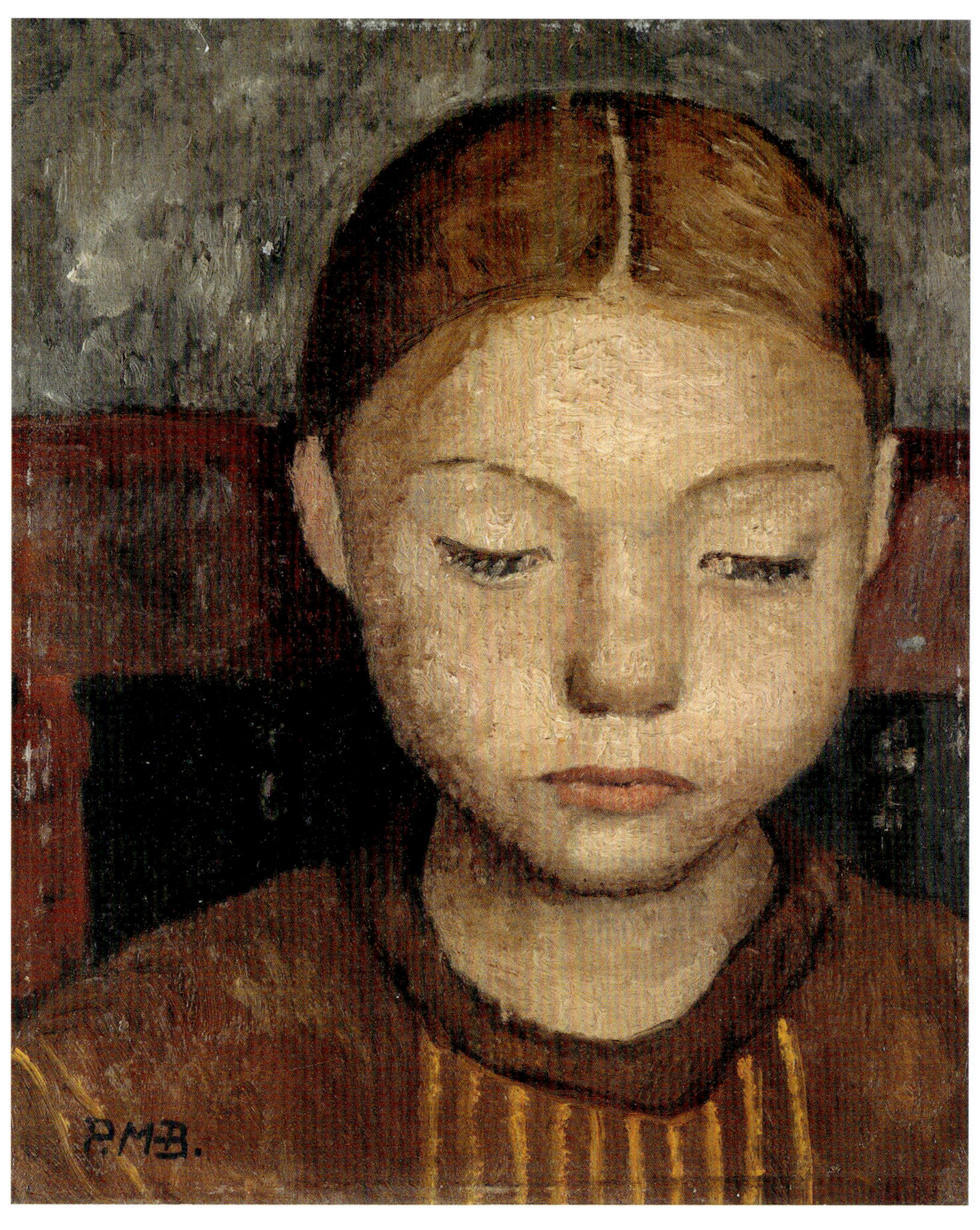

Kopf eines auf einem Stuhl sitzenden Mädchens / Head of a Girl Sitting on a Chair, 1905

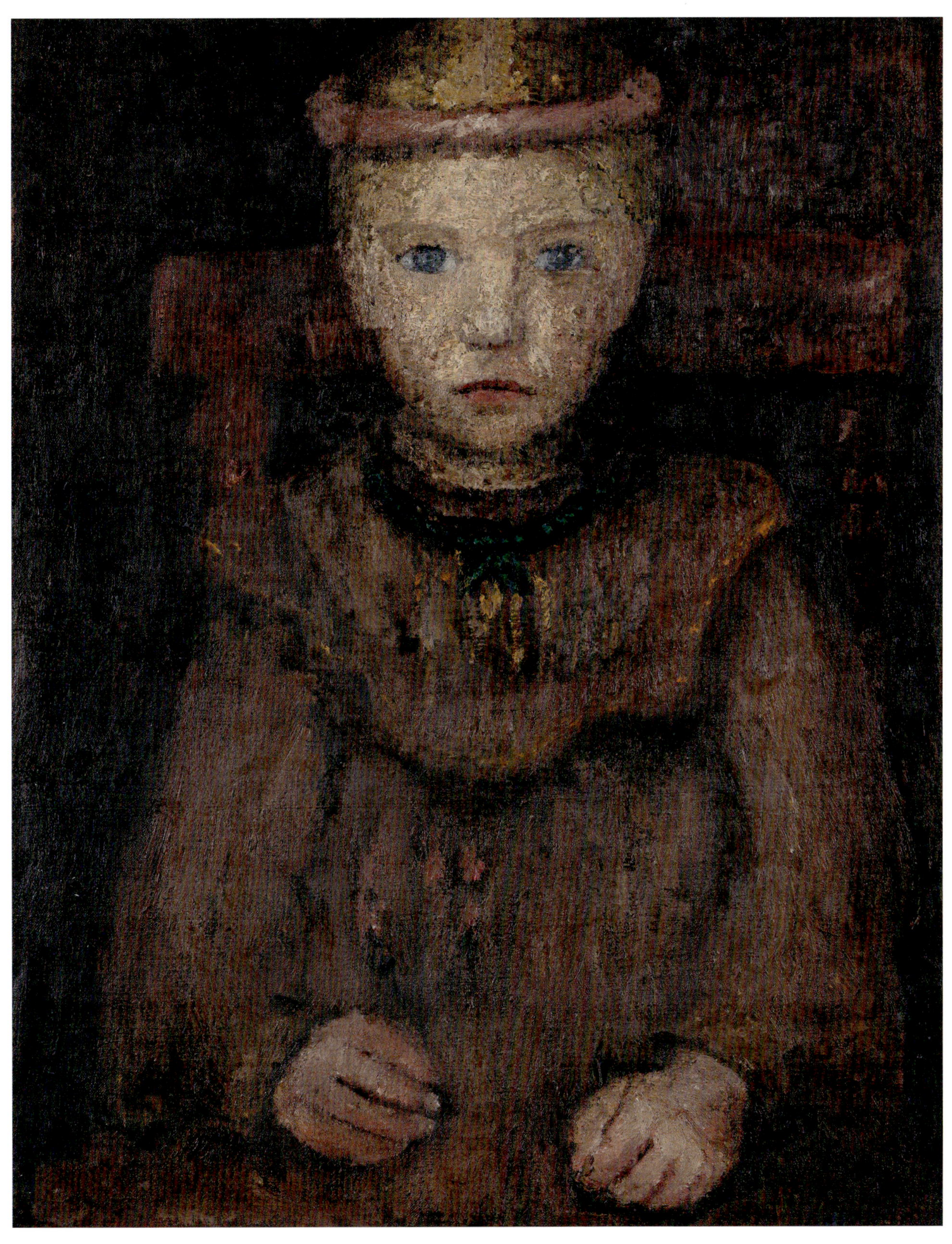

Sitzendes Mädchen mit grüner Kette / Seated Girl with Green Necklace, c. 1904

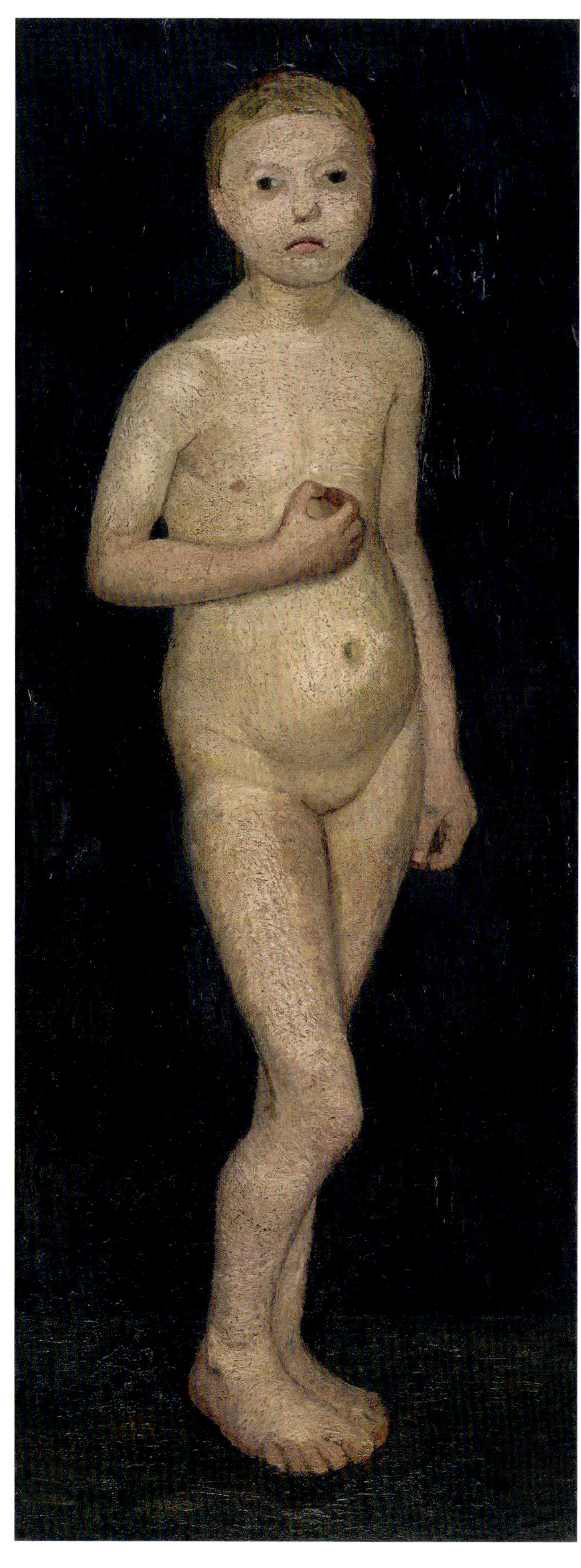

Großer stehender Mädchenakt / Large Standing Nude Girl, 1905/6

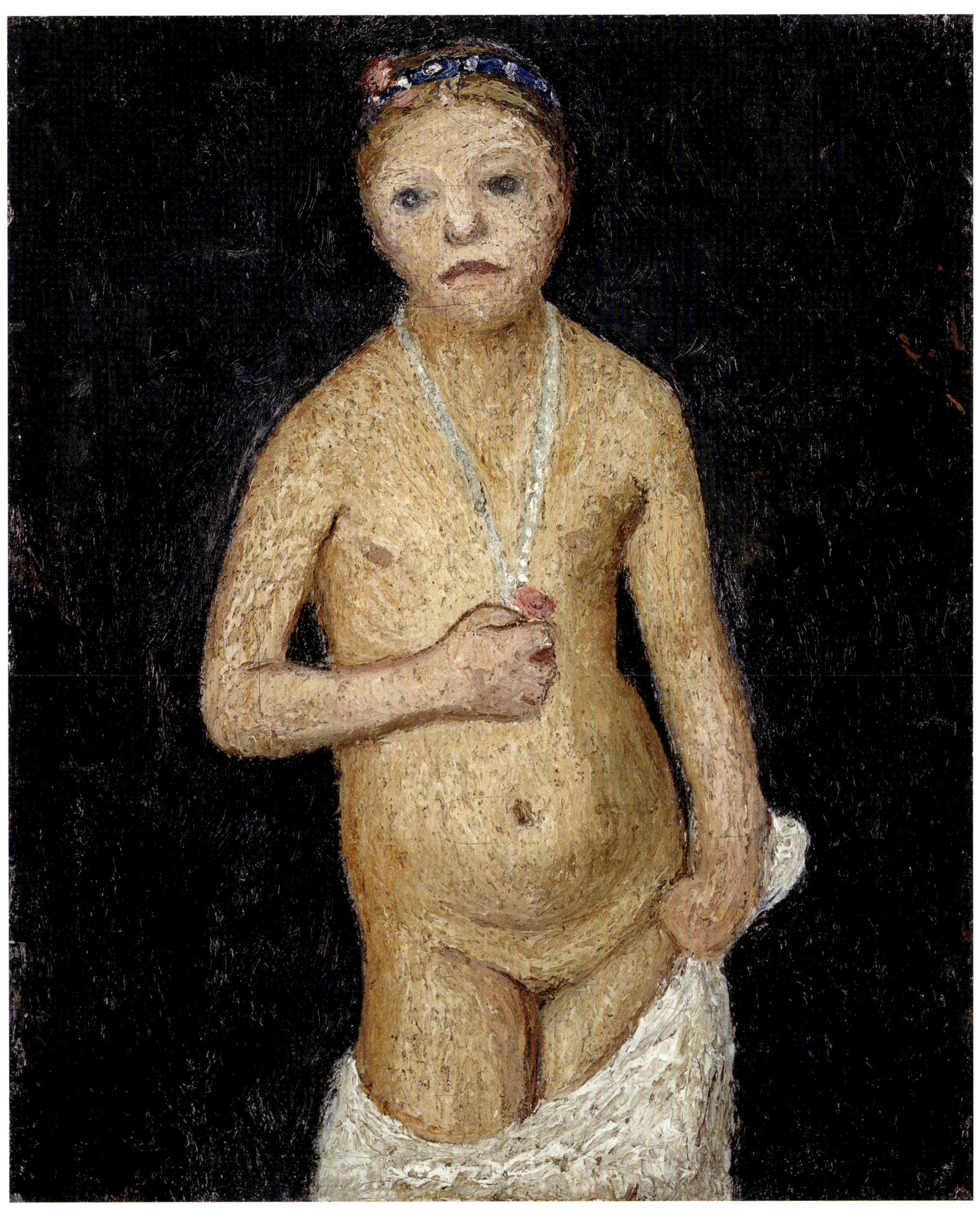

Kleiner stehender Mädchenakt mit Halskette und Rose / Small Standing Nude Girl with Necklace and Rose, 1906

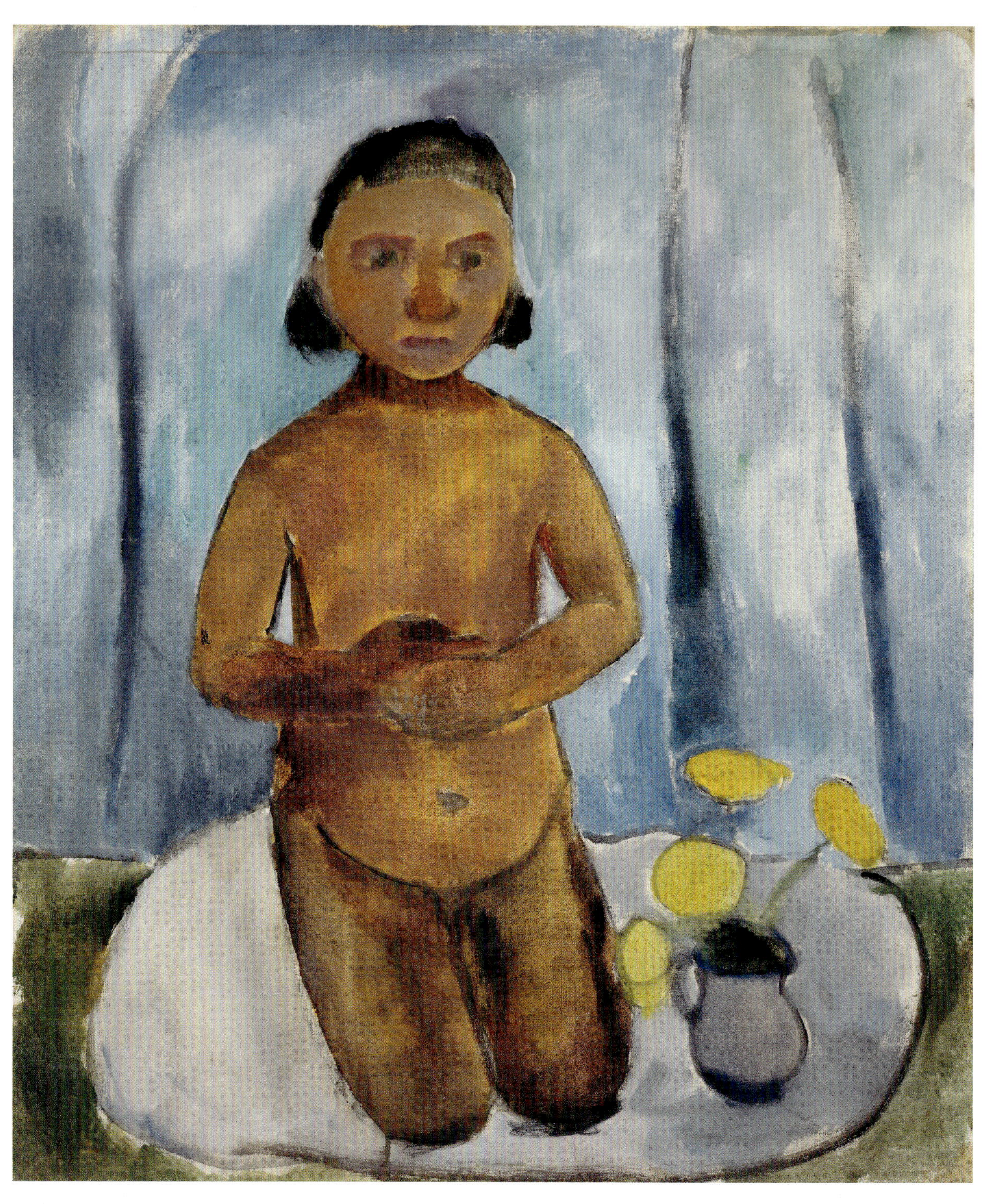

Kniender Mädchenakt vor blauem Vorhang / Nude Girl Kneeling in Front of a Blue Curtain, 1906/7

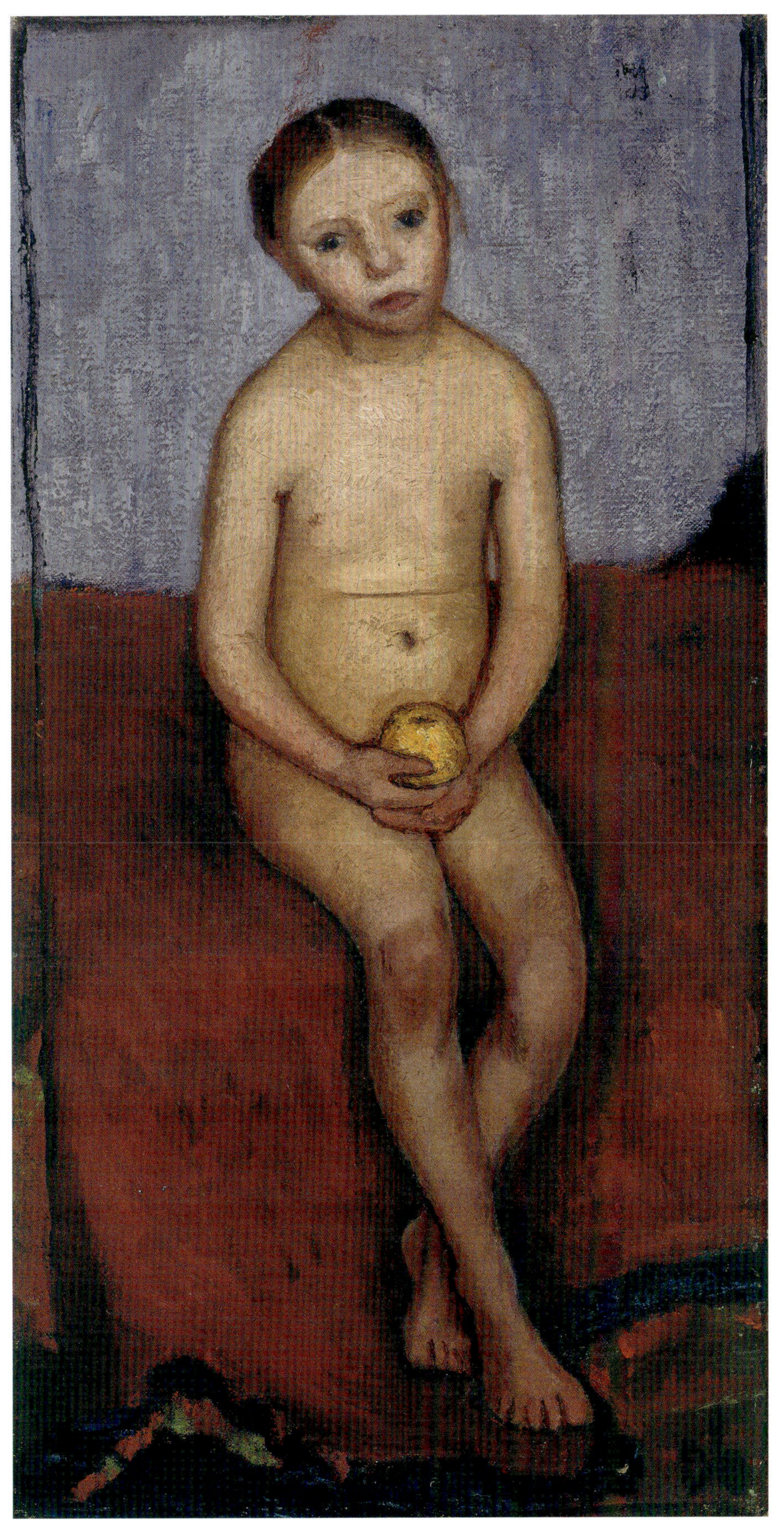

Sitzender Mädchenakt mit Apfel / Seated Nude Girl with an Apple, 1906

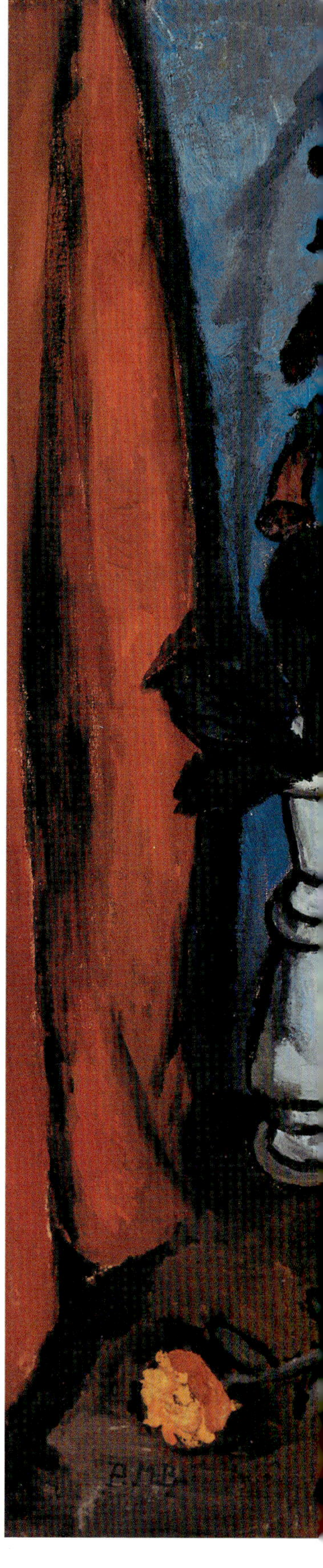

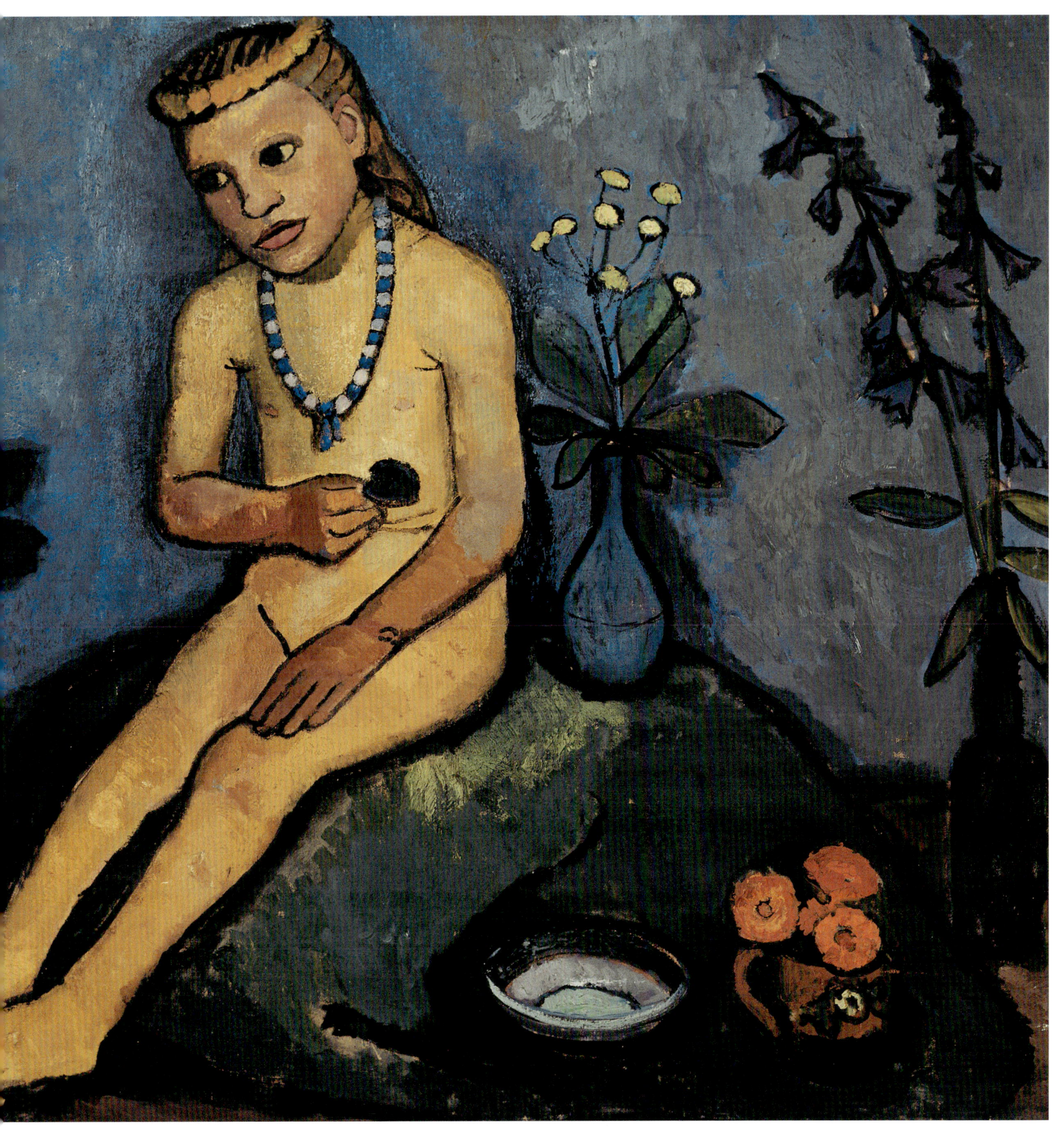

Mädchenakt mit Blumenvasen / Nude Girl with Flower Vases, 1906/7

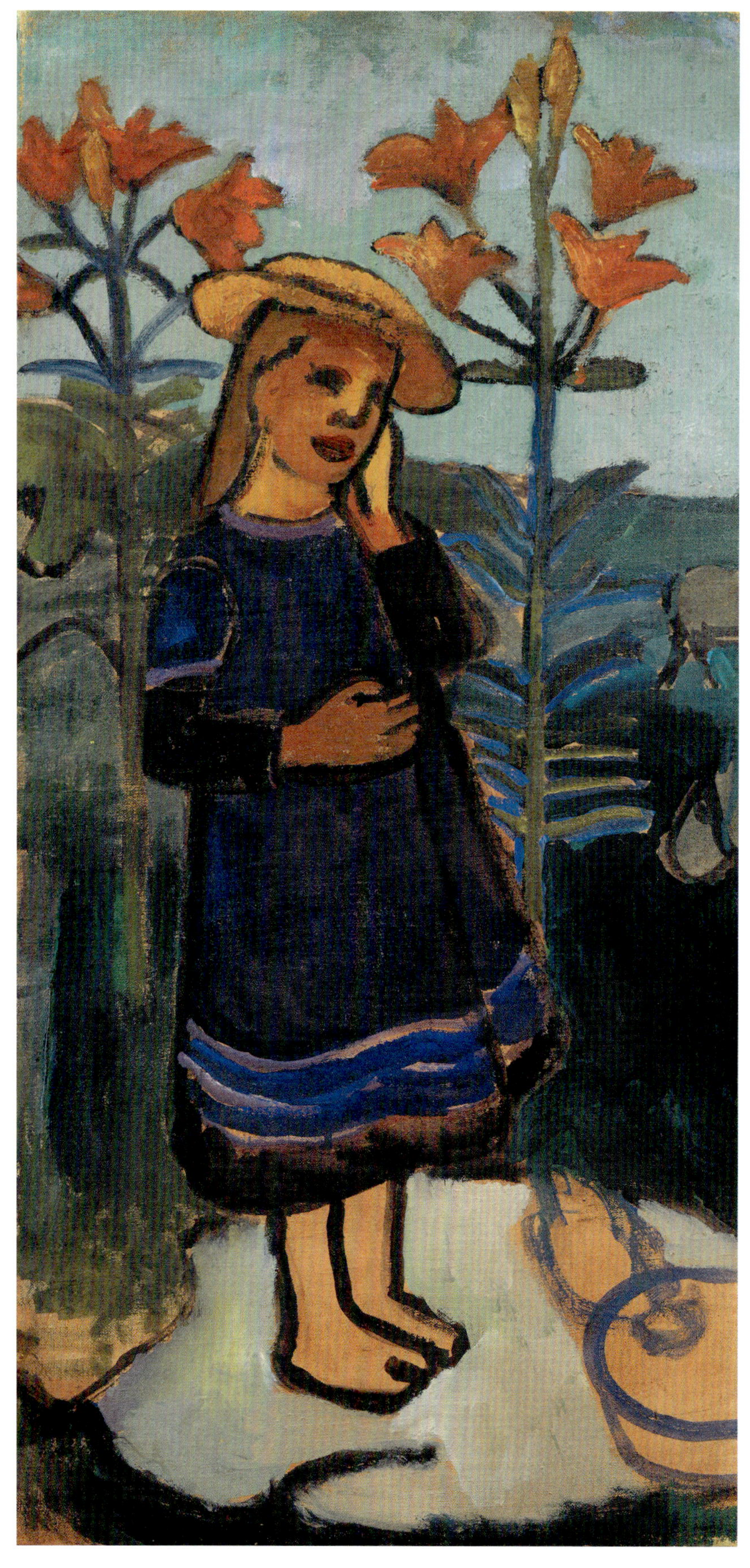

Elsbeth zwischen Feuerlilien / Elsbeth among Fire Lillies, 1907

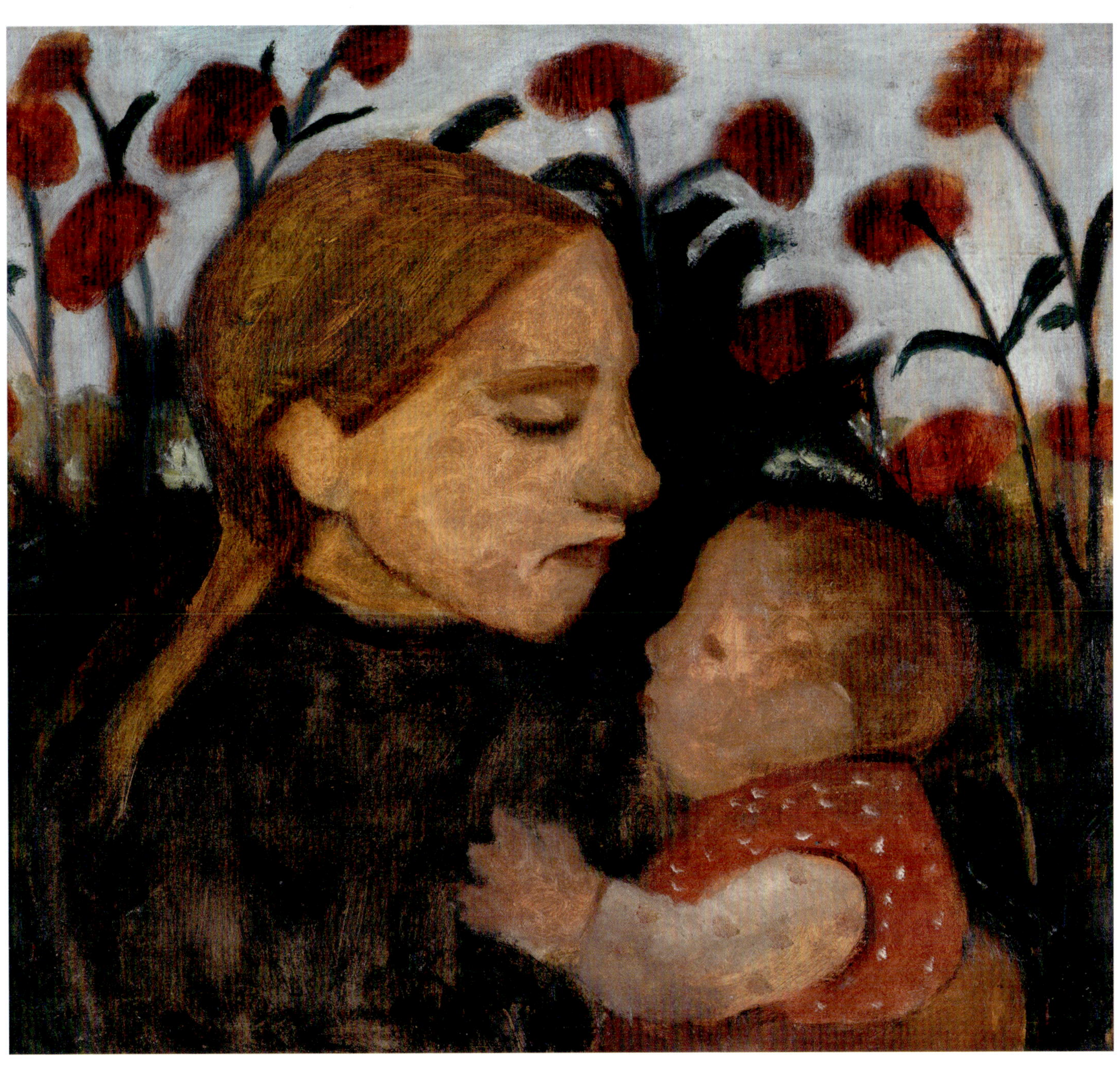

Mädchen mit Kind vor roten Blumen / Girl with Child in Front of Red Flowers, 1902

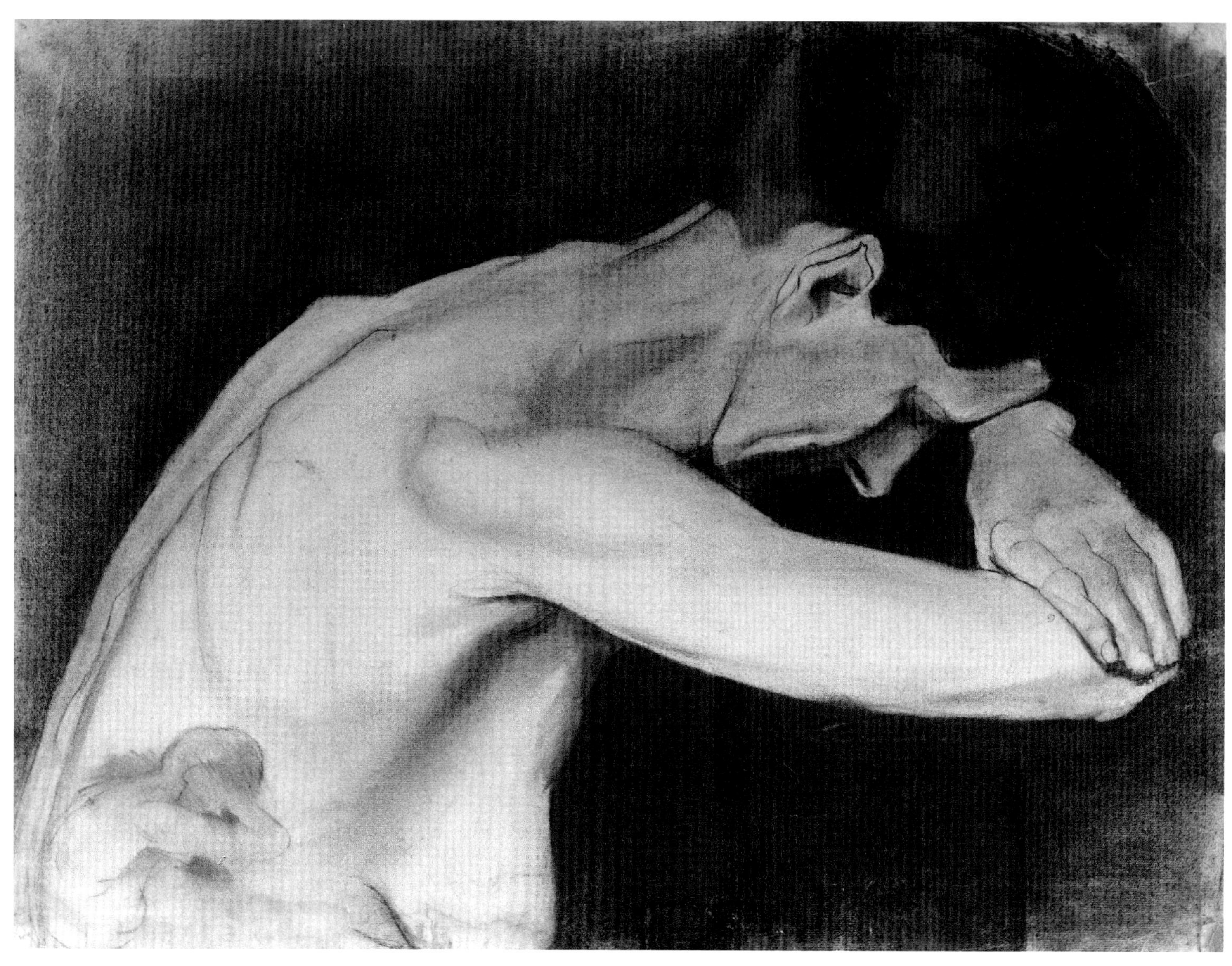

Oberkörper eines nach rechts gebeugten weiblichen Aktes sowie eine kleine Skizze desselben Motivs /
Torso of a Female Nude Bent Forward to the Right and a Small Sketch of the Same Motif, 1898

YEARS OF STUDY AND TRAVEL

PAULA MODERSOHN-BECKER'S STUDIES IN LONDON, BERLIN, AND PARIS

ANNA HAVEMANN

Paula Modersohn-Becker was an artist who signed and dated her works early on, so that roughly 150 works, predominantly on paper, can be attributed to her time as an art student. Her years of study began in London in October 1892, continued in Berlin, and ended in Paris in June 1900.[1] If the London period can be described as a preparatory course and the Parisian period as advanced education, then her two-year study period at the Drawing and Painting School of the Verein der Berliner Künstlerinnen (Association of Female Berlin Artists) falls into the role of the main study period.[2] The astonishing thing about Becker's artistic career is that she received academic training despite the fact that women were not admitted to art academies at that time. She completed her training at the school of the Association of Female Berlin Artists.[3]

According to her biographers, the artist discovered her enthusiasm for drawing by chance. At the age of sixteen, Paula Becker was sent to live with wealthy relatives in England in order to learn how to be confident in social interaction and homemaking and thus increase her chances of finding a suitable husband.[4] She received her first private drawing lessons at her aunt's country estate. Because of her immediately apparent talent and interest, she continued drawing lessons at a private art school in London. In mid-October 1892, she began working according to a strict curriculum at St. John's Wood Art School every other day from 10:00 am to 4:00 pm. Drawings from this period based on plaster casts of Greek busts are preserved in the artist's estate.[5]

1—For more detailed information on her early work, see, among others: Anne Röver, "Laienzeichnen – Akademisches Zeichnen – Freies Zeichnen," in: exh. cat. Bremen 1985, pp. 1–10; Stamm 2007.
2—At its founding, it called itself "Verein der Künstlerinnen und Kunstfreundinnen zu Berlin," from 1919 onwards "Verein der Künstlerinnen zu Berlin," and since 1948 "Verein der Berliner Künstlerinnen 1867 e. V." (VdBK); see: Havemann 2019; exh. cat. Berlin 1992.
3—See: D. Fuhrmann and K. Jestaedt, "Die Zeichen- und Malschule des Vereins der Berliner Künstlerinnen," in: exh. cat. Berlin 1992, pp. 353–366; see also the archive of the VdBK in the Akademie der Künste, Berlin.
4—See, among others: Stamm 2007. Becker lived with Marie Hill, her father's half-sister, from April to December 1892.
5—The estate is maintained by the Paula-Modersohn-Becker-Stiftung, Bremen.

Back in Bremen, both she and her older sister Milly were urged to complete a two-year teacher training course.[6] Her parents took the modern view that their daughters also needed to be financially independent. They financed additional drawing lessons with the aim of giving her the opportunity to work as a drawing teacher (fig. 1).[7] A career as a professional artist was not part of their plan; on the contrary, they asked her in numerous letters to discontinue her art studies and seek employment as a teacher. But Becker had only one desire from the very beginning: to become a painter. "You are indeed alive, you are happy, your life is intense, which is to say: You are painting. Oh, were it not for painting!" one can read in the diary of the then twenty-one-year-old.[8] Throughout her entire training, she expressed to her parents how happy her art studies made her and how grateful she was for the support she received. She attempted to provide proof of her progress by frequently sending artworks home for inspection.

Paula Becker worked in a time of great social change, in which the exclusion of women artists from the art world became increasingly evident. Among other things, women were not permitted to study at art academies or participate in public competitions. They were excluded from being elected as academy members and had no access to many exhibition forums. Even established women artists had to defend themselves against accusations of dilettantism.[9]

1 Plein-air painters in Worpswede, led by Fritz Overbeck, photographed by Hermine Rohte 1896

2 The women's studio led by William Bougereau at the Académie Julian, 1893

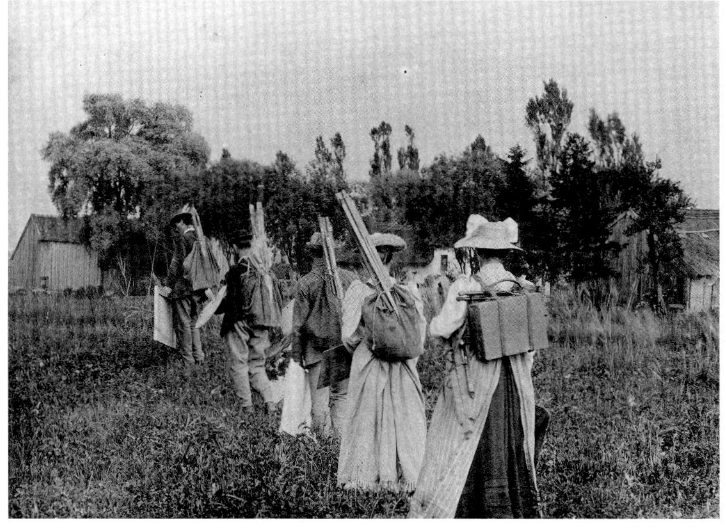

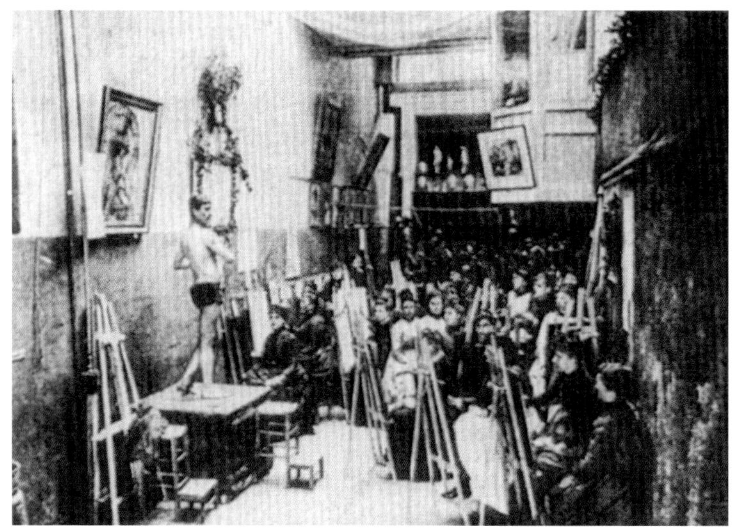

6—See, for example, the letter from her father, dated May 11, 1896 in: Busch / Reinken 1979, p. 81. After her father's early retirement, financial worries burdened the family. Her mother even took in a well-paying American woman as a pensioner in order to be able to continue financing Becker's art studies; see the letter from her mother, dated December 5, 1896, in: ibid., p. 86.
7—The drawing lessons that the parents organized for her during her teacher training are difficult to verify.
8—Diary, Worpswede, July 24, 1897, in: Busch / Reinken 1979, pp. 100f. [translated].
9—For more information, see: Berger 1982; Havemann 2015.

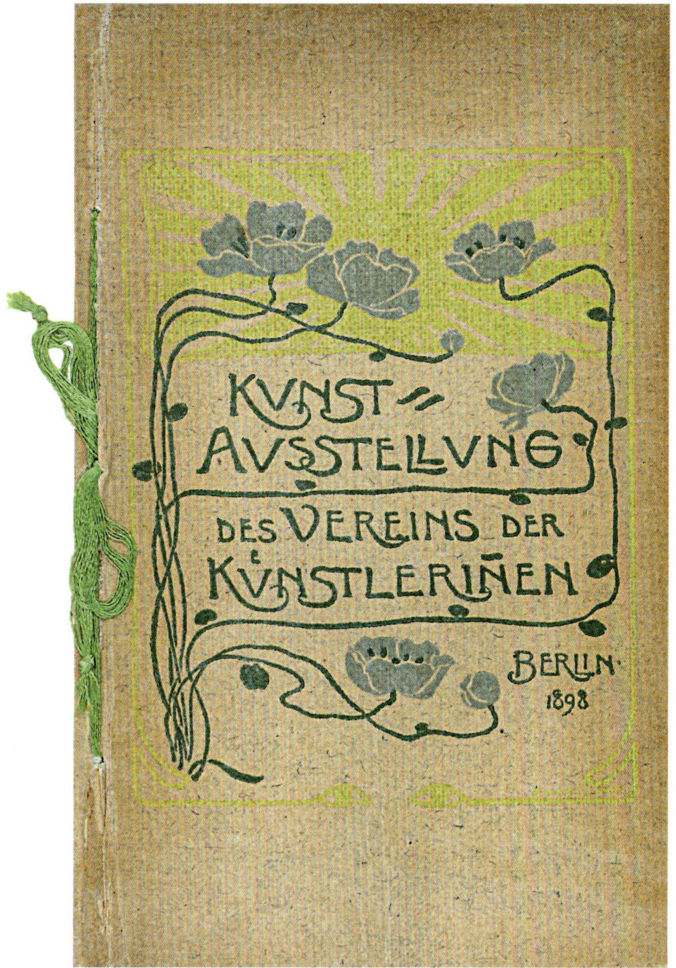

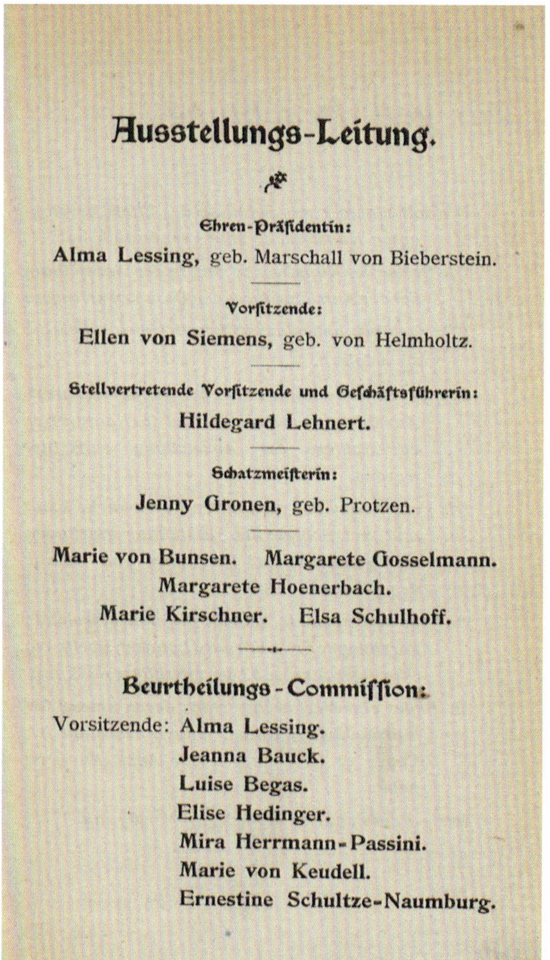

Ausstellungs-Leitung.

Ehren-Präsidentin:
Alma Lessing, geb. Marschall von Bieberstein.

Vorsitzende:
Ellen von Siemens, geb. von Helmholtz.

Stellvertretende Vorsitzende und Geschäftsführerin:
Hildegard Lehnert.

Schatzmeisterin:
Jenny Gronen, geb. Protzen.

Marie von Bunsen. Margarete Gosselmann.
Margarete Hoenerbach.
Marie Kirschner. Elsa Schulhoff.

Beurtheilungs-Commission:

Vorsitzende: Alma Lessing.
Jeanna Bauck.
Luise Begas.
Elise Hedinger.
Mira Herrmann-Passini.
Marie von Keudell.
Ernestine Schultze-Naumburg.

3 Catalog of the exhibition of the Association of Female Berlin Artists, 1898

From the mid-nineteenth century onwards, women fought their way with great courage into less conservative educational institutions, such as the newly founded arts and crafts schools. Sensing opportunities to earn money, additional private art schools opened in many places and admitted women artists for overpriced tuition. In some cases, the tuition was six times higher at private schools than at the state-supported academies (fig. 2).[10] For Becker, the art school of the Association of Female Berlin Artists in particular was of crucial importance. After obtaining a reduction in school fees, she studied there from April 1896 to May 1898, interrupted only by a few trips to visit relatives, as well as study visits to Worpswede, where she was taught by Fritz Mackensen. During this time, she was supported not only by her parents but also by other relatives, some of whom she stayed with, while others supported her financially. Although the art school of the Association of Female Berlin Artists is mentioned in the biographical texts on Becker, neither the historical uniqueness of this institution nor the role it played in the life of the young artist is emphasized (fig. 3).

10 —Cf. Röver 1985, p. 10.

The Association of Female Berlin Artists was founded in 1867 at a time when women were forbidden to organize themselves or be politically active. As if the founding members had suspected that women would not be admitted to state-supported art academies until 1919, they opened an art school for women as early as October 1868. It was the first of its kind and within a very short time advanced to become the central training center for women painters and sculptors. During its seventy-six-year existence, it was headed exclusively by female directors. In 1871, a state-approved seminar for the training of female drawing teachers was added. Since the association had financially strong and well-connected supporting members, it was also able to organize social security for female artists. To raise additional funds, it organized sales fairs and festivals, among other things. The entrance fees to the costume balls, which were introduced in 1891 and in which only women were allowed to participate, were a reliable source of income.

4 Stehender männlicher Akt / Standing Male Nude, c. 1897/98, charcoal on paper, 62.1 x 42.8 cm, Paula-Modersohn-Becker-Stiftung, Bremen

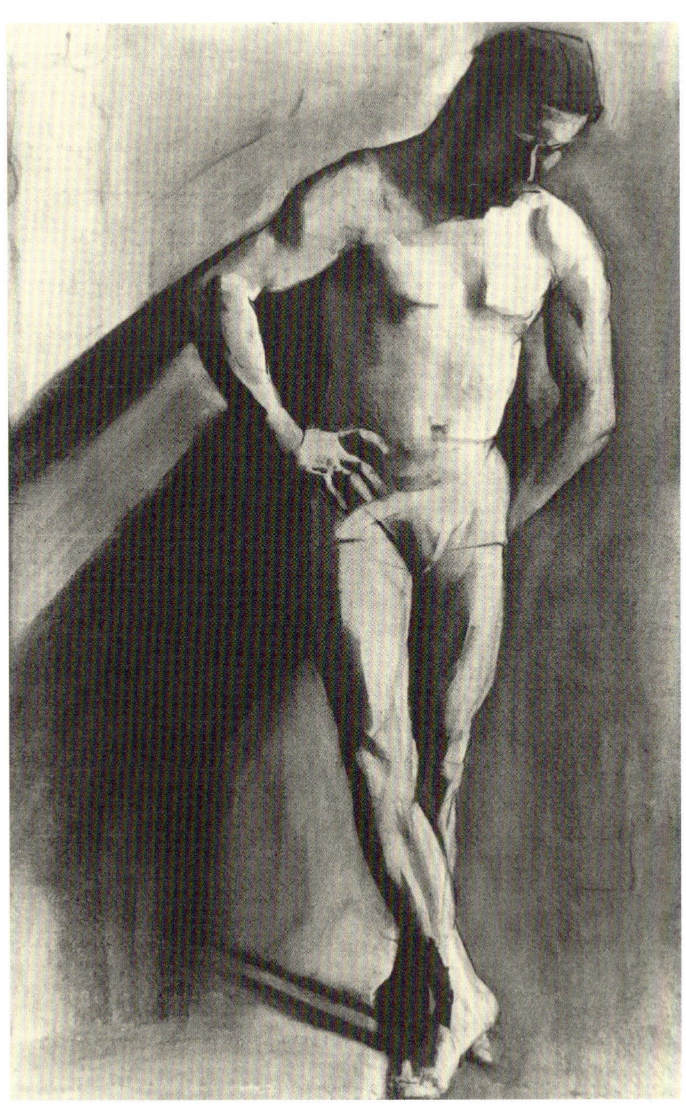

The balls were a cultural highlight of the winter season. Becker attended the event in 1897. She described the evening to her parents, during which 2,800 women celebrated exuberantly with each other: "The costume ball of the female artists is one of my most beautiful memories. I can still feel it in my whole body, and my heart leaps with joy [...] There was dancing with passion. A fine evening!"[11]

It is a special historical achievement of the Drawing and Painting School of the Association of Female Berlin Artists that it was structured according to a strict academic curriculum in order to make the female students competitive with male artists. What was innovative was that, in addition to drawing courses, various artistic techniques and genres such as landscape, portrait, and flower painting were offered, as well as theoretical subjects such as perspective, anatomy, and art history. It was also groundbreaking that, from 1875 onwards, there was a nude drawing class in which only aspiring professional women painters were admitted. It should also be emphasized that, unlike many private studios, several professors—above all, female professors—taught here.

11—Letter to her parents, Berlin, February 19, 1897, in: Busch / Reinken 1979, pp. 120f. [translated].

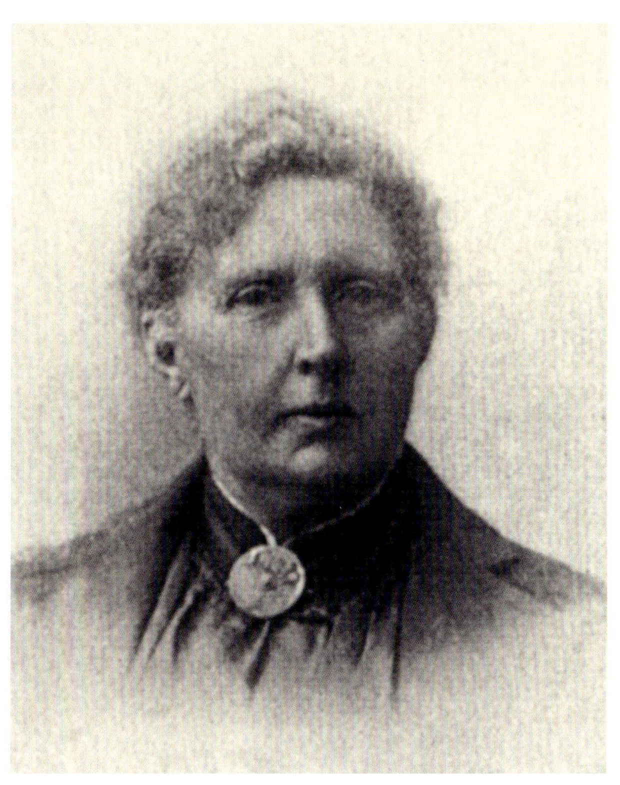

5 Jeanna Bauck, 1902

Becker studied together with 420 other students who were divided into twenty-two classes and could choose from 748 different subjects.[12] From 1895 onwards, the school was located in a prime location on Potsdamer Strasse, in its own building constructed for this purpose, with six 90-square-meter study rooms.[13] In contrast to the cramped conditions in London or Paris, the working conditions here were ideal. Becker wrote to her younger sister Herma in November 1897: "I wish you could be with me just for a moment so that I could show you my school. We have [...] classrooms [...] with very large windows. There are [...] many easels [...]. All along the walls, paintings hang to dry. This makes the whole atmosphere so cheerful and colorful. Between classes, when we eat our breakfast, we are [...] merry [...]. Sometimes, we even waltz."[14] The large skylight hall was also used by the association. Meetings, social gatherings, and lectures were held here. Becker attended a lecture in January 1897, about which she reported: "Last Friday, after the life drawing class, I attended a lecture: 'Goethe and the Women's Emancipation.' The lecturer, Fräulein von Milde, spoke very clearly and very well—and also quite sensibly."[15]

In Berlin, Becker completed a large workload. She studied daily from morning to night, attending lectures in between and using every free hour to visit museums and galleries. Thanks to her prior studies in London, she was able to start working directly from a live model. She initially drew portraits of mostly old men and women in red chalk and charcoal, which were highly praised. As a result, she was permitted to switch to the nude drawing class in the winter of 1896 (fig. 4).

During this time, she created numerous drawings of nude women and semi-nude men, which testify to her intensive study of anatomy. Becker continued these even after her school years in Berlin, as evidenced by a drawing of a nude child with its skeleton visible (p. 116). In her medium-format nude drawings, she focused on the postures and body tension of the models; bone structure and musculature are clearly discernible. Detailed sections are juxtaposed with generously treated surfaces. Outlines define the bodies, which are otherwise treated in a painterly fashion (pp. 148–151). Significantly, until the early twentieth century, male models in nude drawing classes for women were required to wear bathing trunks or loincloths.[16] In contrast, the genitals of female models were not covered in nude drawing classes for men.

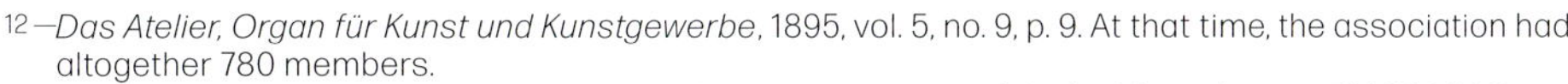

12—*Das Atelier, Organ für Kunst und Kunstgewerbe*, 1895, vol. 5, no. 9, p. 9. At that time, the association had altogether 780 members.
13—According to newspaper advertisements, the purchase price of the building plot was RM 200,000. The Victoria Lyceum, founded in 1869, also moved into the building as a partner.
14—Letter to Herma Becker, Berlin, November 13, 1897, in: Busch / Reinken 1979, pp. 109f. [translated].
15—Letter to her parents, Berlin, January 10, 1897, in: ibid., pp. 87f. [translated] The lecturer was the author Nathalie von Milde (1850–1906), who was active in the women's movement.
16—For more information, see: Berger 1982, p. 103. This is also true of the private art academies in Paris and London.

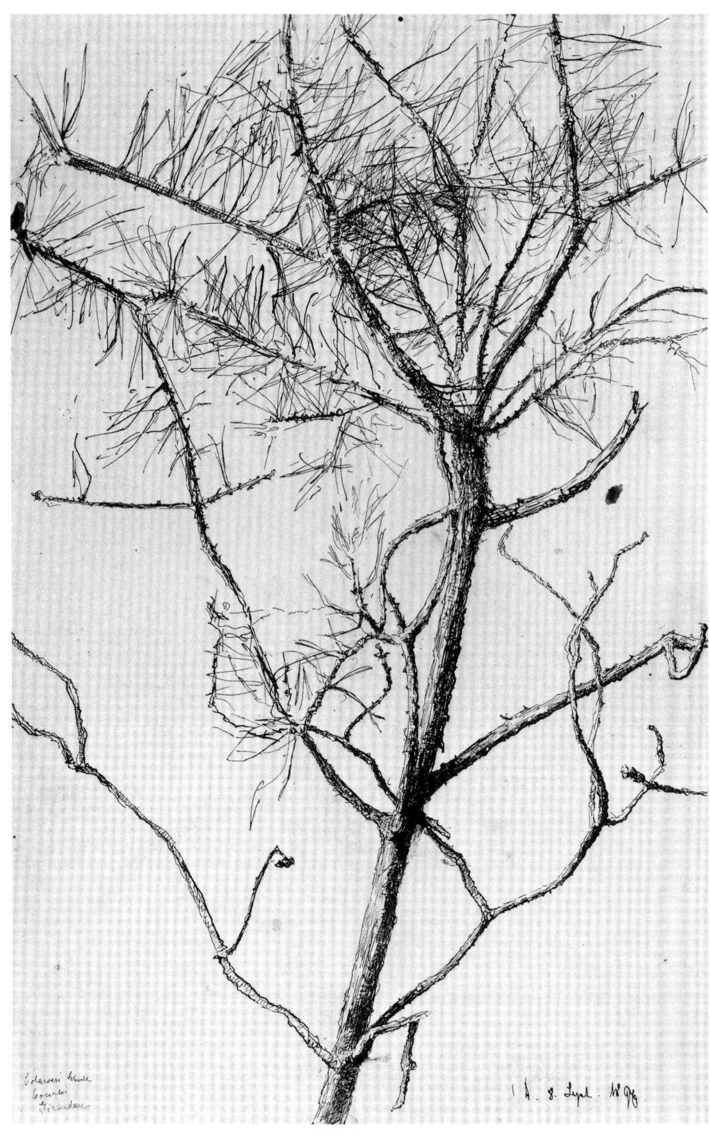

6 Studie eines kahlen Zweiges / Study of a Bare Branch, 1897, pen on paper, 32.9 x 21 cm, Paula-Modersohn-Becker-Stiftung, Bremen

In the fall of 1897, Becker transferred to the portrait class of the Swedish artist Jeanna Bauck (fig. 5). According to her letters, the independent spirit of her teacher made a great impression on her. One can speak of one of the first female teacher-student relationships in an institutional context. Bauck was a great inspiration and role model for Becker on several levels. Becker discerned that it was possible to establish oneself as a woman painter, to found a private school, to live in different European cities, and that it was possible to choose a life for art independent of external constraints. On the small pen and ink drawing of a bare branch dated September 8, 1897, she inscribed "Colarossi School Courtoi[s] Girardeau" (fig. 6). These notes testify to the fact that Bauck reported on her Parisian experiences in her class and encouraged her students to continue their studies there.

Little is known about Jeanna Bauck today.[17] She studied from 1863 onwards at private painting schools in Dresden, Düsseldorf, and Munich and from 1879 onwards spent longer periods in Paris. From 1880 onwards, she exhibited regularly at the Paris Salon. Becker held her teacher in high esteem, both personally and professionally: "Bauck [...] is completely modern, by which I mean, in a good sense, ebulliently youthful. She has retained this despite her fifty years. I love her very much."[18] Becker gratefully accepted her rigorous teaching methods. Although the artistic views of the two women were fundamentally different, Becker's devotion to depicting people can perhaps be traced back to these lessons. Bauck was uncompromising in her support of her students. She was particularly devoted to Becker and even invited her to her studio. "I always look forward to my lessons with Jeanna Bauck. [...] Recently, I visited [...] Bauck in her studio. [...] Fabulous things were hanging there: portraits and landscapes—there is a grand and simple conception in each painting, and yet they are not mannered. Fine, fine!"[19] Their work together came to an abrupt end, however, when Bauck was dismissed at the end of 1897 due to dissonances with the school's principal Margarethe Hoernerbach.[20]

17 —Jeanna Bauck (Stockholm 1840–Munich 1926); see: Corinna Reich, "Zwischen zwei Jahrhunderten – Jeanna Bauck und Paula Modersohn-Becker," in: exh. cat. Buchheim 2020, pp. 13–23.
18 —Letter to her parents, Berlin, October 28, 1897, in: Busch / Reinken 1979, pp. 106f. [translated]
19 —Letter to her parents, Berlin, May 7, 1897, in: ibid., p. 98 [translated].
20 —Margarethe Hoernerbach held the position between 1890 and 1909. Becker reported on the dissonances in a letter to the parents, Berlin, November 7, 1897, in: ibid., pp. 108f.

Shortly afterwards, in May 1898, Becker's time in Berlin also came to an end. From September 1898 onwards, she once again lived and worked in Worpswede and took lessons again with Mackensen. She worked together with several young female artists who had also previously studied at schools run by women artists' associations, such as Marie Bock, Clara Westhoff, and Hermine Rohte Particularly impressive life-size nude drawings from this period (pp. 148, 149) are preserved in Becker's estate.[21]

In this self-set task, she radically dispensed with the loincloth for the male models. She would maintain this bold style of depiction in the years to come (pp. 151, 152). The models, whose physical characteristics are particularly emphasized, are pushed to the foreground. In their monumentality, they almost burst the format. The bodies are not developed as a sum of details but are conceived as a whole. The artist dispensed with spatial relationships and descriptive details. Through this abstraction and a dramatic light-dark contrast, she achieved the strong expression of these works, which would become typical of her later works.

On New Year's Eve 1900, Paula Becker traveled to Paris. Recalling the advice of her teacher Bauck, she enrolled in nude drawing courses at the Académie Colarossi. Her professors were Gustave Courtois and Georges Girardeau. Here as well, she benefited from the struggles of her predecessors, who had won access to the men's studio in 1896.[22] Becker was inspired by the city and became enthusiastic about the Exposition Universelle that was taking place at the time. She visited museums and exhibitions—for, by this time, she was no longer interested in learning craft and techniques, but rather in forming her own artistic conception.

21—See the diary entry dated November 11, 1898, in: ibid., p. 141.
22—For more on Becker's time in Paris, see: Berger 2007.

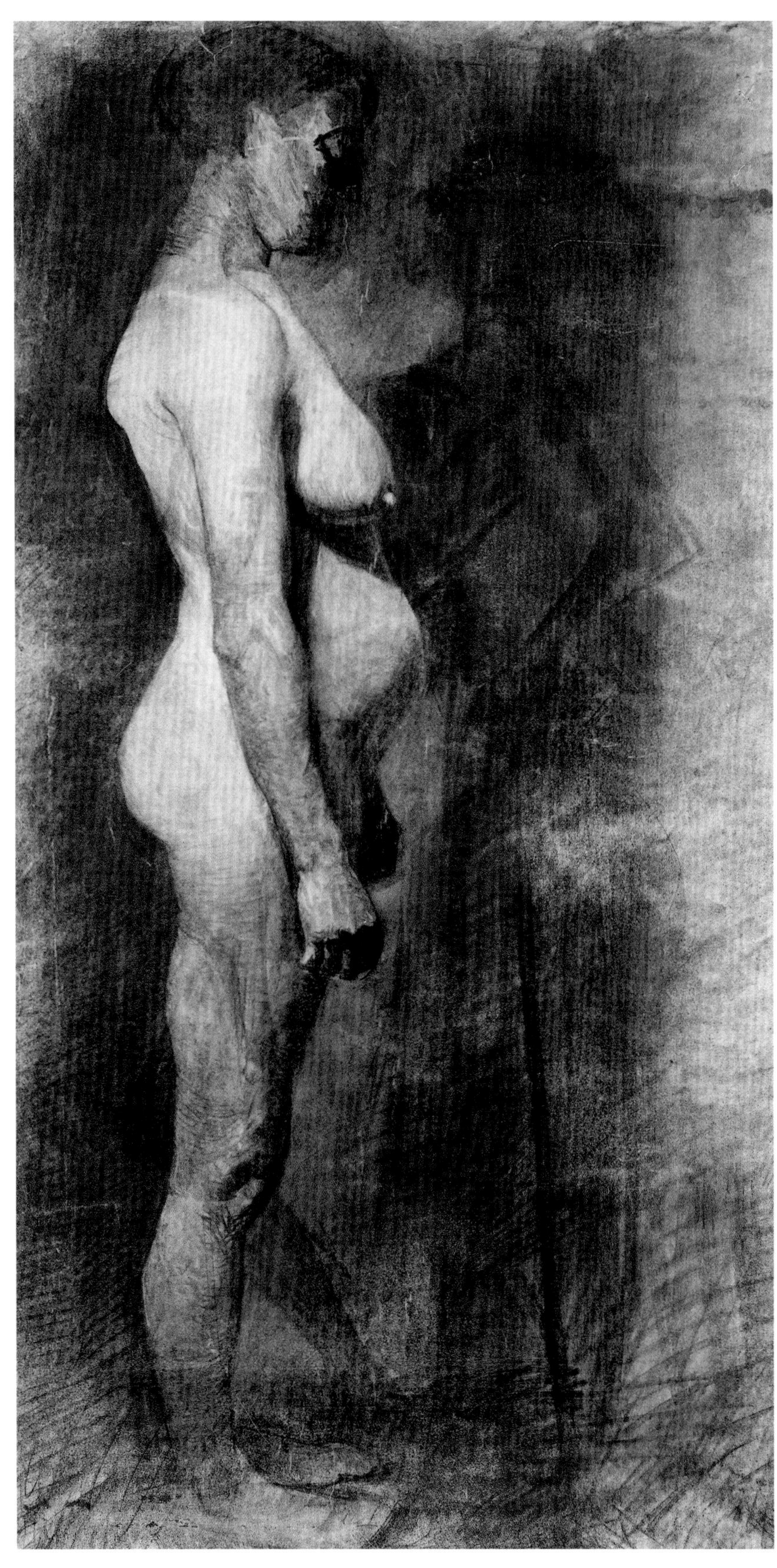

Stehender weiblicher Akt im Profil nach rechts /
Standing Female Nude in Profile, Turned to the Right, 1898

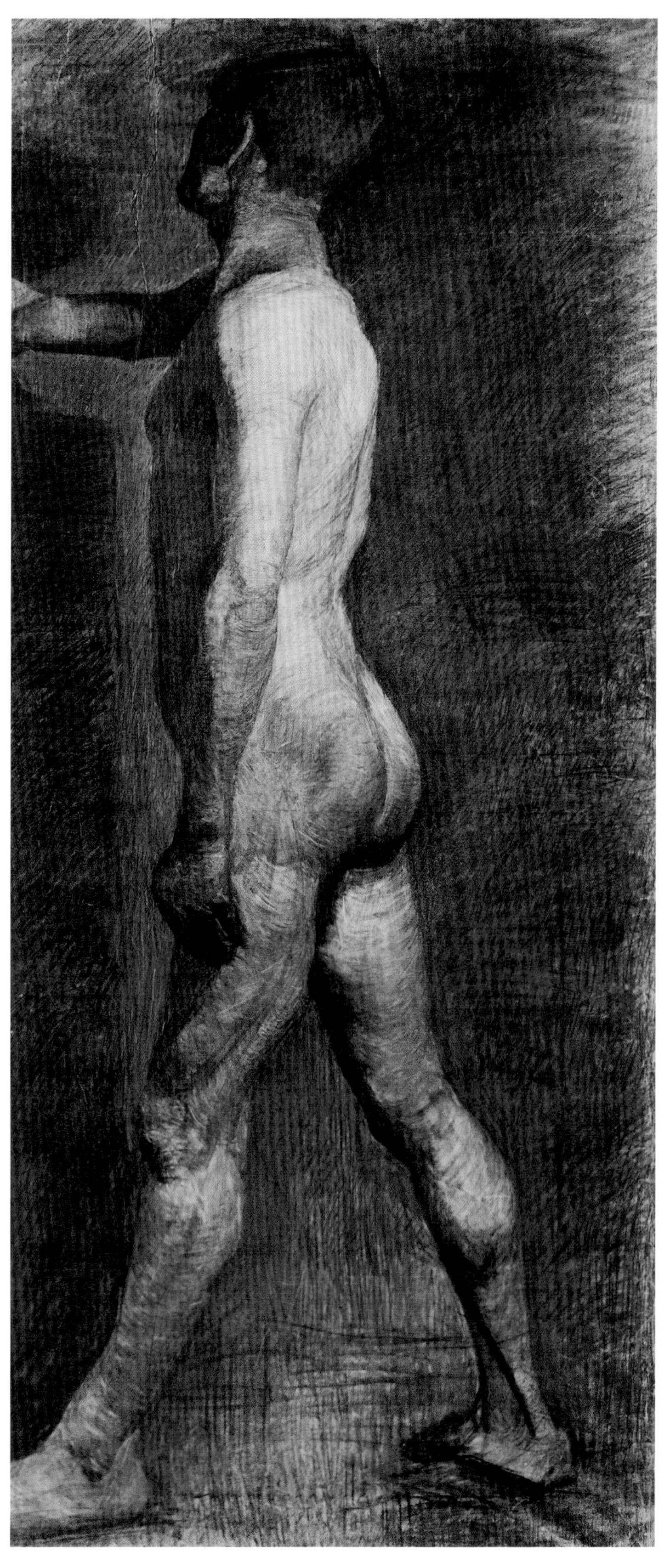

Stehender männlicher Akt nach links /
Standing Male Nude Turned to the Left, 1898

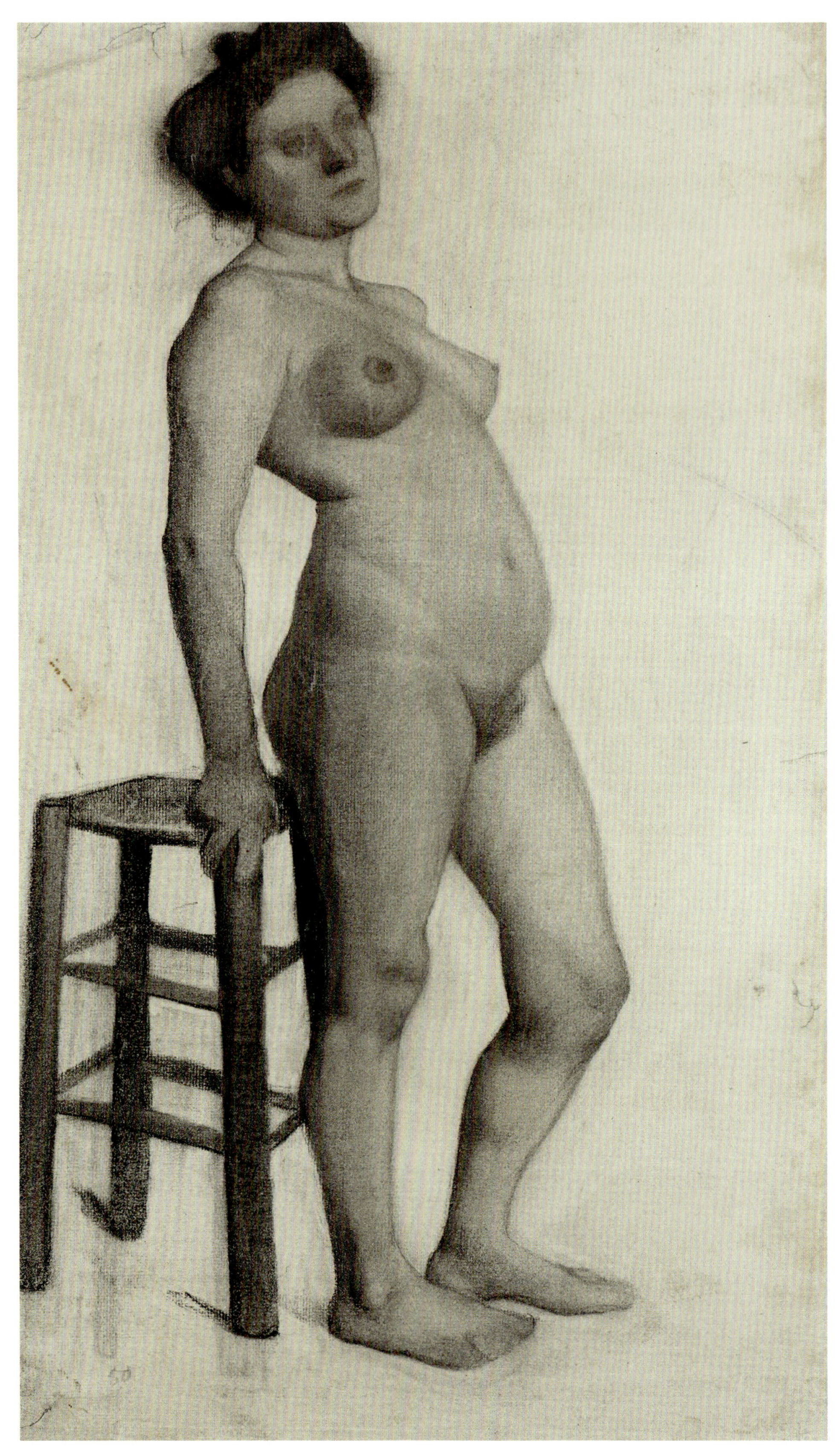

Stehender weiblicher Akt nach halbrechts, auf einen Hocker gestützt /
Large Standing Female Nude, Turned to the Right, with Studio Stool, c. 1906

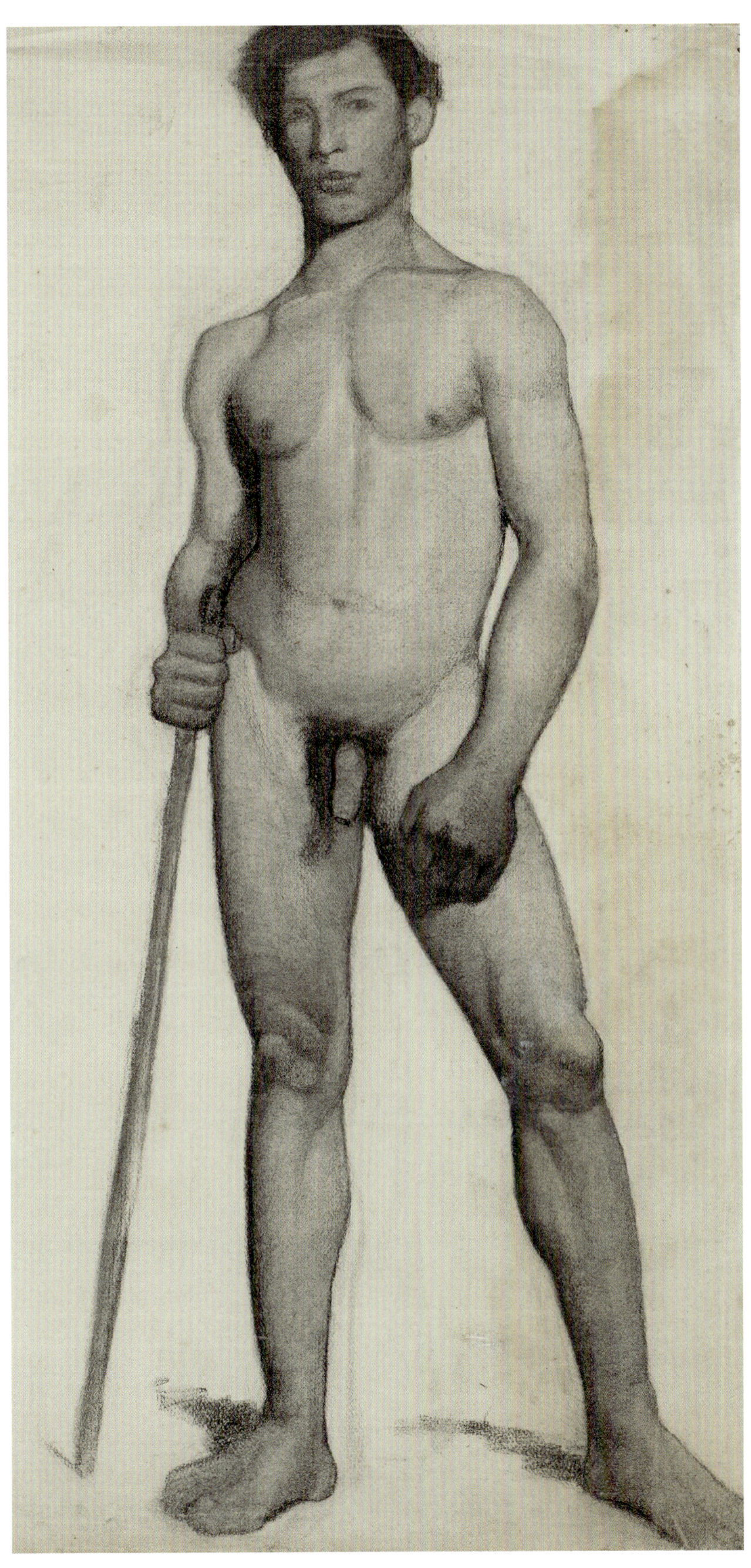

Stehender männlicher Akt frontal, in der Rechten einen Stab /
Frontal Standing Male Nude with a Staff in His Right Hand, c. 1906

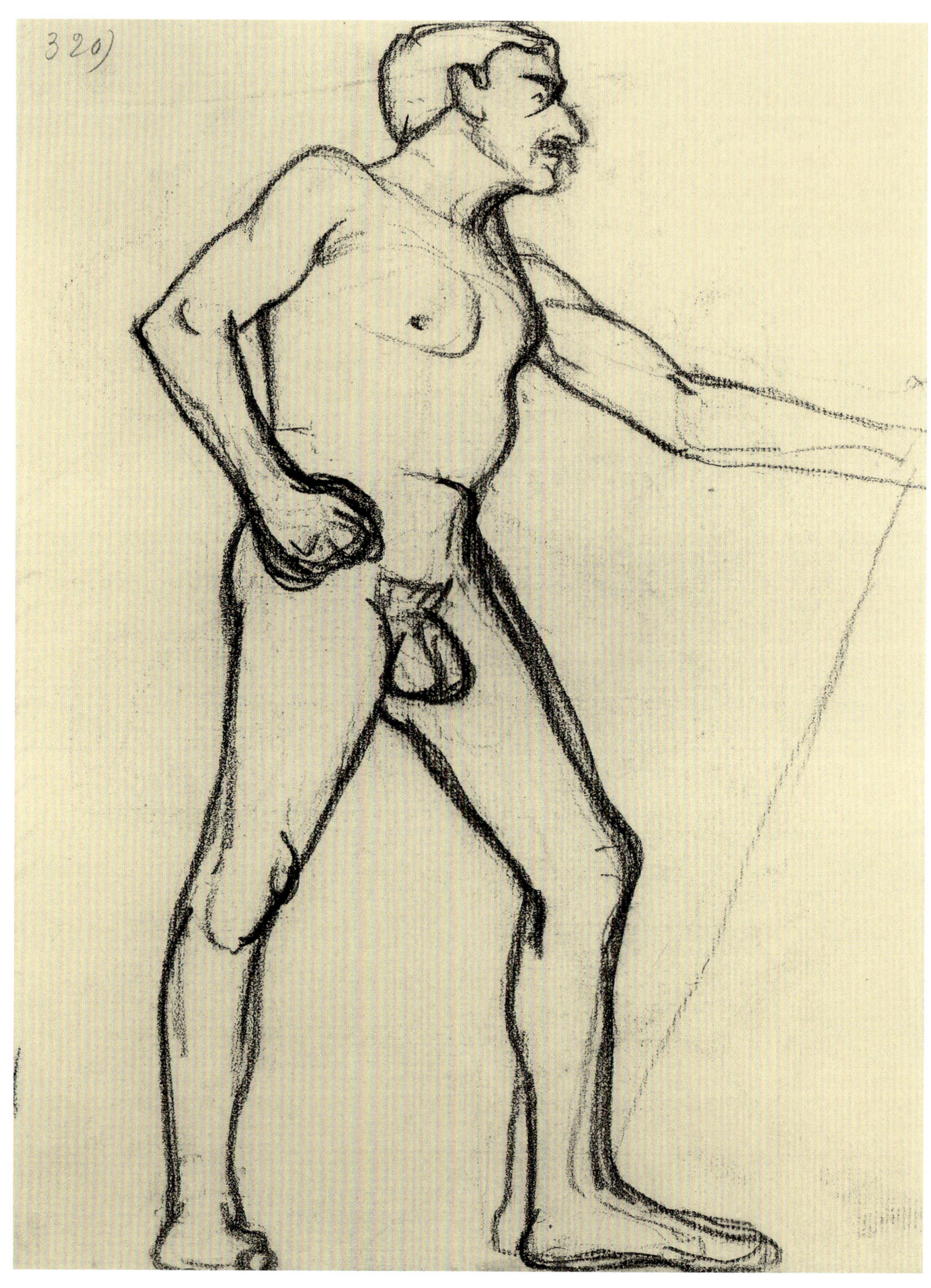

Stehender männlicher Akt nach rechts / Standing Male Nude, Turned to the Right, Paris 1905

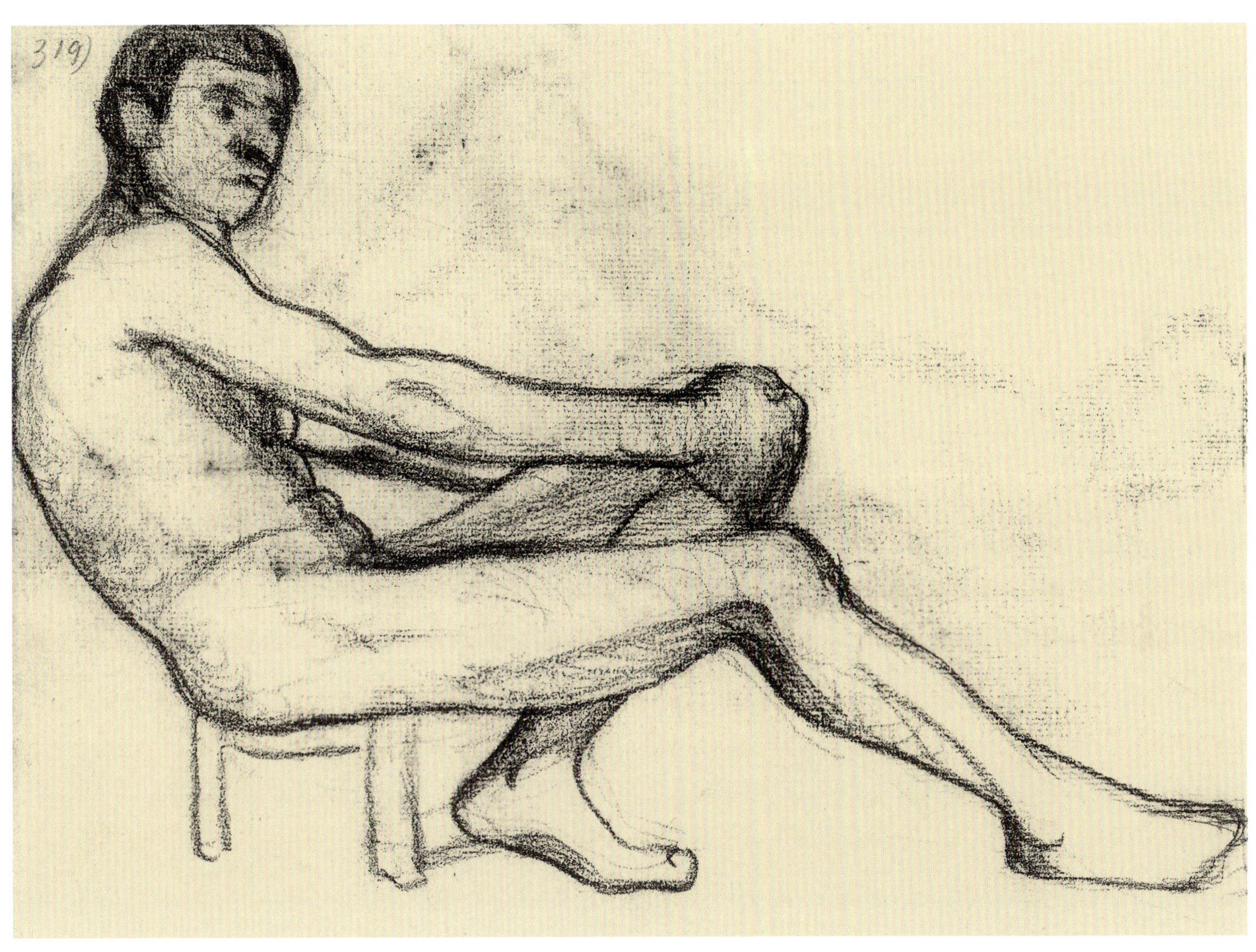

Auf einem niedrigen Hocker sitzender männlicher Akt nach rechts / Male Nude Seated on a Low Stool, Turned to the Right, Paris 1905

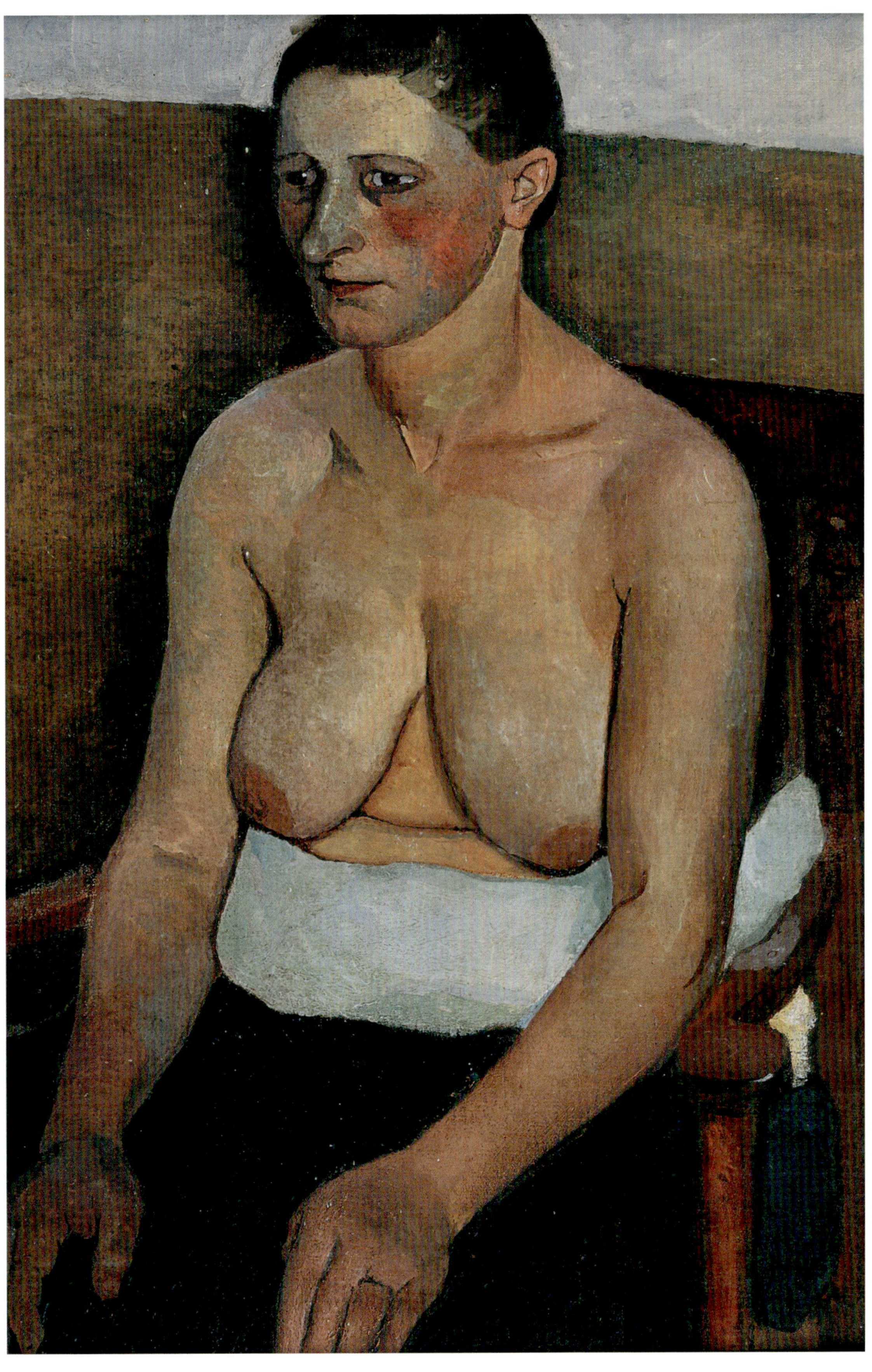

Halbakt einer sitzenden Bäuerin / Half-Length Nude of a Seated Peasant Woman, 1900

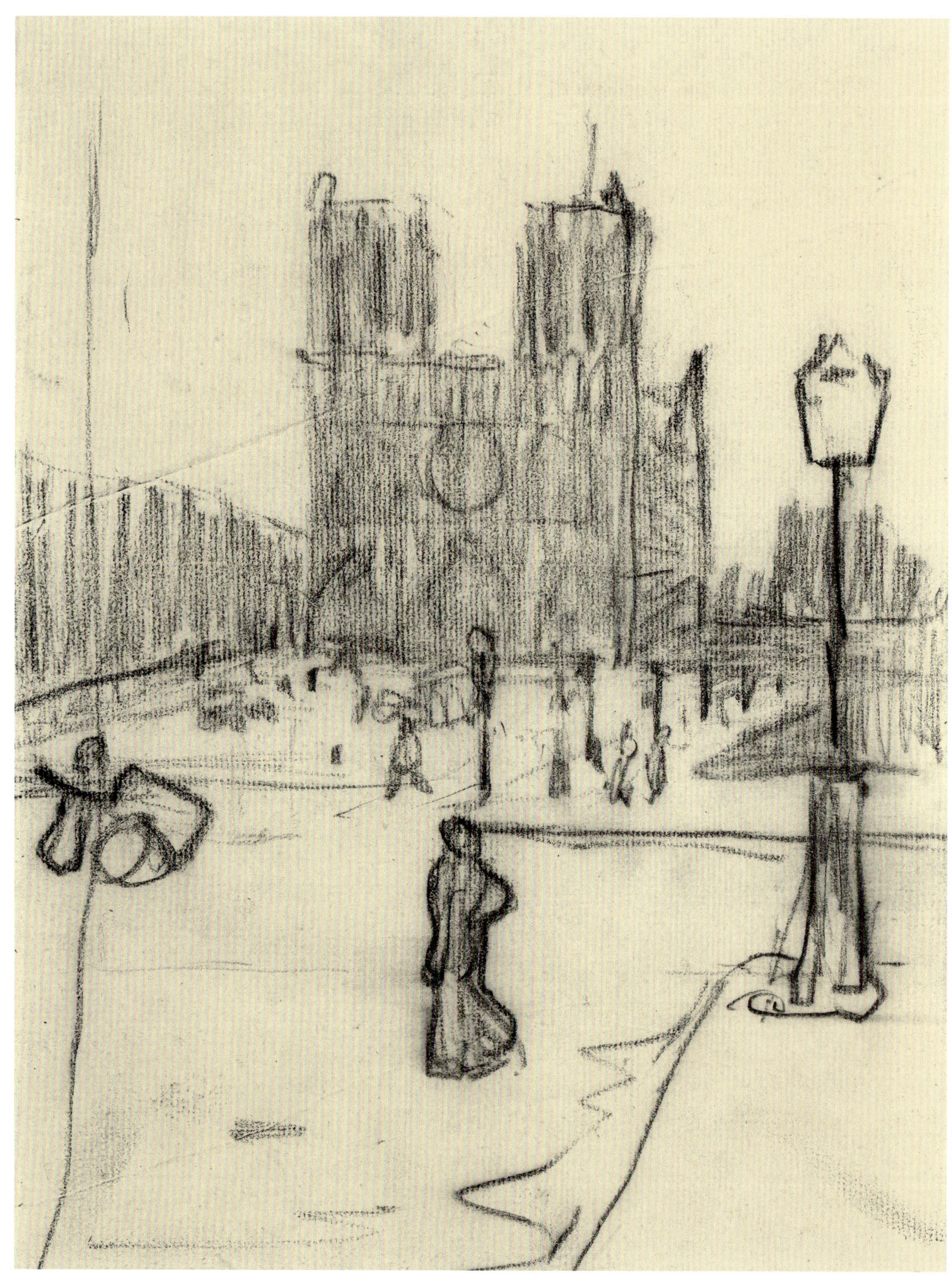

Fassade Notre-Dame (recto) Notre Dame von der Seine her gesehen (verso) /
The Façade of Notre-Dame (recto) Notre-Dame seen from the Seine (verso), c. 1905/6

PARALLEL PHENOMENA

PAULA MODERSOHN-BECKER AND MODERNISM

RAINER STAMM

On the occasion of the major exhibitions marking the centenary of Paula Modersohn-Becker's death in 2007, the *Frankfurter Allgemeine Zeitung* ran an article proudly and somewhat bewilderedly titled: "Germany's Picasso is a Woman." Alongside the astonishment that the pioneer of modernism was a woman, the formulation marked a change in the perception of the artist and her works: no longer was the attention directed at the woman from Worpswede, who had further developed the Secession style of the artists' colony with birch and moor landscapes, but now at a woman artist who, at the beginning of the twentieth century, had liberated painting from its illustrative function and sought new forms. The name "Picasso" was synonymous with the departure into the adventure of the avant-gardes, and indeed some of Modersohn-Becker's pictorial creations, especially from her last sojourns in Paris in 1905 and 1906/7, touch on Picasso's works in a startling way. But equally the name of Matisse could have been invoked, whose works were simultaneously seeking new formulations.

As early as 1903, the artist reflected on the desire for a radical simplification of her painting through the solidification of contours and surfaces. In February of that year, she noted in her journal: "The great simplicity of form – that is something wonderful. Ever since I can remember, I have tried to give the simplicity of nature to the heads I paint or draw. Now I feel deeply how I can learn from the heads of antiquity."[1]

1—Journal entry dated February 20, 1903, in: Günter Busch and Liselotte von Reinken (eds.), *Paula Modersohn-Becker in Briefen und Tagebüchern*, (Frankfurt am Main 2007), p. 410 [translated].

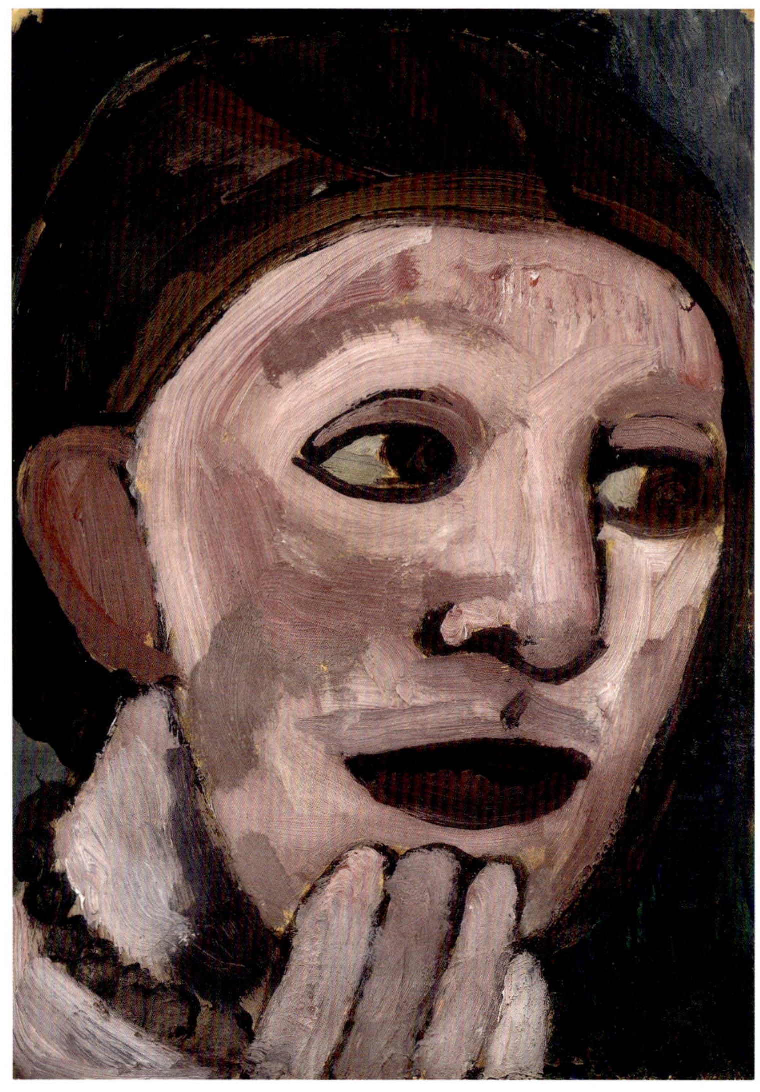

1 Selbstbildnis nach halbrechts, die Hand am Kinn / Self-Portrait Turned to the Right, with Her Hand at Her Chin, summer 1906, oil tempera on paper on cardboard, 27 x 18.7 cm, Private Collection

After the heyday of Impressionism and *plein air* painting in France and Germany, the search for a classical clarity was an issue that preoccupied numerous painters. After the works of Claude Monet, Alfred Sisley, and Camille Pissarro, who had virtuously dissected reality into brushstrokes, and the subsequent varieties of Divisionism, through which forms and surfaces were further dissolved—even as far as pointillist dots—a countermovement had begun: The painters of the Nabis, Émile Bernard, Paul Sérusier and Maurice Denis, combined forms into color surfaces. In so-called Cloisonnism, these were delimited—as by the metal stems in enamel work or stained glass—with the help of black lines, in order to create areas of color and to contain forms. After a brief phase of Fauvism, Henri Matisse had also taken up this impulse and framed his self-portrait of 1906—like Picasso's self-portrait with his upper body exposed of the same year—with black lines (figs. 1, 2).

While Paula Modersohn-Becker put her reflection on the search for the "great simplicity of form" into words in her diary, Matisse expressed himself publicly in his *Notes of a Painter* (1908), in which he wrote about the aspiration of his art to overcome the Impressionist dissolution: Impressionism had rendered "fleeting impressions"; what he was now striving for was a new "stability" and a "more lasting interpretation" of reality. He insisted on reproducing not a superficial impression, but on composing a picture: "If there is order and clarity in the picture, it means that from the outset this same order and clarity existed in the mind of the painter, or that the painter was conscious of their necessity. [...] What I dream of is an art of balance, of purity and serenity, devoid of troubling or depressing subject matter."[2]

The return of painting to composition, to a quasi-architectonic structure and—after the dissolution of Impressionism—to a new sense of coherence and commitment was an aspect that was particularly important to Paula Modersohn-Becker, as it was to her contemporaries Ferdinand Hodler and Karl Hofer. In her still life and figure

2—Henri Matisse, "Notes of a Painter," in: Jack D. Flam, *Matisse on Art* (New York 1978), pp. 35–40, here p. 38.

paintings, she combined objects and figures into compositions, the logic of which followed only the laws inherent in the picture. Whereas, in Worpswede, she had made the simplicity and clarity of the landscape fruitful for her work, in her last months of creative work in Paris it was above all the simple physicality of things and people that she stylized into timeless compositions.

Like Matisse and countless other painters working in Montparnasse at the time, she made use of the youthful models who offered themselves at the "model market" at the intersection of Rue de la Grande Chaumière and Boulevard Montparnasse: Across from the private art academies Colarossi and Grande Chaumière, "every Monday morning there was a throng of Italian models and the painters who looked at them and engaged them,"[3] recalled the painter Friedrich Ahlers-Hestermann, who came to Paris in 1907. Like Matisse and Ahlers-Hestermann, Modersohn-Becker worked with the young girls of immigrant families who modeled for pay.

2 Henri Matisse, Self-Portrait, 1906, oil on canvas, 55 x 46 cm, SMK – Statens Museum for Kunst, Copenhagen

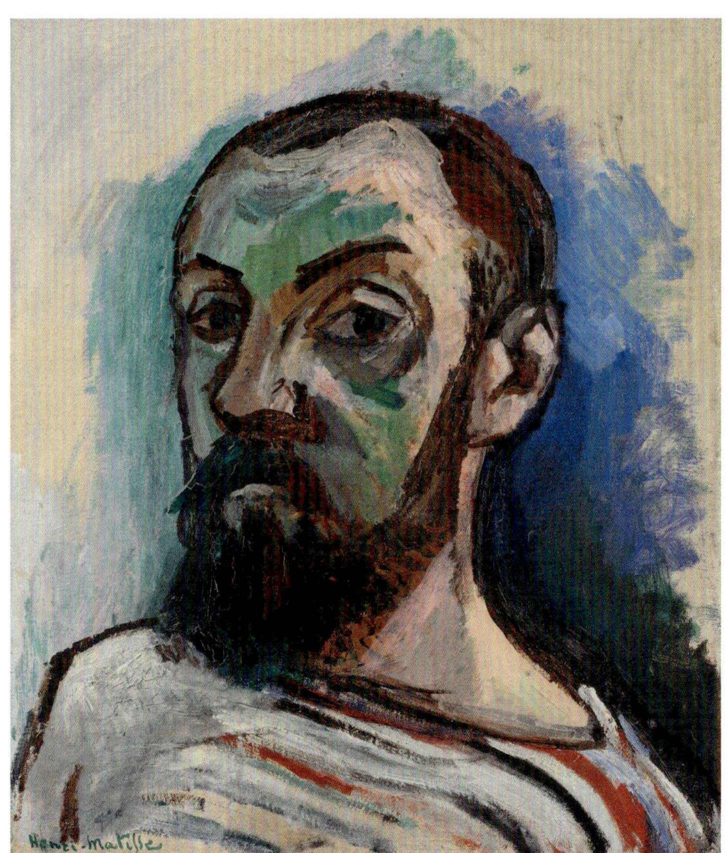

What Ahlers-Hestermann also remembered applies to the *Nude Girl Kneeling in Front of a Blue Curtain* (p. 134), which Modersohn-Becker stylized into a still life in 1906/7: she "was hardly more than a child, brownish, austere, and silent. She sat like a bronze."[4] Without attributes or any action and deprived of any narrative gesture, the girl kneels on a cloth next to a vase of flowers. With this, the painter erased the boundaries between still life and nude painting. The depiction is not embedded in any allegorical context, nor can it be explained by any iconographic tradition. Yet the nude is also not erotically charged as in related works by male painters. In Modersohn-Becker's nude composition, the human creature and its integration into the pictorial space become the subject. The representation of the body reaches its "most detached version," as the art historian Walter Müller-Wulckow put it in 1927, on the occasion of the opening of the museum dedicated to Paula Modersohn-Becker: In her radical simplification, the artist achieved images "that have the magically compelling power inherent in cult images."[5]

3—Friedrich Ahlers-Hestermann, *Pause vor dem dritten Akt* (Hamburg 1949), p. 111 [translated].
4—Ibid., p. 129 [translated].
5—*Die Paula Becker-Modersohn-Sammlung des Ludwig Roselius in der Böttcherstraße in Bremen*, ed. Walter Müller-Wulckow, exh. cat. Bremen 1927, p. 16 [translated].

Although many of Modersohn-Becker's pictorial inventions seem almost without precedent, the artist was in fact a self-confident recipient of the contemporary art of her time: Her friend Clara Rilke-Westhoff attested that she had already discovered Cézanne's works during her first stay in Paris in 1900—at a time when Cézanne's name was still largely unknown even in artistic circles. In 1903, with a recommendation from Rilke, Modersohn-Becker introduced herself to Auguste Rodin, who also showed her the erotic watercolors in his studio in Meudon, which would later cause a scandal when they were exhibited at the Großherzogliches Museum in Weimar a few years later.

3 Pablo Picasso, Egyptian Sacrificial Priestess, c. 1906/7, black chalk, 16 x 9.6 cm, Private Collection

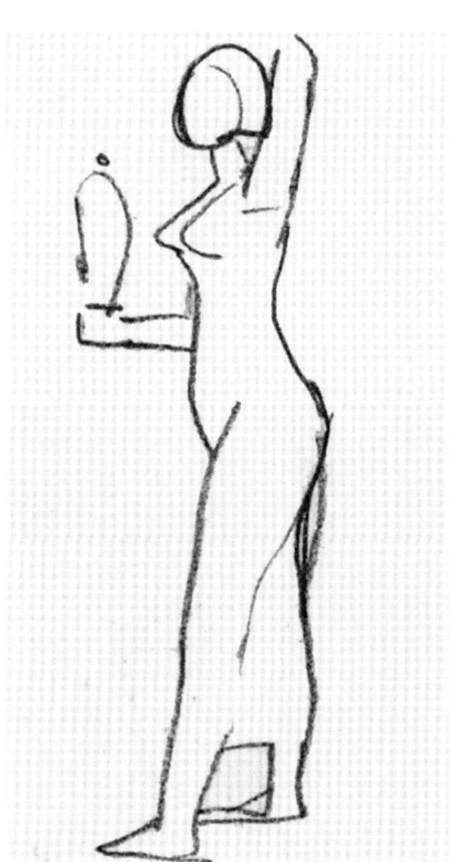

Together with her sister Herma, Paula Modersohn-Becker visited Maurice Denis in his studio in Saint-Germain-en-Laye in March 1906. Like her, Denis was searching for simplification and clarity: "It requires a very strong *simplification*, of the colors, of the tonal values, of the drawing—of everything,"[6] Denis told Harry Graf Kessler in 1902 on the occasion of their joint viewing of his murals in the church in Le Vésinet, which Modersohn-Becker also visited with her sister.

Finally, on the occasion of her visit to Gustave Fayet's collection of works by Paul Gauguin, she experienced essential encouragement on the path of developing of her painting: In view of these works, the "deeply colored array of Gauguin's southern figures, quiet and noble as if shining forth from the depths of a tapestry,"[7] she must have experienced a similar "shock of confirmation"[8] as Picasso did a short time later when he discovered the clearly contoured, expressive forms of African sculpture.

The search for simplicity, contour, and expression undertaken by Denis, Matisse, and Modersohn-Becker also took place in contemporary sculpture. From 1905 at the latest, Aristide Maillol and Bernhard Hoetger, who had been living in Paris since 1900, attempted to liberate themselves from Rodin's overpowering influence. Both turned away from the jagged, impressionistic surface design on which light could play, toward clearer, closed forms. "He was sick and tired of Rodin's muscular knottiness," the painter Franz Nölken reported with surprise on a visit to Hoetger's Parisian studio: "now it must be the exact opposite."[9] From 1906 onwards, Hoetger, who had initially created sculptures in the manner of Rodin, depicting beggars, ragpickers, blind people, and dancers in motion, developed expressive sculptures with Symbolist pathos formulas. That same year, Paula Modersohn-Becker visited the sculptor in his studio on Rue de Vaugirard and found in him one of her most important supporters.

6—"Ce qu'il faut, c'est seulement une très grande *simplification*, des tons, des valeurs, du dessin, de tout"; cf. Rainer Stamm, *"Ein kurzes intensives Fest." Paula Modersohn-Becker. Eine Biographie* (Stuttgart 2018), p. 170.
7—Ahlers-Hestermann 1949 (see note 4), p. 119 [translated].
8—Cf. Werner Spies, "Der Bildausbruch aus dem Abendland," in: *Frankfurter Allgemeine Zeitung* (*Bilder und Zeiten*), June 9, 2007, pp. Z1f. [translated].
9—Ahlers-Hestermann 1949 (see note 4), p. 110 [translated].

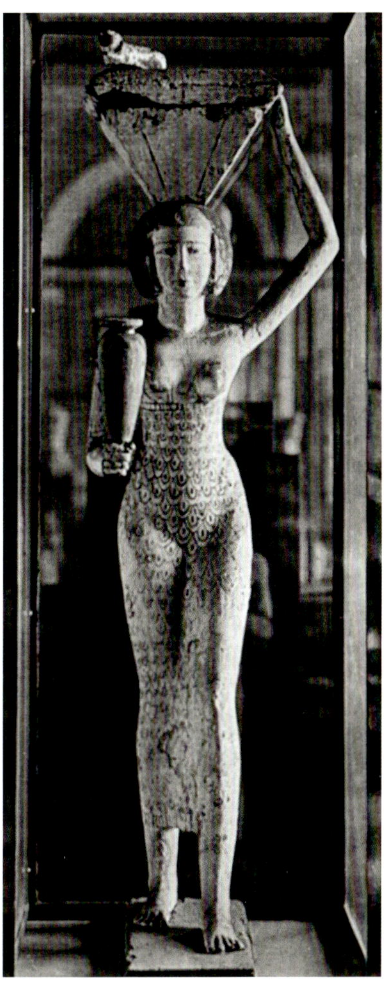

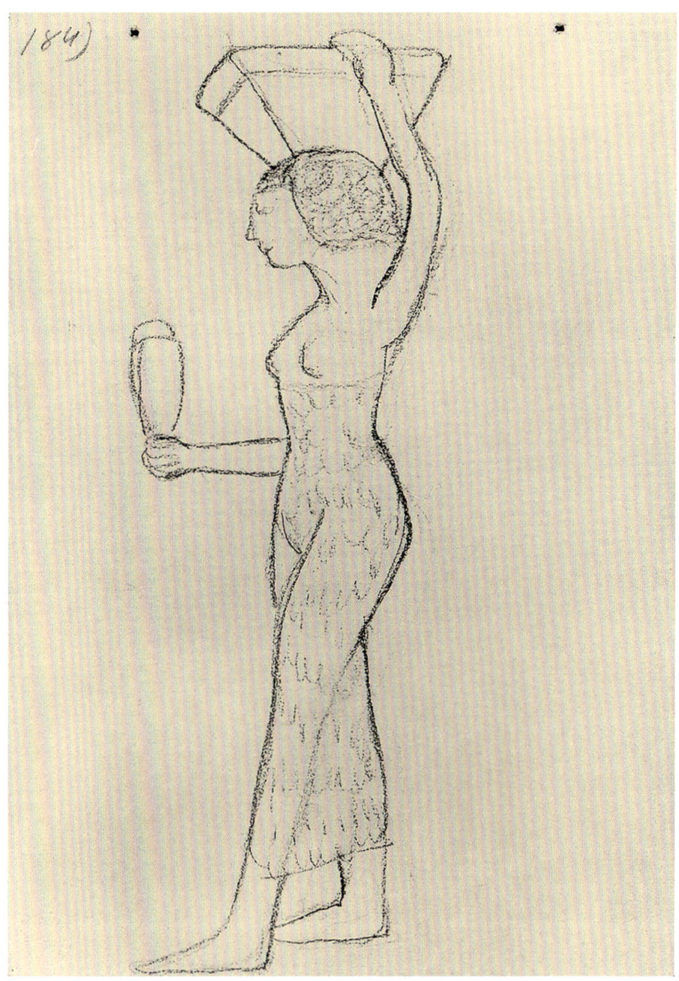

4 Statue of a servant, 2150/2001 BC, Musée du Louvre, Paris, Département des Antiquités égyptiennes

5 Ägyptische Opferpriesterin / Egyptian Sacrificial Priestess, c. 1903, Charcoal on paper, 25.4 x 17.6 cm, Kunsthalle Bremen - der Kunstverein in Bremen, Kupferstichkabinett

"We became more and more good friends," Hoetger later recalled, "we felt each other's contemplative eye as a deep pleasure, confirmation, and strength. [...] She thought of monumental painting, of liberating compositions."[10]

With the abandonment of the fleeting observation of Impressionism and the search for expression and monumentality, new themes also emerged in Modersohn-Becker's art. The subject matter of history painting was just as obsolete for her as the motifs of classical mythology or Christian iconography. Unlike Käthe Kollwitz and Jeanne Mammen, for example, she was not interested in motifs of social engagement or the genre-like observations of a city flaneur. Nor was she interested in narrative painting of the kind she had encountered in the works of Hans Thoma and Max Klinger. Instead, she was looking for the creation of timeless motifs. The motif of "*maternité*" offered itself to her, the creation of supra-individual motherhood, to which contemporaries such as Eugène Carrière, Pablo Picasso, and Aristide Maillol[11] also devoted themselves.

10—Bernhard Hoetger, "Erinnerungen an Paula Modersohn," in: C. E. Uphoff, *Paula Modersohn* (Leipzig 1919), pp. 12–15, here pp. 13f. [translated].
11—See the essay by Inge Herold in this volume, pp. 97–103.

As inspiration and models for her figure paintings, she was fascinated—as were Picasso, Matisse, and Karl Hofer—by the expressive statuary of Egyptian sculpture: "By removing oneself from the literal representation of movement one attains greater beauty and grandeur," Matisse stated: "Look at an Egyptian statue: it looks rigid to us, yet we sense in it the image of a body capable of movement and which, despite its rigidity, is animated."[12] Like Picasso, Modersohn-Becker was fascinated by the *Statue of a servant* in the Louvre, which both artists captured in sketches (figs. 3-5).

In works such as these, they found a "simplicity of form" and the animated statuary that Paula Modersohn-Becker worked through in countless paintings. In the search for timeless subjects, a symbolism beyond iconographic codes thus emerged, which artists such as Hodler, Hoetger, and Hofer also cultivated parallel to her.

6 Pablo Picasso, Jeune homme au bouquet / Young Man with Bouquet, 1905, gouache on cardboard, 67 x 52.5 cm, Basil and Elise Goulandris Foundation Collection, Athens

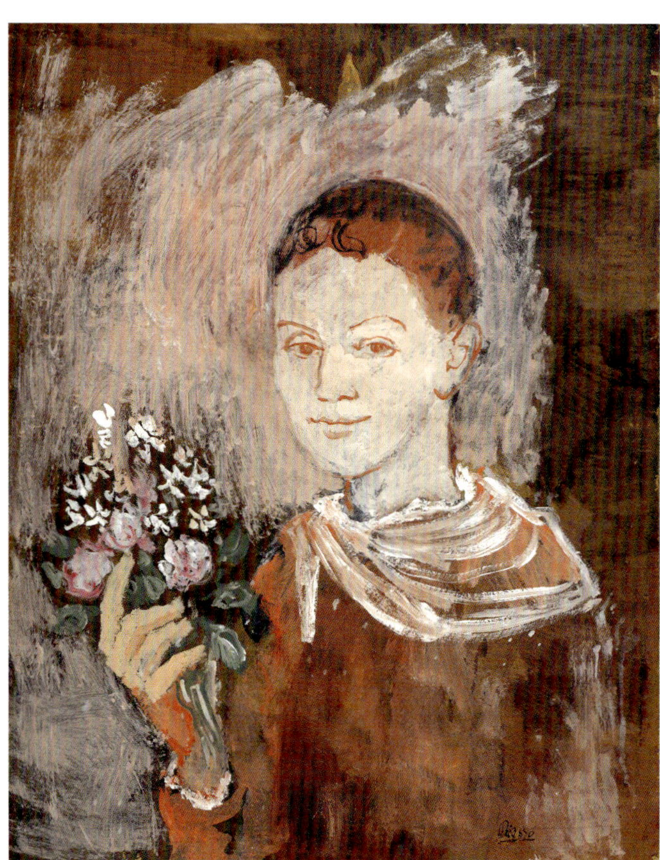

The early recipients were well aware of the innovative nature of this painting. When Heinrich Vogeler viewed the artist's estate in Worpswede, he confessed with emotion: "Only now does one completely see what she was, how she struggled [...]. All smallness fell from her; her visions became grand and festive; the last were new paths to a great monumental painting."[13] Collectors such as Karl Ernst Osthaus and August von der Heydt acquired paintings from the artist's Parisian period; and only seven years after her death, Wilhelm Hausenstein included her in his volume on contemporary art history, *Die bildende Kunst der Gegenwart*: "She, by far the most important of the harmless colony of Worpswede [...] had begun with banal folk art and greatly admired conservative people such as Karl Vinnen and Fritz Mackensen. Then she went to Paris: [...] there began in this German woman, as in many German forces who had taken the same path to Paris, a spiritualization of contemplation."[14]

While her art was later associated primarily with Worpswede, with landscape painting and peasantry, her work was received in the very first decade after her death as both a peculiar and self-evident part of "The New Art." In Frankfurt am Main, one of her paintings was shown for the first time in 1917: In the exhibition of

12—Matisse 1909 (see note 3), p. 37.
13—Quoted in: Stamm 2018 (see note 7), p. 237 [translated].
14—Wilhelm Hausenstein, *Die bildende Kunst der Gegenwart* (Stuttgart et al. 1914), p. 270 [translated].

works from private collections in Frankfurt, *Die Neue Kunst* (The New Art), organized by the Vereinigung für Neue Kunst (Association for New Art) and presented at the Kunstverein on Junghofstrasse, her *Head of a Girl II*, (c. 1905) was hung in close proximity to paintings by van Gogh, Gauguin, Picasso, Matisse, Hodler, and Hofer.[15] "It is only natural that a lively forward-moving age such as ours should emphasize the opposition to what was, to what has been handed down, in order to assert the values it has found," Eduard von Bendemann stated, explaining the ambition of the exhibition. He pointed out that the "opposition to Impressionism" did not automatically have to lead to Expressionism: "The present exhibition strives to promote an understanding of how consistent a development painting has undergone in the thirty years since van Gogh"[16] (fig. 6).

The painter and collector Pauline Kowarzik (1852–1930) was one of the first in Frankfurt to recognize the connection between the works of Paula Modersohn-Becker and the aspirations of the latest art. Her collection included Modersohn-Becker's *Head of a Girl II*[17] as well as works by Sérusier, Hodler, Gauguin, Rousseau and Picasso. The loan from her collection made Paula Modersohn-Becker's contribution to "The New Art" visible in Frankfurt, long before, one hundred years later, her self-portrait of 1907 (fig. 7) entered the avant-garde canon at The Museum of Modern Art in New York.

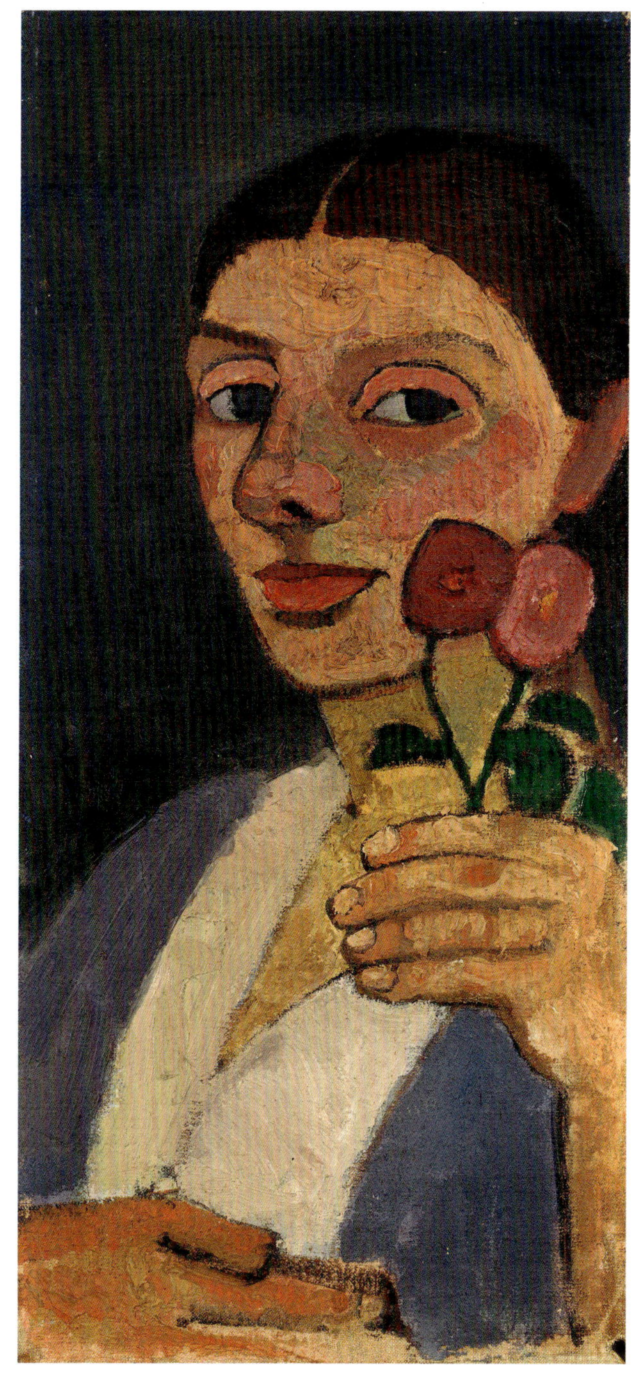

7 Paula Modersohn-Becker, Selbstbildnis mit zwei Blumen in der erhobenen linken Hand / Self-Portrait with Two Flowers in Her Raised Left Hand, Paris 1907, oil tempera on canvas, 55.2 x 24.8 cm, jointly owned by The Museum of Modern Art, New York, gift of Debra and Leon Black, and Neue Galerie New York, gift of Jo Carole and Ronald S. Lauder

15 —Cf. *Die Neue Kunst ausgewählt vorwiegend aus Frankfurter Privatbesitz*, exh. cat. Vereinigung für Neue Kunst, Frankfurt am Main, 1917, cat. 66.

16 —Eduard von Bendemann, "Die neue Kunst," in: *Frankfurter Zeitung*, June 1, 1917 [translated].

17 —Kowarzik's collection included, in addition to *Head of a Girl II* (Busch / Werner 566), Modersohn-Becker's painting *Peasant Woman with Child at her Breast in Front of a Landscape*, (Busch / Werner 384). Both pictures were acquired by the Städel Museum in 1926 and confiscated there in 1937 as "degenerate." They are now in the collections of the Kunsthaus Zürich and the Hamburger Kunsthalle respectively.

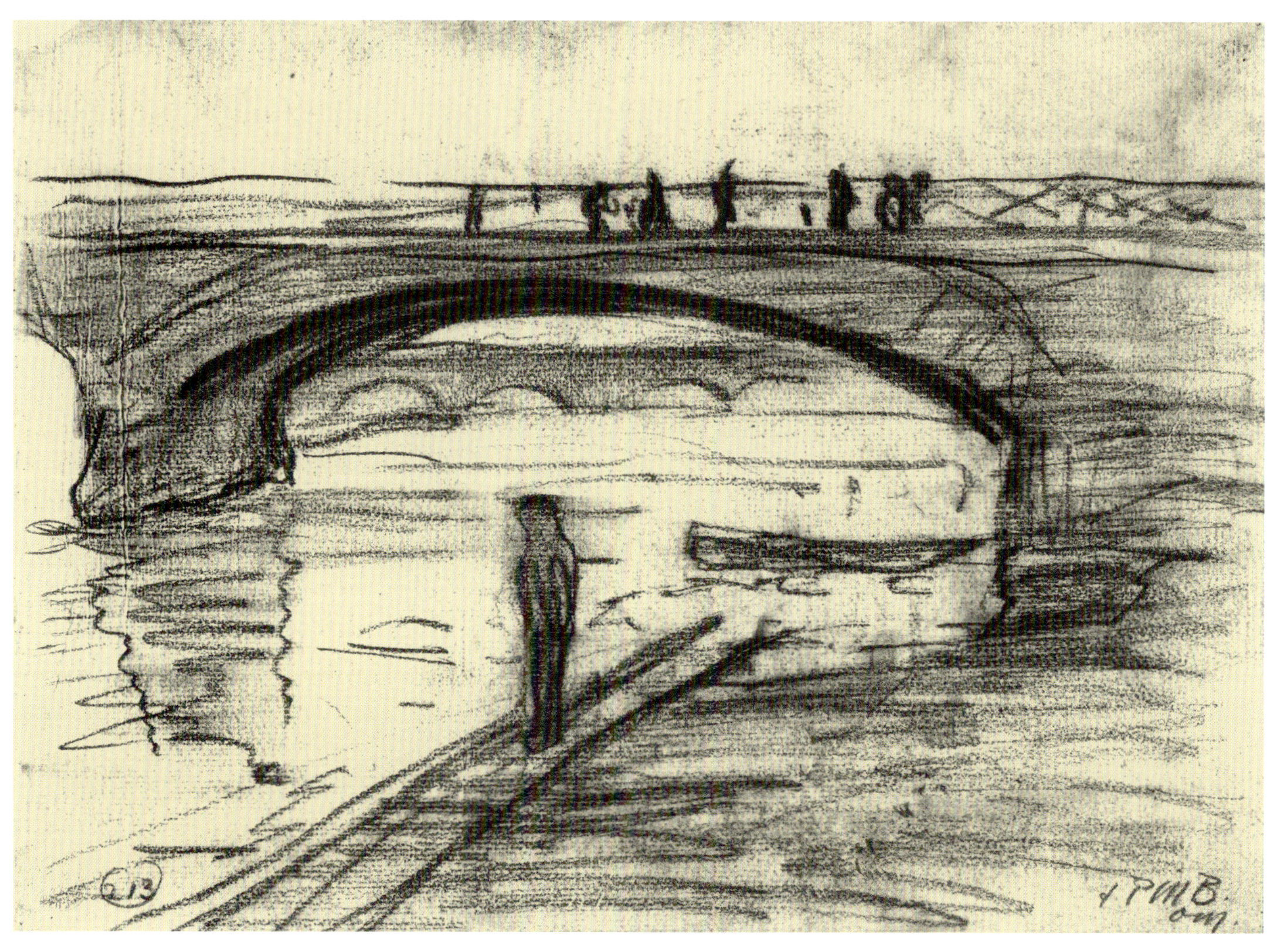

Seine-Brücken in Paris / Bridges over the Seine in Paris, 1905

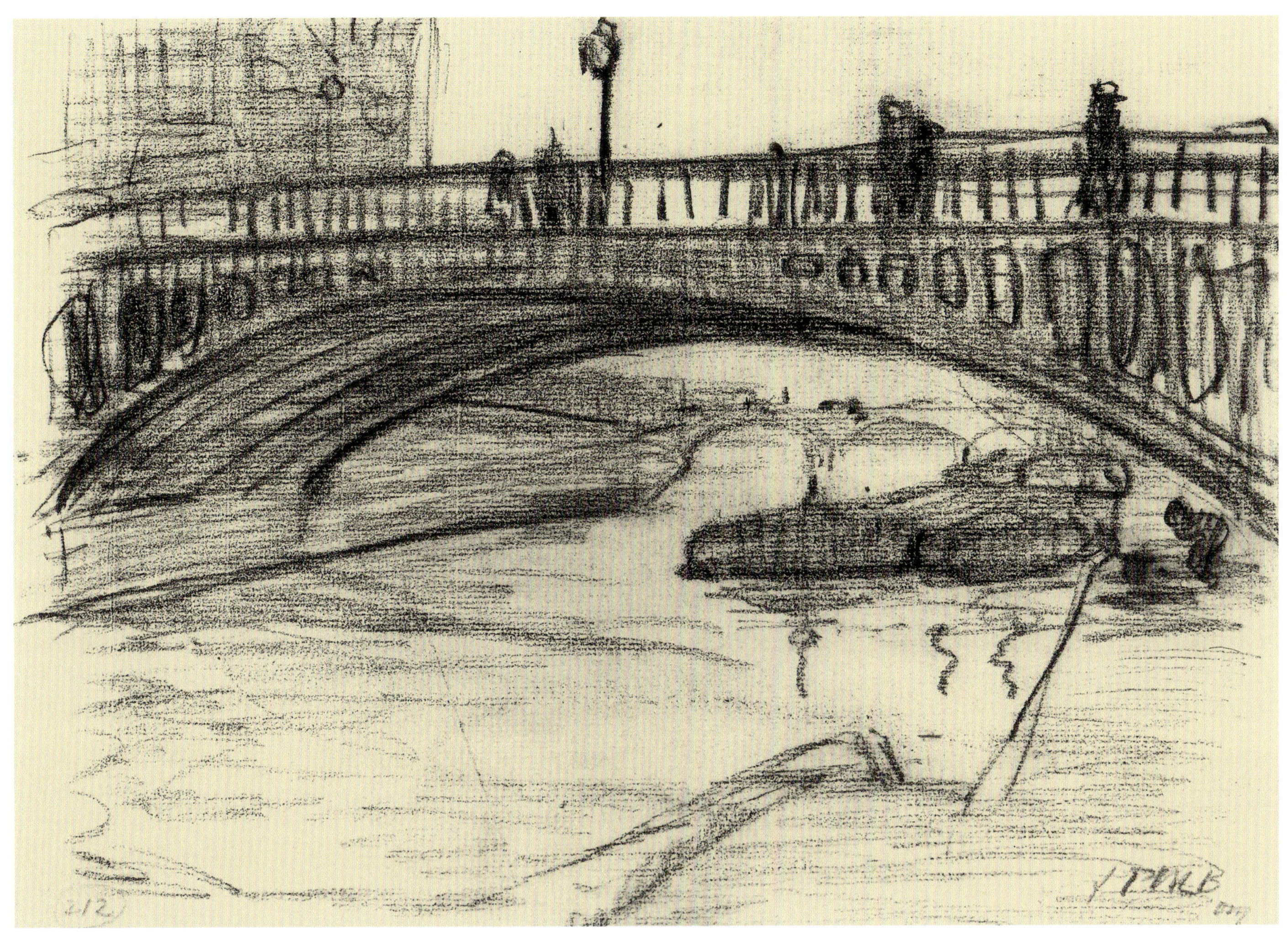

Seinebrücke / Bridge over the Seine, 1905

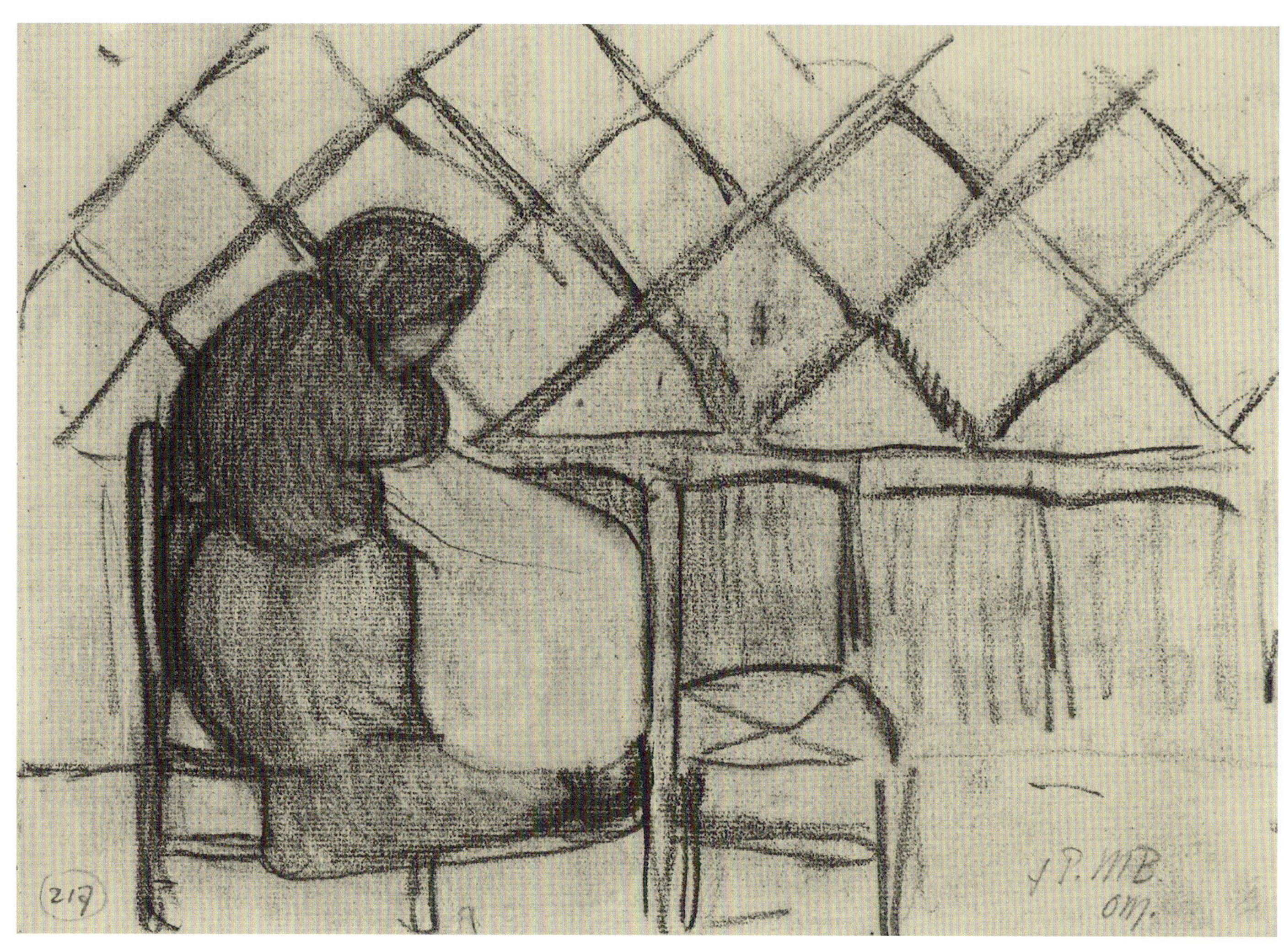

Sitzende Frau nach rechts vor einer Wand mit Gitterwerk / Seated Woman with Apron in Front of a Latticework, c. 1905

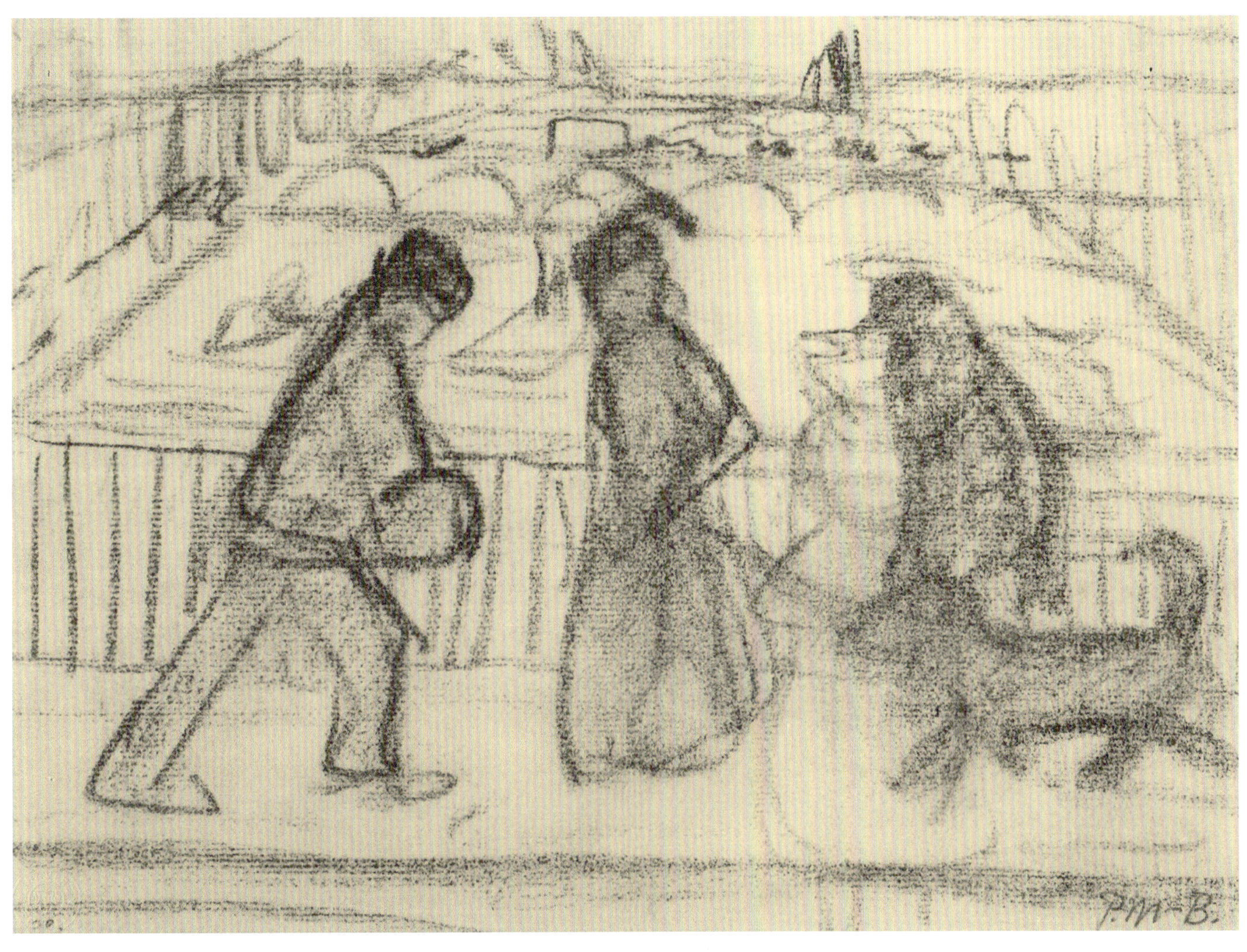

Figuren mit Hund auf einer Seinebrücke in Paris / Figures with Dog on a Bridge over the Seine in Paris, 1906

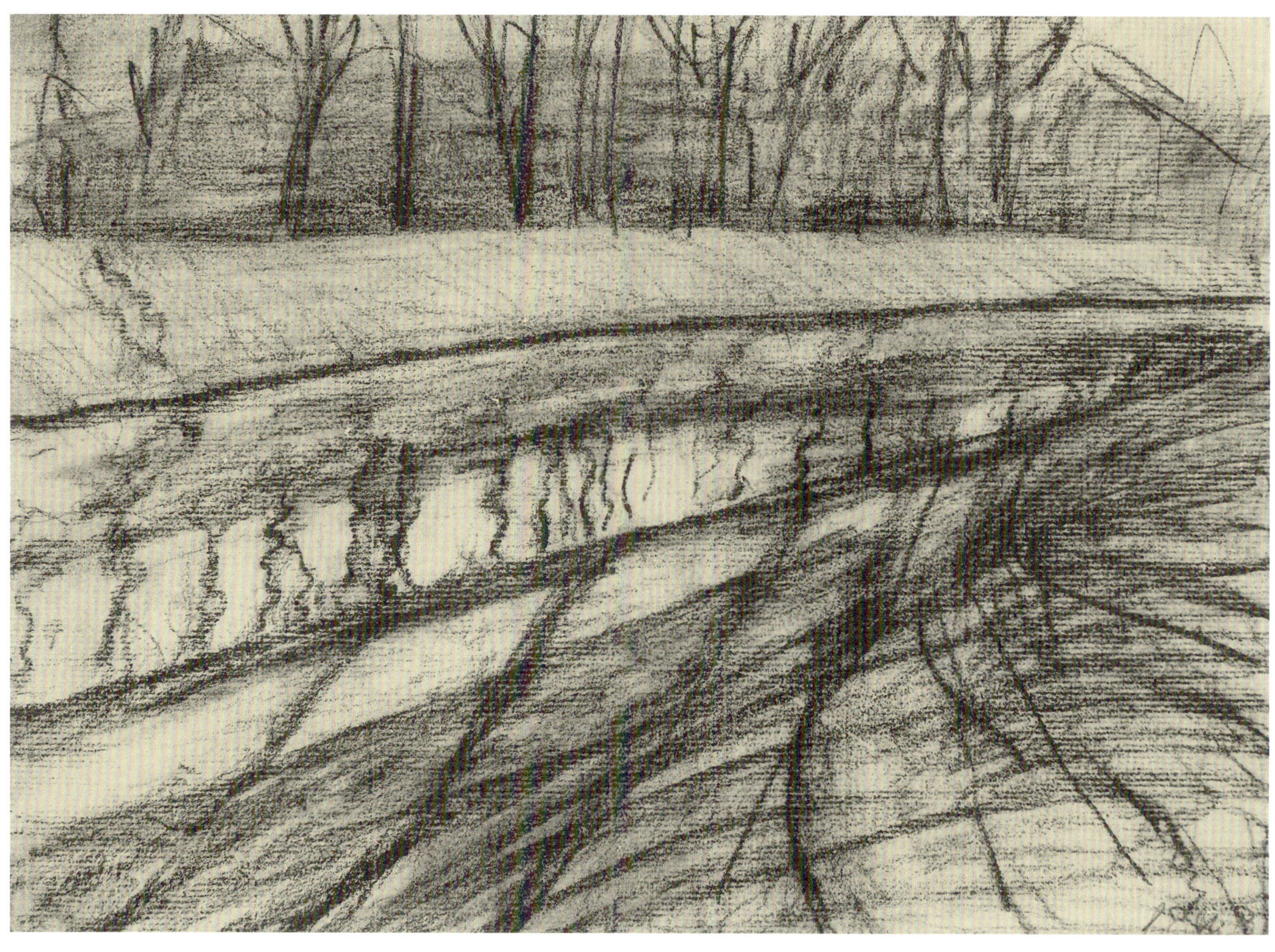

Kanal mit sich spiegelnden Bäumen / Canal with Trees Reflected in the Water, 1905

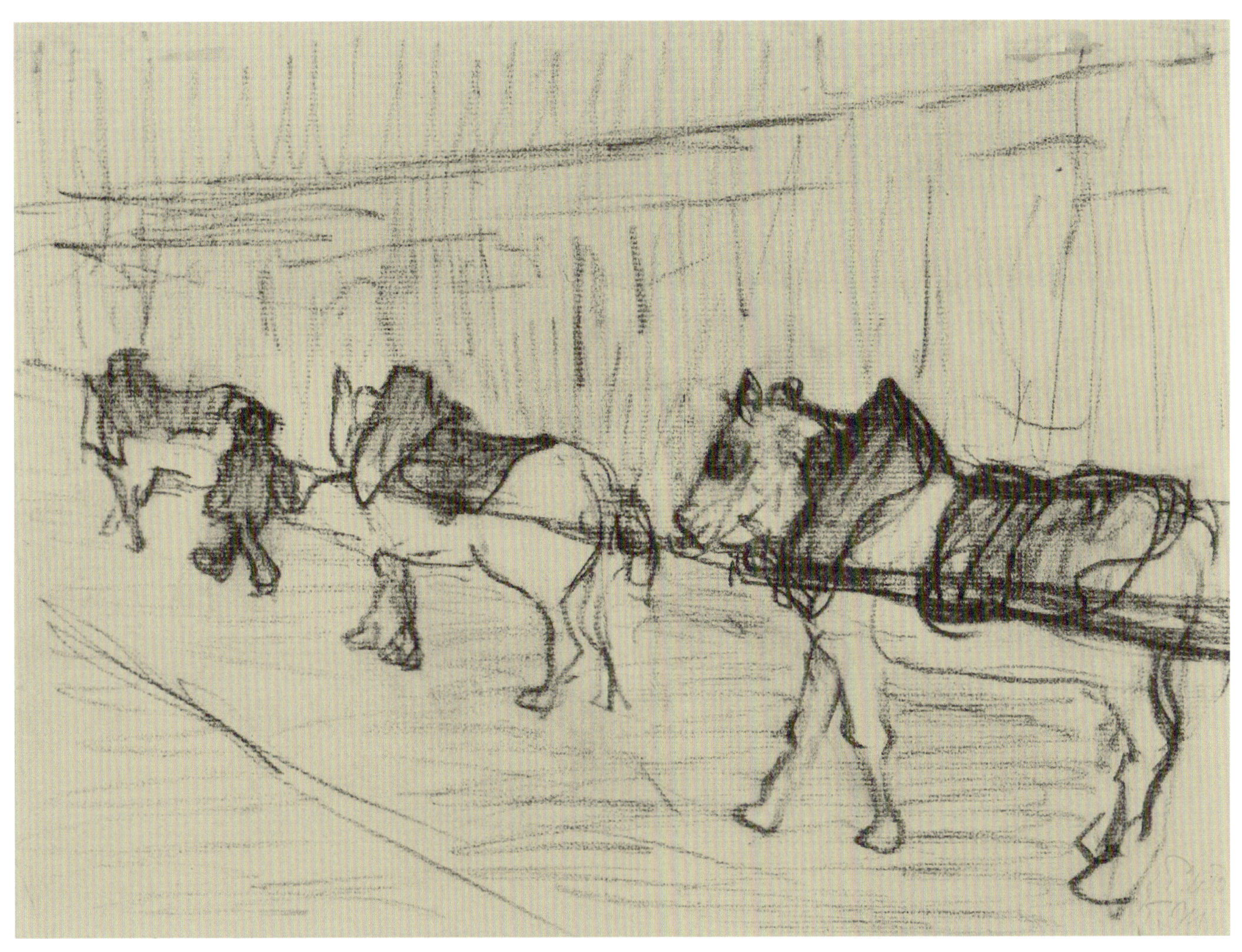

Dreispänniger Pferdelastzug / Carriage Yoked with Three Horses, 1905

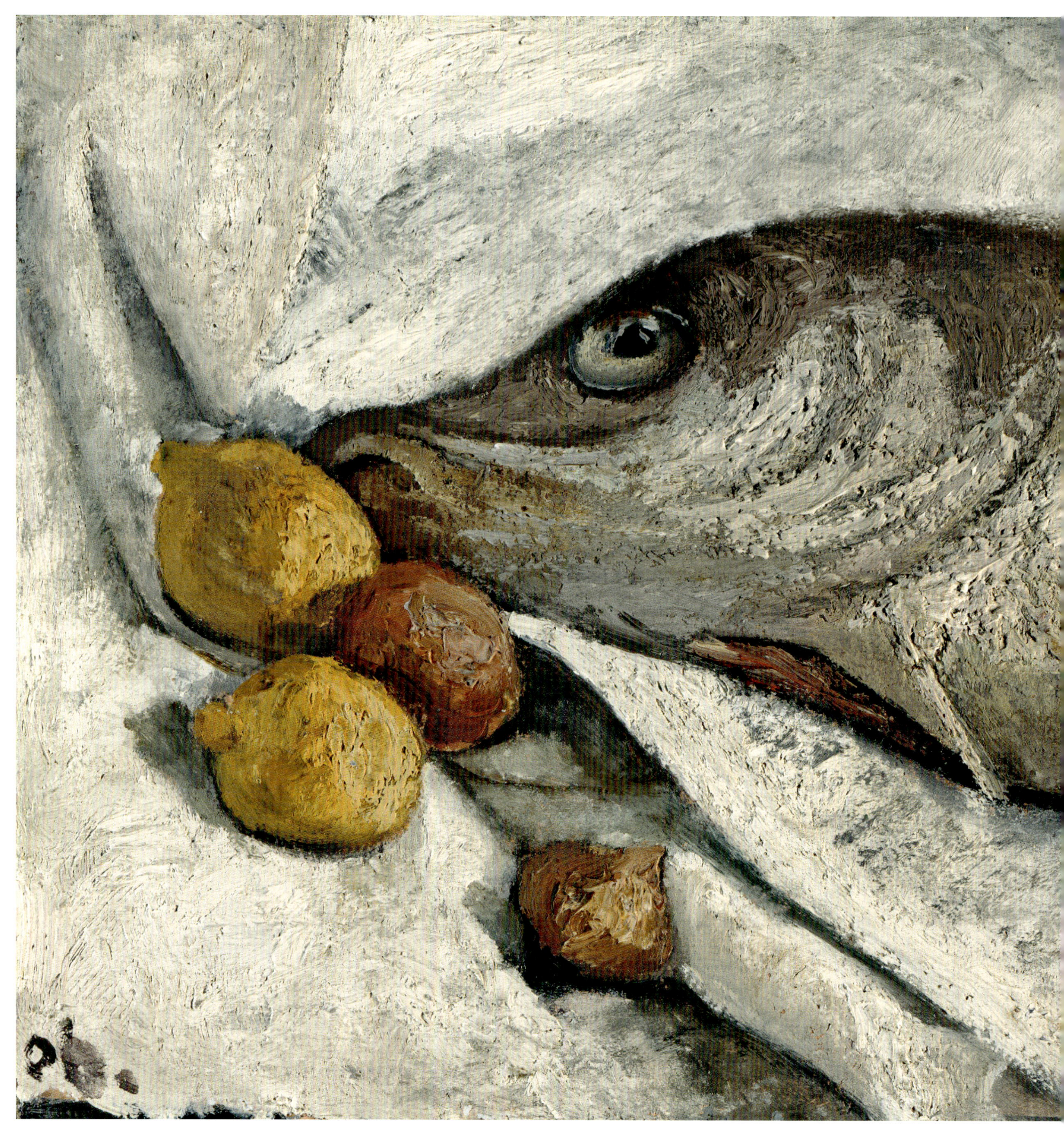

Stillleben mit Fisch / Still Life with Fish, winter 1906

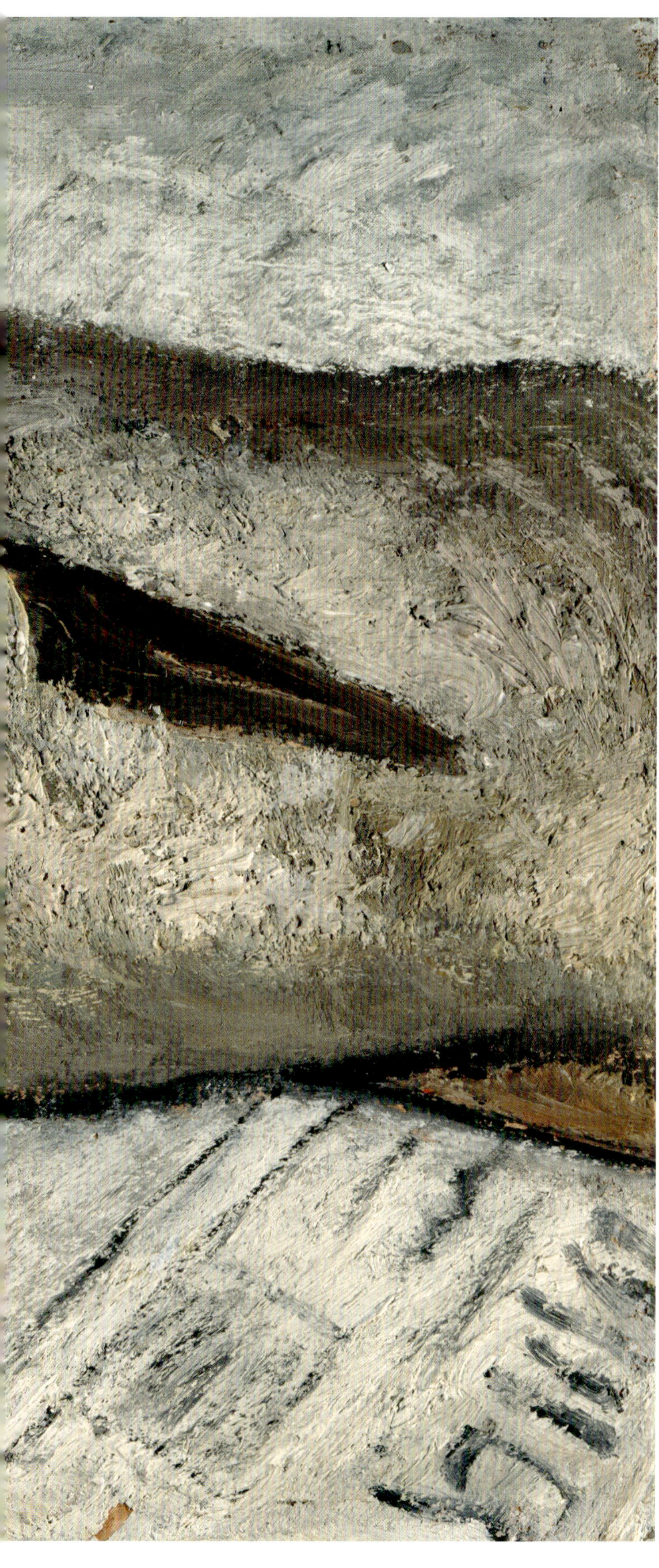

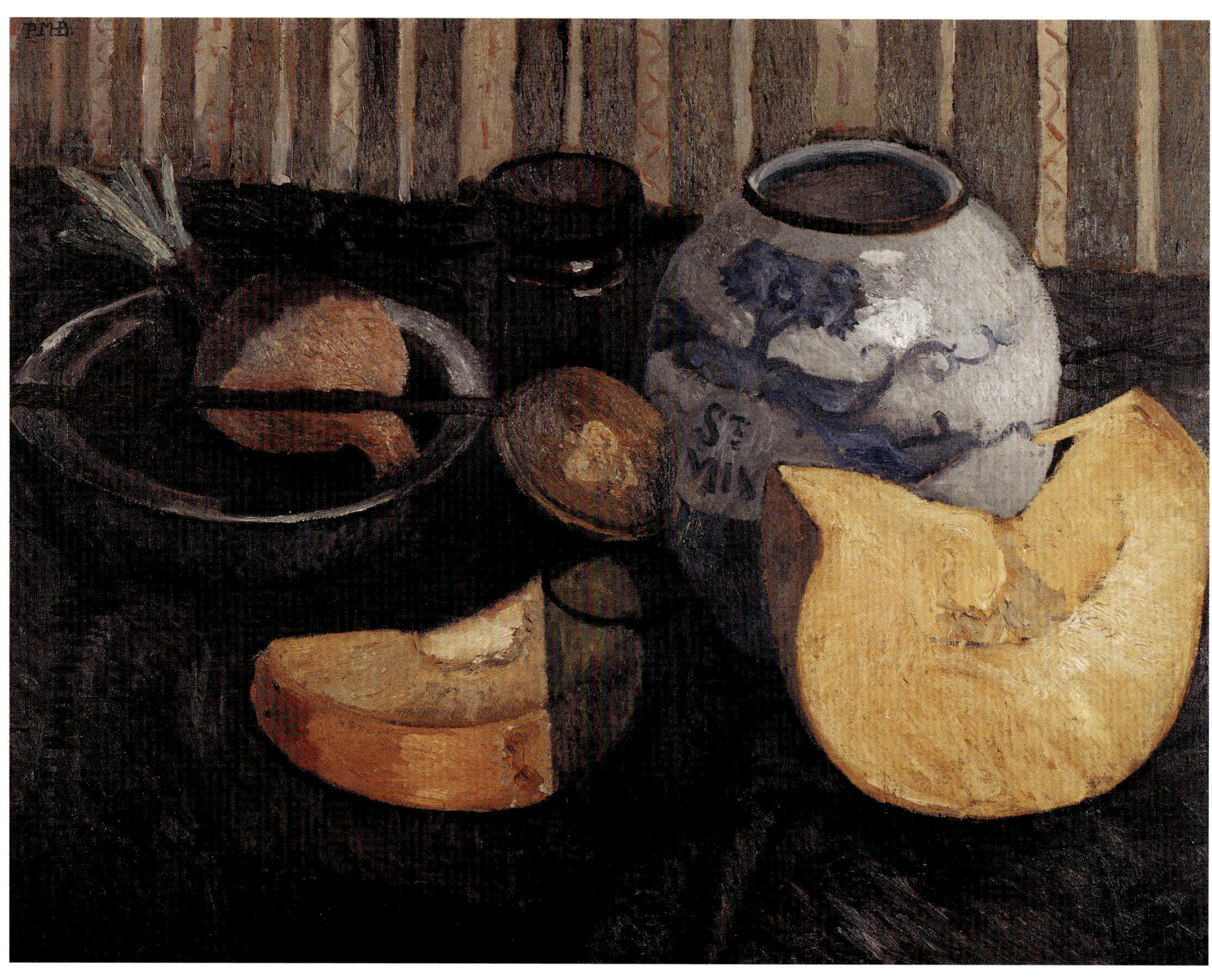

Stillleben mit Kürbis / Still Life with Pumpkin, c. 1905

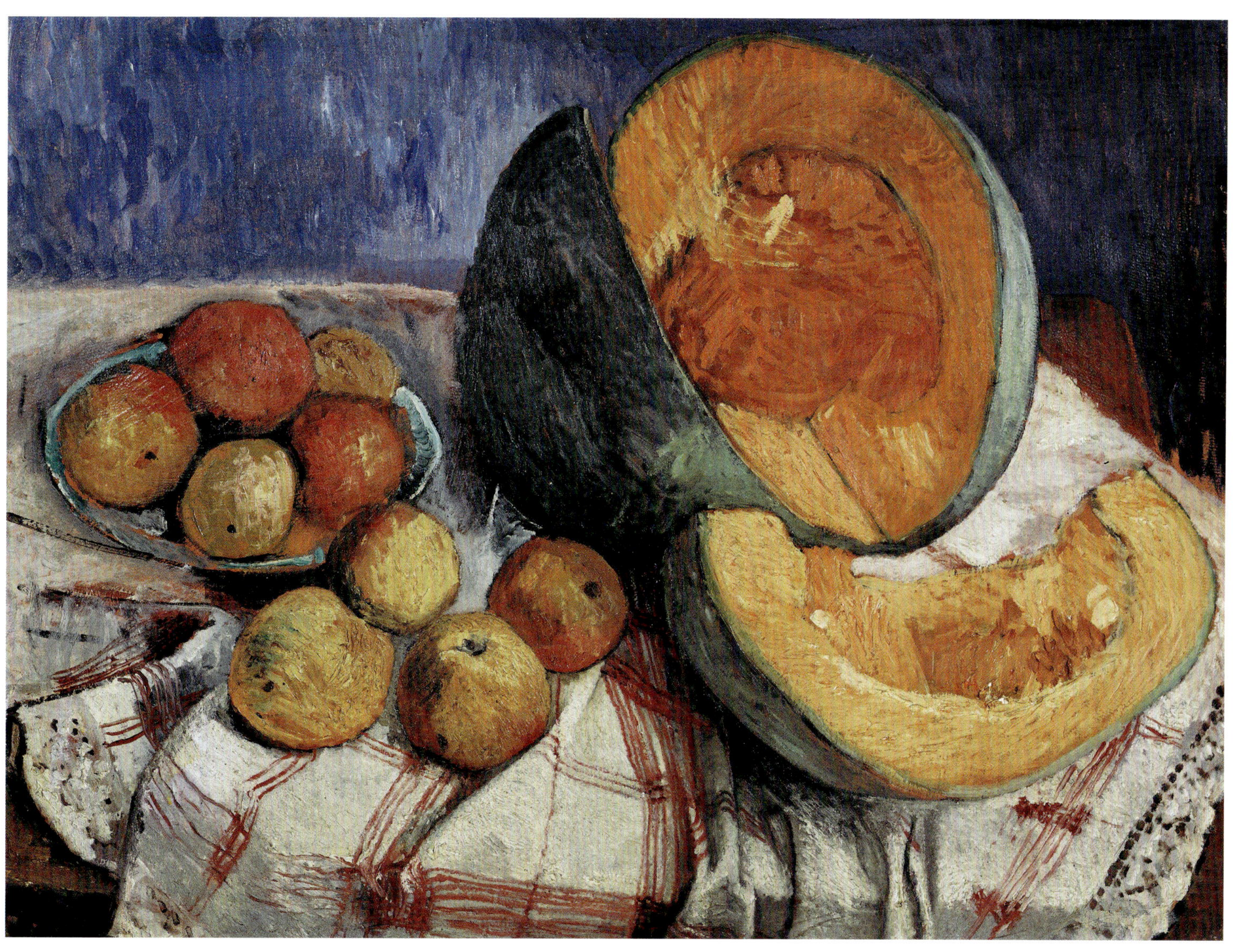

Stillleben mit Kürbis / Still Life with Pumpkin, c. 1905

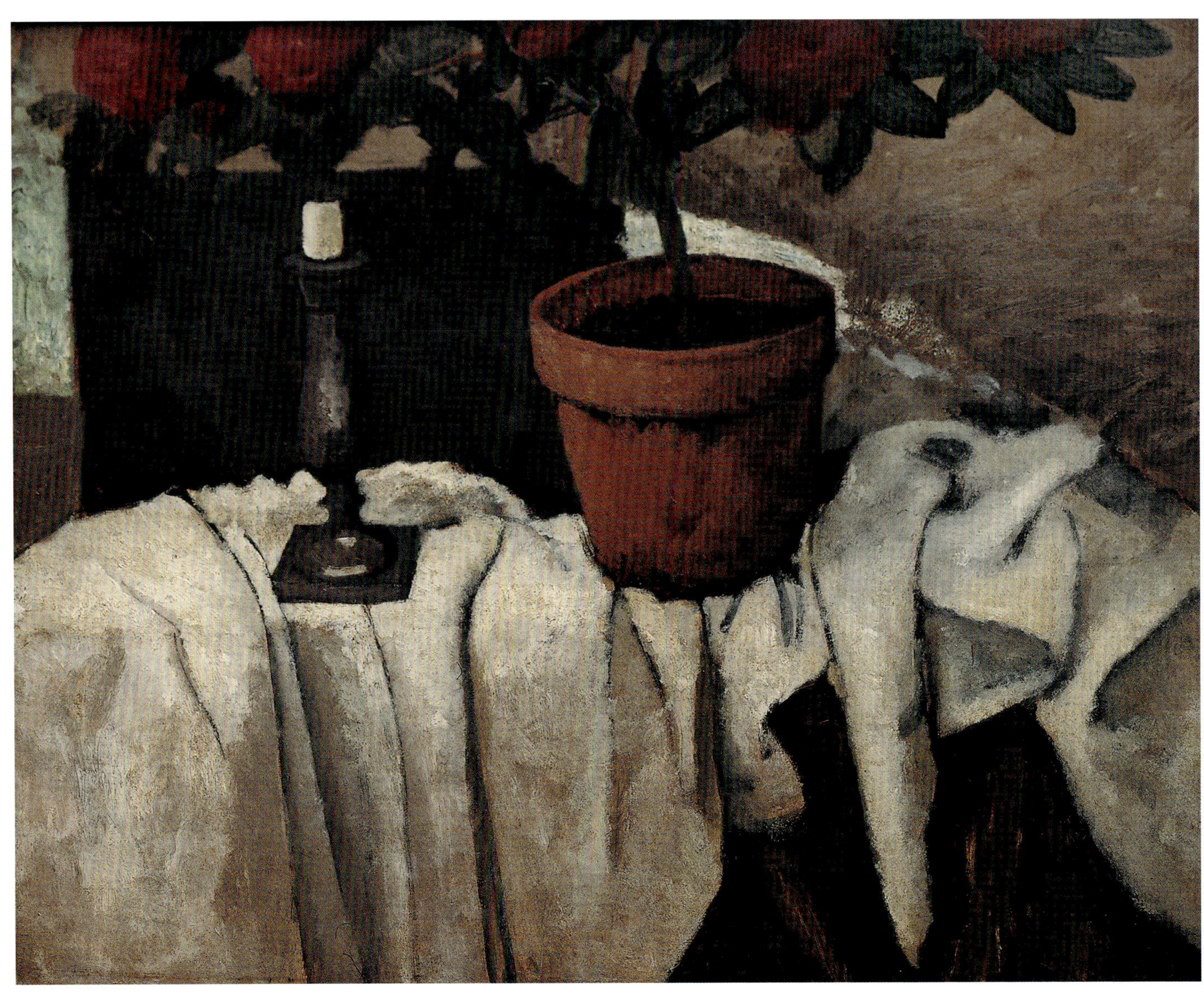

Stillleben mit Rhododendron / Still Life with Rhododendron, 1907

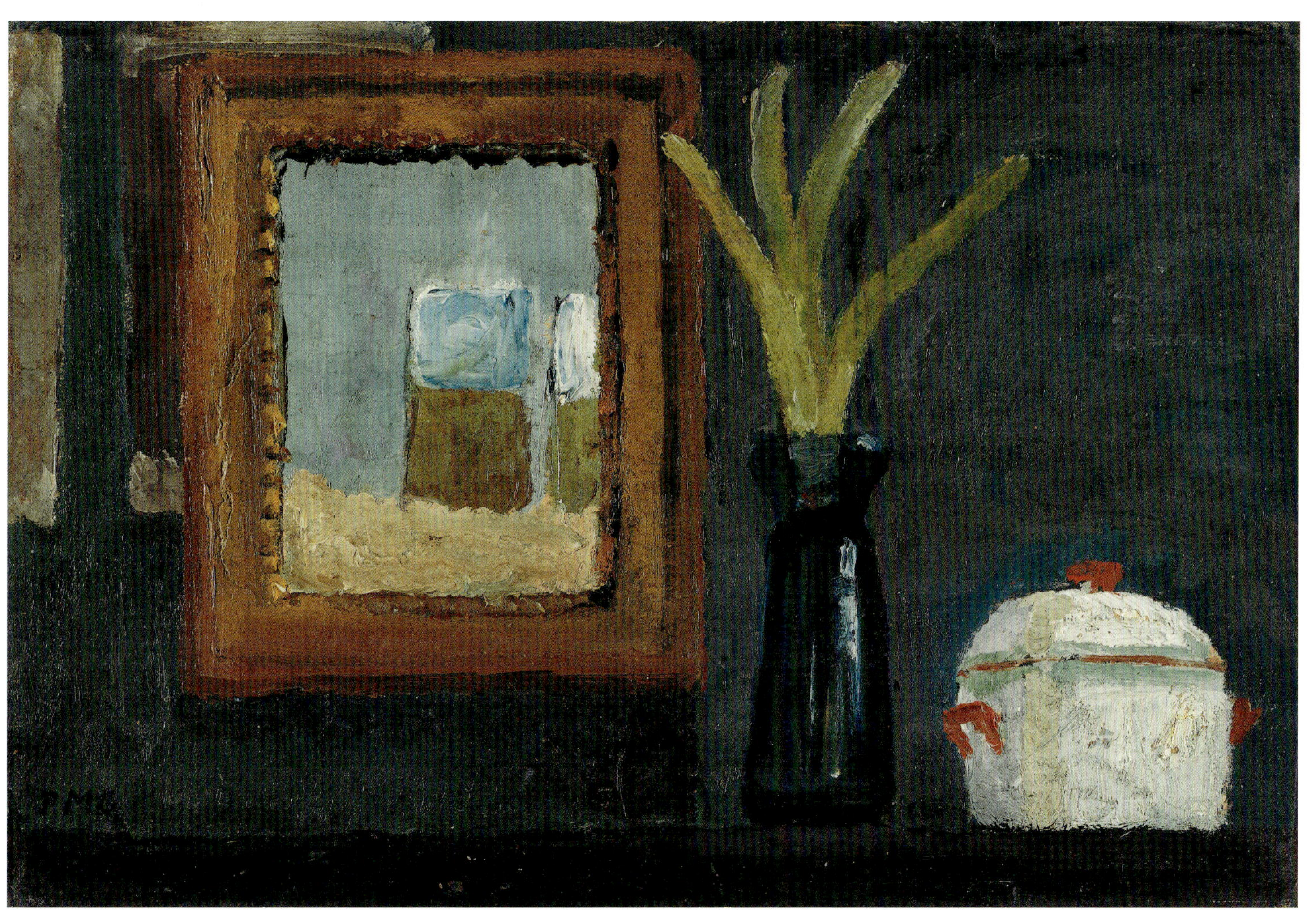

Stillleben mit Zuckerdose und Hyazinthe im Glas / Still Life with Sugar Bowl and a Hyacinth in a Glass, c. 1905

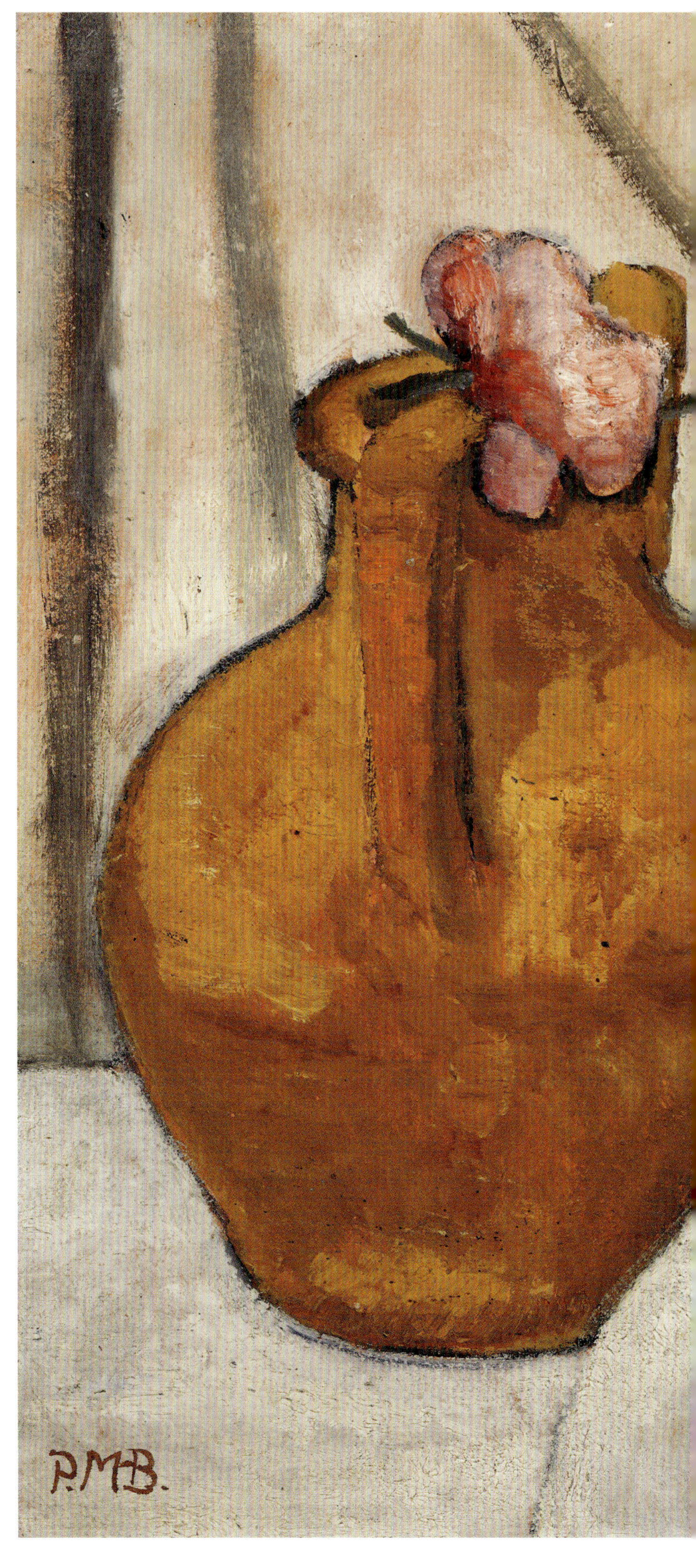
P.M.B.

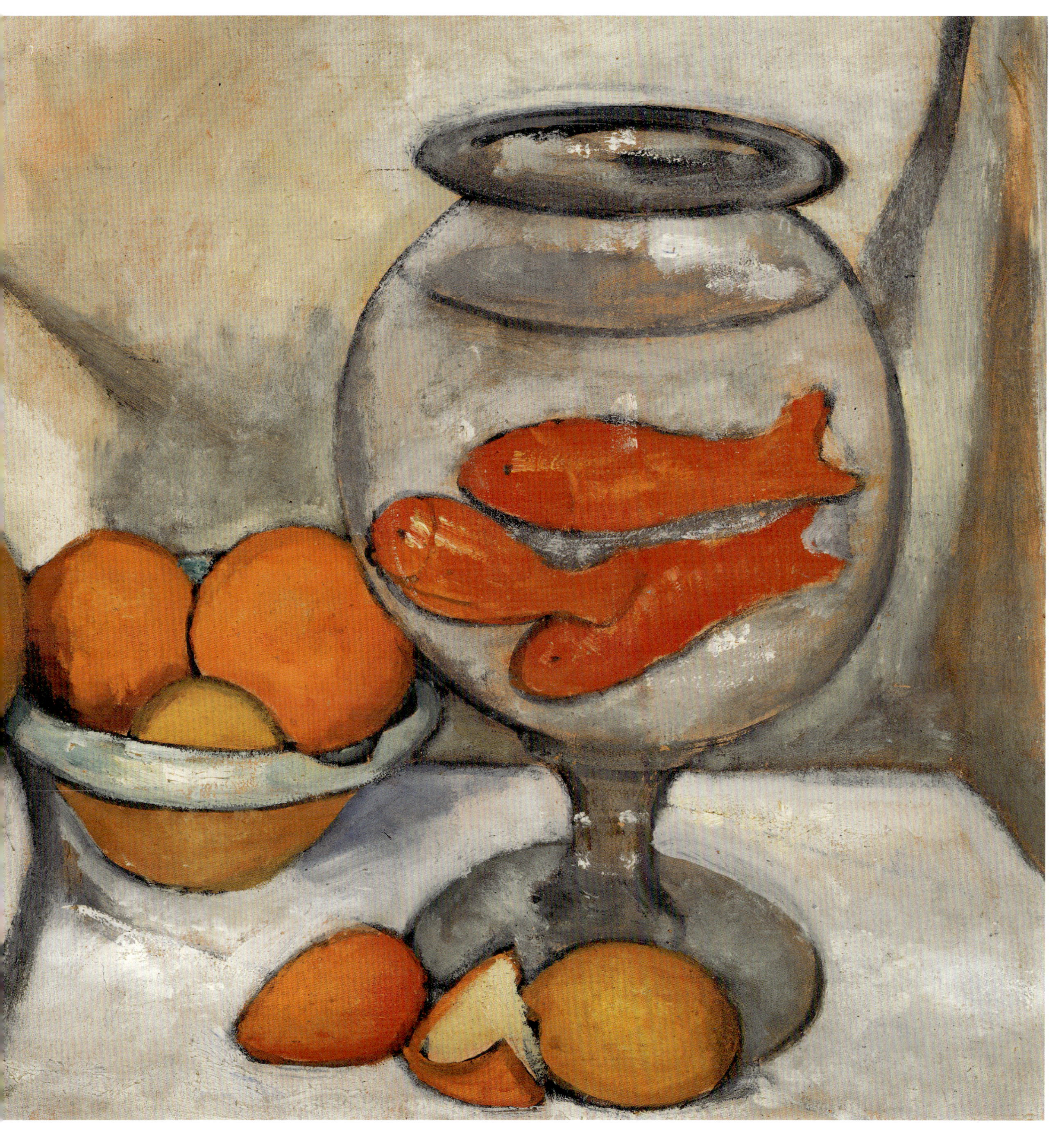

Stillleben mit Goldfischglas / Still Life with Goldfish Bowl, May/June 1906

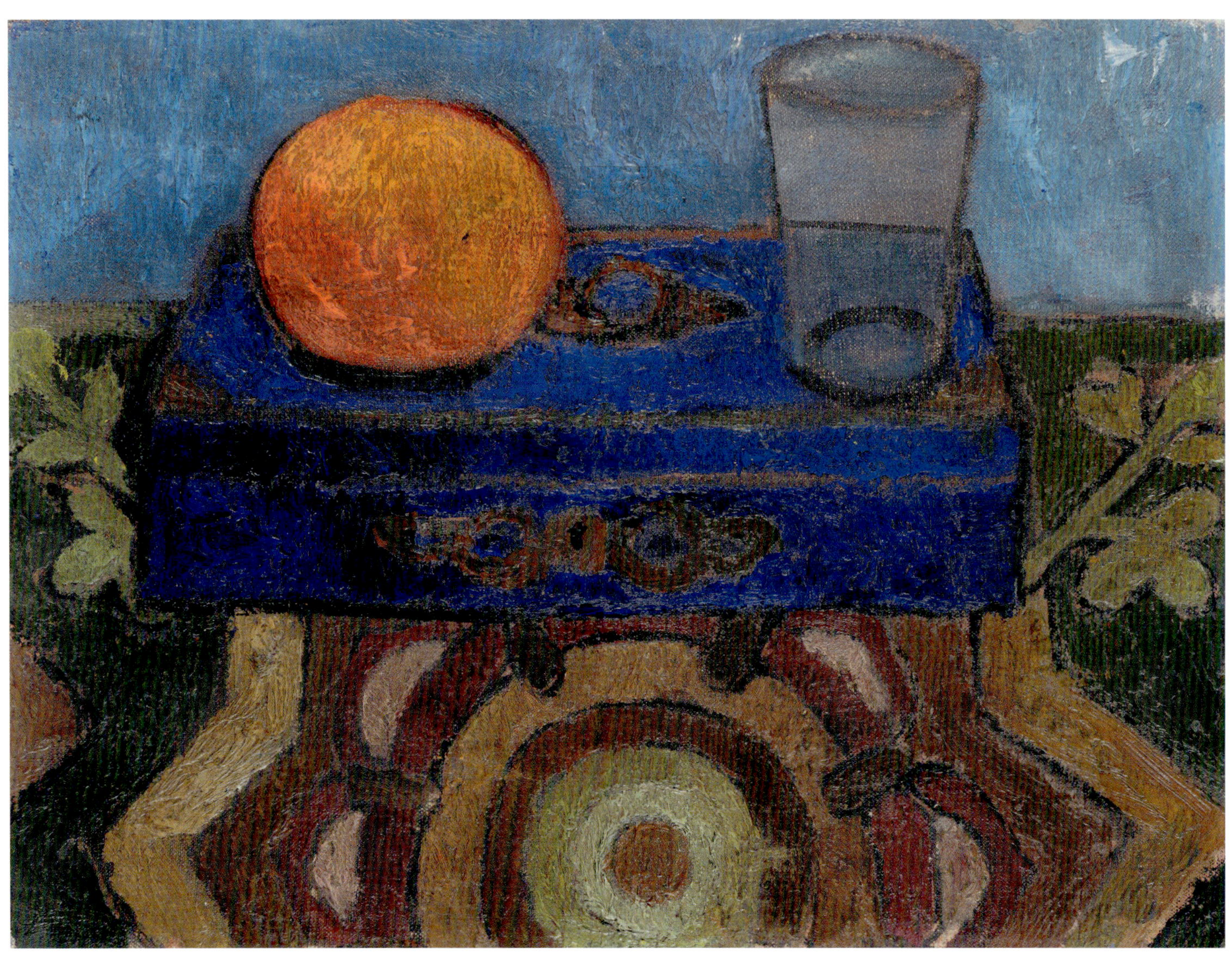

Stillleben mit blauem Kasten / Still Life with a Blue Box, 1907

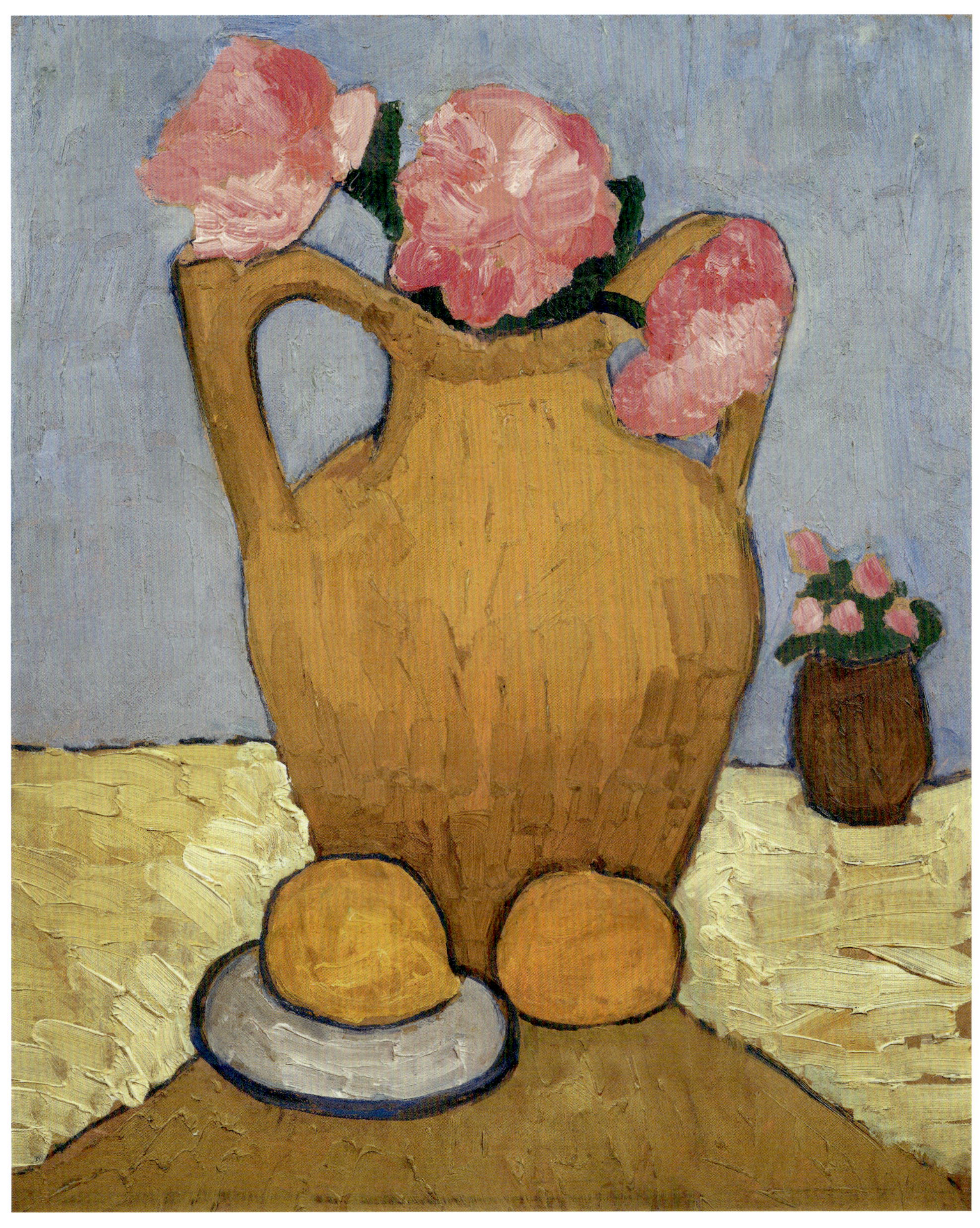

Stillleben mit Tonkrug, Pfingstrosen und Apfelsinen / Still Life with Clay Jug, Peonies and Oranges, May/June 1906

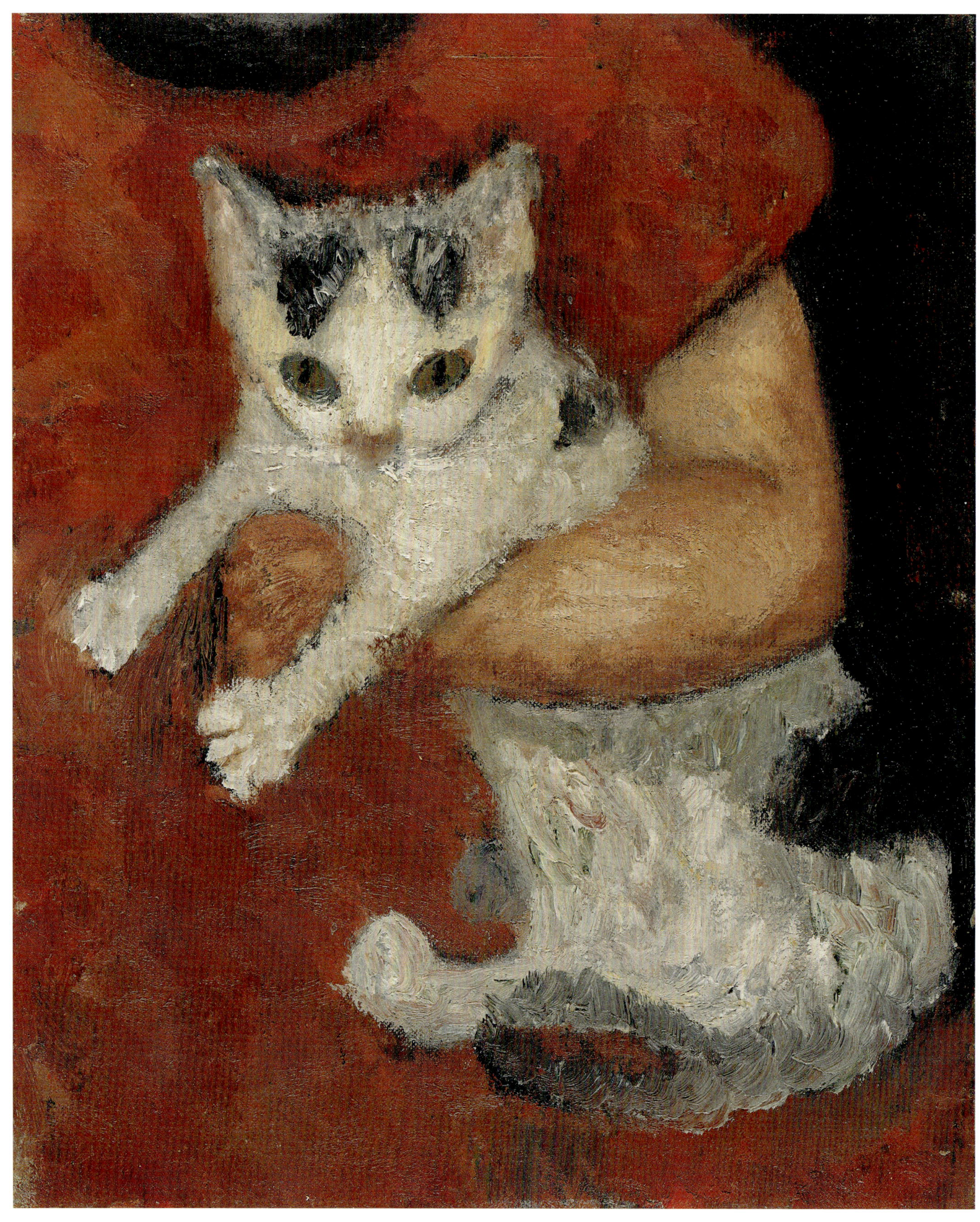

Katze in einem Kinderarm / Cat in a Child's Arm, c. 1903

REST IN MOTION

ON THE POSSIBLE IN THE WORK OF PAULA MODERSOHN-BECKER

KARIN SCHICK

"The painter with her picture / She strikes out like a savage." With these words and a corresponding drawing, Otto Modersohn characterized his wife to her mother, Mathilde Becker, in the fall of 1905 (fig. 1). Paula Modersohn-Becker was always described by family members, acquaintances, and friends as lively and active, and this impression is confirmed when reading her letters and diaries: She liked to speak of life and her work as a "roaring" and "whirring." In search of motifs, she restlessly roamed the fields around Worpswede and the streets of Berlin, collecting impressions of nature and people and seeking to translate them into pictures. Her first trip to Paris in 1900 was followed by three more up to 1906, and thus began an ongoing back and forth between a concentrated country life and an existence in a metropolis that both attracted her and took her breath away. Like her contemporaries, Modersohn-Becker experienced the years around 1900 as a time of change and acceleration—in politics, society, work, technology, communication, art, the humanities, and the natural sciences—and saw herself as part of this new world.

At the beginning of the twentieth century, many artists strove to capture dynamism as a key moment of modernism in their works: Dancers, bathers in nature, and vaudeville were among the preferred motifs of the Brücke artists' association, founded in 1905; in their 1909 manifesto, the Italian Futurists celebrated "movements of aggression," "the double march," and "the beauty of speed." The avant-garde found inspiration in technology, became enthusiastic about experiments in film and photography, and redefined their own intentions. In contrast, Modersohn-Becker did not address modern perception, nor did she translate it directly into art. When she visited the Exposition Universelle in Paris in May 1900 with the motto "Balance of a Century" and awards were given for the diesel engine or the telegraphone, she enthused at length in her letters about the great art shows but did not mention a word about the attractions that electrified fifty million people: the newly opened Métro, rolling sidewalks, the Palace of Electricity, a Ferris wheel 100 meters in diameter, Edison's kinetoscope, or the large projections of the Lumière brothers.

Around 1900 and also in later years, depictions of spinning carousels (p. 80), trotting horsemen, or farmers at work (p. 69) are rare in Modersohn-Becker's work. Indeed, in her numerous figure paintings, portraits, and self-portraits, the standing or seated models often appear as motionless as the inanimate objects in her still life paintings. Furthermore, her most important point of reference in Paris was not the galleries of modern art with the shimmering paintings of the Post-Impressionists, but rather the Louvre. Here, she studied the Old Masters as well as works of past epochs, ancient Greek and Egyptian objects. In them, she found the "depth," "grandeur," and "simplicity" she sought for her own work, a timeless quality that withstood any acceleration. Did she distrust the speed of her time? In any case, a reference to film as a moving image is nowhere to be found in Modersohn-Becker's work, and yet her enigmatic works also reflect its aesthetic. They by all means deal with movement, but indirectly and suggestively—as a pausing, approaching, and halting, as a concentrated in-between, as a point on the axis of time.

1 *Bilder aus dem Familienleben / Pictures of Family Life* by Otto and Paula Modersohn for Mathilde Becker's birthday on November 3, 1905, charcoal on paper, Paula-Modersohn-Becker-Stiftung, Bremen

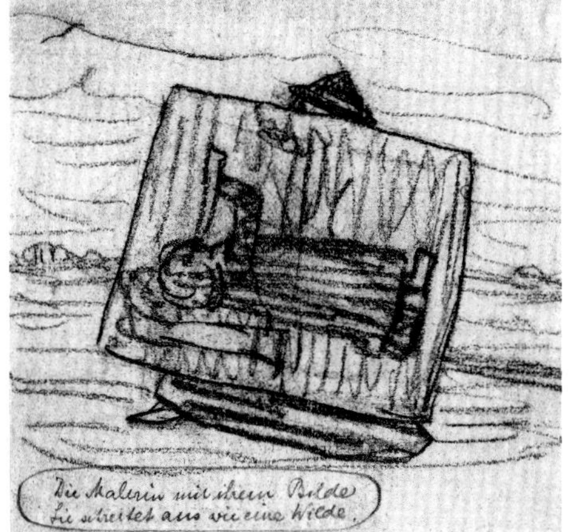

PAUSING – *SCENE STILL*

A favorite motif of Paula Modersohn-Becker was young women and girls.[1] Standing or sitting, they often hold an object in their hands; and often, this connection between person and object appears mysterious: In one self-portrait, the painter, standing alone in a landscape, carries a blue glass in her hand (p. 23); in an interior, she demonstratively raises a bowl and a glass in the air (p. 21)—is she part of a group of people in the garden or house, invisible in the picture? In another depiction, a girl has received yellow flowers and placed them in a jar (p. 129), but her flushed cheeks could also be the result of her own picking. Has a child braided the wreath of yellow flowers herself; why does she hold the delicate flower firmly with both hands; does her gaze reveal a sense of defiance or fear (p. 120)? Perhaps the girl in the landscape with the pigtail, turned to the side, is only

1—See: Karin Schick, "Das Bild als Kosmos. Zu einigen späten Werken von Paula Modersohn-Becker," in: *Paula Modersohn-Becker. Der Weg in die Moderne*, ed. Uwe M. Schneede and Kathrin Baumstark, exh. cat. Bucerius Kunst Forum, Hamburg (Munich 2017), pp. 58–69.

pondering (p. 122); perhaps she strides purposefully in one direction—and also carries something with her.

The models are almost always depicted as half-figures or busts, so that the concentration is entirely on them. A setting and contextual connection are missing in the pictures; only the objects unfold their narrative potential: The flowers, vases, or bowls cannot be held aloft forever; they were once raised upwards and will be lowered again. Modersohn-Becker makes her scenes seem like still images, like moments from an unknown course of events; and even when she allows her figures more surroundings, the girls' relationship to their world remains strangely unclear. In *Nude Girl with Flower Vases* (pp. 136/137) and *Nude Girl Kneeling in Front of a Blue Curtain* (p. 134), the children are placed next to or in front of a curtain as if on a stage. Does the fabric hide a window, a door, or an audience, and what will happen when it opens? The pausing figures could then become acting figures; but at the moment, they are still waiting, surrounded by a supply of flowers, fruits, and vessels.

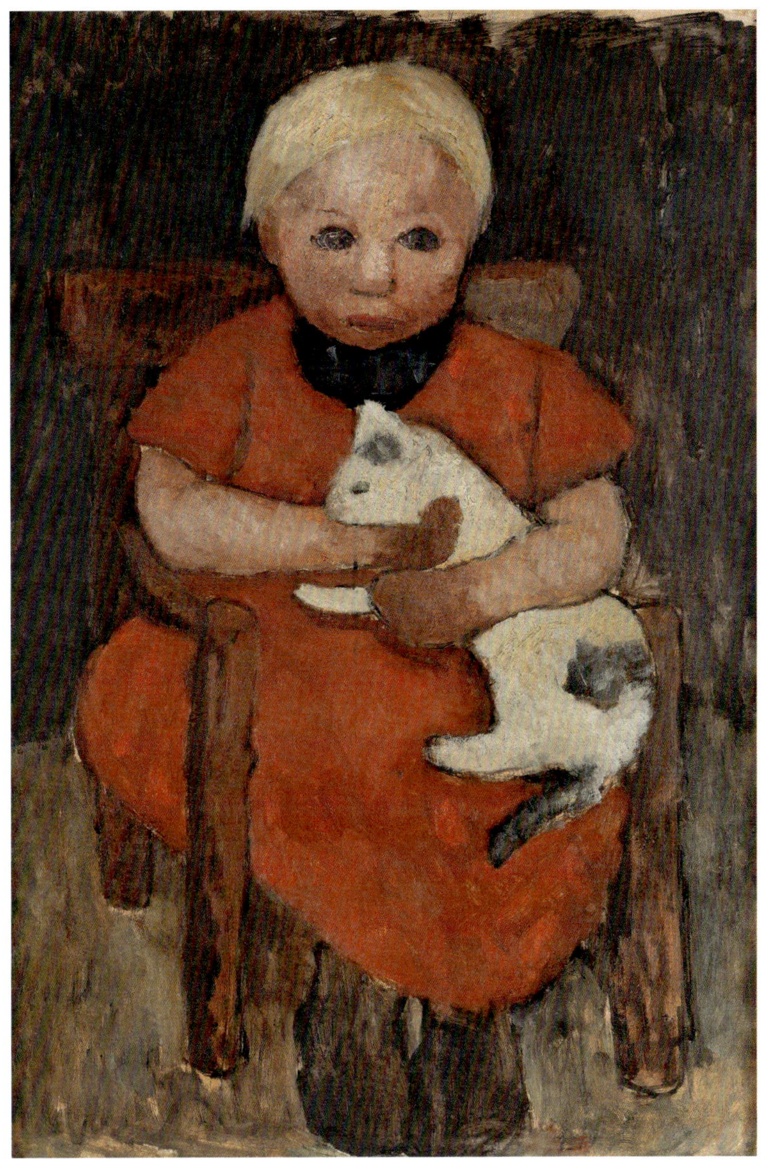

2 Sitzendes blondes Mädchen mit Katze im Arm / Seated Blonde Girl with a Cat in Her Arms, c. 1905, oil tempera on cardboard, 72.5 x 49 cm, Private Collection

As a woman, Paula Modersohn-Becker always saw herself in the roles of wife and mother, but she also single-mindedly pursued her profession as a painter. Her letters and her diary bear witness to an inner conflict and the longing to be simultaneously provided for and free, secure in a community and yet independent, to have a fixed place and to be able to leave at any time. As early as the spring of 1898, possibly in admiration of a courageous cousin, she had written: "How this girl fascinates me! She creates a powerful, beautiful world for herself from within, a world like that of a young boy who enters life with great plans. [...] She is still a bud—still waiting to develop. She does not suspect it, but she waits with a beating heart. [...] I love this simple greatness. It is refreshing, reassuring, like classical antiquity. And yet much more natural, more pulsating. Because it is reality. It is life—modern life."[2] At least in art, she was able to offer a bouquet of possibilities and an open future to girls who were unsure or not yet aware of their abilities.

2—Günter Busch and Liselotte von Reinken (eds.), *Paula Modersohn-Becker in Briefen und Tagebüchern* (Frankfurt am Main 2007), presumably January 1898, pp. 138f. [translated].

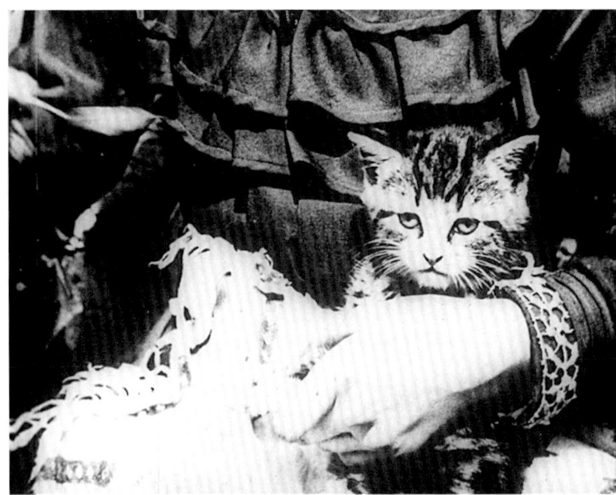

3 George Albert Smith, Sick Kitten, 1903, film still

APPROACHING – *CLOSE-UP*

Around 1905, Paula Modersohn-Becker painted a girl with a cat in her arms (fig. 2). In the center of the picture is the frontally seated toddler with her roundish forms; clumsily, she presses the animal against herself, with the cat threatening to slide down off her lap. With its light fur, it stands out significantly against the red dress, but it is depicted in a very simplified way—its body, face, and extremities are hardly defined and without expression. Quite different is the small cat in a painting with the same color scheme (p. 180): With wide eyes, pointed ears, trembling whiskers, and splayed claws, it gazes curiously out of the picture. Now the cat is the sitter, and its presence is so strong that the child holding it fades completely into the background.

If Modersohn-Becker had been interested in the first film experiments, she might have known the works of a contemporary, the British film pioneer George Albert Smith (1864–1959). The eccentric, who was also active as a hypnotist and mentalist, had attended screenings by the Lumière brothers in London in 1896, acquired a camera, and had begun producing his own works. He used the means of film editing and close-ups in an innovative way and later invented one of the first color film processes. For the short films *Grandma's Reading Glass* and *As Seen Through a Telescope*, produced in 1900, Smith used different camera angles and, for the first time, the close-up technique: The close-ups, framed by a black border, not only enlivened the narrative structure of his films, but they also embraced the main characters, brought their facial expressions and gestures into focus, and invited viewers to identify with them. As in reality, one did not see the people or objects one was close to in their entirety, but rather only in parts.

In 1903, Smith made a short film in which a boy and a girl care for a sick kitten. In a wide-angle shot, *Sick Kitten* shows a furnished interior and the accompanying mother cat, while the close-up focuses solely on the little patient: In front of the girl's dress and in her bent arm, the kitten lies with outstretched paws (fig. 3). Not only is the scene closely related to Modersohn-Becker's painting in terms of motif; the film, presumably made in the same year, refers to a new, modern way of perception: The intimate view of a figure implies moving closer to it and further away from it, later resolved cinematically by the sliding zoom. In the close-up, this time span of movement is not depicted, but its effect is contained within it. In the same way, the painter played with the effect of immediacy, an ostensibly sudden contact, in cropped, close-up images such as *Hands with Chamomile Flower* (p. 190).

GRIPPING – *SUSPENSE*

Paula Modersohn-Becker took every opportunity to paint portraits and found the most diverse models in rural Worpswede. She captured old women and men in numerous pictures: Weary, the figures sit indoors (pp. 66, 67) or, like the old woman from the poorhouse, outdoors in the landscape (p. 74); they surrender to their own heaviness as if they never want to stand up again. However, when Modersohn-Becker drew an old woman with a goose, she executed several movement studies on one sheet, which she framed pictorially (fig. 4). From today's perspective, they resemble the individual frames of a filmstrip or a comic, and the changes in direction of the two striding figures at different distances seem to create a lively sequence.

4 Studien zur Radierung *Die Frau mit der Gans / Sitzende mit linker Hand vor dem Gesicht*, Studies for the etching *The Woman with the Goose / Seated with Left Hand in Front of Face*, c. 1899, Pencil on paper, 26 x 40.3 cm, Paula-Modersohn-Becker-Stiftung, Bremen

The togetherness of human and animal inspired the painter so much that she repeated the theme in numerous variations between 1902 and 1905—but now exclusively with children and young animals. In these depictions, she not only had goats surround her stepdaughter Elsbeth sitting in the field (p. 110) or a rabbit hopping across the meadow at the feet of a girl, but she also usually placed the kids, lambs, chicks, cats, and rabbits directly in the arms of little boys and girls. Thus, in selecting her pictorial subjects, she deliberately focused on two beings whose disposition is movement and who rarely radiate tranquility. When contemplating her paintings, one is aware of the illusion contained in them, because in reality this unity would be short-lived and the probability high that either the animal would run off into the distance or the child's interest would wane.

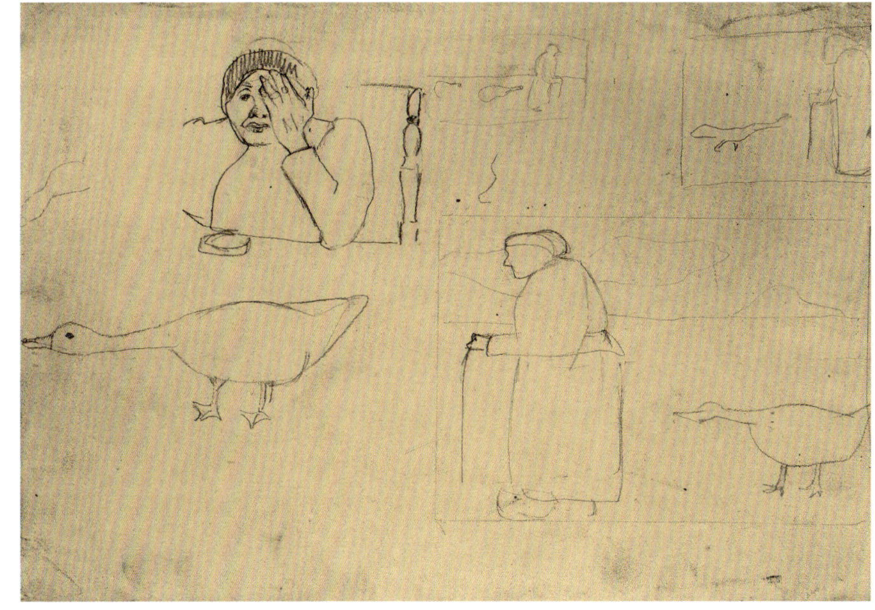

The inherent tension of the motif presumably also fascinated Modersohn-Becker because it corresponded to her sensibility and artistic intention.

As early as January 1899, she noted in her diary: "Inside me, I feel it like a gentle weaving, a vibration, a beating of wings, a trembling state of rest, a holding of breath: If I am able to paint one day, I shall paint that."[3] In February 1903, she reasserted: "I must learn how to express the gentle vibration of things. [...] I must strive to achieve this strange sense of waiting [...] in its great, simple beauty. In general, I must strive for the greatest simplicity through the most intimate observation. That gives greatness."[4]

The quavering holding of breath is impressively conveyed in the painting *Girl with a Rabbit in Her Arms* from 1905: Freely and rapidly placed brushstrokes animate the two bodies and faces, making the landscape that surrounds them vibrate (fig. 5). The head of the girl, who holds the animal protectively against her, is surrounded by an aureole of white sky; her face is slanted upward, and her eyes are directed toward a point outside the picture. Regardless of what she expects from there, one empathizes with her.

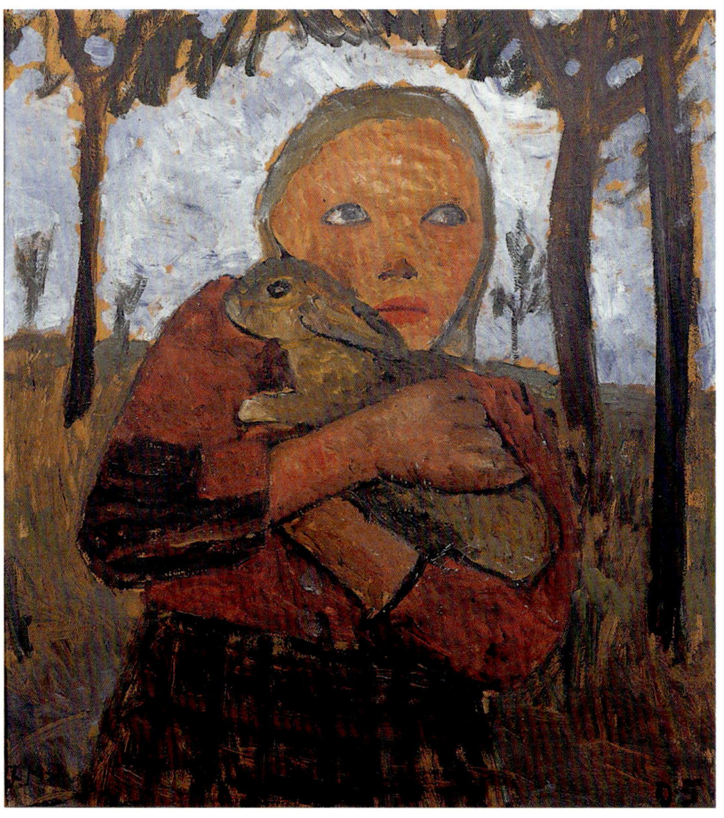

5 Mädchen mit Kaninchen im Arm / Girl with a Rabbit in Her Arms, 1905, oil tempera on cardboard 61 x 55.5 cm, Von der Heydt-Museum, Wuppertal

LETTING GO – *BIRD'S EYE VIEW*

Presumably in the winter of 1905/6, a unique work within Modersohn-Becker's oeuvre was created: the depiction of a cat in the snow (fig. 6). In the small-format picture, painted in one sitting, the animal with reddish-brown fur is seen from a bird's eye view, running across white snow and between two green-brown tree trunks towards the right edge of the picture. The cat could also be lying down, but the tight high cropping and the oblique shadows cast by the trees create such a strong impression of movement that this does not seem to be an option: The blue diagonals painted with powerful brushstrokes cross the horizontal running direction of the cat and the verticals of the trees. The composition seems bold, abstract, almost non-representational. The snow provides the light ground for a formation of lines of varying width; the animal's body is reduced to the extreme, and the trunks are barely recognizable as such. In its momentary randomness, in the unusual top view, which conveys distance and authority at the same time, the small picture is one of the freest representations in Modersohn-

3—Ibid., January 19, 1899, p. 177 [translated].
4—Ibid., February 20, 1903, p. 409 [translated].

Becker's work. It shows an aspect of her talent that she had not been able to pursue until then and that she was not able to develop further right up to her death in November 1907.

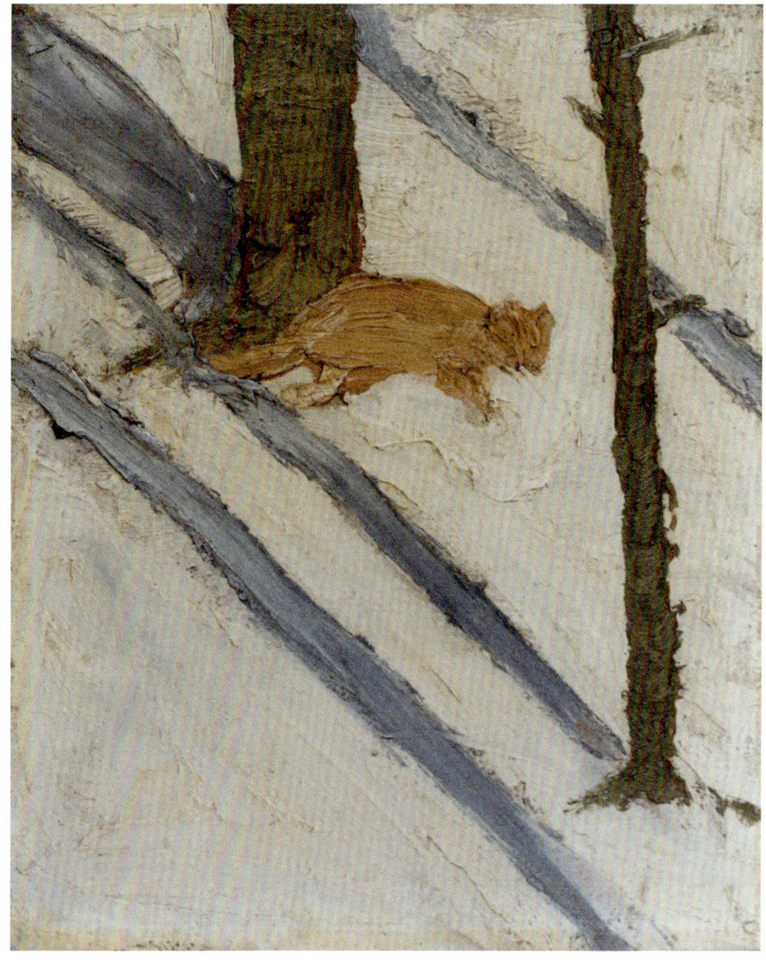

6 Katze im Schnee / Cat in the Snow, c. 1905, oil tempera on cardboard, 26 x 20.7 cm, Private Collection

In January 1906, shortly before she abandoned her husband and moved to Paris to devote herself entirely to art, she wrote to her mother: "This incessant racing towards a goal is the most beautiful thing in life. There is nothing else like it. I ask you to bear in mind that, when I occasionally appear to be lacking in love, I am racing towards my own goal, always, incessantly, only occasionally resting in order to race again towards that goal. It is a concentration of my energies on that one thing."[5] In his *Metaphysics*, Aristotle formulated that everything that exists is conceived in a purposeful movement from the possible to the actual. Capacity—ancient Greek *dýnamis*, Latin *potentia*—is a central concept of ancient philosophy; it designates the property of a substance to be able to change itself or something else. Only through change can something new come into being. It is precisely this potential, the as-yet-to-be-redeemed reality, which seems to charge Paula Modersohn-Becker's paintings with so much mystery and meaning. Her waiting girls and trembling animals carry the future of life and of art—as possibilities of being.

5 —Ibid., January 19, 1906, pp. 516f. [translated].

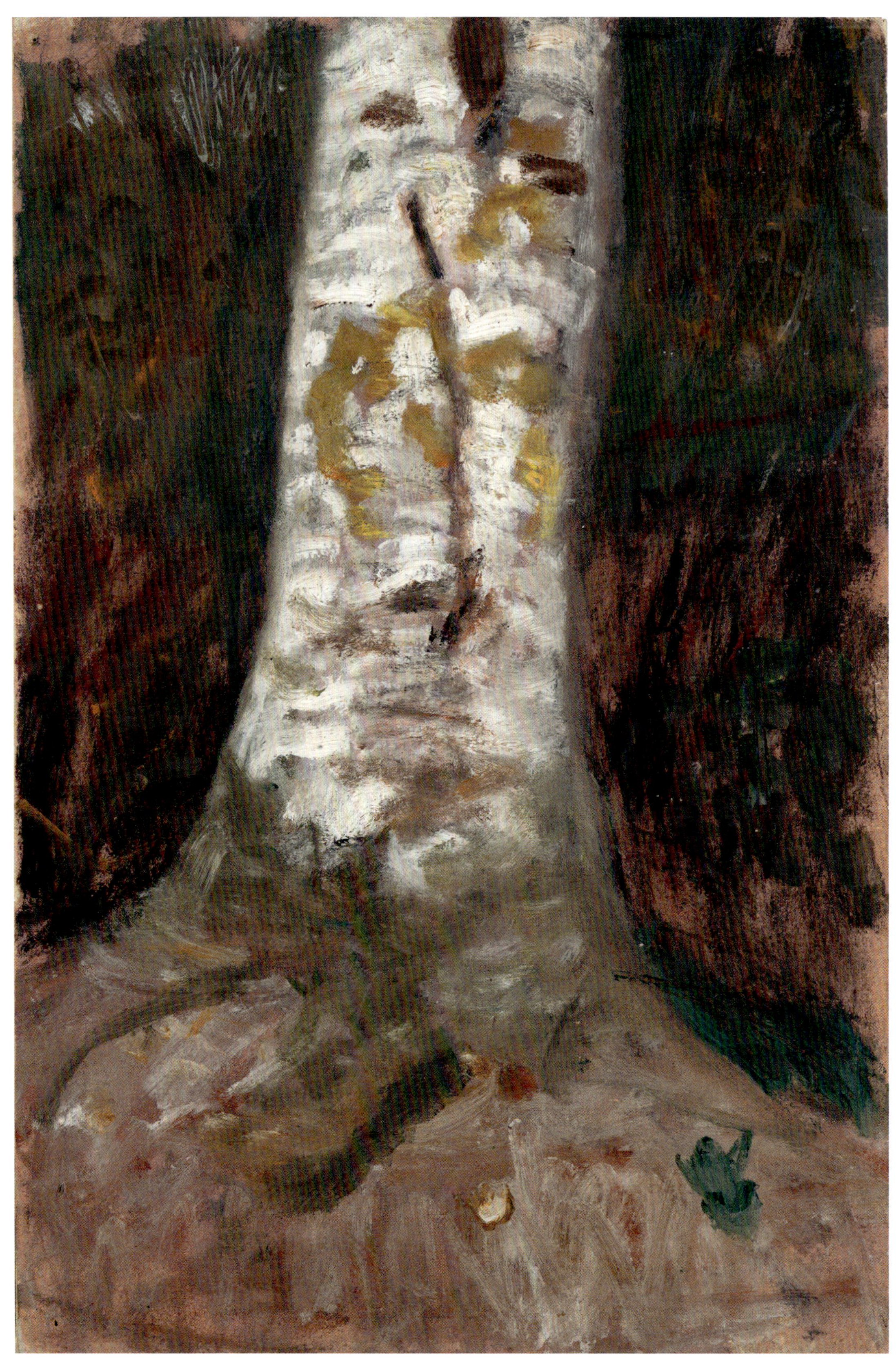

Birkenstamm / Birch Trunk, c. 1902

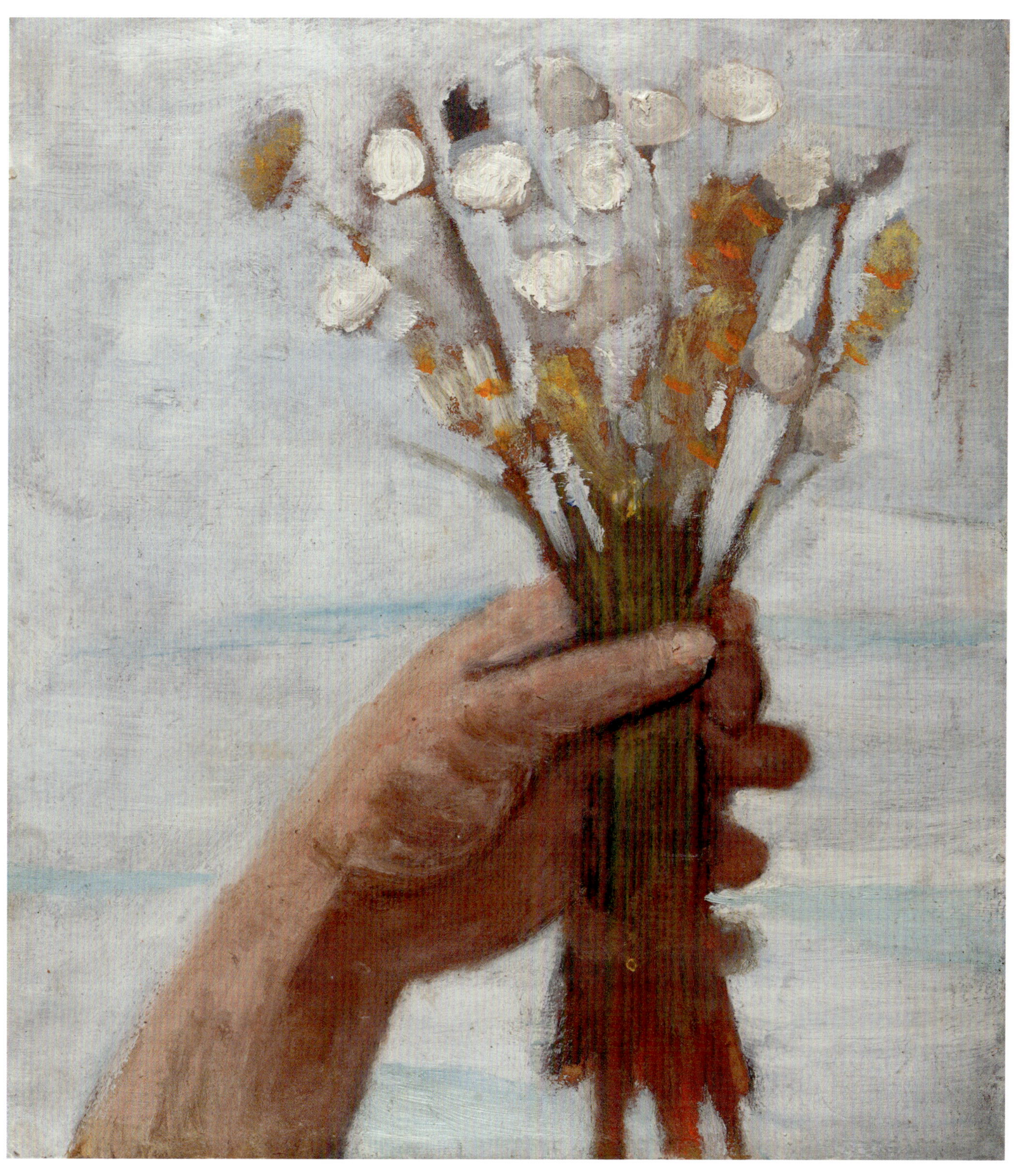

Hand mit Blumenstrauß / Hand with Flower Bouquet, c. 1902

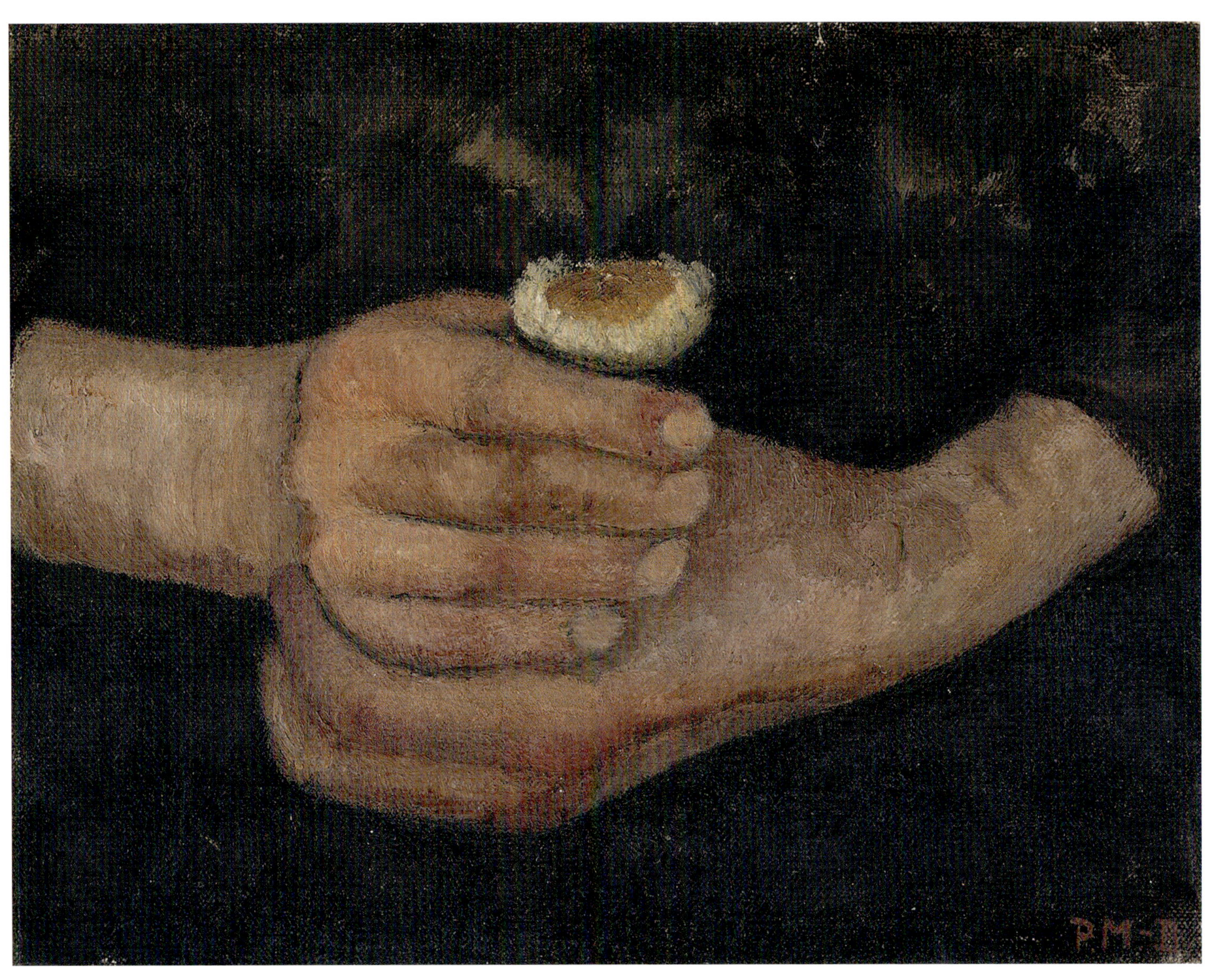

Hände mit Kamillenblume / Hands with Chamomile Flower, c. 1902

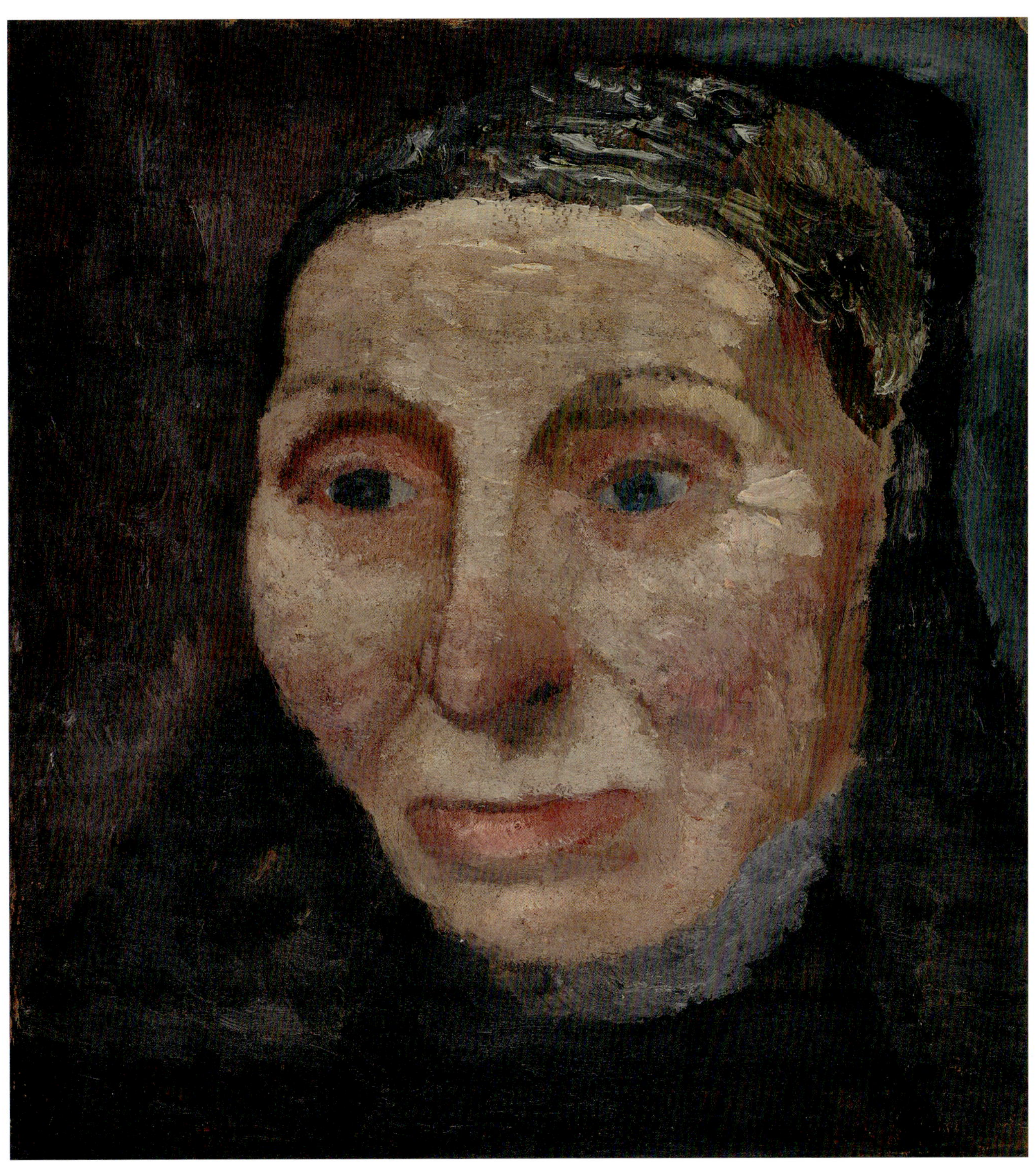

Kopf einer Bauernfrau / Head of a Farmer's Wife, c. 1903

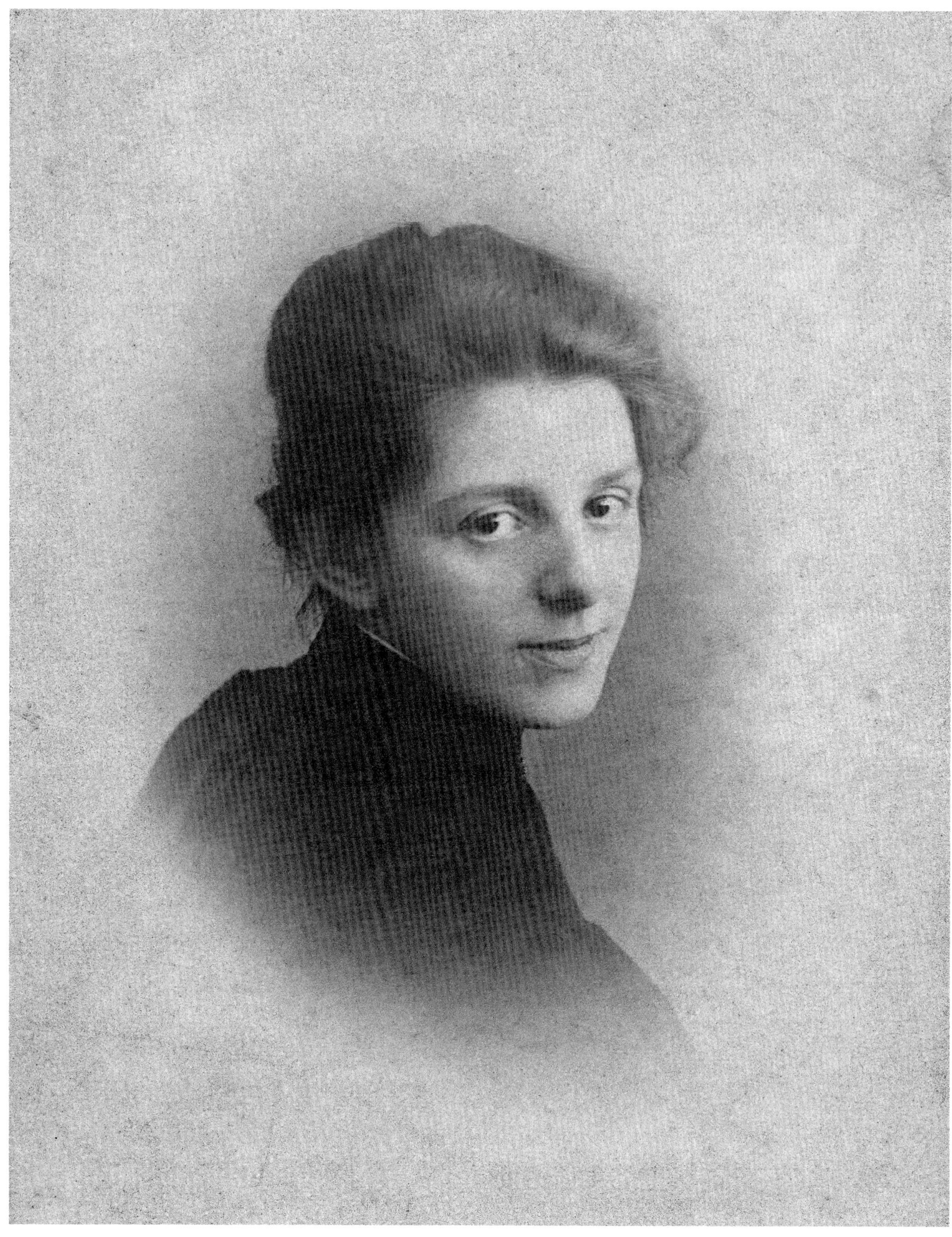

1 Paula Becker, c. 1895

PAULA MODERSOHN-BECKER

A BIOGRAPHY BETWEEN WORPSWEDE AND PARIS

SIMONE EWALD AND WOLFGANG WERNER

1876–1891 Minna Hermine Paula Becker is born in Dresden on February 8, 1876, the third of seven children. Her father Carl Woldemar Becker (1841–1901) is a construction inspector with the Berlin-Dresden railroad, later in Bremen a construction councilor of the Prussian railroad administration. Her mother Mathilde Becker (1852–1926) comes from the aristocratic Thuringian von Bültzingslöwen family. In 1888, the family moves to Bremen, where they take an active part in the city's literary and artistic scenes.

1892 Seven-month sojourn in England with her aunt Marie Hill on a country estate near London. First drawing lessons at St. John's Wood Art School.

1893–1895 At the request of her father, she attends the teacher's training college in Bremen and graduates in September 1895. In addition, she takes painting and drawing lessons with the Bremen-based painter Bernhard Wiegandt. In April 1895, she visits the first exhibition of Worpswede painters in the Kunsthalle Bremen. She mentions Fritz Mackensen, Otto Modersohn, and Heinrich Vogeler.

1896 In the spring, she participates in a course at the School of Drawing and Painting of the Verein der Berliner Künstlerinnen und Kunstfreundinnen (Association of Female

Berlin Artists and Art Lovers), founded in 1867. In October, she begins her one-and-a-half-year studies there. She uses her free time to visit museums: "I am becoming very familiar with the German masters now, and with Holbein—but Rembrandt still remains the greatest." Summer trip to Hindelang in the Allgäu with a stop in Munich to visit the Pinakothek and the Schackgalerie.

1897 In February, she joins the portrait painting class of the Swedish-German painter Jeanna Bauck, which has a lasting influence on her. Frequent visits to exhibitions in the Schulte, Gurlitt, and Keller & Reiner galleries. At the Berlin Kupferstichkabinett (Collection of Prints and Drawings), she studies drawings by Michelangelo and Botticelli's illustrations of Dante's *Divine Comedy*. First stay in Worpswede from the end of July to the end of August. In early October, she travels to Dresden for the Internationale Kunstausstellung (International Art Exhibition) with works by Degas, Monet, Pissarro, Sisley, Böcklin, Hodler, Klinger, Segantini, and the Worpswede artists. She participates in the semester exhibition of the School of Drawing and Painting. In early December, she travels to Vienna and visits the museums there, including the Liechtenstein Galerie. In her letters, she mentions Titian, Rubens, Dürer, Cranach, Holbein, da Vinci, and van Dyck.

1898 Continuation of her studies in Berlin. In March/April, she is fascinated by the exhibition of lithographs at the Kunstgewerbemuseum (Museum of Decorative Arts), featuring works by Klinger, Menzel, Thoma, Manet, Pissarro, Sérusier, Signac, Toulouse-Lautrec, Vallotton, and Munch. At the gallery of Fritz Gurlitt, she sees paintings by Rippl-Rónai and at Galerie Eduard Schulte the Berlin-based artist group known as the "Elfer" (Eleven), including Liebermann and Klinger; in her letters, she mentions Leistikow. At the Keller & Reiner gallery, there is a Munch exhibition in April. On a trip to Leipzig, she visits Klinger's studio. At the end of May, she completes her studies in Berlin, after which she spends the summer in Norway with her uncle Wulf von Bültzingslöwen. In September, she settles in Worpswede. She writes to her aunt Cora von Bültzingslöwen about her first evening in Worpswede: "I'm savoring my life with every breath I take; and in the distance, Paris gleams and shimmers." She receives critique of her life-size model drawings in charcoal and red chalk from Fritz Mackensen, who had already accepted Clara Westhoff and Marie Bock as pupils. Friendship with the sculptor Clara Westhoff.

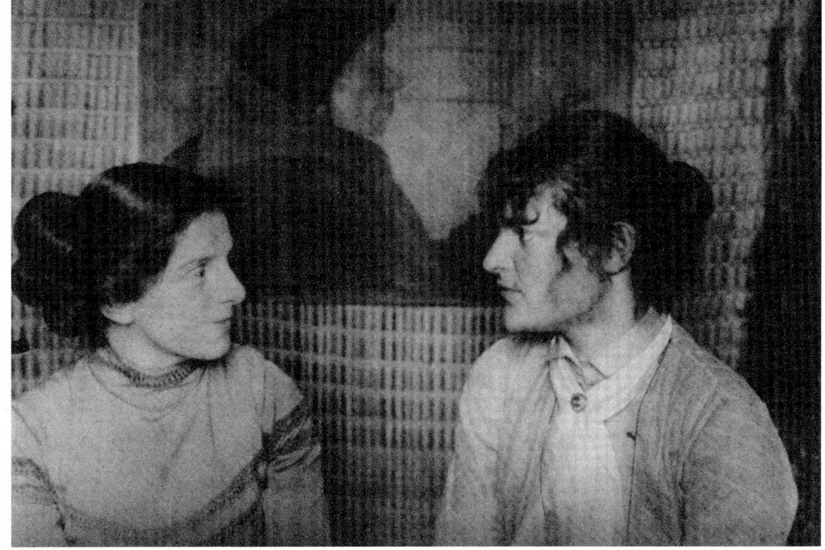

1899 Her sketchbooks are filled with landscape drawings, figure studies, and compositional sketches. She creates her first paintings and a series of etchings, which she prints by hand at Vogeler's home, the Barkenhoff. She reads a great deal, especially J. P. Jacobsen and Henrik Ibsen, in addition to older literature. In August, she travels to Switzerland. The return trip takes her via Munich, Nuremberg, and Leipzig, where Clara Westhoff is working with Klinger, and to Dresden for the Deutsche Kunstausstellung (Exhibition of German Art), in which the Worpswede artists participate. In December, together with Marie Bock and Clara Westhoff, she exhibits several studies in the Kunsthalle Bremen, which are scathingly reviewed by the painter and critic Arthur Fitger.

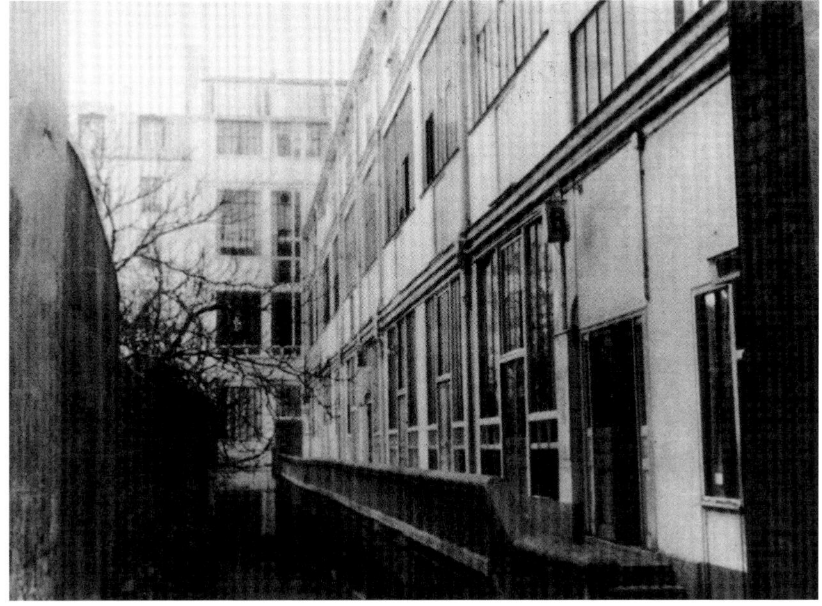

2 Paula Becker and Clara Westhoff in Paula's studio, c. 1899

3 Paula Becker's studio apartment at 9 Rue Campagne Première, 1900

1900 On New Year's Eve, Paula Becker travels to Paris for the first time and meets Clara Westhoff, who wishes to study at the sculpture school established by Rodin. She moves into a studio at 9 Rue Campagne Première and participates in the life drawing class at the Académie Colarossi, where she wins the "concours" medal of her semester. She also attends anatomy classes at the École des Beaux-Arts together with Clara Westhoff. At the gallery of the art dealer Ambroise Vollard, the young artist discovers paintings by Cézanne, which greatly impress her. Numerous visits to the Louvre, where she draws copies of paintings and sculptures. In her letters, she mentions Titian, Botticelli, Fiesole (Fra Angelico), Velázquez, Rembrandt, Holbein, della Robbia, and Donatello. Of the more recent masters, she mentions Corot, Rousseau, Millet, Daubigny, Degas, Puvis de Chavannes, Courbet, and Monet. In the gallery of Georges Petit, she sees works by the Breton painters Lucien Simon and Charles Cottet. *La Revue Blanche* presents a comprehensive Seurat exhibition in March. Encounter with Emil Nolde and the painter Emmi Walther from Dachau. In June, Otto Modersohn, Fritz and Hermine Overbeck, and Marie Bock come

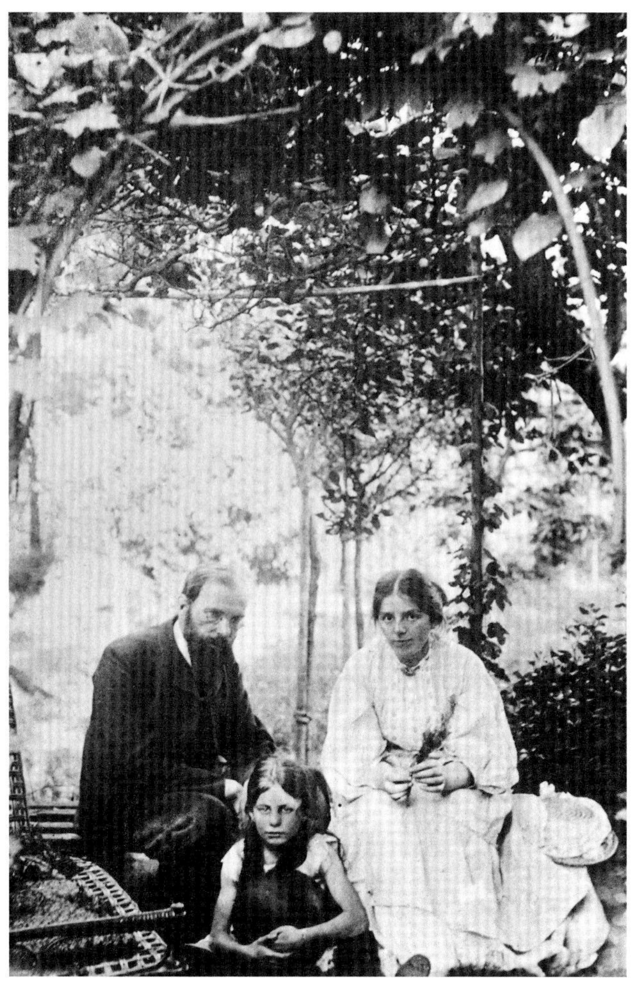

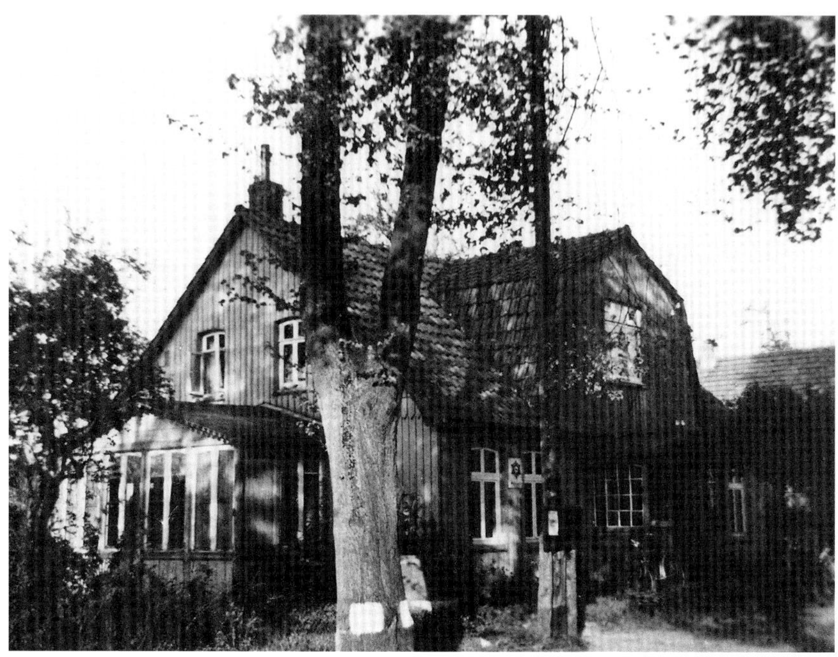

4 Paula, Otto, and Elsbeth Modersohn at the Barkenhoff, c. 1904, photo: Ernst Portig

5 The residence of Paula and Otto Modersohn in Worpswede, c. 1902

from Worpswede to Paris. Joint visit to the Exposition Universelle and Rodin's sculpture pavilion at the Pont de l'Alma. Death of Modersohn's wife Helene in Worpswede.

At the end of June, Paula Becker returns to Worpswede. On Sundays, the circle of friends who call themselves the "family" meets in the White Hall of Vogeler's Barkenhoff: Otto Modersohn and Paula Becker, Heinrich Vogeler and his later wife Martha Schröder, Clara Westhoff, Marie Bock, and Paula's sisters Milly and Herma. The poets Carl Hauptmann and Rainer Maria Rilke are frequent guests. In September, Paula Becker and Otto Modersohn become engaged. Apart from a few figure paintings, she paints almost exclusively landscapes.

1901 In January and February, at the request of her parents, she takes cooking lessons in Berlin. During visits to museums, her interest is focused on Rembrandt,

Velázquez, and Verrocchio, as well as on Dürer, Hans Baldung Grien, the Master of Messkirch, and Goya. She draws further copies of the Old Masters. In the Berlin galleries, she sees the Daumier exhibition at Cassirer's and paintings by Böcklin at Gurlitt's. Frequent meetings with Rilke.

On May 25, she marries Otto Modersohn, who brings his three-year-old daughter Elsbeth into the marriage. The honeymoon takes her via Berlin, Dresden, and Schreiberhau, where they visit Carl Hauptmann, as well as to Prague, Munich, and Dachau. She keeps her room with the farmer Brünjes to use it as a studio.

1902 In her paintings, she deals predominantly with the theme of figures embedded in the landscape and occasionally paints with Otto Modersohn in front of the same motif. She is intensively preoccupied with her own painting and deliberates on color and pictorial composition: "I dream of movement in the color, of a gentle shimmering, vibration, of one object setting another in motion through color."

1903 In February, she travels to Paris for a second time and enrolls once again in a life drawing class at the Académie Colarossi. Joint visits with the Rilkes to the art galleries on Rue Lafitte; at the Hôtel Drouot, they view old Japanese paintings and sculptures from the Hayashi Collection. She sketches in the Louvre on an almost daily basis. In addition to Rembrandt and Veronese, she is interested in antiquity, especially in the late antique Fayum mummy portraits. After a visit to the Musée du Luxembourg, she mentions Manet, Renoir, Zuloaga, Cottet, and Degas. Through Rilke's mediation, she visits Rodin, who shows her his watercolors. In March, she returns to Worpswede. The Modersohn family spends the summer on the island of Amrum. In the winter of 1903/4, she creates only a few paintings and reads, mainly French literature.

1904 In a critical examination of what she had previously created, Modersohn-Becker seeks new pictorial forms, which she prepares in

6 Detail: Paula Modersohn-Becker in the porch of her house, c. 1901, photo: Atelier Schaub, Hamburg

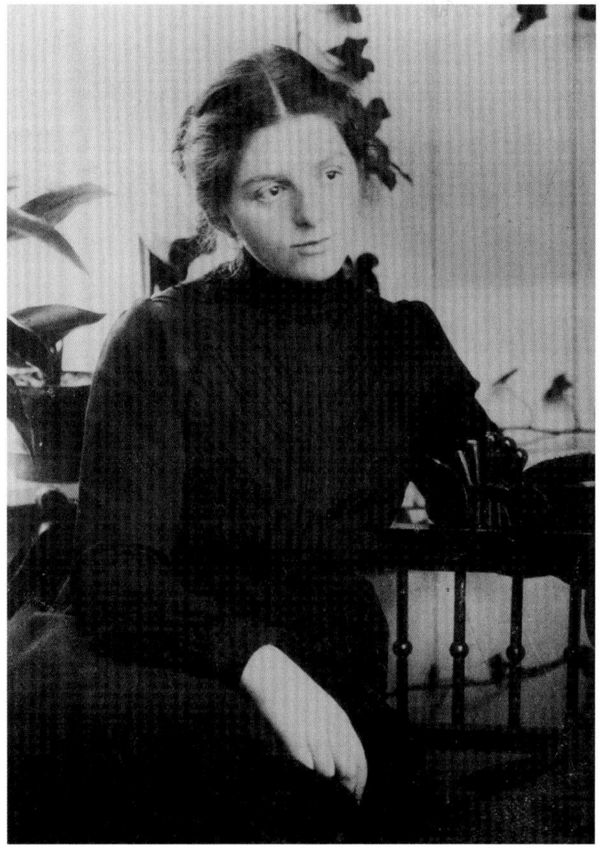

her drawings. A central pictorial theme of the years 1904/5 are figures embedded in the landscape, such as the *Girl Blowing a Flute in the Birch Forest* (p. 118). Summer trip with Otto Modersohn via Berlin to Dresden, where they visit the Große Kunstausstellung (Great Art Exhibition), featuring a retrospective of nineteenth-century French masters, as well as to Kassel, and Braunschweig (Rembrandt). She largely withdraws from her Worpswede painter colleagues.

1905 In February, she travels for the third time to Paris. She enrolls for one month at the Académie Julian, where Gauguin and the Nabis had studied in the 1890s, to paint "from life from eight to eleven each day." Through Rilke, she makes the acquaintance of the Norwegian writer couple Johann and Ellen Bojer. She visits the studios of the Nabis Édouard Vuillard and Maurice Denis, as well as of Charles Cottet, and sees sculptures by Aristide Maillol. The Galeries Serrurier organize a Picasso exhibition with paintings of the *Saltimbanques* (Jugglers). She asks Otto Modersohn to send her addresses of private collections in Paris from Meier-Graefe's *Entwicklungsgeschichte der modernen Kunst* (History of the Development of Modern Art, 1904). At the Salon des Indépendants, she sees paintings by Matisse and the Fauves, as well as the retrospectives of Seurat and van Gogh. In late March, Otto Modersohn, Milly Becker, and Martha and Heinrich Vogeler come to Paris. Together, they visit Gustave Fayet's Gauguin collection and take a trip to Meudon to see Rodin. In April, they return to Worpswede. She asks her sister Herma in Paris to send her prices of various publications about Gauguin, including *Noa Noa*.

7 Paula Modersohn-Becker's studio at 14 Avenue du Maine

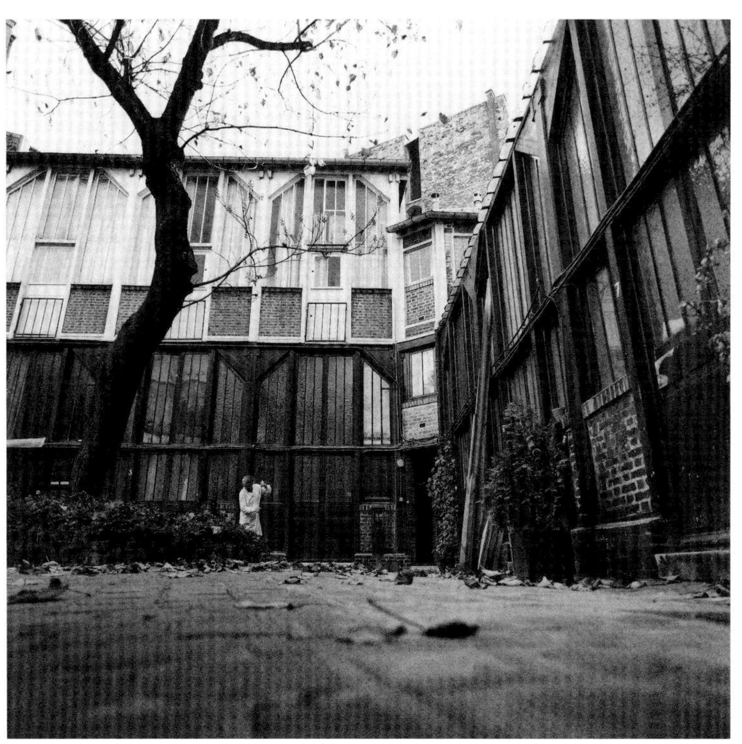

In November, Paula and Otto Modersohn, together with Heinrich Vogeler, visit Karl Ernst Osthaus and his wife in Hagen to view their Museum Folkwang. At Christmas, Rilke is in Worpswede and acquires the painting *Infant with Its Mother's Hand* (p. 104) during a studio visit. At the turn of the year, the Modersohns travel to Schreiberhau at the invitation of Carl Hauptmann. There, they meet, among others, the sociologist Werner Sombart and, during an excursion to Dresden, the painter Otto Mueller.

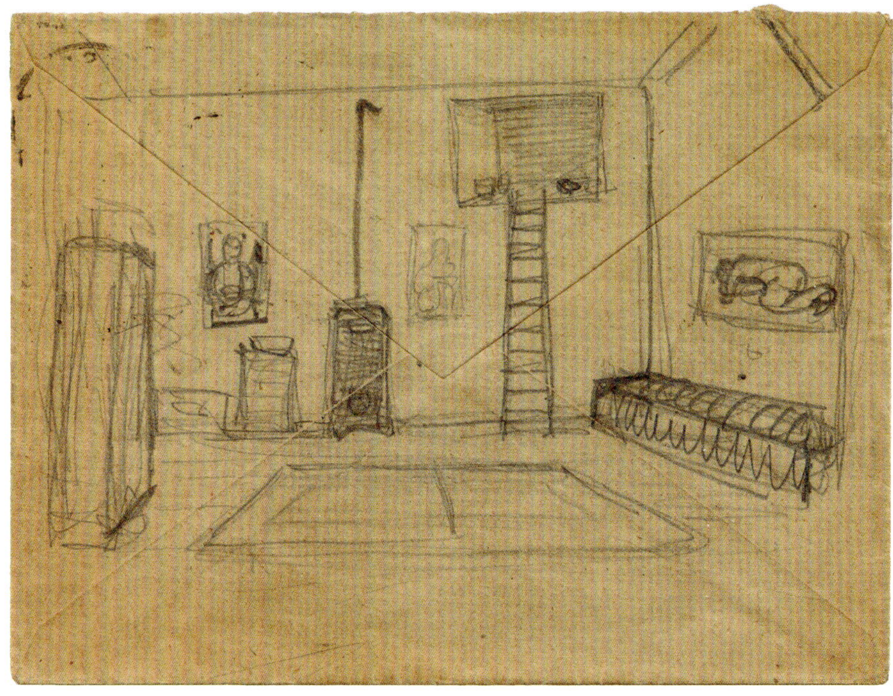

8 Sketch by Paula Modersohn-Becker of her last Parisian studio at 49 Boulevard Montparnasse, 1906; on the walls, the pictures Busch / Werner 685, 695, 657

1906 The return journey from Schreiberhau takes them via Dresden and Berlin. They visit the Kaiser-Friedrich-Museum and the Jahrhundertausstellung deutscher Kunst aus der Zeit von 1775–1875 (Centenary Exhibition of German Art from the Period 1775–1875) in the Nationalgalerie. She mentions Leibl, Trübner, Böcklin, Feuerbach, and Marées.

On February 23, Paula Modersohn-Becker turns her back on Worpswede—and with this also on Otto Modersohn—and moves to Paris. She now intends to devote herself exclusively to her own work without external constraints and realize in paintings what she had gradually worked out in her studies and drawings over the past years. Although she writes to Carl Hauptmann on April 22, 1906, that "it [has] probably been the five most beautiful years of my life that I have been in Worpswede," she concludes with the postscript: "It's too cramped for me."

In early March, she rents space in the artist's studio courtyard at 14 Avenue du Maine, and initially for one month attends the anatomy and life drawing classes at the École des Beaux-Arts, to which women are now admitted. The Galerie Druet exhibits Matisse paintings, and at Vollard works by Cézanne are once again on view. She writes to Otto Modersohn about her exhibition visits: "I've seen wonderful Courbets; I am sorry that he is now the latest fashion. I think he is greater than either Manet or Monet."

In early April, she goes on excursions with Rilke, occasionally joined by Ellen Key and the Bojers. She paints portraits of Rainer Maria Rilke and Werner Sombart, who is also in Paris. In mid-April, she spends Easter with her sister Herma in St. Malo in Brittany. Here, she sees the naïve, strongly colored sculptures that Abbé Fouré had carved into the rocks near Rothéneuf in the nineteenth century; they become one of the sources of inspiration for her late figure paintings. Back in Paris, Rilke and Paula Modersohn-Becker attend the unveiling of Rodin's *Thinker* in front of the Panthéon on April 22 with

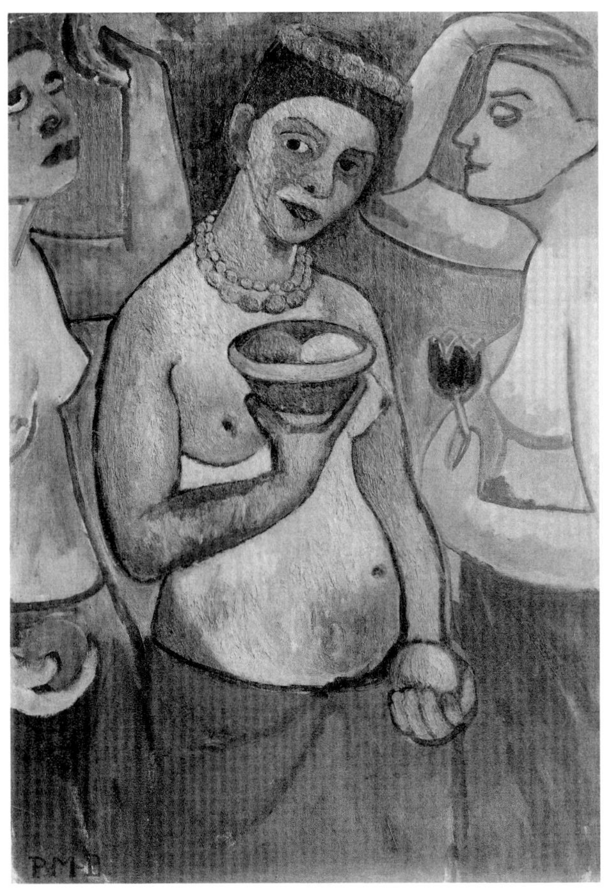

9 Composition with three female figures; in the center, a self-portrait, 1906/7, oil tempera on cardboard, 110 x 75 cm, lost during the war (Part of the von der Heydt collection was burned and destroyed during the air raid on Elberfeld on June 24, 1943 in the family's ancestral home at Kerstenplatz 6)

other artists, including Maillol. She meets the sculptor Bernhard Hoetger and his wife Helene (Lee). In early May, Hoetger visits the painter in her studio and is convinced of her great talent. Weeks of intensive work on the monumental figure compositions follow. First comes the self-portrait completed on May 25, 1906, with the programmatic inscription: "I painted this at age 30 / on my 6th wedding day," which she signs "P. B." (Paula Becker) (p. 32). Her sister Herma, who is also in Paris, informs her mother: "Her thirtieth year will give her pause for thought, she had after all set it as a goal for herself for her painting."

That same month, she begins to prepare her nude compositions in a multitude of quickly executed, very abbreviated drawings. For this purpose, she has Italian mothers with children come to the studio, who she orders at the model market on Rue de la Grande-Chaumière at the beginning of each week. In June/July she executes the large paintings with mother and child motifs, some lying and other standing. She reports to her friend Martha Vogeler in Worpswede: "I love to fall asleep among my paintings and wake up with them in the morning. With faith in God and myself, I'm painting life-size nudes and still lifes."

In August, inspired by the pictorial world of the painter Henri Rousseau, whose studio she visits with the Hoetgers, she begins the large half-figure painting *Lee Hoetger in Front of a Floral Background* (p. 63). On November 18, her sister Milly enquires about this portrait and whether it should be exhibited in the spring. Paula Modersohn-Becker thus presumably intended to show it at the Salon des Indépendants. Regarding two other paintings of Lee Hoetger, she informs Heinrich Vogeler on August 12: "At the moment, I am painting Mrs. Hoetger's portrait. She can look absolutely magnificent, and grave; with an enormous crown of hair, blond, splendidly shaped." These tectonically constructed portraits mark the beginning of her new Proto-Cubist phase of work, with *Kneeling Mother with Child at Her Breast* (p. 101) and *Semi-Nude of an Italian Woman with a Plate in Her Raised Hand*. In the fall, she then works on the mask-like *Self-Portrait with Lemon* (p. 30) and the *Self-Portrait Turned to the Right with Her Hand at Her Chin* (p. 158). The inspiration for this presumably came from African masks that she had seen during a joint visit with Bernhard Hoetger to the Musée de l'Homme. Also with Hoetger, she visits the Gauguin retrospective on view at the Salon d'Automne. In late October, Otto Modersohn comes to Paris to spend the winter with his wife. At the same time, she takes a new studio on Boulevard Montparnasse. In November, the Kunsthalle Bremen shows four of her paintings in the exhibition of Worpswede artists, which then travels on to Fritz Gurlitt's gallery in Berlin.

1907 Before returning to Worpswede at the end of March, she sees the Cézanne collection of Auguste Pellerin. In Worpswede that summer, she executes, in addition to still lifes, the monumental figure paintings *Old Woman from the Poorhouse in the Garden with Glass Globe and Poppies* (p. 38) and *Old Peasant Woman* (p. 77). She communicates her new thoughts on the color composition of her paintings to Bernhard Hoetger: "I have not done much work this summer [...]. In conception, all the work has probably remained much the same. However, the execution, I think, is quite another matter. What I want to produce is something compelling, something full, an excitement and intoxication of color—something powerful. The paintings I did in Paris are too cool, too solitary and empty. [...] We must work with digested and assimilated Impressionism."

In October, Rilke sends her the catalog she has requested of the Salon d'Automne with the Cézanne retrospective. Clara Rilke-Westhoff, to whom he describes his impressions of this exhibition in a series of letters, writes to her heavily pregnant friend on October 18 that she wants to come to Worpswede in the next few days to read to her from it. Paula Modersohn-Becker replies: "My mind has been so much occupied these days by the thought of Cézanne, of how he has been one of the three or four powerful artists who have affected me like a thunderstorm, like some great event. Do you still remember what we saw at Vollard in 1900? [...] Please come soon and bring the letters. Come right away, Monday if you can possibly make it, for I hope soon, finally, to be otherwise occupied. If it were not absolutely necessary for me to be here right now, nothing could keep me away from Paris." On November 2, her daughter Mathilde is born. On November 20, Paula Modersohn-Becker dies of an embolism.

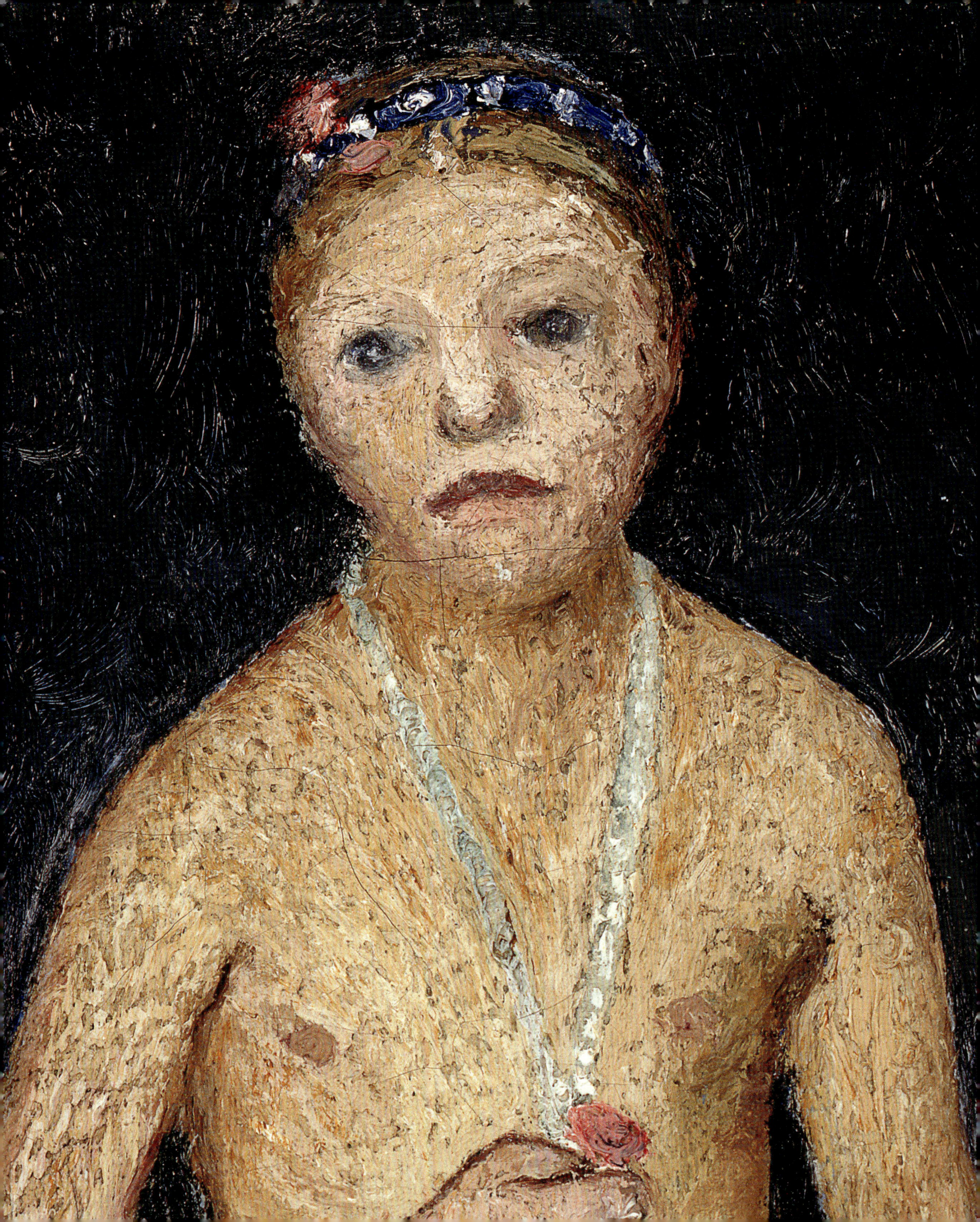

LIST OF EXHIBITED WORKS

Selbstbildnis, c. 1898
Self-Portrait
Oil on cardboard
28.2 x 23 cm
Kunsthalle Bremen – Der Kunstverein in Bremen
Busch / Werner 2
p. 19

Brustbild eines Mädchens in der Sonne vor weiter Landschaft, 1897
Half-Length Portrait of a Girl in the Sun in Front of a Wide Landscape
Oil on cardboard
44.5 x 49 cm
Galerie Haas AG, Zurich
Busch / Werner 12
p. 121

Brustbild einer Frau mit Mohnblumen, c. 1898
Woman with Poppies
Oil tempera on cardboard
57.5 x 46 cm
Museen Böttcherstraße, Paula Modersohn-Becker Museum, Bremen
Busch / Werner 24
p. 57

Blick aus dem Atelierfenster der Künstlerin in Paris, 1900
View from the Window of the Artist's Studio in Paris
Inscribed and dated in pencil (lower right): Paris 1900
Oil tempera on cardboard
48.7 x 37.3 cm
Kunsthalle Bremen – Der Kunstverein in Bremen
Busch / Werner 51
p. 83

Halbakt einer sitzenden Bäuerin, 1900
Half-Length Nude of a Seated Peasant Woman
Oil tempera on canvas
81.7 x 53.7 cm
Bundesrepublik Deutschland
Land Niedersachsen
Kulturstiftung Landkreis Osterholz
Busch / Werner 56
p. 155

Don Quichote, 1900
Don Quixote
Dated in pencil (lower center): 1900
Oil tempera on cardboard
53 x 39.5 cm
Paula-Modersohn-Becker-Stiftung, Bremen
Busch / Werner 66
p. 79

Zwei Männer beim Torfstechen, 1900
Two Men Cutting Peat
Dated in pencil (lower center): 1900
Oil tempera on cardboard
52.5 x 39 cm
Museum am Modersohn-Haus, Worpswede, Sammlung Bernhard Kaufmann
Busch / Werner 71
p. 69

Zwei Bäuerinnen beim Torfstechen, 1900
Two Peasant Women Cutting Peat
Dated in pencil (lower right): 1900
Oil tempera on cardboard
53 x 41 cm
Museum am Modersohn-Haus, Worpswede, Sammlung Bernhard Kaufmann
Busch / Werner 73
p. 68

Moorgraben, c. 1900
(Moorkanal)
Moor Ditch
(Moor Canal)
Oil tempera on cardboard
54.5 x 42 cm
Albertinum | Galerie Neue Meister, Staatliche Kunstsammlungen Dresden
Busch / Werner 102
p. 91

Moorgraben, 1900
Moor Ditch
Dated in pencil (lower left): 1900
Oil tempera on cardboard
39.5 x 53 cm
Paula-Modersohn-Becker-Stiftung, Bremen
Busch / Werner 105
p. 90

Mond über Feldern, 1900
Moon over Fields
Oil tempera on cardboard
39.2 x 53 cm
Paula-Modersohn-Becker-Stiftung, Bremen
Busch / Werner 117
p. 89

Mond über Landschaft, 1900
Moon over Landscape
Oil tempera on cardboard
42 x 55.5 cm
Paula-Modersohn-Becker-Stiftung, Bremen
Busch / Werner 118
p. 88

Dämmerungslandschaft mit Haus und Astgabel, c. 1900
Landscape in Twilight with House and Branch Fork
Oil tempera on cardboard
42.5 x 55.7 cm
Kunsthalle Bremen – Der Kunstverein in Bremen
Busch / Werner 120
p. 82

Birkenallee im Herbst, 1900
Birch Avenue in Autumn
Dated in pencil (lower right): 1900
Oil tempera on cardboard
37 x 46.6 cm
Paula-Modersohn-Becker-Stiftung, Bremen
Busch / Werner 141
p. 87

Weg mit Birken, 1900
Path with Birch Trees
Dated in pencil (lower right): 1900
Oil tempera on cardboard
74.2 x 28.6 cm
Paula-Modersohn-Becker-Stiftung, Bremen
Busch / Werner 147
p. 92

Selbstbildnis mit gelbem Kranz, c. 1901
Self-Portrait with Yellow Wreath
Oil tempera on cardboard
31 x 33 cm
Private Collection
Busch / Werner 152
p. 18

Kopf der Schwester Herma mit Marienblümchenkranz auf dem Hut, c. 1901
The Artist's Sister Herma with a Wreath of Daisies on Her Hat
Oil tempera on cardboard
46.5 x 38.5 cm
Galerie Michael Haas, Berlin
Busch / Werner 156
p. 56

Brustbild eines Mädchens mit Kranz und Gänseblume in den Händen, c. 1901
Girl with Yellow Wreath and Daisy
Oil tempera on cardboard
53 x 50 cm
Private Collection, Courtesy Kallir Research Institute, New York
Busch / Werner 158
p. 120

Brustbild eines Mädchens mit Schleier nach rechts gewandt vor Landschaft, c. 1901
Half-Length Portrait of a Girl with a Veil Turning to the Right in Front of a Landscape
(Martha Vogeler)
Oil tempera on cardboard
38 x 49.7 cm
Private Collection
Busch / Werner 163
pp. 58/59

Mädchenbildnis, 1901
(Brustbild eines Mädchens vor Landschaft nach rechts gewandt)
Portrait of a Girl
(Bust of a Girl Turned Right in Front of a Landscape)
Dated (lower right): VII. 1901.
Oil tempera on cardboard overlaid with silver foil
38 x 54 cm
Städel Museum, Frankfurt am Main
Busch / Werner 167
p. 122

Mädchenkopf, 1901
(Kopf eines blonden Mädchens vor Luft
auch betitelt: Bildnis eines kranken Mädchens)
Head of a Girl
(Head of a Blonde Girl in Front of Sky
also titled: Portrait of a Sick Girl)
Dated (lower left): VII. 1901
Oil tempera on canvas mounted on cardboard
35 x 33 cm
LWL-Museum für Kunst und Kultur
Westfälisches Landesmuseum
Busch / Werner 168
p. 123

Drei badende Jungen am Kanal, 1901
Three Boys Bathing by a Canal
Dated (lower right): VII. 1901.
Oil tempera on cardboard mounted on wood
54.2 x 39.2 cm
Worcester Art Museum, Worcester, MA, Stoddard Acquisition Fund, 2019.48
Busch / Werner 180
p. 125

Kinder mit Laternen vor Haus, c. 1901
Children with Lanterns in Front of a House
Oil tempera on cardboard
40.5 x 57.2 cm
Kunsthandel Wolfgang Werner, Bremen / Berlin
Busch / Werner 194
pp. 126/127

Sandkuhle, 1901
Sand Pit
Dated (on the reverse): Aug. 1901
Oil tempera on cardboard
46.6 x 64.8 cm
Paula-Modersohn-Becker-Stiftung, Bremen
Busch / Werner 240
p. 86

Birkenstämme vor Landschaft, c. 1901
Birch Trunks in Front of a Landscape
Oil tempera on cardboard
73.6 x 46.2 cm
Paula-Modersohn-Becker-Stiftung, Bremen
Busch / Werner 250
p. 95

Birkenstämme, 1900
Birch Trunks
Oil tempera on cardboard
47 x 39 cm
Private Collection
Courtesy Kunsthandel Wolfgang Werner, Bremen / Berlin
Busch / Werner 251
p. 94

Birkenstämme vor roter Hauswand, c. 1901
Birch Trunks in Front of a Red House Wall
Oil tempera on cardboard
53 x 39.8 cm
Paula-Modersohn-Becker-Stiftung, Bremen
Busch / Werner 257
p. 93

Selbstbildnis mit blauem Glas, c. 1902
Self-Portrait with a Blue Glass
Oil tempera on cardboard
73.5 x 51.5 cm
Staatsgalerie Stuttgart, acquired 1968
Busch / Werner 266
p. 23

Junges Mädchen mit gelben Blumen im Glas, 1902
Young Girl with Yellow Flowers in a Glass
Dated (upper left): 1902
Oil tempera on cardboard, mounted on wood
52 x 53 cm
Kunsthalle Bremen – Der Kunstverein in Bremen
Busch / Werner 275
p. 129

Elsbeth mit Ziegen, c. 1902
Elsbeth with Goats
Oil tempera on cardboard
40 x 55 cm
Private Collection
Busch / Werner 290
p. 110

Zwei nackte Jungen am Ufer hockend I, c. 1902
Two Naked Boys Squatting on the Shore I
Oil tempera on cardboard
60.5 x 45.5 cm
Kunsthandel Wolfgang Werner, Bremen / Berlin
Busch / Werner 304
p. 124

Dreebeen mit Ziege und Hühnern, 1902
Old Peasant Woman with Goat and Chickens
Dated (lower right): VI. 1902
Oil tempera on cardboard, mounted on plywood
51 x 71.5 cm
Saarlandmuseum – Moderne Galerie, Saarbrücken
Stiftung Saarländischer Kulturbesitz
Busch / Werner 309
p. 75

Jahrmarkt am Weyerberg, 1902
Funfair at the Weyerberg
Dated (lower left): 1902
Oil tempera on cardboard
54 x 73 cm
Kunsthandel Wolfgang Werner, Bremen / Berlin
Busch / Werner 319
p. 85

Mädchen mit Kind vor roten Blumen, 1902
Girl with Child in Front of Red Flowers
Dated (lower left): XI. 02
Oil tempera on cardboard
45.3 x 50.5 cm
Kunstmuseum Den Haag, The Hague, Netherlands
Busch / Werner 323
p. 139

Birkenstamm, c. 1902
Birch Trunk
Oil tempera on cardboard
53 x 34.5 cm
Paula-Modersohn-Becker-Stiftung, Bremen
Busch / Werner 353
p. 188

Hände mit Kamillenblume, c. 1902
Hands with Chamomile Flower
Oil tempera on canvas
22.5 x 27.4 cm
Private Collection
Courtesy Kunsthandel Wolfgang Werner, Bremen / Berlin
Busch / Werner 363
p. 190

Hand mit Blumenstrauß, c. 1902
Hand with Flower Bouquet
Oil tempera on cardboard
35 x 31 cm
Private Collection
Busch / Werner 364
p. 189

Selbstbildnis vor Landschaft mit Bäumen, c. 1903
Self-Portrait in Front of Landscape with Trees
Oil tempera on painting board
28.2 x 41 cm
Sprengel Museum Hannover, on loan from a private collection
Busch / Werner 366
p. 20

Brustbild eines Bauern, den Kopf auf die rechte Hand gestützt, c. 1903
Half-Length Portrait of a Peasant, His Head Resting on His Right Hand
Oil tempera on cardboard
38.3 x 43.5 cm
Nordfriesland Museum. Nissenhaus Husum
Busch / Werner 373
p. 71

Kopf einer Bauernfrau, c. 1903
Head of a Farmer's Wife
Oil tempera on cardboard
27 x 24.8 cm
Sammlung Sander
Busch / Werner 374
p. 191

Säugling mit der Hand der Mutter, c. 1903
Infant with Its Mother's Hand
Oil tempera on canvas
31.3 x 26.7 cm
Kunsthalle Bremen – Der Kunstverein in Bremen
Busch / Werner 386
p. 104

Katze in einem Kinderarm, c. 1903
Cat in a Child's Arm
Oil tempera on canvas
32.5 x 25.6 cm
Kunsthalle Bremen – Der Kunstverein in Bremen
Busch / Werner 391
p. 180

Sitzendes Mädchen mit schwarzem Hut und Blume in der rechten Hand, c. 1903
Seated Girl with a Black Hat and a Flower in Her Right Hand
Oil tempera on canvas
69.8 x 44.7 cm
Galerie Michael Haas, Berlin
Busch / Werner 393
p. 119

Liegender Mann unter blühendem Baum, 1903
Man Lying under a Blossoming Tree
Dated in red chalk (on the reverse): 1903
Oil tempera on cardboard
52 x 74 cm
Städel Museum, Frankfurt am Main
Busch / Werner 444
p. 84

Selbstbildnis, Halbfigur nach links, eine Schale und ein Glas haltend, c. 1904
Self-Portrait, Half-Length Figure Turned to the Left, with a Bowl and a Glass
Oil tempera on cardboard
67 x 46 cm
Sammlung Sander
Busch / Werner 453
p. 21

Sitzender Mädchenakt mit angezogenen Beinen I, c. 1904
Seated Girl Nude, Her Legs Pulled Up I
Oil tempera on canvas
68 x 57 cm
Private Collection
Busch / Werner 455
p. 115

Kind an der Mutterbrust, c. 1904
(Säugling an der Brust)
Infant, Breastfeeding
(Infant at the Breast)
Dated (lower right): 04
Oil tempera on canvas
23.8 x 28.5 cm
Niedersächsisches Landesmuseum Hannover, on long-term loan from the Rut- und Klaus-Bahlsen-Stiftung
Busch / Werner 458
p. 109

Kind in der Wiege, c. 1904
Child in Cradle
Oil tempera on canvas
51.5 x 57 cm
Von der Heydt-Museum Wuppertal
Busch / Werner 459
p. 108

Sitzendes Mädchen mit grüner Kette, c. 1904
Seated Girl with Green Necklace
Oil tempera on canvas
55 x 42 cm
Kunsthalle Mannheim
Busch / Werner 462
p. 131

Schützenfest mit Karussell II, 1904
Festival with Carousel II
Dated (lower right): 04.
Oil tempera on cardboard
56 x 73 cm
Museen Böttcherstraße, Paula Modersohn-Becker Museum, Bremen
Busch / Werner 526
p. 80

Schützenfest in Worpswede I, 1904
Festival in Worpswede I
Dated (lower left): 04
Oil tempera on cardboard
53.5 x 73.5 cm
Von der Heydt-Museum Wuppertal
Busch / Werner 527
p. 81

Selbstbildnis mit roter Rose, c. 1905
Self-Portrait with a Red Rose
Oil tempera on cardboard
66 x 46.5 cm
Private Collection
Busch / Werner 534
p. 22

Selbstbildnis mit Bernsteinkette, c. 1905
Self-Portrait with Amber Necklace
Oil tempera on canvas
34.5 x 27.3 cm
Paula-Modersohn-Becker-Stiftung, Bremen
Busch / Werner 535
p. 24

Die Bildhauerin Clara Rilke-Westhoff, November 1905
(Brustbild der Bildhauerin Clara Rilke-Westhoff)
The Sculptress Clara Rilke-Westhoff
(Bust of the Sculptress Clara Rilke-Westhoff)
Oil tempera on canvas
52 x 36.8 cm
Hamburger Kunsthalle, acquired 1920
Busch / Werner 537
p. 61

Otto Modersohn mit Strohhut im Profil nach rechts, c. 1905
Otto Modersohn with Straw Hat in Right-Headed Profile
Oil tempera on cardboard
44.8 x 43 cm
Kunsthalle Bremen – Der Kunstverein in Bremen
Busch / Werner 541
p. 54

Alte Frau mit schwarzem Strohhut, c. 1905
Old Woman in a Black Straw Hat
Oil tempera on canvas
35 x 41.5 cm
Von der Heydt-Museum Wuppertal
Busch / Werner 554
p. 70

Kopf eines auf einem Stuhl sitzenden Mädchens, 1905
Head of a Girl Sitting on a Chair
Oil tempera on cardboard
26 x 21 cm
Private Collection
Busch / Werner 556
p. 130

Mädchenkopf, c. 1905
(Kopf eines blonden Mädchens)
Head of a Girl
(Head of a Blonde Girl)
Oil tempera on canvas
24.5 x 21 cm
Städel Museum, Frankfurt am Main
Busch / Werner 569
p. 114

Kinderwagen mit Kindern unter Bäumen, 1905
Stroller with Children Under Trees
Dated (lower right): 05.
Oil tempera on cardboard
36.6 x 55 cm
Paula-Modersohn-Becker-Stiftung, Bremen
Busch / Werner 584
p. 111

Zwei sitzende Mädchen in der Landschaft, 1905
Two Girls Sitting in Landscape
Dated (lower right): 05
Oil tempera on cardboard
72.4 x 42.5 cm
Private Collection, Courtesy Kallir Research Institute, New York
Busch / Werner 592
p. 113

Mädchen in rotem Kleid am Baumstamm vor Wolkenhimmel, c. 1905
Girl in a Red Dress by a Tree Trunk in Front of a Background of a Cloudy Sky
Oil tempera on canvas
56 x 58 cm
Sammlung Sander
Busch / Werner 594
p. 112

Alte Armenhäuslerin, c. 1905
(Alte Armenhäuslerin im Garten sitzend)
Old Pauper
(Old Woman from the Poorhouse Sitting in the Garden)
Oil tempera on canvas
126 x 94 cm
Von der Heydt-Museum Wuppertal
Busch / Werner 600
p. 74

Armenhäuserin, 1906
(Alte Armenhäuslerin)
Woman from the Poorhouse
(Old Woman from the Poorhouse)
Oil tempera on cardboard
90 x 71 cm
Hessisches Landesmuseum Darmstadt
Busch / Werner 601
p. 76

Flöte blasendes Mädchen im Birkenwald, 1905
(also: Mädchen mit Tutehorn)
Girl Blowing a Flute in the Birch Forest
(also: Girl with Horn)
Oil tempera on canvas
110.4 x 90.2 cm
Museen Böttcherstraße, Paula Modersohn-Becker Museum, Bremen
Busch / Werner 602
p. 118

Stillleben mit Zuckerdose und Hyazinthe im Glas, c. 1905
Still Life with Sugar Bowl and a Hyacinth in a Glass
Oil tempera on cardboard
35.5 x 51.5 cm
Kunsthalle Bremen – Der Kunstverein in Bremen
Busch / Werner 608
p. 175

Stillleben mit Kürbis, c. 1905
(Stillleben mit Kürbis und Ingwertopf)
Still Life with Pumpkin
(Still Life with Pumpkin and Ginger Jar)
Oil tempera on canvas
75 x 95 cm
Von der Heydt-Museum Wuppertal
Busch / Werner 622
p. 172

Stillleben mit Kürbis, c. 1905
Still Life with Pumpkin
Oil tempera on cardboard
69.5 x 89.5 cm
Museum Ludwig, Cologne /
Sammlung Haubrich 1947
Busch / Werner 625
p. 173

Selbstbildnis mit weißer Perlenkette, 1906
Self-Portrait with White Pearl Necklace
Oil tempera on cardboard
41.5 x 26 cm
LWL – Museum für Kunst und Kultur
Westfälisches Landesmuseum
Busch / Werner 627
p. 25

Selbstbildnis am 6. Hochzeitstag, May 25, 1906
Self-Portrait on the Sixth Wedding Day
Inscribed in the fresh paint (lower left):
Dies malte ich mit 30 Jahren / an meinem 6. Hochzeitstag / P.B. (I painted this at the age of 30 / on my 6th wedding anniversary / PB)
Oil tempera on cardboard
101.8 x 70.2 cm
Museen Böttcherstraße, Paula Modersohn-Becker Museum, Bremen
Busch / Werner 628
p. 32

Selbstbildnis als stehender Akt mit Hut, summer 1906
Self-Portrait as Standing Nude with Hat
Oil tempera on canvas
40 x 19.5 cm
Private Collection
Courtesy Kunsthandel Wolfgang Werner, Bremen / Berlin
Busch / Werner 629
p. 28

Selbstbildnis als stehender Akt, summer 1906
Self-Portrait as Standing Nude
Oil tempera on canvas
169.7 x 69.7 cm
On loan to the Albertinum | Galerie Neue Meister, Staatliche Kunstsammlungen Dresden
Busch / Werner 630
p. 29

Großer stehender Mädchenakt, 1905/6
Large Standing Nude Girl
Oil tempera on canvas
135.6 x 50.8 cm
Museen Böttcherstraße, Paula Modersohn-Becker Museum, Bremen
Busch / Werner 632
p. 132

Sitzender Mädchenakt mit Apfel, 1906
Seated Nude Girl with an Apple
Dated (lower right): 06
Oil tempera on canvas
45.4 x 23.2 cm
Museen Böttcherstraße, Paula Modersohn-Becker Museum, Bremen
Busch / Werner 633
p. 135

Kleiner stehender Mädchenakt mit Halskette und Rose, 1906
Small Standing Nude Girl with Necklace and Rose
Oil tempera on canvas
35.3 x 28.5 cm
Museen Böttcherstraße, Paula Modersohn-Becker Museum, Bremen
Busch / Werner 634
p. 133

Bildnis Rainer Maria Rilke, May/June 1906
Portrait of Rainer Maria Rilke
Oil tempera on cardboard
32.3 x 25.4 cm
Paula-Modersohn-Becker-Stiftung, Bremen, on loan from a private collection
Busch / Werner 643
p. 60

Zwei Mädchen in weißem und blauem Kleid, May/June 1906
Two Girls in White and Blue Dresses
Oil tempera on cardboard
54.5 x 36 cm
Milwaukee Art Museum, Maurice and Esther Leah Ritz Collection
Busch / Werner 646
p. 128

Mutter und Kind, May/June 1906
(Sitzende Mutter mit Kind auf dem Schoß)
Mother and Child
(Seated Mother with a Child on Her Lap)
Dated (lower left): 06.
Oil tempera on cardboard
105.5 x 75 cm
Von der Heydt-Museum Wuppertal
Busch / Werner 655
p. 105

Stillleben mit Fisch, winter 1906
(Stillleben mit Schellfisch)
Still Life with Fish
(Still Life with Haddock)
Dated (lower left): 06.
Oil tempera on cardboard
26.7 x 38.2 cm
Niedersächsisches Landesmuseum Hannover
Busch / Werner 662
pp. 170/171

Stillleben mit Goldfischglas, May/June 1906
Still Life with Goldfish Bowl
Oil tempera on cardboard
50.5 x 74 cm
Von der Heydt-Museum Wuppertal
Busch / Werner 668
pp. 176/177

Stillleben mit Tonkrug, Pfingstrosen und Apfelsinen, May/June 1906
Still Life with Clay Jug, Peonies and Oranges
Oil tempera on cardboard
61.5 x 49 cm
Kunsthandel Wolfgang Werner, Bremen / Berlin
Busch / Werner 669
p. 179

Selbstbildnis nach halblinks, summer 1906
Self-Portrait, Turned to the Left
Oil tempera on paper mounted on cardboard
26.8 x 21.4 cm
Private Collection
Busch / Werner 675
p. 27

Selbstbildnis mit rotem Blütenkranz und Kette, 1906/7
Self-Portrait with Red Floral Wreath and Necklace
Oil tempera on canvas
50.4 x 45.2 cm
Niedersächsisches Landesmuseum Hannover, on long-term loan from the Rut- und Klaus-Bahlsen-Stiftung
Busch / Werner 680
p. 31

Selbstbildnis mit Zitrone, 1906/7
Self-Portrait with Lemon
Oil tempera on cardboard
50 x 27.5 cm
Private Collection
Busch / Werner 683
p. 30

Bildnis Lee Hoetger vor Blumengrund, August 1906
Lee Hoetger in Front of a Floral Background
Oil tempera on canvas
92.4 x 73.5 cm
Museen Böttcherstraße, Paula Modersohn-Becker Museum, Bremen
Busch / Werner 685
p. 63

Bildnis Lee Hoetger und Clara Haken, July/August 1906
(Lee Hoetger und Clara Haken)
Portrait of Lee Hoetger and Clara Haken
(Lee Hoetger and Clara Haken)
Oil tempera on paper
36.5 x 46.5 cm
Museum Ostwall im Dortmunder U, Dortmund
Busch / Werner 686
p. 62

Otto Modersohn schlafend, winter 1906/7
Otto Modersohn Sleeping
Oil tempera on canvas
39.7 x 46.3 cm
Paula-Modersohn-Becker-Stiftung, Bremen
Busch / Werner 689
p. 55

Mutter mit Kind auf dem Arm, Halbakt II, autumn 1906
Mother with Child in Her Arms, Half-Length Nude II
Oil tempera on canvas
80 x 59 cm
Museum Ostwall im Dortmunder U, Dortmund
Busch / Werner 692
p. 96

Kniender Mädchenakt vor blauem Vorhang, 1906/7
Nude Girl Kneeling in Front of a Blue Curtain
Oil tempera on canvas
72 x 60 cm
Landesmuseum für Kunst und Kulturgeschichte Oldenburg
Busch / Werner 698
p. 134

Mädchenakt mit Blumenvasen, 1906/7
(Sitzender Mädchenakt mit Blumenvasen)
Nude Girl with Flower Vases
(Seated Nude Girl with Flower Vases)
Oil tempera on canvas
74.5 x 52 cm
Von der Heydt-Museum Wuppertal
Busch / Werner 699
pp. 136/137

Selbstbildnis mit Blume, 1907
Self-Portrait with Flower
Oil tempera on cardboard
38 x 24 cm
Private Collection
Courtesy Kunsthandel Wolfgang Werner, Bremen / Berlin
Busch / Werner 712
p. 26

Elsbeth zwischen Feuerlilien, 1907
Elsbeth among Fire Lillies
Oil tempera on canvas
70.7 x 34 cm
Museen Böttcherstraße, Paula Modersohn-Becker Museum, Bremen,
on loan from a private collection
Busch / Werner 718
p. 138

Alte Bäuerin mit auf der Brust gekreuzten Händen, 1907
Old Peasant Woman
Oil tempera on canvas
75.7 x 57.7 cm
Detroit Institute of Arts, Gift of Robert H. Tannahill
Busch / Werner 719
p. 77

Stillleben mit Rhododendron, 1907
Still Life with Rhododendron
Oil tempera on cardboard
69.5 x 85.5 cm
Von der Heydt-Museum Wuppertal
Busch / Werner 724
p. 174

Stillleben mit blauem Kasten, 1907
Still Life with a Blue Box
Oil tempera on canvas
27.3 x 35.7 cm
Paula-Modersohn-Becker-Stiftung, Bremen
Busch / Werner 732
p. 178

DRAWINGS

Oberkörper eines nach rechts gebeugten weiblichen Aktes sowie eine kleine Skizze desselben Motivs, 1898
Torso of a Female Nude Bent Forward to the Right and a Small Sketch of the Same Motif
Charcoal and chalk on paper
48 x 62.5 cm
Paula-Modersohn-Becker-Stiftung, Bremen
p. 140

Stehender weiblicher Akt im Profil nach rechts, 1898
Standing Female Nude in Profile, Turned to the Right
Charcoal on paper
169 x 87 cm
Paula-Modersohn-Becker-Stiftung, Bremen
p. 148

Stehender männlicher Akt nach links, 1898
Standing Male Nude Turned to the Left
Charcoal on paper
189.5 x 84.5 cm
Paula-Modersohn-Becker-Stiftung, Bremen
p. 149

Bäuerin, eine Astgabel tragend, c. 1898/99
Peasant Woman Carrying a Branch Fork
India ink, pastel, and pencil on cardboard
44.5 x 74.5 cm
Private Collection, Berlin
p. 73

Skizzenblatt mit Kompositionsskizze
für *Sitzende Alte*, 1899
Composition sketch for *Seated Old Woman*
Pencil on paper
26 x 40.3 cm
Kunsthalle Bremen – Der Kunstverein in Bremen, Kupferstichkabinett
p. 72

Alte Bäuerin, 1899
Old Peasant Woman
Charcoal on paper
123 x 73 cm
Kunsthalle zu Kiel, Grafische Sammlung
Schleswig-Holsteinischer Kunstverein e. V.
p. 67

Alter Bauer, 1899
Old Peasant Man
Charcoal on paper
127 x 73 cm
Kunsthalle zu Kiel, Grafische Sammlung
Schleswig-Holsteinischer Kunstverein e. V.
p. 66

Stehender Kinderakt mit eingezeichnetem Skelett sowie Knochenstudien, June 1899
Standing Child Nude with the Skeleton Drawn in and Bone Studies
Charcoal on paper
145 x 111 cm
Paula-Modersohn-Becker-Stiftung, Bremen
p. 116

Stehender Mädchenakt nach links, mit verschränkten Armen, c. 1899
Standing Girl Nude, Turned Left with Crossed Arms
Charcoal, red chalk, and green pastel crayon on paper
136 x 68 cm
Private Collection
Courtesy Kunsthandel Wolfgang Werner, Bremen / Berlin
p. 117

Stehender männlicher Akt nach rechts, Paris 1905
Standing Male Nude, Turned to the Right
Charcoal on paper
29.7 x 21.8 cm
Paula-Modersohn-Becker-Stiftung, Bremen
p. 152

Auf einem niedrigen Hocker sitzender männlicher Akt nach rechts, Paris 1905
Male Nude Seated on a Low Stool, Turned to the Right
Charcoal on paper
21.8 x 29.7 cm
Paula-Modersohn-Becker-Stiftung, Bremen
p. 153

Dreispänniger Pferdelastzug, 1905
Carriage Yoked with Three Horses
Charcoal on paper
21.8 x 29.5 cm
Private Collection
Courtesy Kunsthandel Wolfgang Werner, Bremen / Berlin
p. 169

Kanal mit sich spiegelnden Bäumen, 1905
Canal with Trees Reflected in the Water
Charcoal on paper
22 x 29.6 cm
Private Collection
Courtesy Kunsthandel Wolfgang Werner, Bremen / Berlin
p. 168

Sitzende Frau nach rechts vor einer Wand mit Gitterwerk, c. 1905
Seated Woman with Apron in Front of a Latticework
Charcoal on paper
21.8 x 29.7 cm
Private Collection
Courtesy Kunsthandel Wolfgang Werner, Bremen / Berlin
p. 166

Seine-Brücken in Paris, 1905
Bridges over the Seine in Paris
Charcoal on paper
21.7 x 29.7 cm
Kunsthalle Bremen – Der Kunstverein in Bremen, Kupferstichkabinett
p. 164

Seinebrücke, 1905
Bridge over the Seine
Charcoal on paper
21.9 x 29.8 cm
Kunsthalle Bremen – Der Kunstverein in Bremen, Kupferstichkabinett
p. 165

Fassade Notre-Dame (recto) Notre Dame von der Seine her gesehen (verso), c. 1905/6
The Façade of Notre-Dame (recto)
Notre-Dame seen from the Seine (verso)
Charcoal on ribbed handmade paper
29.5 x 21.5 cm
Saarlandmuseum – Moderne Galerie, Saarbrücken
Stiftung Saarländischer Kulturbesitz
p. 156

Liegende Mutter mit Kind, 1906
Reclining Mother with Child
Charcoal on paper
23 x 31.3 cm
Kunsthalle Bremen – Der Kunstverein in Bremen, Kupferstichkabinett
p. 106

Figuren mit Hund auf einer Seinebrücke in Paris, 1906
Figures with Dog on a Bridge over the Seine in Paris
Charcoal on paper
20.6 x 27.5 cm
Kunsthalle Bremen – Der Kunstverein in Bremen, Kupferstichkabinett
p. 167

Stehender weiblicher Akt nach halbrechts, auf einen Hocker gestützt, c. 1906
Large Standing Female Nude, Turned to the Right, with Studio Stool
Charcoal on paper
59 x 35 cm
Paula-Modersohn-Becker-Stiftung, Bremen
p. 150

Stehender männlicher Akt frontal, in der Rechten einen Stab, c. 1906
Frontal Standing Male Nude with a Staff in His Right Hand
Charcoal on paper
60 x 33 cm
Paula-Modersohn-Becker-Stiftung, Bremen
p. 151

Kniender Frauenakt mit Kind, c. 1906
Kneeling Female Nude with Child
Charcoal on paper
32.2 x 23.3 cm
Kunsthaus Zürich, Collection of Prints and Drawings, Gift of Sophie Fohn, 1980
p. 107

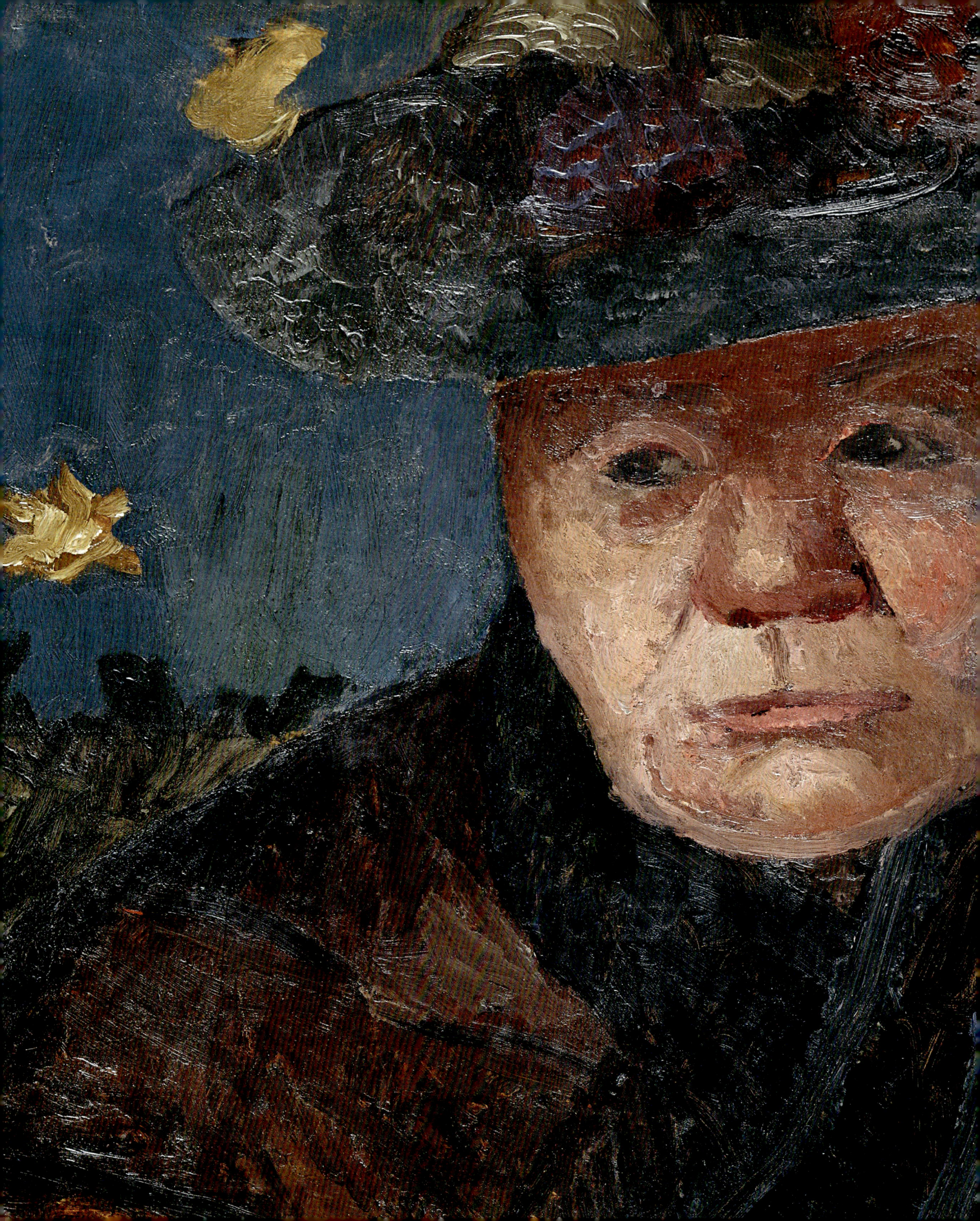

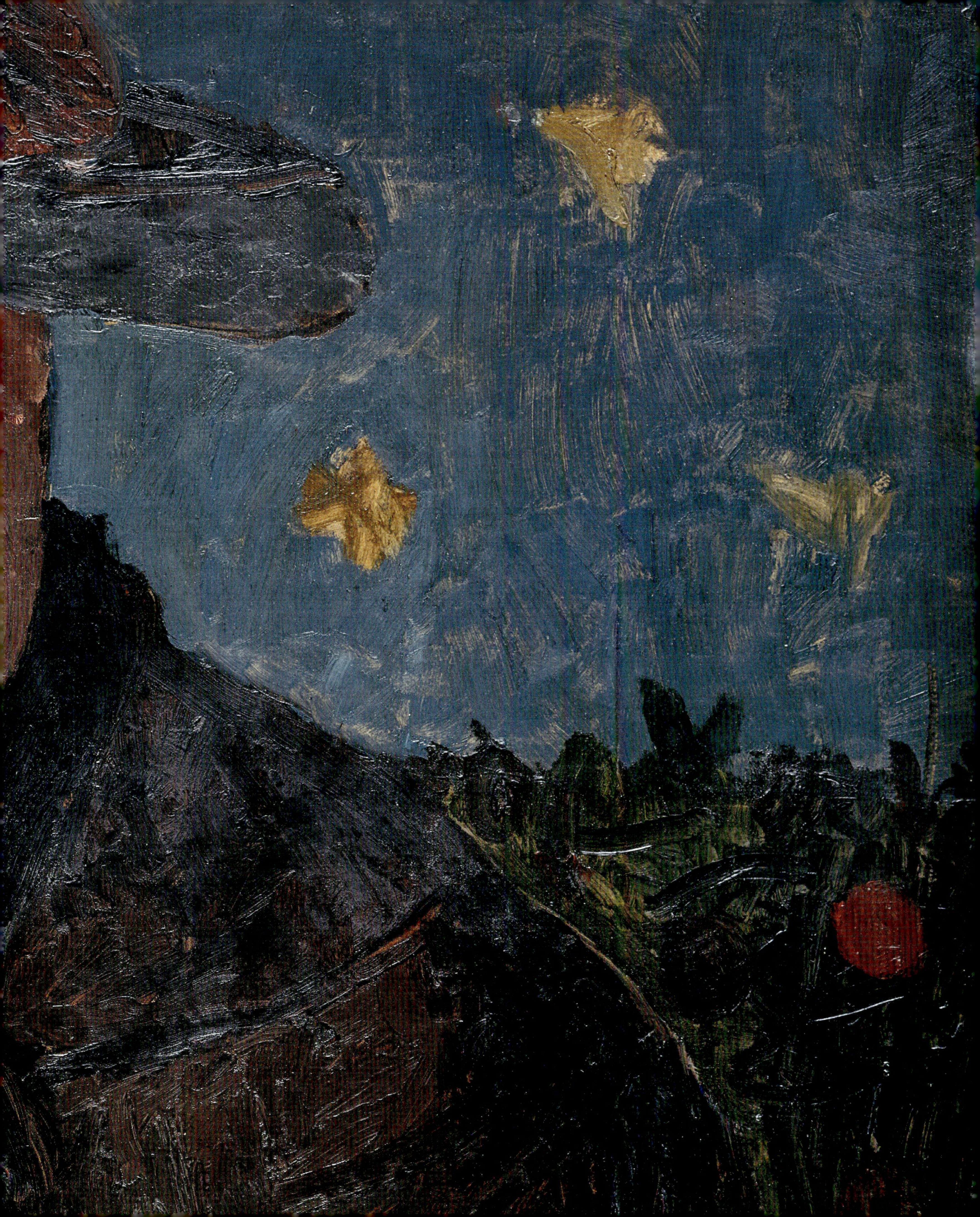

BIBLIOGRAPHY
(SELECTION)

CATALOGUE RAISONNÉ

Paula Becker-Modersohn, Katalog ihrer Werke, Gemälde, Studien, Zeichnungen und Radierungen, ed. Curt Stoermer, Worpswede 1913

Gustav Pauli, Paula Modersohn-Becker. Mit einem Werkverzeichnis (= Das neue Bild. Bücher für die Kunst der Gegenwart 1), Leipzig 1919

Paula Modersohn-Becker 1876–1907. Oeuvreverzeichnis der Graphik, ed. Wolfgang Werner, Bremen 1972

Paula Modersohn-Becker 1876–1907. Werkverzeichnis der Gemälde, ed. Günter Busch and Wolfgang Werner, 2 vols., Munich 1998

LETTERS AND DIARIES

Eine Künstlerin. Paula Modersohn-Becker. Briefe und Tagebuchblätter, ed. Sophie Dorothea Gallwitz, Bremen 1912

Paula Modersohn-Becker. Briefwechsel mit Rainer Maria Rilke, ed. Rainer Stamm, Frankfurt am Main 2003

Paula Modersohn-Becker in Briefen und Tagebüchern, ed. Günter Busch and Liselotte von Reinken, revised and expanded edition ed. Wolfgang Werner, Frankfurt am Main 2007

Paula und Milly. Eine Erzählung in Briefen zum hundertsten Todestag von Paula Modersohn-Becker, ed. Gabriele Werner, Dresden / Munich 2007

Paula Modersohn-Becker – Otto Modersohn. Der Briefwechsel, ed. Antje Modersohn and Wolfgang Werner, Berlin 2017

MONOGRAPHS

Carl Emil Uphoff, Paula Modersohn (= Junge Kunst 2), Leipzig 1919

Die Paula Becker-Modersohn-Sammlung des Ludwig Roselius in der Böttcherstraße in Bremen, ed. Walter Müller-Wulckow, Bremen 1927

Paula Modersohn-Becker. Ein Buch der Freundschaft (= Die Zeichner des Volkes 4), ed. Rolf Hetsch, Berlin 1932

Günter Busch, Paula Modersohn-Becker. Handzeichnungen, Bremen 1949

Otto Stelzer, Paula Modersohn-Becker (= Die Kunst unserer Zeit 12), Berlin 1958

Paula Becker-Modersohn. Mutter und Kind (= Werkmonographien zur bildenden Kunst 62), ed. Carl Georg Heise, Stuttgart 1961

Christa Murken-Altrogge, Paula Modersohn-Becker. Kinderbildnisse, Munich / Zurich 1977

Gillian Perry, Paula Modersohn-Becker. Her Life and Work, London 1979

Christa Murken-Altrogge, Paula Modersohn-Becker. Leben und Werk, Cologne 1980

Günter Busch, Paula Modersohn-Becker. Malerin, Zeichnerin, Frankfurt am Main 1981

Liselotte von Reinken, Paula Modersohn-Becker mit Selbstzeugnissen und Bilddokumenten, Reinbek 1983

Peter J. Harke, Stilleben von Paula Modersohn-Becker, Lilienthal 1985

Gert Claußnitzer, Paula Modersohn-Becker, Dresden 1986

Boda Hülsmann, Paula Modersohn-Becker. In Freiheit zu sich selbst, Stuttgart 1988

Brigitte Uhde-Stahl, Paula Modersohn-Becker. Frau, Künstlerin, Mensch, Stuttgart / Zurich 1989

Diane Josephine Radycki, Paula Modersohn-Becker: The Gendered Discourse in Modernism, Diss. Harvard University 1994

Doris Hansmann, Akt und nackt. Der ästhetische Aufbruch um 1900 mit Blick auf die Selbstakte von Paula Modersohn-Becker, Weimar 2000

Renate Berger, Paula Modersohn-Becker. Paris – Leben wie im Rausch. Biografie, Bergisch-Gladbach 2007

Rainer Stamm, "Ein kurzes intensives Fest". Paula Modersohn-Becker. Eine Biografie, Stuttgart 2007

Kai Artinger, Paula Modersohn-Becker. Der andere Blick, Berlin 2008

Paris, Paris! Paula Modersohn-Becker und die Künstlerinnen um 1900, ed. Renate Berger and Anja Herrmann, Stuttgart 2009

Diane Josephine Radycki, Paula Modersohn-Becker. The First Modern Women Artist, New Haven / London 2013

Doris Hansmann, Paula Modersohn-Becker, Cologne 2015

Marie Darrieussecq, Being Here Is Everything. The Life of Paula M. Becker, Cambridge 2017

Diane Radycki, Paula Modersohn-Becker - Self-Portrait, MoMA, New York, 2018

EXHIBITION CATALOGS

Paula Modersohn-Becker (130 Gemälde, Zeichnungen und Radierungen 1895–1907), Kestner-Gesellschaft Hannover 1934

Paula Modersohn Becker, Kunsthalle Bremen 1947

Paula Modersohn-Becker, Gemeente-museum's-Gravenhage, The Hague 1952

Paula Modersohn-Becker, 1876–1907, Kunst und Museumsverein Wuppertal 1954

Paula Modersohn Becker, Steinernes Haus, Frankfurt am Main 1963

Paula Modersohn-Becker zum hundertsten Geburtstag, Kunsthalle Bremen and Kunstsammlungen Böttcherstraße, Bremen 1976

Paula Modersohn-Becker. Zeichnungen, Pastelle, Bildentwürfe, Kunstverein Hamburg 1977

Paula Modersohn-Becker. Die Landschaften, Kunsthalle Bremen 1982/83

Paula Modersohn-Becker. Das Frühwerk, Kunsthalle Bremen 1985

Paula Modersohn-Becker 1876–1907. Retrospektive, Städtische Galerie im Lenbachhaus, Munich 1997

Käthe Kollwitz, Paula Modersohn-Becker. Zwei Künstlerinnen zu Beginn der Moderne. Kunstsammlungen Böttcherstraße, Paula Modersohn-Becker Museum, Bremen 2000

"rücksichtslos geradeaus malend", Paula Modersohn-Becker, Marie Bock, Clara Rilke-Westhoff. Die Ausstellung in der Kunsthalle Bremen 1899, Kunstsammlungen Böttcherstraße, Bremen 2003

Paula Modersohn-Becker, Chabot Museum, Rotterdam 2007

Paula Modersohn-Becker und die ägyptischen Mumienporträts. Eine Hommage zum 100. Todestag der Künstlerin, Kunstsammlungen Böttcherstraße, Paula Modersohn-Becker Museum, Bremen 2007

Paula Modersohn-Becker und die Kunst in Paris um 1900 – von Cézanne bis Picasso, Kunsthalle Bremen 2007

Paula Modersohn-Becker und Otto Modersohn. Ein Künstlerpaar um 1900, Niedersächsisches Landesmuseum, Hannover 2007

Paula Modersohn-Becker. Pionierin der Moderne, Kunsthalle Krems 2010

Sie. Selbst. Nackt. Paula Modersohn-Becker und andere Künstlerinnen im Selbstakt, Museen Böttcherstraße, Paula Modersohn-Becker Museum, Bremen 2013

Paula Modersohn-Becker. Berlin–Worpswede–Paris, Museen Böttcherstraße, Paula Modersohn-Becker Museum, Bremen 2014

Paula Modersohn-Becker, Louisiana Museum of Modern Art, Humlebæk 2014

Paula Modersohn-Becker. L'intensité d'un regard, Musée d'art moderne de la Ville de Paris 2016

Emil Nolde trifft Paula Modersohn-Becker, Museen Böttcherstraße, Paula Modersohn-Becker Museum, Bremen 2016

Sammler der ersten Stunde. August von der Heydt entdeckt Paula Modersohn-Becker, Museen Böttcherstraße, Paula Modersohn-Becker Museum, Bremen 2017

Paula Modersohn-Becker. Der Weg in die Moderne, Bucerius Kunst Forum, Hamburg 2017

Paula Modersohn-Becker zwischen Worpswede und Paris, Von der Heydt-Museum Wuppertal 2018

Paula Becker & Otto Modersohn. Kunst und Leben, Museen Böttcherstraße, Paula Modersohn-Becker Museum, Bremen 2018/19

Ich bin Ich. Paula Modersohn-Becker – Die Selbstbildnisse, Museen Böttcherstraße, Paula Modersohn-Becker Museum, Bremen 2019/20

Avantgarde. Bernhard Hoetger und Paula Modersohn-Becker in Paris. Ed. Frank Schmidt in conjunction with the Paula-Modersohn-Becker-Stiftung, Bremen, Museen Böttcherstraße, Paula Modersohn-Becker Museum, Bremen 2021

Tausche Cranach gegen Monet / Tausche Monet gegen Modersohn-Becker, Museen Böttcherstraße, Paula Modersohn-Becker Museum / Arp Museum Bahnhof Rolandseck, 2021/22

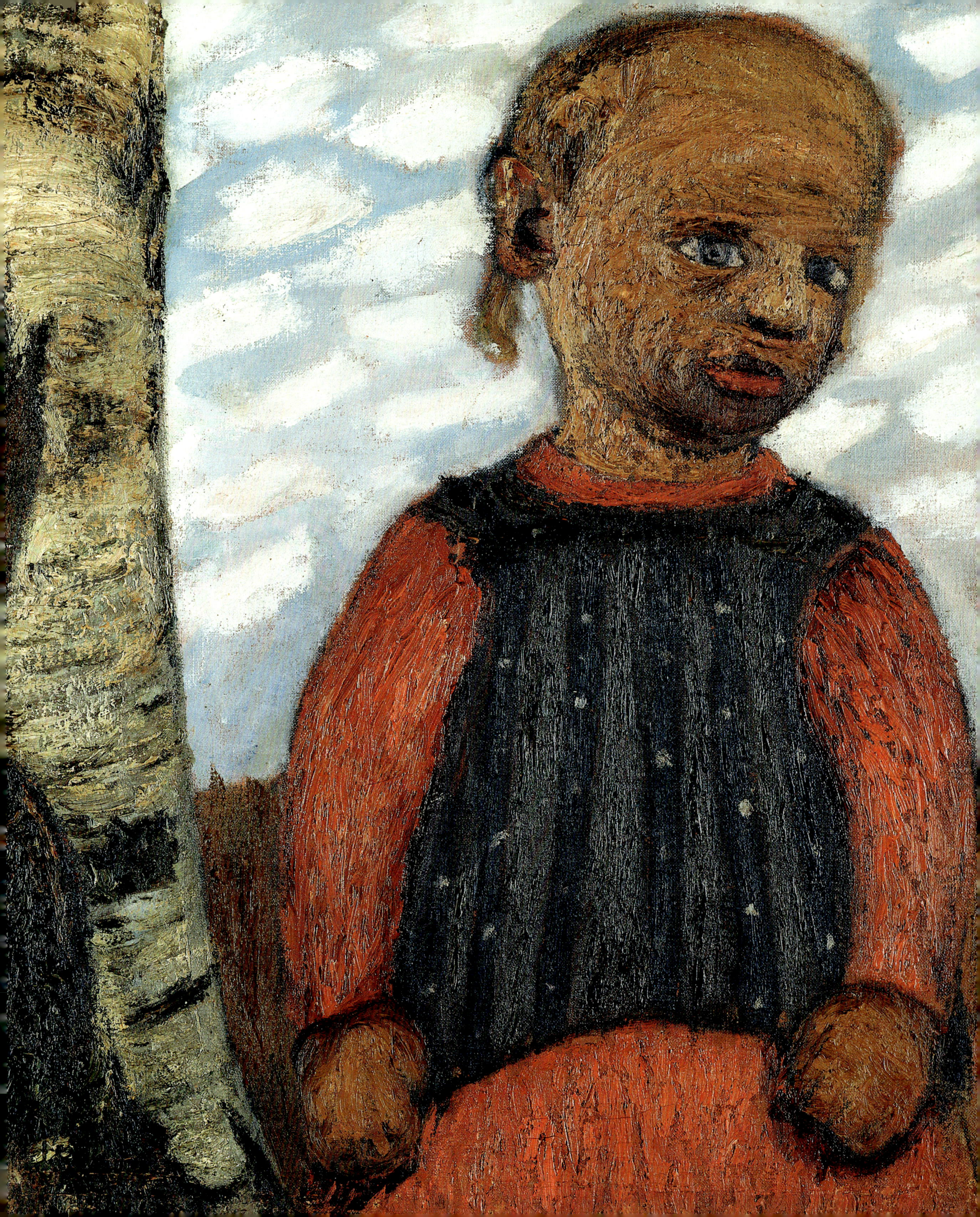

IMAGE CREDITS

© Archiv Böttcherstraße Bremen, p. 51
© Bildarchiv Foto Marburg, p. 161
© bpk/Kunstbibliothek, SMB, p. 143
© bpk/Saarlandmuseum – Moderne Galerie, Saarbrücken, Stiftung Saarländischer Kulturbesitz, pp. 75, 156
© Courtesy of the BFI National Archive, p. 184
© Courtesy Galerie St. Etienne, New York, pp. 53, 113, 120
© Photo: Jürgen Spiler, Dortmund, p. 62
© Photo: Dr. Eike Knopf, pp. 68, 69
© Frauen-Daheim, Nr. 33, 17. May 1902, p. 145
© Galerie Michael Haas, photo: Lea Gryze, p. 56
© Hessisches Landesmuseum Darmstadt, photo: Wolfgang Fuhrmannek, pp. 76, 210/211
© Kunsthalle Bremen – Lars Lorisch – ARTOTHEK, p. 54
© Kunsthalle Mannheim, photo: Margita Wickenhäuser, p. 131
© Kunsthandel Wolfgang Werner, Bremen / Berlin, pp. 85, 124, 126/127, 179, 216/217
© Landesmuseum für Kunst und Kulturgeschichte Oldenburg, photo: Sven Adelaide, p. 134
© Landesmuseum Hannover – ARTOTHEK, pp. 31, 98, 170/171
© Museumsverband Nordfriesland, photo: Sönke Ehlert, p. 71
© Photo: Chris Doulgeris, p. 162
© Sammlung Sander, p. 191
© SMK Photographer, SMK Photo / Jakob Skou-Hansen, p. 159
© Städel Museum, Frankfurt am Main, photo: U. Edelmann, p. 122
© Städel Museum, Frankfurt am Main – ARTOTHEK, p. 84
© Städel Museum, Frankfurt am Main, photo: U. Edelmann – ARTOTHEK, p. 114
© Paula-Modersohn-Becker-Stiftung, Bremen, pp. 2, 4/5, 8, 10, 16/17, 18, 19, 20, 21, 22, 23, 24, 25, 26, 27, 28, 29, 30, 32, 36, 37, 38, 40, 42, 43, 45, 46, 47, 48, 50, 51, 55, 57, 58/59, 60, 61, 63, 64/65, 66, 67, 72, 73, 77, 79, 80, 81, 82, 83, 86, 87, 88, 89, 90, 91, 92, 93, 94, 95, 96, 100, 101, 102, 103, 104, 105, 106, 107, 108, 109, 110, 111, 112, 115, 116, 117, 118, 119, 121, 123, 128, 129, 130, 132, 133, 135, 136/137, 138, 139, 140, 142, 144, 146, 148, 149, 150, 151, 152, 153, 155, 158, 161, 163, 164, 165, 166, 167, 168, 169, 172, 173, 174, 175, 176/177, 178, 180, 182, 183, 185, 186, 187, 188, 189, 190, 192, 195, 196, 197, 198, 199, 200, 202, 214, 220
© Von der Heydt-Museum Wuppertal, photo: Antje Zeis-Loi, Medienzentrum Wuppertal, pp. 70, 74

DETAIL IMAGES

Endsheets: Various covers of exhibition catalogs on the work of Paula Modersohn-Becker from the years 1913–1961
p. 2: detail: Selbstbildnis nach halblinks / Self-Portrait, Turned to the Left, summer 1906
pp. 4/5: detail: Brustbild eines Mädchens in der Sonne vor weiter Landschaft / Half-Length Portrait of a Girl in the Sun in Front of a Wide Landscape, 1897
p. 8: detail: Birkenstämme / Birch Trunks, 1900
p. 10: detail: Mutter mit Kind auf dem Arm, Halbakt II / Mother with Child in Her Arms, Half-Length Nude II, autumn 1906
pp. 16/17: detail: Paula Modersohn-Becker in her studio on the Brünjes farmstead, c. 1905, photo: Karl Brandt
p. 53: detail: Zwei sitzende Mädchen in der Landschaft / Two Girls Sitting in Landscape, 1905
pp. 64/65: detail: Paula Modersohn-Becker, 1905, photo: Karl Brandt
p. 202: detail: Kleiner stehender Mädchenakt mit Halskette und Rose / Small Standing Nude Girl with Necklace and Rose, 1906
pp. 210/211: detail: Armenhäuserin / Woman from the Poorhouse, 1906
p. 214: detail: Mädchen in rotem Kleid am Baumstamm vor Wolkenhimmel / Girl in a Red Dress by a Tree Trunk in Front of a Background of a Cloudy Sky, c. 1905
pp. 216/217: detail: Jahrmarkt am Weyerberg / Funfair at the Weyerberg, 1902
p. 220: detail: Bildnis Lee Hoetger vor Blumengrund / Lee Hoetger in Front of a Floral Background, August 1906

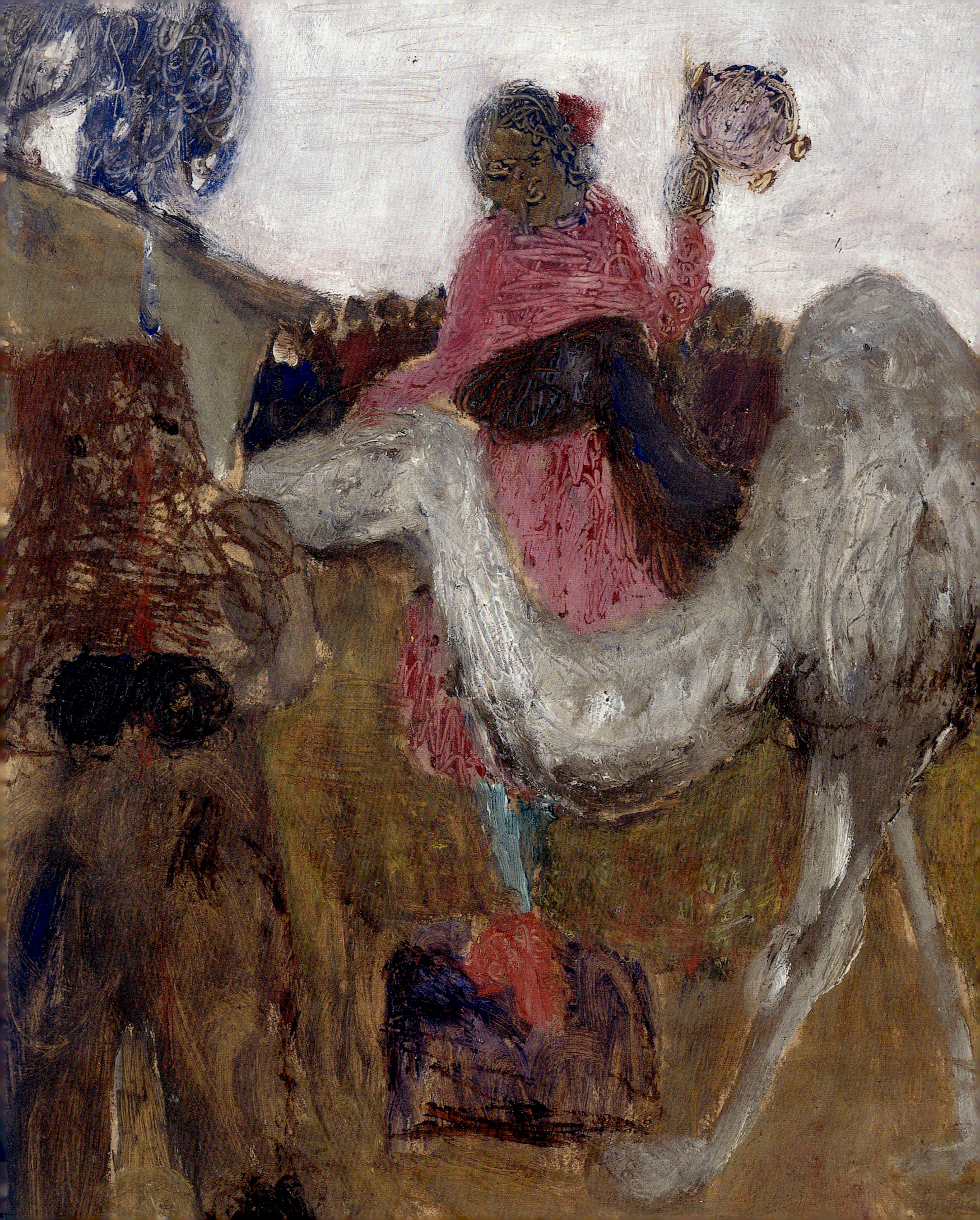

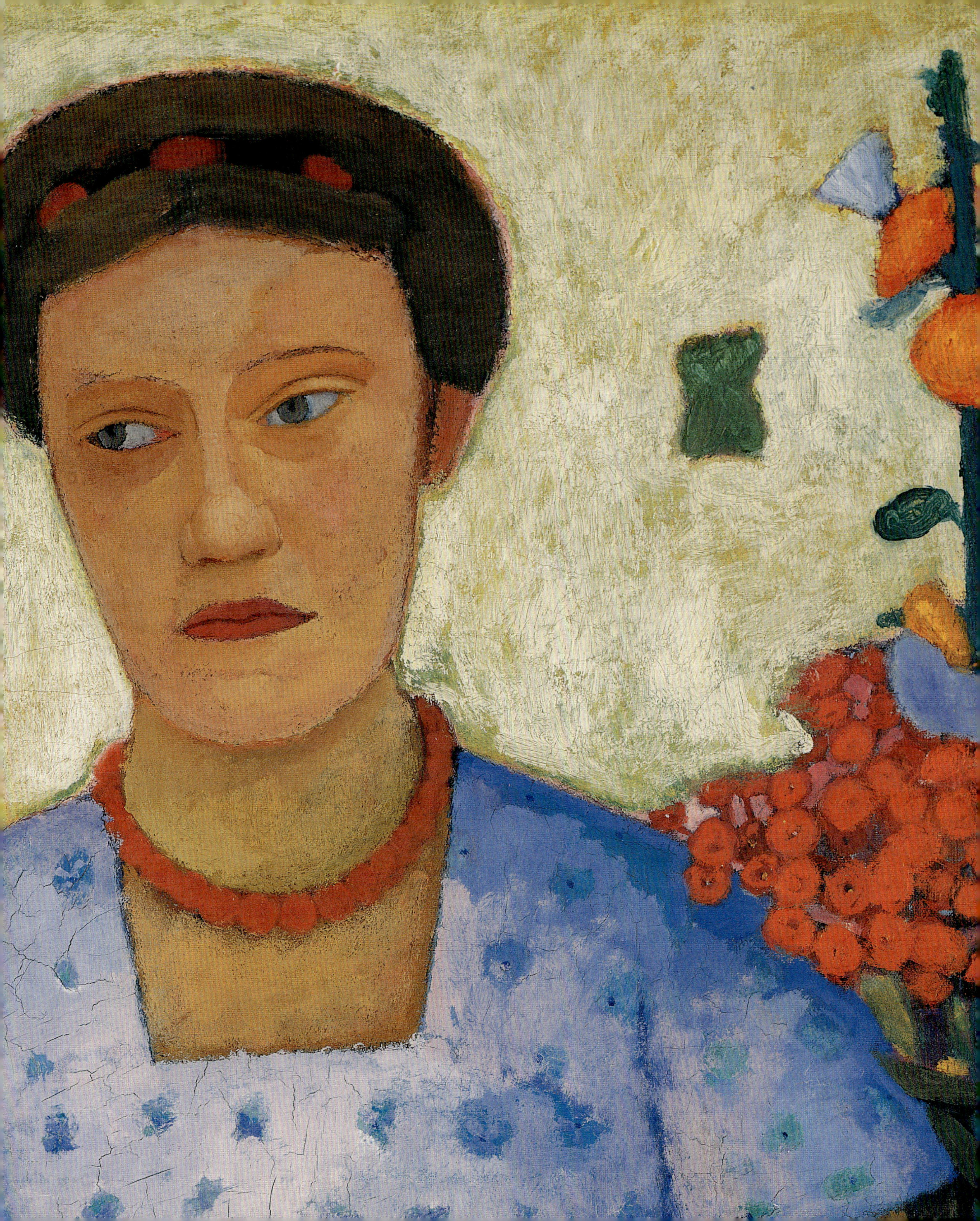

Education
Chantal Eschenfelder, Simone Boscheinen, Laura Heeg, Olga Schaetz, Anna Haag

Events & Visitor Management
Ute Seiffert, Alena Flemming

Administration
Heike Berndt, Hina Ahmad, Boris Deckelmann

Assistant Head of Exhibitions
Luise Leyer

Assistant to the Director
Samira Koch, Marejke Fries

Administrative Assistant
Andrea Canthal

Cleaning Supervision
Rosaria La Tona

Reception
Bettina Beyermann, Vanessa Bernhardt

FRIENDS OF THE SCHIRN KUNSTHALLE E. V.

Executive Board
Antje Conzelmann (Chairman)
Jan Bauer
Philipp Demandt
Sylvia von Metzler

Board of Trustees
Florian Schilling (Chairman)
Clemens Börsig
Andreas Dombret
Armin von Falkenhayn
Diego Fernández-Reumann
Jürgen Fitschen
Peter Gatzemeier
Joachim Häger
Helmut Häuser
Elisabeth Haindl
Gerhard Hess
Marli Hoppe-Ritter
Catharina Jurisch
Wolfgang Kirsch
Gisela von Klot-Heydenfeldt
Salomon Korn
Renate Küchler
Jörg Kukies
Christoph Mäckler
Andreas Muschter
Lutz R. Raettig
Tobias Rehberger
Horst Reinhardt
Michael Riedel
Petra Roth
Martin Scholich
Willi Schoppen
Doris Maria Schuster
Wolf Singer
Claudia Steigenberger
Bettina Volkens
Eberhard Weiershäuser
Susanne Zeidler
Matthias Zieschang
Rolf-E. Breuer (honorary member)

Schirn Contemporaries
Jan Bauer and Lena Wallenhorst
Oliver and Nicole Behrens
Olaf Gerber and Nicole Emmerling de Oliveira
Markus Hammer and Birgit Heller
Shahpar Oschmann
Björn and Kim Robens
Jörg Rockenhäuser and Vasiliki Basia
Reiner Sachs and Brigitta Bailly
Julia Schönbohm and Ralf Böckle

Corporate Members
Deutsche Bank AG
Deutsche Beteiligungs AG
Deutsche Börse AG
DWS Investments GmbH
Europäische Zentralbank
Fraport AG
Gemeinnützige Hertie-Stiftung
Landwirtschaftliche Rentenbank
Lufthansa Group
Morgan Stanley Bank AG
Nomura Bank (Deutschland) GmbH
ODDO BHF AG
UBS Europe SE
Verianos AG

Management
Tamara Fürstin von Clary

PARTNERS

Corporate Partners of the Schirn Kunsthalle Frankfurt
Bank of America
Bloomberg L. P.
Commerz Real AG
HEUSSEN Rechtsanwaltsgesellschaft mbH
Le Méridien Frankfurt
Messe Frankfurt GmbH
Oliver Wyman GmbH
PPI AG
PwC

Partners of the Schirn Kunsthalle Frankfurt, the Städel Museum, and the Liebieghaus Skulpturensammlung
Allianz Global Investors
Fraport AG

Cultural Partner
hr2-kultur

COLOPHON

This catalog is published in conjunction with the exhibition

PAULA MODERSOHN-BECKER

Schirn Kunsthalle Frankfurt
8 October 2021 – 6 February 2022

Editor
Ingrid Pfeiffer

Editing
Ingrid Pfeiffer and Anna Huber

Publication Management
Renate Voget

Head of Project, Hirmer Publishers
Kerstin Ludolph

Project Management, Hirmer Publishers
Jutta Allekotte

Copyediting
Vanessa Magson-Mann, So to Speak, Icking
Olivia Parkes, Berlin

Translation into English
Gérard Goodrow

Graphic Design, Typesetting, and Production
Sabine Frohmader, Hirmer Publishers

Pre-Press and repro
Reproline mediateam, Unterföhring and SMS | Scheer Medien Service, Bremen

Paper
Luxo Satin, 130 g/m^2

Typeface
Forma DJR

Printing and binding
Firmengruppe Appl, aprinta Druck, Wemding

Printed in Germany

Bibliographic information published by the Deutsche Nationalbibliothek
The Deutsche Nationalbibliothek lists this publication in the Deutsche Nationalbibliografie; detailed bibliographic data are available online at http://dnb.de.

ISBN 978-3-7774-3723-1 (English Edition)
ISBN 978-3-7774-3722-4 (German Edition)

www.hirmerpublishers.com
www.hirmerpublishers.co.uk

Cover Illustration
Front: Selbstbildnis mit rotem Blütenkranz und Kette / Self-Portrait with Red Floral Wreath and Necklace, 1906/7
Back: detail: Stillleben mit Kürbis / Still Life with Pumpkin, c. 1905

EXHIBITION
SCHIRN KUNSTHALLE FRANKFURT

Director
Philipp Demandt

Deputy Director & Head of Exhibitions
Esther Schlicht

Curator
Ingrid Pfeiffer

Curatorial Assistant
Anna Huber, Rebecca Herlemann

Registrars
Karin Grüning, Elke Walter

Supervision Installation Crew
Andreas Gundermann

Technical Services
Christian Teltz, Oliver Taschke, Stefan Schell

Exhibition Architecture
Karsten Weber

Exhibition Design
John Russo, Studio Heyhey

Press
Johanna Pulz, Julia Bastian, Elisabeth Pallentin, Clara Nicolay

Schirn Magazine
Anuschka Berthelius

Marketing
Luise Bachmann, Isabel Reiche, Heike Stumpf, Angelika Schäfer

Sponsoring
Julia Lange, Miriam Werner, Hannah Ruiz

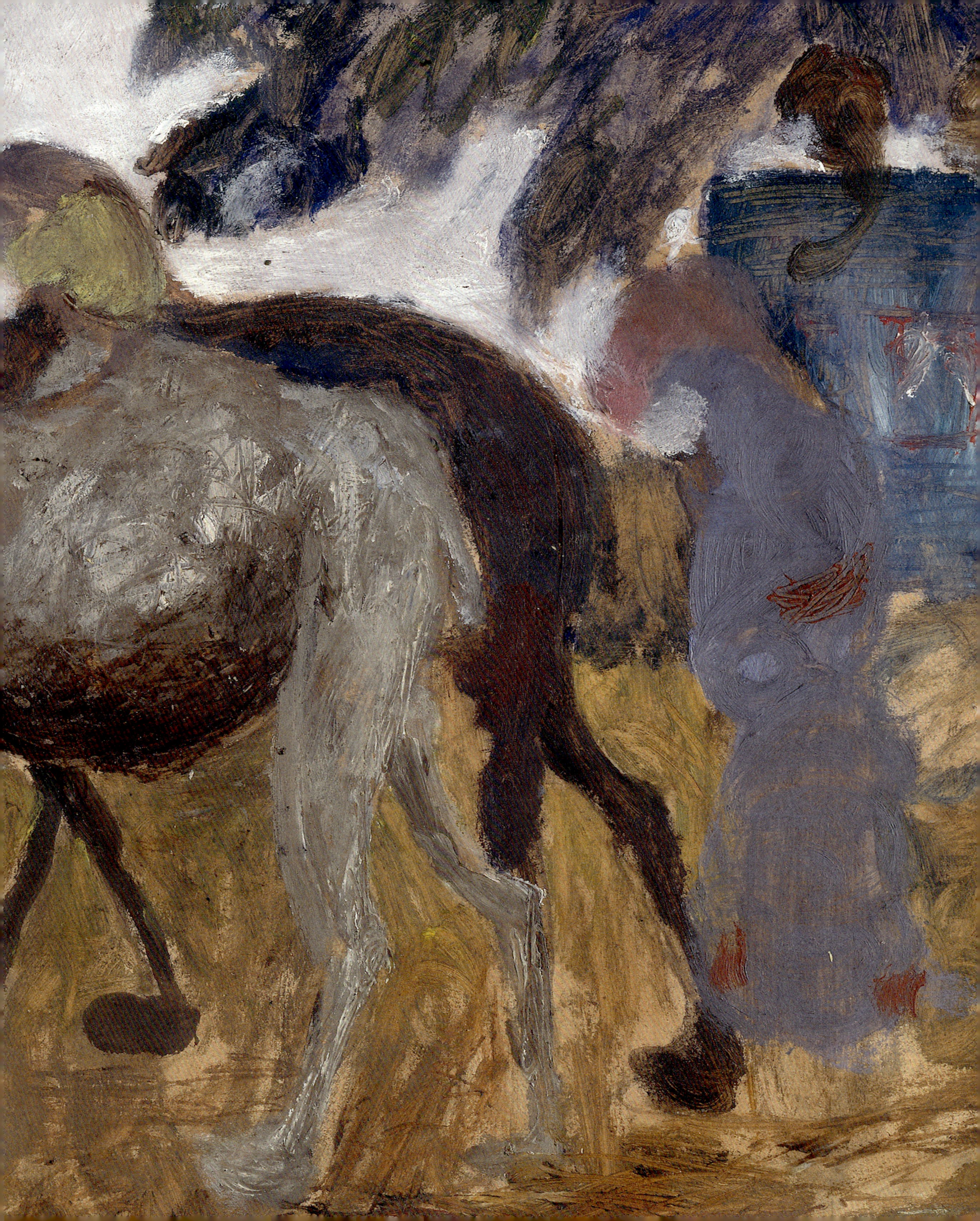

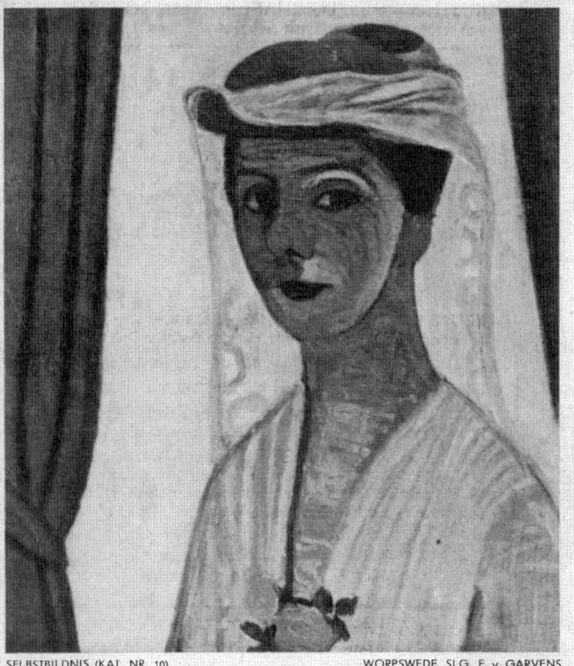

SELBSTBILDNIS (KAT. NR. 10) WORPSWEDE, SLG. E. v. GARVENS

PAULA MODERSOHN-BECKER
5. OKTOBER BIS 4. NOVEMBER 1934
KESTNER-GESELLSCHAFT HANNOVER

Ausstellung
Paula Modersohn-Becker
im Rahmen
nordwestdeutscher Kunst

Im Landesmuseum in Oldenburg
Februar—März 1925

KEES VAN DONGEN
FRAUEN

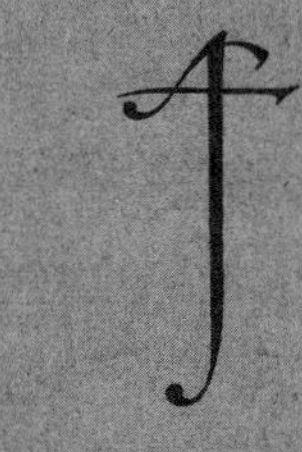

GALERIE ALFRED FLECHTHEIM
DÜSSELDORF · KÖNIGSALLEE 34

RECLAM
PAULA BECKER-
MODERSOHN
MUTTER U. KIND

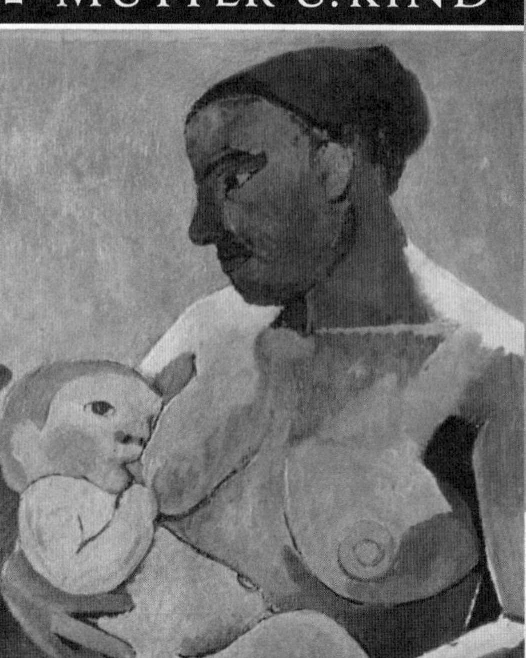

PAULA
MODERSOH
BECKER

KESTNER-G

KUNSTHALLE BERN
8. APRIL BIS 3. MAI 1936

PAULA MODERSOHN-BECKER

GEDÄCHTNISAUSSTELLUNGEN
EMIL ANNER
ERNST LINCK
GUSTAV VON STEIGER

ADOLF FUNK, AQUARELLE

DAS NEUE BILD

PAULA
MODERSOHN-
BECKER

KURT WOLFF VERLAG

KESTNER-GESELLSCHAFT E.V.

PAULA
MODERSOHN †
/ GEMÄLDE /
ZEICHNUNGEN
RADIERUNGEN

X. SONDERAUSSTELLUNG

PAULA
MODERSOHN-BECK
(1876-1907)

PAINTINGS
•
DRAWINGS
•
ETCHINGS

March—April, 1958

GALERIE ST. ETIENNE
46 West 57th Street
New York City

HANDZEICHNUNGEN

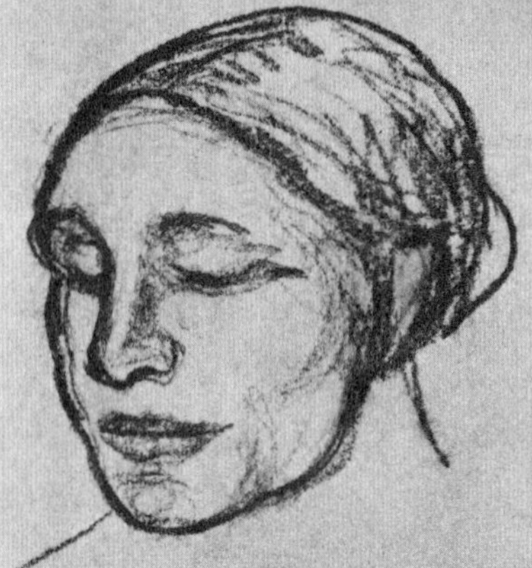

PAULA
MODERSOHN-BECKER

P. BECKER-MODERSOHN
KATALOG IHRER WERKE
GEMÄLDE / STUDIEN / ZEICHNUNGEN UND RADIERUNGEN
M. 6 ABBILDUNGEN VERSEHEN

I. LIEFERUNG.

ZUSAMMENGESTELLT UND
HERAUSGEGEBEN V. HOREN-
VERLAG / WORPSWEDE 1913.

Paula Modersohn-Becker

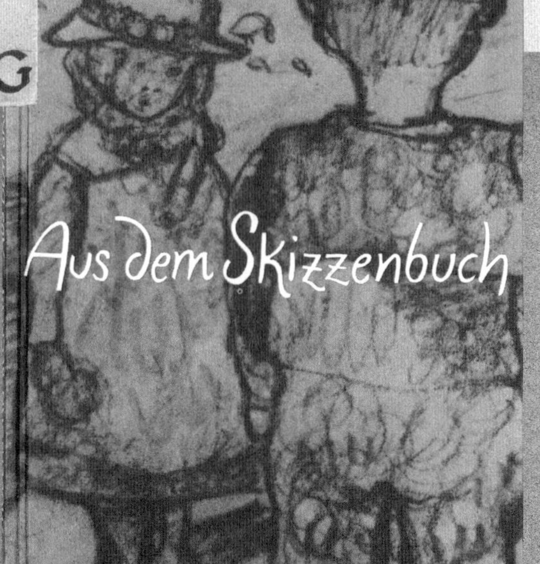

Aus dem Skizzenbuch

Piper-Bücherei

KUNSTHA

PA
MODERSO
187

AUGUS
188